Our Comfort in Dying

Our Comfort in Dying

Civil War Sermons by R. L. Dabney, Stonewall Jackson's Chief-of-Staff

Transcribed and Edited by
Jonathan W. Peters

Our Comfort in Dying
Civil War Sermons by R.L. Dabney,
Stonewall Jackson's Chief-of-Staff
© 2021 Jonathan W. Peters
www.solafidepublications.org

ISBN: 978-0-9972666-4-1

Prepared for publication by www.greatwriting.org.

Cover art:
"Boast Not Thyself of Tomorrow" by Julia Smith

Book layout and design: www.greatwriting.org

Unless noted otherwise, Scripture quotations are taken from The Authorized (King James) Version of the Bible.

SOLA FIDE PULICATIONS
Destin, Florida

SF/LS/20210727

Appreciations

Too few Christians know Dabney as one of 19th-century America's greatest theologians. Fewer yet know him as one of its most gifted and practical preachers. In *Army Sermons* Jonathan Peters has assembled a rich collection of Dabney's work from the Civil War era. Peters' glossary makes these sermons accessible to readers of all ages, and his introduction weaves a rich historical background. As you read Dabney's words, place yourself among his original hearers – thousands of men in battlefield encampments, many hearing the saving truth of the Gospel and the imperative of holy living for the last time before their deaths. *Army Sermons* is a must-read in our own chaotic times: It will focus the mind on the things that are eternally vital.
– Dr. Paul Elliott, Founder and President of TeachingTheWord Ministries

Jonathan Peters and Sola Fide Publications have done a great service in publishing the *Army Sermons* of Robert Lewis Dabney. Those of us who have benefited from reading Dabney's *Sacred Rhetoric* will also benefit from reading some of his own sermons, which tell us nearly as much about Dabney's audiences as they do about Dabney. The sermons are remarkably precise, especially when they address ethical matters; they are also thorough in their coverage of their topics, and they are cogently reasoned. Peters's endnotes and glossary are helpful throughout, without cluttering the manuscript or disrupting Dabney's thought, and his Introduction is a nice mini-biography of Dabney, even while focusing on the military years. *Tolle lege!*
– Dr. T. David Gordon, Professor of Religion and Greek at Grove City College; Author of *Why Johnny Can't Preach: The Media Have Shaped the Messengers*

Rev. Dabney's powerful preaching, depth of doctrinal teaching and precise application of Scriptural truth convict and challenge the mind and heart. Dabney's pleas for repentance, fasting, and prayer ring out from a time of prosperity in the 1850's and a time of great peril in the 1860's. His gospel preaching sowed the seeds of repentance and revival in the nineteenth century that continue to bear fruit today . . . This work is a valuable record of spiritual heritage from the Civil War period.
– Brett Keefer, Guidance Officer and Sr. High History Teacher at Upper Bucks Christian School

It is a marvelous fact of history that sermons had an incalculable impact on the warp and woof of American society in previous generations. And especially potent are the sermons that are delivered during seasons of national distress. Such is the case with this rare collection of sermons preached during the years of America's Civil War, one of the saddest eras of our nation's history. This book has been compiled with painstaking attention to detail and accuracy. The reader will find that Dabney's sermons read like something out of the Westminster Confession of Faith for their deep insight and wisdom; yet they maintain a penetrating practical application aimed at the heart of the hearers. It is no wonder that the conscience of society in this period of America's history was so singularly shaped by the pulpits of such preaching.
– Steven Lee, Founder of SermonAudio

Dabney's sermons, transcribed by Jonathan Peters from the original manuscripts and buttressed by a helpful introduction and meticulous citations for modern readers, will prove of inestimable value for today's soldier of Jesus Christ. Not only was R.L. Dabney one of the towering theologians of his time and the biographer of Jackson, whom he served briefly in the field in 1862, his army sermons also reveal him to be a soldiers' preacher, a friend of sinners, and as was said of him, "a Chaplain worth having."
– Dr. Forrest L. Marion, Staff Historian at the Air Force Historical Research Agency; Author of *Flight Risk: The Coalition's Air Advisory Mission in Afghanistan, 2005-2015*

The content of the sermons is developed and mature, demonstrating the readiness of mind of the Civil War soldiers to receive didactic and edifying teaching – with constant emphasis on practical living, such as gambling, lying, and stewardship. Peters meticulously documents sources, and goes to great lengths to define and illustrate terms that have fallen out of use in the 21st century. This book is a superb composition to enhance the understanding of how God puts gifted men into places of service at the time and place of His choosing for His glory.
– Col. James May, Retired United States Army Chaplain; Author of *From Farmboy to Fanfares: A Chaplain's Story*

As a non-American, the history is very readable, interesting and informative: as a minister, it is massively challenging and heart-stirring. The sermons that are included in this volume hold the attention and make practical application of weighty gospel truth – an unusual trait in today's world. I have been both humbled and heartened by reading these pages and Jonathan Peters is to be commended for bringing them to a much wider audience.
– Rev. Colin Mercer, Deputy Moderator of the Free Presbyterian Church of Ulster; Author of *For Such a Time as This: The Sovereignty and Goodness of God in the Book of Esther*

Dabney had the gift of making brief comments in passing which shed light on the reasons, consequences, foundations, and ramifications of both the doctrines and behaviors which were found in the texts he was expounding. His sermons are enlightening, reproving, convicting, motivating, and heart-warming. The person who reads these sermons will profit greatly from them even if periodically he may wonder how such a minister could support the Confederate cause. I am happy that Jonathan Peters has gone to the labor of assembling these sermons of a godly and prudent man for our salvation and edification.
– Rev. Kermit L. Minnick, Retired Pastor of West Side Baptist Church, Thomasville, PA

All who have become aware of Robert L. Dabney will be thankful for the work of Jonathan Peters in recovering these rare sermons by one of the most eminent preachers of Virginia, and with them he brings together much little-known and illuminating comment from other sources. Here is a great reminder that, whether in life or death, the word of God is the strength of all who belong to Christ.
– Rev. Iain H. Murray, Co-Founder of the Banner of Truth Trust
Author of *Revival and Revivalism: The Making and Marring of American Evangelicalism 1750-1858*

These sermons by one of America's greatest ministers and theologians are valuable for their content as well as for the important insights into that fratricidal conflict known as the American Civil War. Peters does not side-step the problems with Dabney's views concerning the African slaves, but addresses that problem head-on in his introduction to this volume. Ministers and Christians of many denominational backgrounds will be inspired by these sermons even as were the soldiers who first heard them.
– Dr. Dewey Roberts, Pastor of Cornerstone Presbyterian Church, Destin, FL; Author of *Samuel Davies: Apostle to Virginia*

All of us will die with unfinished business, plans that we would like to have accomplished but never did, such as the books we never wrote. Most of these unfinished plans will remain unknown to all or forgotten by the few who knew of them. In a very few cases, someone will come upon the remnants of these plans, dust them off, fill them in, and bring them to completion.

During the three months I spent in the Archives of Union Theological Seminary in Richmond, Virginia examining Robert Lewis Dabney's sermon manuscripts, I kept thinking that someone should publish them. I even took pictures of many with the idea of doing it myself, but I never got around to the tedious work of transcribing, editing, and setting the sermons in their historical contexts. One set of sermons especially begged for attention, the Army Sermons, since Dabney had himself planned to publish them and made initial efforts to identify, organize, and edit them. Although Dabney never finished the task, more than 150 years later, Jonathan Peters has finally realized Dabney's purpose. With careful editing, close attention to his-

torical details, and helpful explanations of archaic words, Peters has made Dabney's remarkable sermons available to the public.
– Dr. Larry Trotter, Pastor of Florida Coast Church
PhD dissertation, "Blasting Rocks: The Extemporaneous Homiletic of Robert Lewis Dabney"

Dabney was not known among the 19th century men as "the preacher." Palmer and Girardeau were the leading pulpiteers among the Presbyterians of that era. Among the leading theologians, Thornwell was the most highly regarded preacher. And thus yet another reason why Dabney has fallen off the reading list for many. Yet, when you read Dabney's sermons there is a simplicity and straight forwardness that warms the heart as it informs the mind. Take the prayer of the importuning widow in Luke 18. Perseverance is the theme, says Dabney. Then he works through the various lessons we learn concerning a faith that glorifies God. But always the theologian, he brings us to an "intelligent" faith when he presses home such truths as: "although [God] is independent and perfectly glorious and blessed in himself, and sufficient for himself, yet it is certain that the promotion of his own declarative glory in the acts and events of his creation, is a grand motive of his determinations." Here, with a quick defense of God's divine simplicity, he shows that the doctrine in no way diminishes our responsibility to bring Him ever more glory. Dabney's sermons deserve our consideration; they will promote our spiritual health. It is good to have them available. Set aside any prejudices you may have and grow in grace.
– Dr. C. N. Willborn, Professor of Historical Theology at Greenville Presbyterian Theological Seminary

Jonathan Peters' work on Dabney's wartime sermons is a gem among Civil War chaplaincy research. While these sermons have existed in various separate forms, Peters is the first to organize them into one, well-researched monograph. I commend Peters for this important step and whole-heartedly recommend this work to any historian.
– Dr. Brett Williams, Provost/Executive Vice President at Central Baptist Theological Seminary

About the Editor

Jonathan W. Peters labors at Reformation Bible Church and Harford Christian School (Darlington, MD) as an administrative assistant, middle school soccer coach, and 5th grade Civil War instructor. Since 2016, he has led numerous tours of Gettysburg for church and school groups, now costumed as a Union major. He was also interviewed by Brady Crytzer on *Battlefield Pennsylvania: Battle of White Marsh*, which aired on the Pennsylvania Cable Network in September 2019.

To my friend,
Lloyd Scarborough, III

Table of Contents

Editor's Preface

In *Christ in the Camp, or Religion in the Confederate Army*, author J. William Jones declared:

> I do not believe that Dr. Burrows, Dr. Stiles, Dr. Hoge, Dr. Dabney, Dr. Pryor, Dr. Lacy, Dr. Moore, Dr. Read, Dr. Duncan, Dr. Granberry, Dr. Rosser, Dr. Doggett, Dr. Edwards, Dr. John A. Broadus, Dr. Pritchard, Dr. Wingate, Dr. Andrew Broaddus, Dr. Jeter, Dr. A. B. Brown, or any of the missionaries or chaplains were ever able, before or since, to preach sermons of such power as they were stirred up to preach in the army [during the American Civil War]. If any man had any capacity whatever to preach, it would be developed under circumstances which would have stirred an angel's heart; and if he knew anything about the Gospel at all, he would tell it to these congregations. . . . And so, when the preacher stood before these congregations of veterans, his very soul was stirred within him, and he "determined to know nothing among them save Jesus Christ and Him crucified."[1]

While Jones detailed the effects of this soul-stirring preaching throughout his book, he did not present any of the actual camp sermons.

Thankfully in the 1880s, Robert Lewis Dabney began compiling twenty of his wartime sermons, some of which were still in outline form.[2] The content of these sermons "were formed indelibly impressed upon [his] memory, as to the whole train of thought," so he decided to write them out in full "on uniform sheets[,] . . . mark[ing each manuscript] with a unique series of Roman numerals in the sermon title." He was careful to make "no changes. . . except unimportant verbal ones," so that they were "substantially the same which were delivered" during the war. Dabney hoped to publish this set of sermons as:

Army Sermons,

OR

Discourses.

Delivered by Rev. R.L. Dabney, D.D.

of Union Theological Seminary, Pr. Edward, Va.,

in the Armies of the Valley and of Northern Virginia

in the years 1860-1865.

By 1882, he completed the title page, preface, and "12 vo." worth of sermons. In the 1890s, he had a few of his wartime sermons published as a part of his multi-volume *Discussions*, but he never saw the *Army Sermons* set published. Union Seminary eventually received the introductory material and twelve completed manuscripts from this set, and preserved them in its library in Richmond. They lay there, forgotten for a century, until David Coffin discovered them "wrapped in a distinctive paper band." Coffin soon perceived that these twelve *Army Sermons* would be "of great interest to the student of Dabney's preaching, for [they give] an insight into his sense of calling, his theoretical commitments concerning preaching, and his practice in the midst of the most extraordinary circumstances."[3] Union Seminary then digitized each page of the sermons and uploaded them to its website. Log College Press combined all these scanned pages into one PDF, and also posted it on the internet.

While studying the life of Dabney in March 2020, I came across the *Army Sermons* online.[4] During the next several months, I transcribed these sermons along with 1) six sermons previously published in the *Discussions*, 2) two unpublished, antebellum sermons from the archives of Union Seminary, and 3) a recently discovered sermon from *The Central Presbyterian*.[5] Although Dabney may not have envisioned all of these for his original compilation, I found them to be pertinent to the Civil War or military life in general. To all these sermons, I added modernized spelling, missing words/punctuation, and a glossary to assist readers with understanding Dabney's language and theology. I also included eyewitness accounts in the endnotes and introductory essay, to illuminate Dabney's effectiveness as a minister of the Protestant faith in the Confederate armies. Sola Fide Publications kindly agreed to publish all of this, with a new title, appendices, and bibliography. Julia Smith also lent her brush to provide a delightful painting for the cover.

Thanks are due to the following for their labors in helping me research, proofread, and/or publish this book: Ryan Douthat and Paula Skreslet (William Smith Morton Library, Union Presbyterian Seminary), David Coffin (New Hope Presbyterian Church), Larry Trotter (Florida Coast Church), Christina Dean (University of Virginia Library), Joan M. Wood (Handley Library), Erin Weinman (New-York Historical Society), Sarah Almond (Botz Library, Hampden-Sydney College), Sharon H. Byrd (E. H. Little Library, Davidson College), Iain Murray and John Rawlinson (The Banner of Truth Trust), Bob Kuykendall (Tinkling Spring Presbyterian Church), Marc Brodsky (Newman Library, Virginia Tech), Janet Tillman (Robert L. Powell Library, The Master's University), Jessica Sheets, Justine Melone, and Thomas Buffenbarger (U.S. Army Heritage and Education Center), Casey Billhimer (Elkton Historical Society), Keith Gibson (Virginia Military Institute), Jonathan Eaker and Mike Klein (Library of Congress), Mark Chaney (Antietam National Battlefield), Will Meeks and Madhu Nainani (Hanover Branch, Pamunkey Regional Library), Jim Holmes, Dewey Roberts, Kermit Minnick, Forrest Marion, Wayne Owens, Ruth Edwards, Adam Eshleman, John Wilson, Carolyn Peters, and my darling esposita, Andri-Ellen.

Dabney's Preface

This little volume of sermons is offered to my former comrades, and in general, to the surviving soldiers of the Southern armies, as an humble tribute of affection and respect. The primary object of its publication with the author, it is hoped, is the desire to glorify God in Christ, and to bless the souls of men, by giving further currency, in the way, to the doctrines of redemption. But in consistency with this, several subordinate motives have concurred in prompting it. Of these, the chief one is the belief, that many Christian men, who heard a part of these discourses, when delivered, will read them with a tender and pensive pleasure, as they revive the recollections of the impressive scenes which they will recall, and of the comrades who then worshipped beside us, and are now in the General Assembly on high. A second consideration of some weight, is that of self-defense. It has been often charged, that the clergy of the South were as delinquent as those of the North, in desecrating the pulpit to political agitation; and that in fact, they were the chief instigators of the war. Now, so far as the author's limited reputation has extended, it is well known that no Southern clergyman was, or could be, more thoroughly identified, both by principles and position, with the great movement for the defense of the constitution, made by our people. And if any temptations could be supposed to swerve a minister of the gospel from the strict line of professional instructions, it would be that besetting an army chaplain. The public may now see, in my volume, what proportion secular topics held in the pulpit teachings of the Southern clergy; and what sort of politics they preached. It will of course be understood, that a collection of twenty discourses must form a very small part of the whole number delivered in the army, in a diversified ministry, as chaplain and missionary. But the selection represents the tenor of my preaching fairly, save that the sermons which have direct application to secular duties and interests, bear a[6] larger proportion to the others, in the volume, than they did in my ministry.[7]

The reader will also understand, of course, that very few of these sermons were preached from written manuscripts. Where the temple was a forest, or a camp, and the pulpit an empty barrel or a stump, these formal methods were out of place. But in reducing the oral discourses to writing, no changes have been made, except unimportant verbal ones. Having been preached *memoriter* from full manuscripts, or from careful briefs, all of which are still in my possession, they were formed indelibly impressed upon my memory, as to the whole train of remark. They may now be received as substantially the same which were delivered.

Two discourses[8] are introduced into these "Army Sermons," which were delivered before the outbreak of the revolution. The apology for their insertion is, that events speedily gave a peculiar importance to the truths there discussed. In explanation of the predictions contained in these, and a few others, as the 14th of the series[9] (predictions fulfilled even more speedily and sorrowfully, although not more accurately, than the author feared), he would say, that he is "neither a prophet, nor a son of the prophets": but he was guided to these prognostications of coming events, solely by his habit of accepting the sacred Scriptures as an infallible book, and sure guide on every subject on which it professes to treat; and by faithfully and humbly applying its principles to current events, in preference to the shallow and vain glorious boasts of the humanitarian philosophy, now prevalent.

In conclusion, every intelligent reader outside the late Confederate States, will perceive, from the topics and methods of discussion in these sermons, that the author at least, supposed himself to be addressing highly intelligent audiences. Often they were rough in exterior, travel-soiled, worn with battle and toil, ill clad, and unkempt; but he always felt that he was in the main, addressing assemblages of cultivated gentlemen. It will ever be his belief, that these volunteer armies of Southern citizens, while including not a few bad men, present the noblest aggregate of mental and moral cultivation, Christianity, manly honour, patriotism, and gallantry, which this age can assemble from the civilized earth. And the author will ever esteem it the chief honour of his life, next to that belonging to the Lord Jesus Christ, that he served as a soldier and minister of the everlasting Gospel, in these armies; that he shared the dangers of these heroic men on many a well fought field, and followed them to their bivouacs and hospitals, with the consolations of the faith.

Introduction

Robert Lewis Dabney ministered in Virginia for the majority of his adult life. Born in 1820 in Louisa County, Dabney received his early education at three log cabin schools before going on to study at Hampden-Sydney College, the University of Virginia, and Union Theological Seminary, which was also located in the town of Hampden-Sydney in Prince Edward County, Virginia.[10] The West Hanover Presbytery licensed Dabney to preach on May 4, 1846, and a month later, he completed his divinity degree. His first charge was as a missionary to his home county in central Virginia. In July 1847, he took up his first pastorate at Tinkling Spring Church near Waynesboro, and married Lavinia Morrison in March of the following year.

While at Tinkling Spring, he grew burdened for the souls of his people and mourned their spiritual lethargy. His mentor, Rev. William S. White, urged him to "preach as if your preaching was everything, and then pray as if it were nothing." His friend, Rev. C. R. Vaughan, also counseled him to "to pray and trust and preach straight at the conscience . . . Preach earnestly, no matter if your manner may seem harsh."[11] Dabney continued to labor zealously, and in 1850, a revival broke out at Tinkling Spring.

Dabney ministered there for another three years, and then returned to Union to become, at first, the Professor of Ecclesiastical History, and eventually, the Professor of Systematic and Polemic Theology. Two years into his first professorship, Dabney received one of the heaviest blows of his life: the loss of two of his sons within two weeks' time (another would die in 1862). This had a powerful effect on his preaching in chapel and the pulpits he would later occupy. Formerly, Dabney's preaching "savored" God's just punishment of unrepentant sinners; but now, without neglecting God's judgment, he tenderly entreated contrite sinners to find rest in Christ's atoning work on their behalf.[12] Three years after this strange providence, Dabney took on the additional responsibility of co-pastor of College Church, a post he would share with his brother-in-law for sixteen years.

Dabney gained notoriety in the United States, both as a preacher and professor. In early 1860, he received job offers from two prominent ministries in the North. Fifth Avenue Presbyterian Church in New York City was solicitous of making Dabney a candidate to replace the late James W. Alexander, but he demurred. Upon the death of Joseph A. Alexander at Princeton Seminary, Charles Hodge wanted to restructure the curriculum and make Dabney the chair of Ecclesiastical History. Dabney respectfully declined on April 10, stating:

> My refusal to serve [Princeton] will not arrest her prosperous career. She will scarcely feel the jostle; but will continue on her way, honored, well-attended and useful. . . . But, on the other hand, in all human view, my desertion of my post here [at Union] would initiate changes which would speedily reduce our thirty-six [students] to eleven, the number I found here seven years ago, or possibly to none, and that in a place where a home-bred ministry is more direfully necessary than in your section.[13]

Almost one year later to the day, the American Civil War erupted, and Dabney, with his native state of Virginia, sided with the Southern Confederacy in defense of Negro slavery and state sovereignty.[14] Dabney noted in his unpublished autobiography that "nearly all of the young men in College Church volunteered at once." Several of these men enlisted in the Prospect Rifle Grays, which:

> held a meeting [on April 23, 1861] to drill and to raise a subscription to buy uniforms and blankets for the poorer members. I [Dabney] was requested to go up and make them an address, which I did. When I got there the company was in the church, with their full equipment, and a house full of their neighbors, wives, sisters and children. There was most intense feeling. I gave them various good advices, seeking rather to quiet than to agitate their feelings; and then made an appeal to people for aid, as did a Methodist minister who was there. The people then raised about seven hundred dollars in cash, and handed it to their captain; and also promised full assistance to the dependent wives and children left behind. So we dismissed them with prayers, among universal tears and sobs. This company is composed of middle-class men; most of them Presbyterians or Methodists, and a few gentlemen. They are a stalwart set of fellows, sun-burned, raw-boned and bearded; but they all wept like children. They will fight none the less for that.[15]

The Grays soon left for Richmond to receive further training, and to band together with other Southside companies to form the 18th

Virginia Infantry Regiment, commanded by Col. Robert E. Withers. After a month of training, Withers received orders to move his regiment to Manassas Junction, a strategic railroad depot twenty-two miles southwest of Washington D.C. (the Federal capital). The regiment garrisoned at Camp Pickens upon arrival, and became a part of the 3rd Brigade under Gen. Philip St. George Cocke.[16]

Dabney greatly desired to minister to the soldiers from Hampden-Sydney (now Company D), so he discussed a plan with his session that would allow him to take a leave of absence during his summer vacation from the seminary. He convinced them that he could serve as the chaplain of the 18th Virginia, while his brother-in-law maintained the work at College Church. Dabney then applied for a state commission, and was accepted. He joined the regiment at Manassas Junction on Saturday, June 8, and boarded with an old man named Weir. Since Weir's quarters were a mile outside of Camp Pickens, Dabney sought closer accommodations, and within a few days, he was able to lodge with Dr. Richard Walton in his tent.[17]

On June 13, the 18th Virginia assembled for a special worship service in recognition of a National Fast Day proclaimed by President Jefferson Davis. Dabney described the service in a letter to *The Central Presbyterian* newspaper:

> Over head there is no roof besides the azure of the heavens. – The place of worship is nothing but an oblong area between two rows of tents; and the pulpit a rude box to elevate the minister a step from the earth, with a rough board before him, draped with nothing richer than a soldier's blanket. On either hand are clusters of glittering arms stacked, soldiers reclining on their pallets, and the open doors of tents, filled with their occupants. The signal of divine worship is the rattle of the drum, the soldier's substitute for the bell; and they come from every side to the meeting-place, some singly, some by twos and threes, some marching in companies with measured tread; rough-bearded men, bronzed and weather-beaten, and almost unrecognizable as the trim gentlemen, who a month or two ago would have been seen at similar occasions, going in holiday attire to their churches. Some bring camp-stools in their hands, some stand, some are seated on logs of wood, some on mother earth.
>
> But see; the man of God [Dabney] has risen and stretched forth his hands in prayer. Instantly every head is reverently uncovered; and bowed in prayer; while Jehovah of Hosts is implored to bless our bleeding country, to crown our arms with success, and to protect the beloved

ones at home. Then follows an old, familiar psalm. – There are no strains of woman's sweeter melody to mingle with the stern melody of the men; but the wind sighing through the pine trees around us is the accompaniment, not unfitting, to the hundreds of manly voices which roll the hymn to the heavens. Then follows the sermon, short and informal, but swallowed with solemn eager faces.[18]

Dabney delivered many such sermons that summer (and throughout the war) from reduced sketches or memorized manuscripts, lasting approximately twenty-five minutes in length. When he reached the makeshift pulpit (sometimes "an empty barrel or a stump") to preach,[19] he stood

stalwart in form[,] . . . six feet in height . . . with an expansive and nobly shaped brow, powerful, deeply set dark eyes, a well shaped nose, expressive mouth and lips, a lower face speaking of the utmost will power, standing with feet adjusted to give him the stablest equilibrium, this whole stalwart frame often quivering from the mighty soul fires within. His speech was the speech of a great teacher, rapid, but not too rapid for every word to be heard, his words chosen for their didactic power, the stream of this didactic eloquence colored by allusion, classic and other, spiced by illustration, sometimes homely, but always apt, sometimes witty, often without much more than feeble signs of suppressed feeling, sometimes aglow with heat, and sometimes white with intense passion.[20]

Dabney believed that while his camp listeners "were rough in exterior, travel-soiled, worn with battle and toil, ill clad, and unkempt," they were also "cultivated gentlemen." He therefore treated his listeners with due respect.[21]

Like most evangelical chaplains during the Civil War, Dabney preached on:

the attributes of an infinite and jealous God and his perfect law; . . . [the] fatal lapse which "brought death into the world and all our woe;" the immortal soul, with its destiny of endless bliss or pain; the tomb, the resurrection trump, the righteous Judge, the glories of heaven and the gloom of hell, the gospel's cheering sound, the tears of Gethsemane, the blood of Calvary, and the sweet and awful breathings of the Holy Ghost.

Dabney recognized that "[his] mission [was] to lay hold of his fellow men, as they h[u]ng over the pit, and draw them from perdition by the love of the Redeemer."[22] He therefore urged the soldiers to "fear

[God], which after he hath killed hath power to cast into hell" (Luke 12:5). But in all this, Dabney refused to engage in revivalism.[23] He simply left it in God's hands to convict men "of sin, and of righteousness, and of judgment" (John 16:8).

Thomas Carey Johnson, Dabney's first biographer, noted that "his preaching gripped the men of the line," as well as the officers, many of whom were "won to Christ" or "edified."[24] Dabney wrote his friend and former classmate, Rev. Moses D. Hoge, on June 28, 1861 to say that "he had found the religious sentiment as great as he had ever known it in any community not in actual revival; that the men seemed kind, and pleased to have a chaplain, and that he preached with as much freedom and satisfaction as he had ever felt anywhere."[25]

Dabney did more than just preach that summer. On July 17, the 18th Virginia made a forced march to Bull Run which exhausted some of the men, two of which (from Company G) would die later in the hospital. Dabney, nevertheless, "walked the far larger part of the way, lending [his] horse to fainting soldiers, one of whom [he] undoubtedly saved from captivity or death."[26] Col. Withers noted that four days later at the First Battle of Manassas, Dabney "followed . . . [his] Regiment and with his own hands gathered up the knapsacks and blankets that had been thrown off by [the] men in their advance, piled them up, covered them with oil cloth, and thus saved to the men of the Regiment all their personal belongings. This was really an important service and was highly appreciated by both officers and men." During the bloody battle, he also served as an orderly for Withers as the regiment fought for control of the Henry House Hill. At the close of the conflict, Dabney "rode over the part of the field where [his] regiment fought, to make sure that there were none who needed aid." That summer, he also ministered to the sick and wounded in the hospitals, even catching a little of the camp fever himself. Col. Withers concluded that overall, Dabney "was fearless and faithful in the discharge of every duty. . . . [He] was a Chaplain worth having."[27]

Dabney continued his preaching ministry through the next two months. The Thursday night following the Battle of First Manassas, Dabney preached a thanksgiving message to his regiment, which was instrumental in bringing about Col. Withers' profession of faith.[28] In late August, Dabney received an invitation from Thomas "Stonewall" Jackson to hold a service in his brigade encamped near Centreville.

Dabney chose to speak on the stoning of Stephen from the Acts 7:59, a text which Dabney "hoped . . . would be impressive to those who were out of Christ, and consoling to those who were united by faith to him." Dabney comforted the men with these words:

> Dreary would be the Christian's death-bed, indeed, if the best prospect which could be offered him amidst the decays of nature were but this: that he must pass from the toils of life and the pangs of dying to fiercer pains beyond the grave, of uncertain duration, which could only be abridged by the piety and doubtful care of survivors. Blessed be God, such is not our hope; but when once life's pilgrimage is ended, if we live in faith and love towards God, the eternal peace begins. The pains of our last struggle are the last experience of evil to which the ransomed spirit is called forever.[29]

Stonewall Jackson wrote his wife the next day to tell her how pleased he was with the sermon: "[Dabney] beautifully and forcibly described the death of the righteous."[30]

Around this time, Dabney contemplated whether he should return to Union Seminary during the fall. He and the directors of Union believed it was essential to keep the school open so that ministerial candidates might continue with their five-to-seven year program. Dabney, though, could let others do the work by requesting a furlough to remain in the army, but he considered this "utterly useless." Resigning his seminary post also seemed "a bad bargain in every sense." An army chaplaincy, Dabney thought, might only last a year or two, but a professorship at Union could last a life-time if maintained. Furthermore, an epidemic of typhoid fever broke out in his regiment, which scattered the sick so far and wide that they were "completely out of [Dabney's] power" to visit. He decided it would be best then to resign from his chaplaincy and return to Hampden-Sydney to teach twenty students that fall. He likewise encouraged ministerial candidates in the army to "lay . . . aside the musket, as autumn returns, and com[e] back to their studies, in every case where they can honestly do so," so that the Church would not suffer the "fatal evil of an absolute dearth of ministerial supply at the end of the war."[31]

Shortly after his return, Dabney attended a meeting of the Synod of Virginia in Petersburg to discuss severance from the Presbyterian Church in the United States of America (PCUSA). In May 1861, the General Assembly of the PCUSA passed the Gardner Spring Resolutions obligating all Presbyterian churches "to promote and perpetuate . . . the integrity of these United States, and to strengthen, uphold, and encourage the Federal Government in the exercise of all its functions under our noble Constitution; and to this Constitution in all its provisions, requirements, and principles, we profess our unabated loyalty." Dabney and his fellow Presbyterians from Virginia considered this action to be "unjust" as it 1) sought to bind their consciences against their state and 2) violated the *Westminster Confession of Faith*, Chapter XXXI, Section 4: "Synods and councils are to handle, or conclude nothing, but that which is ecclesiastical: and are not to intermeddle with civil affairs which concern the commonwealth." The Synod of Virginia therefore separated from the PCUSA, and appointed commissioners (including Dabney) to go to Augusta, Georgia on December 4 to assist with the formation of a new General Assembly of the Presbyterian Church in the Confederate States of America.[32]

Dabney was prevented from attending this assembly, for he soon fell ill with a bout of camp fever which lasted from late November 1861 through January 1862. Even in the midst of his sickness, he yearned to rejoin the army for the upcoming summer, and applied for a chaplaincy in Col. Henry Coalter Cabell's Artillery Battalion. He was not able to get that position, but he received other offers just as a new Confederate conscript law emptied the seminary of all but four students.[33] Gen. D. H. Hill wrote to Dabney on March 26, 1862, saying:

> It seems to me that you could do more good as a chaplain than in any other capacity. I am now in command of a division, and would be exceedingly gratified to have you attached to my command. Such a thing as a division chaplain is not recognized; but if you had the appointment of a chaplain without designating the regiment, you would find plenty of work to do in the division.[34]

Stonewall Jackson, on the other hand, wrote Dabney multiple times during the winter and spring of 1862, suggesting that Dabney come to his command either as a chaplain, aide-de-camp, or regular soldier. Jackson said: "I have had a strong desire to have you with me ever since I knew you."

The position of Adjutant-General (i.e. chief-of-staff) became available on Jackson's staff in early April 1862, and Jackson informed Dabney he could have this post with the rank of major, provided he could

1) get the appointment approved in Richmond, 2) stay with Jackson for the duration of the war, 3) be able to rise early in the morning and work hard, and 4) come immediately to Jackson's camp. Jackson also mentioned that he would allow Dabney to preach in the camps on Sabbath days if he became the adjutant-general.[35]

Dabney was reluctant, at first, to accept a parson-adjutant position. He talked the matter over with Dr. John M. P. Atkinson, President of Hampden-Sydney College, who encouraged him "not to reject the offer summarily." Anna Morrison Jackson, second cousin to Dabney's wife and current lodger at the Dabney residence, encouraged him to accept her husband's proposal. The elders of College Church and the directors of Union likewise urged him to take the offered position because they understood that "the Seminary would be closed temporarily, and . . . [Dabney] would neither be able nor willing to lie about home doing next to nothing, with the country in this terrible state, and so many in [the] camps without preaching." Dabney considered this counsel and decided to join Jackson in the Shenandoah Valley, hoping to convince him of a chaplaincy only, due to poor health.[36]

He found Jackson's army encamped between Conrad's Store and Swift Run Gap, arriving at headquarters on Thursday, April 24 amidst a "very inclement" snow storm. He ate a meal with Jackson and his staff, and chatted with Jedidiah Hotchkiss (Jackson's topographical engineer and fellow Presbyterian) about the decrease in students at Union Seminary.[37] After the meal, Jackson pulled Dabney aside for a private conversation:

Jackson: "I am glad that you have come."

Dabney: "I fear I have come uselessly, only to reveal my unfitness, and retire; already half broken by camp-disease, and enervated by student's toil."

Jackson: "But Providence will preserve your health, if he designs to use you."

Dabney: "But I am unused to arms, and ignorant of all military art."

Jackson: "You can learn."

Dabney: "When would you have me assume my office?"

Jackson: "Rest to-day, and study the 'Articles of War,' and begin to-morrow."

Dabney: "But I have neither outfit, nor arms, nor horse, for immediate service."

Jackson: "My quartermaster [Maj. John Harman] shall lend them, until you procure your own."

Dabney: "But I have a graver disqualification, which candor requires me to disclose to you, first of mortals: I am not sanguine of success; our leaders and legislators do not seem to me to comprehend the crisis, nor our people to respond to it; and, in truth, the impulse which I feel to fly out of my sacred calling, to my country's succour, is chiefly the conviction that her need is so desperate. The effect on me is the reverse of that which the old saw ascribes to the rats when they believe the ship is sinking."

Jackson: "But, if the rats will only run this way, the ship will not sink."

Dabney yielded to Jackson's wishes,[38] and Jackson issued General Orders No. 41 to the troops, announcing that Dabney was his new chief-of-staff. Dabney studied hard and went to bed. The next day, he wrote his first order for Jackson, and continued to digest the Articles of War. He also conversed with "the more experienced officers of the Corps" to gain insights on military affairs.[39] He learned that:

[t]he [chief-of-staff] of a corps was actually the administrative secretary of the corps commander. His principal duties were to dispatch the commander's orders to his divisional subordinates, to receive communications from them to the commander, to keep all the records of the corps, and to prepare and forward the daily reports of the corps to [the army commander]. And in addition to these functions the [chief-of-staff], along with other staff officers, irrespective of their official duties, performed on the field of battle any duty which came at hand. They often carried orders from the corps commander to his generals, conducted reconnaissance, participated in charges upon the enemy, and, if necessary, rallied or endeavored to rally wavering troops.[40]

As the officers shared military insights with Dabney, he, in turn, offered them the wisdom of God's Word. He also ministered to the common soldiers in the camps and hospitals,[41] and in time, was able to renew old acquaintances from Union Seminary.[42]

Dabney's work in the army evoked various responses, even before he ascended the pulpit. In an undated letter to his wife, Gen. Jackson exclaimed: "Dr. Dabney is here, and I am very thankful to God for it. He comes up to my highest expectations as a staff-officer."[43] Col. Andrew Jackson Grigsby (27th Virginia) had a different reaction. After a visit to Jackson's headquarters on Friday, April 25, Grigsby's officers asked him what he thought of Maj. Dabney. He replied: "I concluded that old Jack must be a fatalist sure enough, when he put an Ironside Presbyterian parson as his chief of staff, but I have bright hopes of headquarters, seeing they are no longer omniscient."[44] Jackson's own staff had mixed views of Dabney. Hotchkiss believed Dabney to be "a fine man," and Lt. Sandie Pendleton concurred. Two days after Grigsby's visit to headquarters, Pendleton wrote his father to say that Dabney's "sturdy piety . . . is very great, and is felt in the whole army."[45] By contrast, Lt. Henry Kyd Douglas despised Dabney's testimony, believing he was "too old, and too reverend, and too unelastic." The dislike was mutual, for Dabney considered Douglas to be "too bumptious & self sufficient."[46]

On Sunday, April 27, Dabney stepped forth to preach his first two sermons in the Army of the Valley. That morning, Jackson, Dabney, and the bulk of the staff rode to the 2nd Virginia Brigade, where the drummer boys "beat to attention." The soldiers "formed a [semi-] circle and sat on the ground," while Jackson reverently "stood with head uncovered," facing the sun. On this beautiful Sabbath day, Dabney "laid [his Bible] open upon the head of a bass drum" and preached from Proverbs 27:1: "Boast not thyself of to morrow; for thou knowest not what a day may bring forth." He appropriately exhorted his audience: "what is this delay of repentance till tomorrow, but a gambling with your everlasting all, upon the chances of uncertain life? . . . A soldier, a man whose very profession it is to face danger and wounds; whose daily tasks all point to the field of battle, where death holds high revel! Of all men, the soldier can with least reason be thoughtless of his soul." Dr. Harvey Black (4th Virginia) thought it was "a most excellent sermon," and Maj. Frank B. Jones (2nd Virginia) prayed that "the Lord [would] bless the discourse to those who heard it." That evening, Dabney preached to the 5th Virginia on Philippians 4:4-7. Maj. Jones attended again and left this account: "I enjoyed the sermon. It was a great comfort to me. . . . [Dabney] said nothing was too trivial or *too small* to go to God with, but in everything by prayer and supplication with thanksgiving let our requests be made known unto God. Blessed Lord, what a glorious priviledge (sic.), and may I learn more and more to pray with faith and trust." Soldiers would continue to write about Dabney's "great sermons" throughout the rest of the spring.[47]

Hotchkiss noted that on April 30, Jackson and his "staff [were] in the saddle & our Division [was] in motion up the [Shenandoah] river." Dabney was able to acquire a "sober old horse" for this ride, but the quartermaster failed to give him a uniform and sidearms. Dabney was therefore still attired in his black clerical garb and a beaver hat. A torrential downpour began at 3:30 PM, causing the flat country to turn into a sea of mud and quicksand. On this dreary day, the soldiers in the ranks decided to have some light-hearted fun with their beloved commander and adjutant-general. When the soldiers spotted Dabney in his Prince Albert coat carrying an umbrella, they teased him by saying: "Come out from under that umbrella!" "Come out! I know you are under there; I see your feet a-shaking!" "'Fraid you are going to get your beegum spoiled?" "'Fraid you will get wet?" The infantrymen also cheered loudly when they saw Jackson, hoping he would take off his hat in acknowledgement and get his head wet. The General instead galloped off; and the staff, in an attempt to catch up, "had a rather ludicrous race across a quicksand field" and through a neighboring forest. The tree branches destroyed Dabney's hat and umbrella, prompting a staff member to lend him a hat. Within a few days, the quartermaster finally gave Dabney sidearms and "a rather ill-fitting uniform." He held on to his clerical outfit, though, for use when he preached to the troops.[48]

Over the next few of days, Dabney grew more confident in his parson-adjutant position. He wrote to his mother on Tuesday, May 6, saying:

> The adjutant is pretty much the General's secretary; and as he must be near the General's person, he necessarily shares his comforts. I always eat at the same table, and most frequently sleep in the same room. On one occasion I was in a good feather bed, and he on his military pallet. In general, I may say that he treats me with the greatest kindness and consideration; and while he is exact and exacting in an official point of view to all under him, personally he is almost embarrassingly kind. The bargain is that I shall do his army work in the week, and be at liberty to preach to the soldiers on Sundays. I have now been in the camp two Sundays. The first I preached twice to noble congregations. The

second, the whole army was marching, and neither I nor any chaplain could preach at all.[49]

In his autobiography, Dabney recorded that he "soon accompanied [Jackson] through the marches and battles of his splendid Valley Campaign . . . ; to McDowell, Franklin, in Pendleton Co, Frontroyal (sic.), [and to] Winchester." Sabbath interruptions frequented the campaign, to the dismay of Jackson, Dabney, and those of like-precious faith. Dabney was forced at times to preach his sermons the Monday or Tuesday following a victorious battle. Such was the case with the Battle of McDowell (May 8) and the First Battle of Winchester (May 25). Not long after the latter, Dabney fell ill "with disordered bowels, the consequence of the water and fatigue, and was [placed] on the sick list." By early June, he was well enough to join Jackson's army on its retreat to Harrisonburg.[50]

Jackson, his staff, the wagon trains, and a small force of soldiers soon encamped at Port Republic, while the bulk of the army lay across the North River. On Sunday morning, June 8, after breakfast, Dabney asked Gen. Jackson, "I suppose, General, divine service is out of the question to-day?" Jackson replied: "Oh, by no means; I hope you will preach in the Stonewall Brigade, and I shall attend myself—that is, if we are not disturbed by the enemy." Dabney then returned to his tent to change into "the parson's black" and prepare his message. He lay on his cot for some time, mulling over the finer points of his sermon, when suddenly, Jim Lewis (Jackson's servant) ran up to dismantle Dabney's tent. Dabney was baffled to see Lewis "hastily jerking up the tent pins," so he asked him what was going on. Lewis explained that the enemy just made a surprise attack on the village, and Jackson swiftly escaped across the river. Dabney quickly laid aside his clerical garb and sermon, grabbed his major's uniform, sidearms, and horse, and rode out to reconnoiter. He soon recognized that he could not reach Jackson, so he sought to organize what troops he could to save Jackson's supply wagons.[51] By now, even profane men like Col. Grigsby could assuredly say: "Our parson is not afraid of Yankee bullets, and I tell you he preaches like the Devil."[52]

Dabney had to wait until the following weekend to preach again, but he was well rewarded. The evening of June 14 and the morning of June 15, he preached to the Stonewall Brigade, exhorting them to: "Come now, and let us reason together, saith the Lord: Though your sins be as scarlet, they shall be as white as snow: though they be red like crimson, they shall be as wool" (Isaiah 1:18). On Sunday afternoon, he held a communion service in the Third Brigade for two hundred soldiers, including Gen. Jackson. The soldiers hushed to hear Dabney deliver "some excellent remarks" and then receive the elements at his hands. "[M]any . . . drew near to Jesus," and considered it "a spiritual feast indeed."[53]

A few days later, Jackson ordered his men to begin an arduous journey (combination forced march and train ride) to link up with Gen. Robert E. Lee's army near Richmond. Jackson halted briefly at Fredericks Hall on Sunday, June 22, and there, Dabney preached to him and Gen. John Bell Hood's Texas Brigade in the late afternoon. Little did these men know that this was to be Dabney's last message under Jackson's command. A "little wooden church was packed, the open grounds beside it crowded, and the fences and the very trees loaded with human bodies. To provide for the multitude without, General Hood . . . [had Dabney stand], not in the pulpit, but in a side door, where a table was arranged." The men listened "with the strictest decorum" as Dabney solemnly exhorted:

> "Except ye be born again, ye cannot see the kingdom of God." You will never work this new birth of yourselves; you are absolutely dependent on the sovereign inworking of that God against whom you sin hourly. Unless he condescends to stoop and touch your stubborn heart, it will remain ungodly, just as surely as the corpse remains dead. All the zeal of religious teachers, all your own self-righteous resolutions and vows, will be assuredly vain. . . . Will you not now cease fighting against your only deliverer, and begin to cry, "Create in me a clean heart, O God; and renew a right spirit within me?"

After the service was over, Gen. Jackson said to Dabney: "Your subject this evening was of great importance[.] . . . I wish all my men could read your sermon. I should be glad if you would reduce it to writing, when other duties permit—I know you cannot have time for this now, but hereafter, when operations in the field are less urgent—and let me have it. I will print it myself and supply my command." The subsequent events of the war prevented this from happening.[54]

The tireless campaigning and ministering took a toll on Dabney's already frail health, lessening his ability to serve effectively. Jackson noticed this during the Peninsula Campaign, and "insisted on [Dabney] taking a sick leave from Harrison's landing" sometime after the Battle of Malvern Hill on July 1. Dabney eventually traveled home and battled a "long and terrible spell of camp fever, which brought [him] near to death's door. After this came a tedious relapse, followed by long prostration." Surgeon Richard Walton advised Dabney "that [he] would never be fit for the service [again], and would certainly die if [he should go] back." With deep sadness, Dabney sent in his resignation in late August.[55]

During the Second Battle of Manassas that month, Jackson conversed with Dr. Samuel R. Morrison about Dabney's situation. Jackson said: "Major Dabney wishes to resign on account of his health; I hope that after a while he can remain in the field." Dr. Morrison informed Jackson that "active service so exhausted and prostrated [Dabney] as to render [him] unfit for any duty." Jackson reluctantly agreed to accept Dabney's resignation, but said that "he considered [Dabney] the most efficient officer he knew, he was very much pleased with [him] as an adjutant, and knew of no one that could fill [his] place."[56]

Although he could no longer be with the troops, Dabney uplifted them in prayer, first likely in his closet, and then in a "little prayer-meeting [at Hampden-Sydney] . . . which met daily to pray for [the] army." On December 5, Jackson wrote Dabney a letter which must have been a great encouragement to him. The letter said:

> Long have I been desiring to write to you, but up to this time have been prevented. I much regret that your health would not permit you to remain longer in service with the army in the field, but I am very thankful to God for having permitted me to have the privilege of being blessed with your Christian and military labors as long as he did. Whilst we were near Winchester, it pleased our ever-merciful Heavenly Father to visit my command with the rich out-pouring of his spirit. There were probably more than a hundred inquiring the way of life in my old brigade. It appears to me that we may look for [ever] growing piety and many conversions in the army, *for it is the subject of prayer*. If so many prayers were offered for the blessing of God upon any other organization would we not expect the Answerer of prayer to hear the petitions, and send a blessing?[57]

What Jackson saw in Winchester was, in fact, only the beginnings of a great awakening which swept through the Army of Northern Virginia (ANV). By the war's end, over fifteen thousand ANV soldiers professed faith in Jesus Christ (and many more in other armies, North and South).[58] This faith, as Gen. John B. Gordon noticed,

> banished[ed] from the heart all unworthy passions[;] prepared the soldiers for more heroic endurance; lifted them, in a measure, above sufferings; nerved them for the coming battles; exalted them to a higher conception of duty; imbued them with a spirit of more cheerful submission to the decrees of Providence; sustained them with a calmer and nobler courage; and rendered them not insensible to danger, but superior to it.[59]

Although Dabney was absent from the ANV for much of this revival, he was duly credited for sowing some of the seeds which others reaped.[60]

As his health improved during the latter part of 1862 on into 1863, Dabney resumed his responsibilities at Union Seminary and College Church.[61] He also wrote a defense of the Confederate cause and two religious tracts.[62] Meanwhile, Jackson fought and won a great victory at the Battle of Chancellorsville, but at the cost of his life. On the first Sunday of June 1863, Dabney preached a memorial sermon for Jackson at the First Presbyterian Church in Richmond.[63] Shortly thereafter, Anna asked Dabney if he would write a biography of her late husband. Throughout the rest of the war, Dabney devoted much of his energies to researching and writing this book. In the late summer of 1863, Dabney even visited with "his old mess-mates of the Second Corps [at Orange Court House] . . . to talk over the campaigns and battles of Stonewall Jackson," and while there, Dabney took the opportunity to preach to them one more time on the subject of "Faith" on September 6. Dabney returned to the seminary that fall to teach three students.[64]

Over a year later, he decided to become a missionary to the army as he had "next to no students" in the seminary. In early December 1864, Dabney visited Gen. Jubal Early's Army of the Valley encamped at New Market and stayed "[f]or five or six days . . . to assist the chaplains . . . in preaching to the soldiers" of Gen. Gordon's Division, Gen. Cullen Battle's Alabama Brigade, Col. Thomas Munford's Cavalry Brigade, and Lt. Col. William Nelson's Battalion of Artillery. To the former three units, Dabney reused messages he had previously delivered during Jackson's Valley Campaign two years prior. To the latter unit, Dabney reused his message on "The Christian Philosopher," but also preached a relatively new one based on Proverbs 24:10. In this sermon, entitled "Fortitude under Reverses, a Christian Duty," Dabney engaged in a rare case of "secular preaching" in the Confederate army. He claimed: "if the *duties enjoined in S[acred] S[cripture]* happen to have secular relations: [there is] no reason the mouths of God's *heralds* should be sealed. If it very nearly affect[s the] prosperity of God's Church, her officers sh[oul]d speak." He believed the "cause of our country's Independ[ence]" was in defense of "Religious liberty," and therefore encouraged the soldiers to continue to *"defend this cause . . .* of *justice,"* despite the enemy's "Plunderings," "Confiscations," "Emancipation [Proclamation]," and enlistment of "Negro soldiers."[65]

After a brief respite at home, Dabney traveled over to Petersburg, where Gen. Robert E. Lee's army was then besieged. From January to March 1865, Dabney filled the pulpits of Tabb Street Presbyterian Church and the First Presbyterian Church of Petersburg, and preached to a number of soldiers assembled there. He also ventured out to Gen. R. Lindsay Walker's Third Corps Artillery Battalions sometime in March to preach a narrative sermon on I Samuel 24. In this, his last sermon in a Confederate camp, Dabney reminded his listeners of the "magnanimous forbearance" of David towards his unjust persecutor (King Saul), and thereby exhorted the men to have a "Christian forgiveness [towards others] found, not in insensibility, or deadness to one's own just rights; but in an appeal to God."[66]

Petersburg and Richmond (the Confederate capital) fell in early April, and Dabney retreated westward with the army. According to his son, Charles (who was nine years old at the time), Dabney "had been placed in charge [of a shipment] of important books, papers, bonds, and bond plates, and such Confederate money and gold as had been left in the Treasury, and been instructed to run off with it and hide it, for the Government until it was re-established, as it was hoped it would be somewhere in the South." Initially, he may have planned to travel to North Carolina, but after the Confederate debacle at Sailor's Creek on April 6, he decided to bury the treasure in Buckingham (Maysville), Virginia "beneath a carpet of pine needles in a deep forest." Dabney also "hid [himself] a few days in Buckingham, to avoid," he said, "being carried off to [a] Northern prison." Lee's decimated army surrendered a few short miles away on April 9, signaling the end of slavery and the curtailment of state sovereignty. Dabney soon returned to Hampden-Sydney, and "found my wife and children safe, but my home pillaged" by marauders from both armies. While he quickly forgave "the poor hungry" Confederates, he grew bitter toward all Yankees for their thorough destruction of the Old South, and he refused to accept their verdict that the newly liberated slaves should be regarded as equals with the rest of society. At Gen. Lee's suggestion, Dabney did, however, report the whereabouts of the buried treasure. The Federal government sent a detail of soldiers to unearth, repackage, and ship everything to Washington. They left behind some of the original packaging, which Charles later used to make cabinets.[67]

In spite of his depleted resources, Dr. Dabney proceeded with his regular ministerial duties in Hampden-Sydney, becoming, as A. A. Hodge said, "the best teacher of theology in the United States, if not the world" at that time.[68] Several young men attended Union Seminary during the Reconstruction Era to study under the renowned theologian. Some came to finish their education interrupted by the war,[69] while others enrolled for the first time. Many in the latter category "were among those converted in the military encampments under Dr. Dabney's preaching."[70] During the postwar era, Dabney also began publishing books, a few of which were based on his classroom lectures. In 1870, Dabney published a homiletical classic entitled *Sacred Rhetoric,* and in 1871, his pupils published the first edition of his acclaimed *Syllabus and Notes of the Course of Systematic and Polemic Theology,* which he eventually revised and republished himself. He later went on to publish seven additional books: *The Sensualistic Philosophy of the Nineteenth Century Examined* (1875, rev. 1887), a four-volume compilation of smaller works, entitled *Discussions* (1890-92, 1897, edited by C. R. Vaughan), *The Practical Philosophy* (1897), and *Christ Our Penal Substitute* (1898, posthumously).

In 1883, he headed to the University of Texas to become the Professor of Mental and Moral Philosophy. Within three years, Dabney underwent an operation for glaucoma. The procedure was unsuccessful, and Dabney's sight faded into complete darkness by 1890. He eventually had to resign from the University of Texas, but he continued to preach and give lectures, whenever and wherever possible, until he passed away on January 3, 1898. He was buried a few days later in his native state of Virginia, resting alongside his three infant sons in Union's Cemetery.

His wife had I Thessalonians 5:21 inscribed on his tombstone: "Prove all things, hold fast that which is good." Princeton theologian B. B. Warfield strove to do exactly that when he eulogized Dabney in the early 20th century[71]:

> As a preacher, as a teacher and as a writer equally he achieved greatness. . . . Dr. Dabney [was a] . . . forceful, clear, decided advocate of the Evangelical system of truth. . . . It must be confessed that the robustness of his views and the vigor with which he expressed them have, especially outside of the spheres of philosophical and theological matters where his thought was most at home, betrayed him occasionally into extremities of opinion[, particularly against the Negroes]. This will not, however, be permanently remembered against him. When all is said, he was a man of light and leading, who served his own generation well, and if unable to rise wholly above the provincialism powerfully fostered by the circumstances in which his life was passed, yet always worth listening to and always to be learned from. . . . [M]ay not only his memory remain green, but his influence be increased through the coming years!"[72]

Robert Dabney in Uniform
*Courtesy of Special Collections, William Smith Morton Library, Union
Presbyterian Seminary*

Senator Robert E. Withers
Courtesy of the Library of Congress

Lt. Gen. T. J. Jackson & His Staff
MOLLUS-MASS, Volume 87, Page 4390
Courtesy of the U.S. Army Heritage & Education Center

Venable Hall, Union Seminary, Hampden-Sydney, VA
Courtesy of Special Collections, William Smith Morton Library, Union Presbyterian Seminary

College Church, Hampden-Sydney – Built by Dr. Dabney
Courtesy of The Banner of Truth Trust

I, 340   161.

Exercise, No. 39.

Narrative Sermon on I Samuel. 24.
Hist: wisdom teaching by example:
To Introduce; Review Saul's persecution of David. I Sam.
18: 8.9.10.11.21. 19:1.10.11.20. 22:6.8. 23:7. 14.21x
Here was the provocation of pertinacious malice.

In exposition; describe nature & locality of En-Gedi: of
the cave, & the event. v.3. Saul goes into the very
cave, unattended, where David and his men hid, to rest
and sleep- v.4. They plausibly urge him to kill Saul.
v. 5: David only cuts off the skirt of his robe: Why? and
v.6.7. neither hurts him, nor permits his hurt: v.8.
David follows & expostulates. protesting his guiltlessness.
and v.13. proving it by his conduct- v.15: appealing
to God.

Saul. v. 16-19. is temporarily overcome with Davids
forbearance. v.20. prophecies his advancement; & v.
21. exacts of David an Oath to spare his posterity-

David however v. 22. does not put himself in his
power-

This history illustrates strikingly

Proposition.) The magnanimous forbearance of the
true Christian.

I. The provocation had been great. See Introduction.

II. The occasion for revenge tempting to a bad heart.
and its use plausibly urged- v.3.4. Note here; God's
wishes to be interpreted from his precepts, not his Providential dealings- Need of rectitude, humility. self=
denial to walk in difficult providences.

Narrative Sermon on I Samuel 24
*Courtesy of Special Collections, William Smith Morton Library,
Union Presbyterian Seminary*

III. David's loyalty to duty under great provocation —
See his tenderness of conscience. v. 5. Reverential address. v. v. 8–15. no reproaches.

    Note. Loyalty to duty best qualification for
reigning. Here the basis of David's splendid reign—

IV. Christian forgiveness founded. not in insensibility, or
deadness to one's own just rights; but in an appeal
to God. v. v. 12–15. Compare Ps. 7. 35.

    Here vindicate Psalmist fr. revengeful spirit.

V. Christian forgiveness does not make man a fool or
a weakling. v. 22. Matt. 10:16.
In sad contrast. we see the envy and malice of Saul.
Temporary compunction, indeed. v. 16. 17. This is not repentance.   To envy. every virtue is new offence —

In conclusion:
1. Forgiveness is a supernatural grace —
2. Forgiveness is a happy grace. Contrast the influence of David's right conduct here. on the glory & success of his life. with the result of his plucking a guilty
deliverance by revenge. Ps. 4:8. And with the influence of Saul's envy & jealousy on his own career —

Preached at Union Sem. Va. April 1860.
Preached at Pr. Edw, C.H. Va. Jan, 1865.
Preached in 1st Ch. Petersburg. Va. Jan, 1865.
Preached to Mulberry [illegible]. [illegible]. 186[illegible]

Used in Lecture Room. March 1882.

Getting Without Paying[73]

A Sermon

on

Exodus 20:15

"Thou shalt not steal."

Preached at Tinkling Spring Church in August 1851.

The indirect means by which men break the spirit of this command[ment] are so numerous that, if we entered into an extended discussion of even the most common of them, we should become tedious. For this reason, it will be necessary to set out, with some clear and general principle, which by a prompt and easy application, will test the true character of these various acts. Such a principle will be found in the answer to the question: 'what is stealing? What is the essence of this criminal act?' It was shown, last Sabbath, that the thing which constitutes the theft is *the getting without paying*; and without the owner's intelligent consent. It is not the circumstance that the goods were stolen in the dark, or in the owner's absence, that they were taken from his barn, or his pocket, that they we[re] obtained by a falsehood, or by slight of hand, that the owner was conscious or unconscious, which constitutes the act of stealing. It is simply the getting without an equivalent. This equivalent value may be returned, in the honest purchase of any goods, in the form of goods, or of labor, bodily or intellectual, or of money: which men have selected to represent all values. Where the full market value is intentionally not returned in any shape, there is a theft.

It need hardly be said that all the forms of swindling, forging, passing counterfeit money, and selling worthless commodities by the help of lies as to their value, are direct theft. Their baseness is too evident to need any remark. [Therefore, I shall restrict my remarks today to the more subtle forms of theft.][74]

1. The use of false weights or measures is a virtual theft. "Ye shall do no unrighteousness in judgment, in meteyard, in weight, or in measure. Just balances, just weights, a just ephah, and a just hin, shall ye have." (Leviticus 19:35-36) "*Divers* weights, and *divers* measures,[75] both of them are alike abomination to the Lord." (Proverbs 20:10) He who sells by a weight lighter than the honest one gives the purchaser just so much less than his money entitles him to receive. He who buys by a weight heavier than the just, gets for his money so much *more* than he pays for. In each case, the difference between the false weight and the just one, *is so much stolen*. If the merchant's pound weight is two ounces too light, then for every pound he sells, he does just the same thing as if he stole two ounces from his customer. For, he gets from him the *price* of those two ounces, without paying for it. He then who knowingly uses false weights or measures is a thief. His thieving is as perpetual as his buying or selling. But are not weights and measures used often by those who would be loathe to be thought thieves where they are *suspected* to have become too small by use and wear? It is no excuse to say that they were not *intentionally made* too small by the owner. Remember God does not forbid us only, to *design* to do unjustly; he forbids us *to do unjustly*. It is our duty to take all necessary care so as to *assure* ourselves that we are doing right. The mixing or adulterating of commodities, by mingling with them some cheaper or worthless substitute is also an indirect theft. It is implied that the purchaser is receiving the pure commodity for his money: if he receives something less valuable, he is defrauded. This is an iniquity peculiarly prevalent, we are told, among the dealers in spirituous liquors. It is also practiced in regard to medicines, oils, and many other commodities.

2. When one person engages to work for another for wages, whether it is the performance of some mechanical job, or of daily, weekly, or monthly labor, he engages to give his employer, for so much money, so much of his time and bodily strength. He then who labors unfaithfully, he who, as a hireling, wastes his time, or as a mechanic, slights his work,[76] does exactly the same thing with the merchant who uses a false weight and measure. He returns, for his employer's money, a false quantity of the article bargained for, which was his labor. He

procures a part of his employer's money, therefore, without recompense: in other words, he steals it. If he does two thirds of the day's work only, and takes a day's wages, it is just the same as though he had received two thirds of the sum, and then picked his employer's pocket for the other third, or, had sold a bag of corn for so much, and then stolen a bushel out. How many are there who take liberties with their conscience in this way? We fear that there is a vast amount of this thieving, the stealing of time which has been sold to employers. This is peculiarly the sin of servants, who are commanded by God "whatsoever they do, to do it heartily, as to the Lord and not unto men, not with eye service, as men pleasers." But it is a sin which may be committed by any one, however elevated in profession, who engages to work for others. The physician may commit a theft on his patient, by robbing him of a part of the *attention and care*, which he has bargain to sell to him for his fee. The teacher may rob his pupil of a part of the instruction purchased by the tuition money. The lawyer may rob his client of the legal skill and watchfulness which the client has bought of time. Wherever the professional man fails, through laziness, or any other cause, to expend that fair amount of professional skill and attention, which it is commonly understood the employer is to receive for his money, he has committed a virtual theft. *He sells the professional commodity by a false weight and a false measure.* How many men, my friend, act up to the principles of honesty in this respect? Who can say his hands are clean?

3. In the transacting of bargains, many frauds are committed, which are breaches of the eighth commandment. One of these but too common, is, to take advantage of the ignorance of the purchaser to sell for more than the fair price, or of the inexperienced seller, to procure for less than the full value, what he has to sell. In all usual circumstances, the market price is the just price, for the times of every commodity. He who sells for more than this, obtains his purchaser's money fraudulently: and he who buys for less, by the help of the seller's ignorance, gets a part of the goods sold for less than their just value. How many men, yea and females also, calling themselves gentlemen and ladies, when they see the country-man, coming with the products of his farm, and ignorant, in his retired home, that these products have risen in market value, will take advantage of this ignorance, never utter a word of the true state of the markets, and procure

the poor man's property for half or two thirds of its worth? How many will even stoop to the meanness of robbing the poor colored man of the worth of his little poultry, because, in his simplicity and ignorance, he does not know that it would fetch twice as much, if sold in [a] fair and open market? And how many in selling, take advantage of the ignorance of the purchaser, to make him give more than they would dare to ask from a well-informed customer? It is pleaded, in excuse: that *they* do not do any thing to produce this mistake: and it is not their business to teach the opposite party to take care of *his* interests, provided they do not directly deceive him. It is their business: for has not God said: "Thou shalt love thy neighbour as thyself"? Could an honest man take advantage of a little child, to sell him, in his childish ignorance, a pinchbeck watch, for the price of a solid gold one? What would be thought of such baseness? Now *why* would such a trick upon a little child be dishonest? The only reason that can be assigned is, that the child does not know the worth of what he is buying. Neither, in the cases mentioned, does the man. As to this particular transaction, he is a child: for he is in the same condition of defenseless ignorance.

Another dishonest art in selling, is to be silent about secret defects of the thing sold, known to the seller, but not perceived by the purchaser. All the good qualities of his property he displays, and lauds to the skies: but about the bad qualities he says not a word. He satisfies his conscience by saying that he tells no lie about it: that the particulars in which he praises the thing offered for sale, are *true*, and it is the *buyer's* business to find out its defects. These are wretched excuses indeed. Do not all know that, where a piece of property is sold for its apparent market value, without any thing said about defects while much said in praise, *it is implied to be sound*? The *purchaser* certainly understands that it is so implied, if not he would not buy: and the seller permits and encourages him to understand so.[77] Then the seller *acts* a lie, though he does not speak a lie: and the two sins are the same. These concealments are the peculiar sins of that class of men called Jockies. To see their utter dishonesty let us apply the wretched pleas made to justify them, to other callings. Suppose *the merchant* should sell to the Jockey a thick roll of what appeared to be costly broadcloth, unrolling a yard from its outside, vaunting its fineness and gloss, but never whispering, what he knew, that the interior of the roll was rotten. The same pleas would apply. "The merchant has told no lie: he has only said what was true: it is the buyers to scout to find out defects; he has eyes of his own, and must see for himself." Would he be considered an honest merchant?

Another specimen of the same fraud is displayed when men cry down the quality of an article which they wish to buy. "It is naught, it is naught; saith the buyer, but when he is gone his way, then he boasteth." (Proverbs 20:14) This is *positive lying*, and the reduction of price below the fair market value which is gained by it, is so much stolen from the seller. This fraud is exhibited in a most shameful and disgusting form, when the purchaser takes advantage of his superior age, or dress, or reputation for knowledge, to browbeat and reduce the seller who is oppressed by bashfulness, or youth, or inexperience, or urged by his necessities.

So, when we take advantage of the urgent necessities of our neighbor, in buying or selling, we sin, against both honesty and charity. If your neighbor is compelled by his wants to sell some commodity for whatever he can get, that fact does not make that commodity worth less than the market price to *you* who buy it. If he is compelled to have some commodity instantly, whatever it may cost him, that fact does not make it worth more than the market price to you who sell it to him. If, therefore, you take advantage of his necessity to force him to sell you his goods for a less price than you yourself would give, if you could[78] take this advantage, you rob him of the difference. And it is a fraud committed under peculiarly base circumstances. For his necessity, instead of arousing your cupidity, ought to excite compassion. Instead of taking advantage of his necessity, you should charitably aid in relieving them. Such measures are excused, I know, by saying that he makes the bargain voluntarily, or that his necessity makes the price which you give him, actually *worth* to him individually, in his peculiar circumstances, what he gave in exchange for it. To these heartless excuses, there is one answer, which at a touch exposes their worthlessness. "Do unto others as ye would that they should do unto you." How would you like to have *your* necessity thus abused? And yet, how many men are there, who watch, like harpies, for these opportunities, to make, what they call a good bargain?

On this whole subject of buying and selling, there is but *one* general honest rule. By whatever means we obtain our neighbor's goods or money for less than we know to be their fair value, to do so intentionally is to make a fraudulent bargain. He who indulges the wish to buy any article whatever for a less price than he himself believes it is really worth, is guilty of coveting. He has committed theft in his heart. It matters not whether he accomplishes his wish by beating down the seller, by taking advantage of his wants, or his ignorance. And yet, are not these just the bargains which people are perpetually seeking to make: to get things for less than they know they are worth? Are not these just the bargains which industrious housekeepers, and thrifty managers, and prudent mamas *boast of*, as the evidences of their management? A *good bargain*, as the world calls it: what is it usually, but a fraudulent bargain? Alas: covetousness hath blinded the eyes of men!

4. Another class of actions forbidden by the eighth commandment is to avail one's self of legal advantages which the law grants, from motives of public policy and convenience, but which are not founded in morality. Such, for instance, are the acts of limitation, which to cut off sources of litigation, ordain that an open account shall not be recovered by law after five years, nor a bond after a certain longer term. Such was the bankruptcy law, lately in force, which annulled the debts of bankrupts. Such, is the law of usury, which to discourage the wicked practice of thieving, releases the debtor from the payment of the usurious debt. No moral principle teaches that an open account is any the less an honest debt the year after it is five years old than the year before. No honest man will avail himself of this law, to avoid the payment of a debt honestly binding. Every principle of right says, that the stroke of an act of congress cannot wipe out just debts and annul bonds in the eye of conscience: so that the bankrupt, if he afterwards obtains the means, is as much bound to pay his old debts, in the eye of justice, as though no such law has liberated him. And so of the plea of usury: though the demanding of usurious interest in the first instance was sinful: yet, when the borrower has voluntarily promised to pay it, when he has received the usurer's money and enjoyed the use of it, to avail himself of this law for release from his own voluntary obligation, is treachery. He is still bound in the eye of God and conscience, to pay the principal with lawful interest. He who avails himself of *any* of these laws to keep his neighbor's property without compensation, keeps it dishonestly. He is guilty of a breach of the

eighth commandment. For the enactments of human legislators are not the standard of right. They cannot release any human being from moral obligation. The man who professes to let *the law* make his conscience, proves that he has no conscience. Laws vary in different nations; and of course, his conscience would change with them. In Turkey he would be guilty of bigamy. In India he would lie. In [the] Barbary States, [he would] be a pirate. In New Holland he would eat his own mother; for the laws and customs of those nations authorize these several sins. And when he reached the South Sea Islands, where there is no law, he would have *no conscience* at all!

5. Perhaps there is no dishonest conduct now common among those who wish to be considered upright men, than the liberties taken with the public purse and property. In dealing with the treasuries of the county, the commonwealth, and the Federal government, the common rule seems to be, that every one shall get as much as he can. For services rendered to the public, they charge higher prices; for commodities sold, they demand more; and in the settling of accounts, and the claiming of perquisites, the only limit they put upon themselves is that which the facility and laxity of the guardians of the public purse impose. So uniform is this conduct, that it has passed into a maxim of political economy, that every operation must usually cost the commonwealth more than it would cost a private individual. The true motive of all this peculating spirit [is] easily perceived. The public purse belongs to a multitude of citizens in common, so that the particular interest of each one in it is exceedingly small. And if a large sum is taken from it fraudulently, yet the portion of loss shared by each citizen (where the whole number is so great) is trifling. Hence no individual has any strong, *personal* interest in watching over fraud, proclaiming the attempt at peculation, and punishing the thief, as he has in his own private estate.[79] Again, where the sums handled are so large, a theft which would be important in amount to an individual, is small comparatively and less noticed. Thus the public treasury is a creature[80] vulnerable, as well as inviting. It lies like a great whale in shoal water, inviting depredations at once by its helplessness and its fatness. But is there anything in all this, to *justify* a greater license in exacting money from the public? If the sum lost by each individual citizen, in a large peculation, is exceedingly small, still, it is a theft. Certain it is, it does not belong to the peculator. And a multitude of

little thefts aggregated[81] into one, amount to a great theft. The crime is just that of the miller, who accumulated a hogshead of grain, by stealing[82] an eggshell full from each man's grist. The loss to each was imperceptible: yet the hogshead was as much a *stolen hogshead*, as though it had been all stolen from one man's garner. And if the public purse is in an unprotected state, compared with that of the individual, if the public is in a state like that of the rich orphan without a vigilant administrator, so much the baser is it, to take advantage of its orphanage. Undoubtedly, all this conduct is stealing, in the eye of God. His sleepless watchfulness observes all the snaky windiness and every delusive pretext of these workers of iniquity. And, at the last day, many of the great and honorable men of this world will find themselves dragged from their marble tombs to be ranked with the open thieves who will be raked from the graveyards of the gallows and the jail.

6. Another specious form of indirect theft is the heedless contracting of debts. The duty of not taking our neighbor's goods includes also the duty of using all the means and safeguards necessary to avoid the sin. He who creates a debt, without a reasonable certainty of being able to pay it, is guilty of the eighth commandment. It may not be his direct intention to take the creditor's property, at the time the debt is contracted: but he does that which he ought to know, he may know, he *does* know, if he reflects as he should, would lead to this result. There is no difference, whether the debt is contracted by direct borrowing, or by buying or credit: for he who sells on credit virtually makes the purchaser a loan of the value of the article so sold. There is a vast looseness of conscience in this matter of contracting debts: and unfortunately, it is often most general among those who especially claim gentility. Two young people set out in life as husband and wife. They suppose that a certain style of living is necessary to the reputation of gentility: their foolish vanity lays it down as a first principle that they *must* live up to that style; and without counting the cost, or considering whether their income will bear them out, they launch forth. Credit is easy: they buy without paying, and consume; until, after a few years, they are found bankrupt, and a number of just creditors lose their dues. A merchant or businessman sets out with a little nest egg of real capital, or perhaps none at all, and obtains large means by credit. He thinks he is doing a large business, because he

is handling much of other people's capital. And forthwith he concludes that he must live, not according to the *real capital he owns*, but according to the seeming wealth he handles. After a few years, he is a bankrupt, and leaves several thousands of just debts unpaid. He has, in fact, *eaten up*, in luxurious living, the little real capital he owned and more: so that his whole business rests really on a baseless, imaginary foundation: and his credit is a bubble. This is all genteel stealing. It is the duty of every man to know what his *real* income is, and to live within it. Otherwise we *cannot know* that we are not placing ourselves in circumstances where a robbery of creditors will be inevitable. He who does not ascertain his real means, and resolutely live within them, is not an honest man. And the heedlessness with which men contract debts without providing for the pay-day, is one of the most lamentable proofs which make us suspect that the honesty of a multitude of persons is only a selfish regard for appearances.

7. There is another gigantic vice which clearly comes under the eighth commandment: the vice of gambling: but we have left ourselves little room for its discussion. Under this name we include all bets, and horse racing, where money is staked, as well as the playing of games of skill or chance for money. And in the first place, gaming is fraud. It takes our neighbor's goods without returning any equivalent. It has precisely the same effect upon his worldly estate as a direct theft, causing the loss of the property to him. And the winning gamester sees all the misery and want inflicted upon his antagonist, and his family, which a robbery could cause. The gambler plays *in order to gain* his neighbor's property without compensation. This is the wish with which he sits down; and this wish is covetousness: it is the heart sin of which outward theft is the offspring. Let it not be said that gaming is distinguished from stealing by this: that the gamester takes the property of his adversary *openly*. So I answer, does the robber. Nor let it be said that is no theft, because the other party loses it by the game of chance, or bet, *of his own free will*. It is not true, in any proper sense, that the losing gambler *consents* to the loss of his money. No man ever sat down to a game of chance with the *intention* of losing. He does, indeed, expose the money staked by himself, to a chance of loss, of his own free will: but he believes that his luck, or skill, or fraudulent playing will save it from the risk, and make him the winner. No man would play if he did not thus hope. So that the loss is not a voluntary one.

But if it were, has the losing gamester a *right* to cast away the property of which God has made him a steward, and which belongs also to his wife and his babes, in this useless game? Surely not. His willingness to risk it there is wicked, and therefore it cannot be innocent to take advantage of his sin, to take the wasted property from him. If he has no right to *give* it, the winning gambler has no right to take it from him.

Second: gaming breaks the eighth commandment by creating a temptation to fraud, which none are able to withstand. It is well known that *no man* ever games habitually, without at length coming to cheat in playing. Professional gamblers assent this, as the result of their wide experience. I heard a gentleman of years, familiar with the sports of the turf remark, that the more he observed the more he was convinced that no man could be a professed racer and a gentleman. Now to cheat in games of chance, the gambler himself will admit, is stealing. But if the practice tempts and surely leads to this, then it is our duty to avoid it. The duty of being honest requires also that we shall shun the temptations to dishonesty.

Third: Every gamester is ultimately a ruined man. His vice therefore robs God, whose steward he is, robs his dependent family, and wastes his substance. And once more, it is the inlet to all dissipation, to drunkenness, profanity, late hours, and introduces to all bad company. It wears out the mind and spirits, brings care, anxiety, remorse and distress, and leads to suicide. No man can meddle with it in its remotest steps, and be safe or innocent.

And now, having examined these various forms of indirect theft, let us pause, and ask: what is their true moral character, in the sight of God and an honest conscience? Wherein does he who gets his neighbor's goods, without just equivalent, by any of these arts, differ from the direct thief? The motive is the same: in both it is the coveting of their neighbor's possession: the desire to injure him in his worldly estate by getting from him *something for nothing.* The substance of the act is the same in both: taking without paying.[83] The only essential difference is that the direct thief braves the penalty of the law; while those who steal by the various modes above described, more cunning and more cowardly, steal so as to enjoy the wages of the iniquity and at the same time dodge the law. The only difference is a difference of boldness and openness in the crime. How full, then, is the world of covert, but real breaches of the eighth commandment? And how many, who proudly, scornfully slight the convicted thief, must be ranked along side of him in the day of Judgment? Many a thrifty and respectable citizen, as men call him, many a proud and dainty female, many a professor of religion, many of judge and magistrate, who has set in stern judgment to condemn the open offender,[84] many a legislator and statesman, will be placed, by God's discriminating eye, along with that meanest, lowest criminal whom they had professed to scorn and revile, the thief.

This discussion gives us the strongest practical evidence of the depravity of our natures, and the sinfulness of our conduct. We have seen that the true spring and source of this base crime, covetousness, is in all our hearts. *Covetousness is spiritual theft.* Who of us is innocent? And this lust has so generally blinded men's eyes to the guilt of a multitude of arts and tricks which injure the rights of our neighbor, that few can say their hands are clean. Proud sinner: will you not acknowledge that God is true when he says your heart is depraved: seeing that you find in yourself the seeds, yea, the sproutings, of this coarsest, lowest sin?

There are many men who find much fault of ministers of the Gospel, because they preach so much about the theory of redemption, and the inward exercises of the heart. Ministers[85] ought, say they, to preach more on practical morals, if they wish to make men virtuous. They would have us lay down a moral character not only as the evidence, but the meritorious cause of acceptance with God. They desire this because they fancy that *they* possess that moral character: because they are proud of it. Well: to such we would say: Here is a specimen of preaching on practical morality. How like you it? Here is the morality of the gospel. How does your boasted morality stand the comparison? Bible morality requires all that I have pointed out in these sermons, or shall point out in the succeeding ones, it requires *all that can be* pointed out, of purity, justice, and honesty. It requires you to "love your neighbour as yourself." It forbids all the twists and turns, all the shufflings and concealments which I have described. It is not satisfied with an honesty such as yours, which satisfies itself with making the public opinion of a covetous world your guide, making the best bargains you can; and which takes those advantages of a fellow-creature's rights which a respectable reputation will allow. Now let me ask: if your morality cannot stand the test, in this very point on which you most prided yourself, uprightness between man and man, how will you stand in judgment? When questioned as to that great clap of duties, duties towards God, you were compelled always, to avow yourself deficient: but your boast and your reliance was that *towards your fellow men*, you were upright: more upright than many Christians. But if on that very head your morality be found hollow and defective, how will you appear before God?

"Now we know that what things soever the law saith, it saith to them who are under the law: that every mouth may be stopped, and all the world may become guilty before God. Therefore by the deeds of the law there shall no flesh be justified in his sight: for by the law is the knowledge of sin. But now the righteousness of God without the law is manifested, being witnessed by the law and the prophets; even the righteousness of God which is by faith of Jesus Christ unto all and upon all them that believe: for there is no difference: for all have sinned, and come short of the glory of God; [and are] justified freely by his grace through the redemption that is in Christ Jesus." (Romans 3:19-24) "Because thou sayest, I am rich, and increased with goods, and have need of nothing; and knowest not that thou art wretched, and miserable, and poor, and blind, and naked: I counsel thee to buy of me gold tried in the fire, that thou mayest be rich; and white raiment, that thou mayest be clothed, and that the shame of thy nakedness do not appear; and anoint thine eyes with eyesalve, that thou mayest see." (Revelation 3:17-18)[86]

A Warning Against Secular Prosperity[87]

A Sermon

on

Deuteronomy 32:15

"Then he forsook God which made him,
and lightly esteemed the Rock of his salvation."
(with reference to the whole passage, from v. 12 to v. 16)

Preached to a great assemblage, in the 2nd Presbyterian Church of Richmond, Va.[88] on the afternoon of Feb. 21st 1858. The day before the inauguration of the Washington Monument of Va.

Is not this the first occasion within the memory of man, when the temporal prosperity of the people was so great and general, that even complaining politicians were compelled to admit it? Agriculture, the basis of all increase, is successful; harvests are abundant, and markets unusually good. Commerce is expansive and progressive; money is plenty. The general standard of comfort in living is constantly improved; and among the wealthy classes, the stand of luxury is rising, with what we cannot call a rapid improvement; but, at least, with a rapid increase. Meanwhile, our modern Ophir continues to pour in its steady stream of gold. Perhaps such a spectacle of national plenty and increase, was never seen before.

Christians are enjoying their full share in these blessings; if blessings they are. They are in the foremost rank of every lawful business, and of every material comfort and luxury; and are gathering a full part even of the golden harvest of California. Besides this, the Church is free among us, in a sense in which it never enjoyed freedom before. Not only has it the fullest religious liberty, secured by law; but it enjoys the apparent respect of the press, of the government, and of the masses. Surely, "religion walks in her silver slippers." Such a combination of secular advantages was never possessed before by Christians.

If any parallel has ever existed, it was to be formed, probably, in the era of Israel's history which passes before the prophetic eye of Moses, in the text. His language is in the past tense; but the scenes he describes are future: to the divine Spirit, by which he then spoke, future and past have equal certainty. He saw in vision his people, miraculously delivered from Egypt, casting out the inhabitants of Canaan, possessing their fruitful and cultivated country, entering into the occupancy of houses, castles and towns ready built, and of teeming farms and vineyards, enjoying the abundant stores already gathered, and the herds of cattle, and flocks of sheep. They found the vats for wine and oil excavated in the living rock, stored with their rich contents, and even the wilder crags of the mountains, stocked, in the caverns, with the luscious labors of the innumerable bees. Their lands were blessed by God with the early and latter rains; and the results of their tillage were sure and abundant.

But no sooner were these benefits fully enjoyed, then they produced in the unthankful recipients the usual effects, arrogance, carnality, disobedience. According [to] the figure, which was, to a pastoral people, so graphic, "Jeshurun waxed fat and kicked; thou art waxen fat, thou art grown thick, thou art covered with fatness; then he forsook God which made him, and lightly esteemed the Rock of his salvation." This text has been selected, my brothers, as an instance of a sad truth, a truth which the introductory remarks show to be appropriate for our meditation; that *Temporal prosperity usually occasions spiritual decline.*

Is not the sin of Israel here in accordance with all the experience of the Church? Has it ever been able to enjoy such temporal prosperity without being poisoned by it?[89] Let us get the answer to this question from history and from human nature. The past does not furnish an instance, in which the spiritual health of the church has survived a season of high secular abundance. The [Church] has survived the sword and the fire. Like the burning bush, she has been unconsumed by persecutions. The power of kings and commonwealths, and the gates of hell, have not been able to prevail against her; but never, in a single case, has she failed to succumb, sooner or later, before the miasm of carnal ease and plenty. When, under Joshua, God "made Israel ride on the high places of the earth, that he might eat the increase of fields; and he made him to suck honey out of the rock, and oil out of the flinty rock; butter of kine and milk of sheep, with the fat of lambs, and rams of the breed of Bashan, and goats, with the fat of kidneys of wheat; and he did drink the pure blood of the grape"; what was the result? "Jeshurun waxed fat, and kicked"! And again, when the talents and virtues of David, and of David's less noble son, had raised the theocracy to the zenith of its prosperity, so that "Judah and Israel were many, as the sand which is by the sea in multitude, eating, and drinking, and making merry," when the nation became so rich that "silver was nothing accounted of, in the days of Solomon," how long was it before the apostasy of Jeroboam followed, and the idolatry of the calves at Dan and Bethel; yea, and Solomon's own backsliding?

So under the Christian dispensation, as long as the pristine church was oppressed and reviled, it remained comparatively pure and active: but from the very date of its establishment by Constantine, when it received external respect, ease, reverences and honors, began these corruptions, which, in a few centuries, brought on the dark ages. Thence forward, the only communions which had purity and vitality, were downtrodden churches like those of the Waldenses. The pure and active churches of the Reformation were born, and grew strong, amidst reproach, danger and strife. As soon as they became safely established, and Providence had given them rest on every side, their decline began. And where is now the glory of Geneva, of Wittenberg, of Leyden? Obscured by the twilight of Rationalism or Socinianism. Compare the pure zeal, the fraternal charity, the humility, of the Church of England, as it emerged from the fires of Bloody Queen Mary, with its subsequent worldliness, exclusiveness, Arminianism, and Popery. See what has been the effect of outward prosperity and power on the Established Church of Scotland, on Puritanism in New England, and *on ourselves*. Yes; let us count the feeble and retrograding beat of our own spiritual pulse, and note how much weaker is our own religious life, than in the days of [Samuel] Davies and [Gilbert] Tennent.

Looking into man's nature, we shall see some of the reasons for this result. Societies are made up of persons; hence, that which is a customary tendency in the hearts of individual men, will be the tendency of communities. Now, it ought not to be true; but it is true; (such is man's thankless and forgetful nature) that we are likely to feel less gratitude, as the favors we receive are multiplied. Try it my brother, with any neighbor you have. Send him a present this week; and he will return you his hearty thanks for it. But send him the same every week for three months; and then omit it; and he will almost feel that by this cessation, you have robbed him of a right. It will be well, if his politeness suffices to prevent his intimating so much to you. But we treat God in the same thankless way. We speak of the daily bounties which crown our lives, as his "common mercies." Why "common"? Only because they are so multiplied, that they have become habitual. But if they are multiplied, then each repetition should be an addition to our pleasing load of grateful obligation; for each is a dear gift from God. But by virtue of a perversion of the law of habit, in our diseased souls, this very repetition causes the bestowal of the blessing to make less impression upon our hearts; so that the sense of obligation is deadened just in the inverse proportion to our debt. Here then, we have this result; that sluggish, thankless indifference to God's love and benevolence, will naturally grow out of continued prosperity.

Second, it is very evident that worldly success stimulates worldly affections. [90]The more money men have it in their power to make, the more they will love to make money. Gain stimulates the desire of gain. That Christians will win success, is usually ensured by those qualities which accompany godliness, integrity, industry, punctuality, economy. But continued success weakens the sense of dependence on Providence; and the too prosperous Christian begins to "sacrifice to his drag, and burn incense to his net."

Third, when abundance is acquired, how is it likely to be employed? In alms, and pious uses? Or in avaricious hoarding, or the pomps and vanities of life? Alas, the influences which have just been explained are too apt to decide this question adversely. The same love of gain, whetted by success, and increasingly unmindful of God's kindness, which wins these growing acquisitions, will very surely determine their perversion to selfish purposes. The new abundance will either be engrossed by the designs of that covetousness which is idolatry; or they will be devoted to the "lust of the flesh, and the lust of the eyes, and the pride of life." Thus comes in luxury, with its self-indulgence, its enervations, its pride, its impatience of toil, its sensual desires; and spiritually dies, as surely as the lamp goes out in the mephitic air of a cavern.

But fourth, there follows the most fatal cause of all; that the danger arising from temporal ease and plenty, is one which leads the Christian away from his fountain of strength, the mercy seat, just in degree as the danger becomes more imminent. The spiritual life of a Christian, or a church, is like that of the roots of a sturdy oak, which grow more tough by the storm, because then they grasp more tightly the crevices of the rock. It is like the refined gold, which must be purified from its dross in the furnace of fire. It is like the strength and hardihood of the soldier, which are formed by exposure and battle. Let the Christian be persecuted, troubled, or afflicted; his trials, by casting down his heart, bring it to the footstool of grace in humble prayer. And there, he finds a strength which rises elastic and indomitable under every oppression, because it is the strength of God communicated to him. Hence it is, that the Christian is benefited by reproach and affliction; and that the fire of persecution has often been the most prosperous element for the church. That which crushes it down, at the same time brings it into contact with the source of might and life. But alas, just when the forgetful Christian is most endangered by pride, fullness of bread, worldliness, and sensuality, then he is farthest from prayer. Let us borrow an illustration from classic mythology. When Hercules wrestled with the giant Antaeus, son of the Earth, he was baffled by finding that his antagonist rose from every fall with new strength; so that the more he was subdued, the more unconquerable he became. But at last Hercules perceived that it was because Antaeus, as often as he fell upon the bosom of his mother, received new vigor from the contact. And then the god of strength lifted him up in his mighty arms, so that he could no longer touch his mother-Earth; and speedily, crushed him to death in his embrace. So wrestles this mighty and insidious prosperity. So wrestles Satan now with the church, which he has found by other means unconquerable. Finding that the Church has risen with immortal vigor, as often as she has been pressed down upon the bosom of her Savior, and driven out of her pride and self-dependence to the throne of grace by affliction, he now lifts her aloft in carnal abundance, security, and haughtiness; in order that having separated her from the spring of her strength, he may choke her to death in his treacherous embrace.

In a word, since the whole is made up of its parts; the spirituality of the church consists of that of its individual members. But let every true Christian review his own life, and see how nearly his whole spiritual progress has been made in the seasons of trial. Dearly beloved:

have not your steps in advance towards heaven been chiefly taken in the season of private affliction, on the sick bed, in the chamber of bereavement, beside the dying couch or the fresh graves of those you love?

To close up this part of my argument, let us inquire whether the aspect of the Church does not already betray signs of the fatal effects of an unblessed abundance. I point you to the growing and unblushing conformity of Christians to the worldly standard of conduct: to the extravagance of selfish and ostentatious expenditure, which has now become such, that there is no license of luxury, in building equipage or diet, to which the world rushes in the very riot of its rampant prodigality, which Christians are not eager to imitate: to the cold, metallic mercenary spirit, and inordinate greed for wealth, which seem to be the main-springs of effort; to the decline of sober, moderate and devotional habits of life; to the relaxed standard of morals which is adopted, alike, in the realms of business and pleasure. Is there much religious bustle; much almsgiving? Alas! it does not keep pace with the means and obligations, which accrue with our growing wealth; and there is reason to fear that much of it is as foreign to Christianity, as Phariseism was – as much inspired, in many quarters, by ostentation and self-righteousness.

Is it not, then, a most sober and literal truth, that this is a time of more danger than the time of persecution and oppression? We verily believe, that splendid is the grace which carries the martyr to the stake, and sustains him in his baptism of fire; glorious as is the display of Divine power in a church downtrodden but indomitable, persecuted, but not consumed: the grace which should carry a church through a season of continued prosperity and carnal ease, such as we now experienced, would be still more potent. The church has often enjoyed the former grace; she has never yet attained permanently unto the latter. It seems as though this were a height of spiritual attainment, which is reserved for the better days ushering in the millennial glory. But the rule is: that grace is bestowed in answer to prayer. Now, while seasons of persecution are seasons of abounding prayer, this era of carnal plenty is a time of prayerlessness. By how much is the danger more imminent? If then, the approach of oppression or persecution, or the prospect of losing our religious liberties would awaken the voices of the watchmen of our Zion trumpet loud; what should be the action now of those "who have understanding of the times, to know what Israel ought to do"? Should not the teachers and rulers of the church lift their voices in warning, more loudly even, than when [John] Knox called upon his countrymen to stand for their lives against the Pope and tyrants? And should not every Christian gird himself against the danger, with a spirit more earnest, cautious, and prayerful, than if he were counting the cost for a deadly warfare with persecution? True, ours is a danger which, just now, comes with no clamor, no "distress of nations and perplexity," or roaming of the seas of popular commotion. But if it is a danger, the wise man will therefore proclaim it with a voice only the more urgent and startling; because, unlike that class of calamities, it does not proclaim itself. The household which should be awakened at the cold midnight, with the news that an absent member was freezing to death somewhere on the highway, would start from their beds into intense alarm and exertion. But that frost which was fast freezing their brother's blood into fatal sleep, is a thing most quiet and noiseless; as quiet as the general dew! And so, "the pestilence that walketh in darkness," with no outward sign or voice, but the stillness and desertion of the streets, and the muffled roll of the hearse, thrills the hearts of a people with as sharp as an alarm as the clamorous voice of war. And rightly. So, unless we bestir ourselves with a wise alarm and diligence, utterly unlike our present conduct, and entirely above any to which any previous church has ever attained, in the like case, our present ease will be our ruin; and history will date the decline and fall of American Christianity from our generation. But alas! Where is the voice powerful enough to pierce the ear benumbed with this worldly abundance, and to rouse the sleepy, self-indulgent soul of the church, lapped in these folds of seductive ease, to more than the awakened hardihood and prayerfulness of a martyr communion? Can you reasonably flatter yourselves that you shall be an exception to all previous history? To human judgment, your history must be this; either to sink deeper and deeper into formalism, worldliness, heresy, and immorality, with, (perhaps) partial and temporary resuscitations, till our light shall go out in a night which, like that of the seven churches of Asia, is to have no morning: or else, you must expect to be lashed back to duty and to the throne of grace, by the loss of your abused abundance, and religious liberties, by social calamities and political oppressions, until you are restored, purified, and filled to promote the work of God. And if God, in his grace, shall deliver you from both these destinies, if he shall sustain and restore your spiritual life while he leaves you your present outward prosperity; then will that display of divine power and indwelling be more truly new and wonderful, than anything which the church has ever yet experienced. Again I ask, recalling the rule, "he that asketh receiveth"; do you think that there is enough prayer now in the church to justify the expectation of such effusions of the Holy Spirit?

Learn, then, these lessons my brother: from the truth established. Beware of unsanctified prosperity. "Watch and pray, that ye enter not into temptation." Be humble. Repine not at loss or affliction: your Father, may see that it is your necessary medicine. "Honour the Lord with thy substance, and with the first fruits of all thy increase"; so, by sanctifying the first fruits, the remainder may become holy unto you. (Romans 11:16) Beware, I repeat, of that abused bounty of God, in which his goodness, which should have led thee to repentance, being perverted, is treasured up as a material of wrath, against the day of wrath, and revelation of the righteous judgment of God. (Romans 2:4-5) Hear your Redeemer-King say: "As many as I love, I rebuke and chasten: be zealous therefore, and repent." (Revelation 3:19) But if you will not, then be sure this season of deceitful peace, is the time when the bolt is secretly fitting to the string, to pierce you. This is the sultry, relaxing, drowsy, calm which precedes the hurricane, when the storm is spreading its dusky wings in the silence, and preparing its might to wreck the forests and lash the seas into chaos.

Let one humbly beg my brethren, the preachers of Christ, to accept a suggestion touching their duty likewise. If you clearly foresaw a powerful assault about to be made upon the spiritual independence of your charges: if you saw the fires already kindling for those who should refuse to bow the knee to Antichrist: how would you lift up your voices! How would you warn, and adjure the slumbering people! Well; a greater Danger is upon them; greater, because [it is] more insidious, more sure in its mischievous efficacy.[91]

What then, is the remedy for the organized church? By what means is this rescue to be effected, so unusual that it is scarcely to be hoped? We shall find the answer to this question, in asking another: what was God's benevolent design in giving this prosperity? Not, surely, to be a trap and curse to us! This is the secondary use to which his righteous and wise retribution will convert it, if it be abused by us. But surely, he gave it primarily, that we might find our safe and innocent enjoyment in it, by using it for his glory. Here, then, is our escape from its benumbing effects. We must be unlike all the outwardly prosperous churches which have ever gone before us, in the use which we make of our prosperity. We must be as distinguished for our large-hearted liberality, and our expanded plans of beneficence, as we are for temporal riches and privileges. We must burst forth on every side, into a magnificence of missionary enterprise, as marvelous as the growth of our commerce, arts, agriculture, and general prosperity. We must cast the antiquated measures and standards of Christian liberality to the winds. Our prosperity has utterly outgrown them, and calls upon us to adopt new and larger designs. This is our only medicine for the unwholesomeness of our abundance. Thus alone shall we be able to consecrate it and render it harmless. Our only escape is in giving and doing for Christ, on a scale as eminent as that of his liberality to us.

But should God give us the heart to adopt this remedy, how blessed, how splendid would be the aspect of such a church! Such outward means and advantages, armed with such grace, would surely work wonders for Christ, and for man. Perhaps, this conjunction; never yet long maintained by the people of God, is to be the precursor of the *millennium*.[92]

Profaning God's Name[93]

A Sermon

on

Exodus 20:7

"Thou shalt not take the name of the Lord thy God in vain: for the
Lord will not hold him guiltless that taketh his name in vain."

Preached at Union Seminary. October 1859.[94]

According to the Shorter Catechism, the third commandment requireth the holy and reverent use of God's names, titles, attributes, ordinances, word and works: and forbiddeth all profaning or
abusing of *any thing whereby God maketh himself known.*[95] We are
justified in giving this extent of signification to the words *my name*
in the letter of the precept, as including every thing by which God is
made known, or presented to the mind of the hearer, or beholder.
What is a *name*[?] It is a sign spoken or written, which represents
to the mind a certain thing, or Being. The mention of one of God's
titles, as the word 'creator,' or of one of his peculiar attributes, as his
eternity, or of his sacred Scriptures, or the sight of an ordinance of
worship or a sacrament, or even the pointing of the hand to heaven,
may represent to the mind the idea of God; just as truly as the *word*
God, or Jehovah. There is therefore the same reason for the reverent
use of all these things, as for the reverent use of his name. Any thing
by which God is represented to the mind of the hearer or spectator
partakes of the same nature with the names of God, and is therefore
to be reverenced, as his name should be reverenced.

The object of this precept therefore is to secure the reverential
treatment of God: and of all that immediately pertains to and suggests him. Its object is to exclude every thing that is *profane* in the
treatment of God's names, attributes, Scriptures and worship. The
expression 'taking his name in vain,' evidently means, using it in an
unnecessary or in a *light* and frivolous manner. The essential wick-

edness of this making use of his name, or of any thing else that represents him, or suggests him to the mind, is plain from His majesty and greatness, and from the *feelings* of love and fear with which He ought to be regarded in the heart. *Words* are the expression of thoughts and feelings. We ought not therefore to *speak* lightly of him of whom we ought not to *think* lightly. So that this commandment is founded on the First, and follows necessarily from the duty there implied of *having* God for our God, and regarding him with the veneration and love due to a God. When we consider the unspeakable majesty, greatness, and excellence of our God, which cause the most powerful and glorious beings in heaven to serve him with the deepest, most awful reverence, and when we join with this, our puny, weak and guilty condition before him, the obligation to a reverential treatment of him and his affairs appears inexpressibly strong. Levity or irreverence in speaking of a parent or ruler appears highly improper; Consider the immense difference between the most exalted human ruler and Jehovah, and how much greater the sin of levity or disrespect towards Him?

This commandment then, in the first place, requires us to cultivate reverential and adoring *thoughts* of Him[.][96] . . . It requires us to treat his name, and all that refers to, or suggests Him with seriousness and awe: to swear in his name, and in the name of nothing else, when an oath becomes proper and necessary, with truth, sincerity and devotional reverence. It requires us to use and to witness his worship and sacraments with solemnity and sincerity; and to read, repeat or hear his word always with the highest respect and attention.

But the chief practical instruction of the Precept will be gained by discussing the things which are forbidden by it. And here we are met by an interesting question: whether the taking of an oath from the civil magistrate or church officer, with scrupulous truth and reverence, is taking the name of God in vain. It is known, I suppose, to all, that the Quakers, and some other denominations of Christians hold this view, and conscientiously refuse to take the usual form of oath before the courts of the country. This has always been thought by us an unnecessary strictness: as we hold that to take an oath in affairs of suitable importance, and when tendered by lawful authorities, is scriptural and beneficial; provided it be taken with due reverence and truth. Our reasons are the following. Moses expressly commands the people to swear by the name of Jehovah, when they did swear. (Deuteronomy 6:13) This surely implies that there is a right and proper time to swear. The Israelites were carefully instructed how to swear. (Leviticus 19:12) Oaths were appointed to be administered by divine authority in certain cases: and surely God would not require his people to do that which is wrong. (Exodus 22:11, Numbers 5:19) We find that God sware: and "because he could swear by no greater, he swore by himself." And although we are not to presume to do all that it is proper for God to do, yet his example is worthy of mention here. We find also that the apostles, and especially Paul, frequently appealed to God by an oath as the witness of their assertions. (Romans 1:9, II Corinthians 1:23, Galatians 1:20) These expressions involve all the essentials of an oath. Others might be cited. And although it was possible for an inspired apostle to do wrong, as witness Peter; (Galatians 2:11) yet we can hardly suppose that if an oath had been in all circumstances unlawful, Paul would so often have indulged in it: and his oaths would have been left on record in the sacred Scriptures without any expression of blame. But we have a more indisputable example. Jesus Christ took an oath, when it was tendered to him by Caiaphas the High Priest acting as the authorized magistrate (though a wicked one) of the Jewish people. (Matthew 26:63-64) We know that the expressions used by the Hebrew prophet "I adjure thee by the living God," etc., were those in which, at that day, a magistrate administered an oath among the Jews. His addressing these words to a person before him would have been understood by any Jew, as putting him on his oath. (The words *adjure thee* mean, *I swear thee*). Thus understanding him, Christ promptly gave an affirmative answer, (though before he had refused to give any answer) thereby taking the oath tendered to him. Let it be noticed also, that in this, He was acting in his *human capacity*, as a subject to the government of his country. This is an example absolutely satisfactory, proving that an oath may be lawful.

The contrary opinion is founded essentially upon the positiveness of two or three expressions of the New Testament. (Matthew 5:34, 37 and James 5:12) It is asserted that these direct and explicit assertions absolutely exclude all oaths; and that they cannot be explained away or weakened, without treating sacred Scripture with disrespect. To this we answer that if this absolute interpretation be insisted on: all that will be gained will be to make sacred Scripture contradict itself, and to prove that the holy and blessed Savior committed sin: in swearing to the High Priest. The law of Moses on this subject was not repealed by the precept given in the Sermon on the Mount; because the moral law is unchangeable, because Christ said (Matthew 5:17), and this act of his, in taking an oath at the mouth of the Jewish ruler was subsequent to the Sermon on the Mount. A proper understanding of the circumstances of the times will explain the true intention of our Savior's and the Apostle James' language. The Jewish Elders had corrupted the third Commandment by teaching that a man might interlard his common conversation with oaths, and there was no profanity, provided what he swore was true. They also taught that one might swear by any thing else than the name of God, as his temple, or altar, or some of his works, and be innocent. Against *these* corruptions our Savior's precept is aimed. What he forbids is the causeless use of oaths. In our common intercourse with our fellow men, we are not to swear at all: but let our yea be yea, and our nay, nay. The express law of God, the practice of the Apostle Paul in his official character, and of Christ himself prove that this was his intention.

But, on the other hand it should be urgently stated, that it is a great evil for civil governments to multiply the occasions of taking oaths needlessly. An oath is an appeal to our Maker, which should be reserved for times when something of really solemn importance is concerned. To ordain that oaths shall be administered in a multitude of trivial civil concerns, as is too often done, makes the government guilty of profanity: though the citizen who takes the oath with sincerity and reverence is innocent. The heartless and hurried manner in which the oath is often[97] administered, where neither magistrate nor subject pays any true regard to the awful name to which they appeal, makes it often a taking of the name of God in vain.[98]

Among the sins forbidden by this commandment may be classed all irreverent uses of God's holy word. Dictated by the Holy Ghost himself, treating of the most sacred and important of all subjects, and intimately associated with all that is awful in the divine name and character, it[99] should never be alluded to nor cited without solemn respect. The practice of using quotations of sacred Scripture to point a jest, or provoke a laugh by the ingenuity of its application partakes strongly of profanity. It is extremely common to hear our political men dray the expressions of sacred Scripture into their discourse, as though their highest idea of wit was, to degrade God's word by an irrespected application to an unholy subject, and provoke by it the coarse laugh of the multitude. If reverence cannot restrain them in this habit, they would often be wise to forbear from self-respect: for they usually betray in their quotations an ignorance of holy writ as disgraceful as their profanity. This practice has the mischievous effect to associate the various expressions of sacred Scripture so used with a ludicrous idea, which puts to flight all feelings of reverence when those passages are heard again. (Psalm 138:2, II Timothy 3:16)

The sacred name is doubtless often taken in vain, by heartless and formal worship. God has told us that he must be worshipped in *spirit*, that he reads the heart, that he disregards the mere hollow form, and hates it, and that he cannot be mocked. To worship him, with the lips, or the postures of the body alone, is an implied insult to him. How often is his sacred name addressed in prayer, by those whose minds are full of vain and wandering thoughts,[100] with as real levity and emptiness, as it is used by those who employ it for an expletive to their conversations? How often do men call upon God with their lips, when the heart pays no regard to his majesty? Nay, how often do *we* thus take his name in vain?[101]

The spirit of this commandment is broken also by all irreverence or levity in the worship and sacraments. Sacred exercises, and sacred places even, are suggestive of the idea of Him to whom they are dedicated: and should be beheld with reverence. Levity in the presence of divine things partakes of the essential nature of profanity. And especially is this true of that most solemn and touching of all ordinances, the Lord's Supper. To behold this lively representation of the most lovely and awful work of Divine compassion, even as a spectator, with any other than the most solemn respect, is a glaring insult to God whose justice and mercy are there harmonized, and to Jesus Christ there visibly set forth, crucified before us. I doubt not that many a person, the child of pious parents, whose lips would turn pale at the attempt to utter verbal blasphemies, yea many a female who supposes herself to be refined and sensitive, is regarded by God as guilty of a profanity akin to that of the drunken blasphemy, by his levities, smiles, whisperings and inattention in the presence of the sacred emblems.[102]

There are certain kinds of exclamations, and minced oaths, and little harmless imprecations much in use among some professors of religion, which they suppose to be innocent because they contain no mention of the name of our Maker, or his eternal retributions. All such expressions should be retrenched. This disposition to use them arises from a sinful source. (Matthew 5:37) The use of all such expletives gives to the wicked profane, just ground for this disgraceful suspicion;[103] they indicate that you have a hankering after the more thoroughgoing and vigorous curses which they indulge, and would fain use them if you were not forbidden. Now, even a harmless imitation (if there could be a harmless imitation) of any thing so wicked as profaning the name of God, is, at the least, contemptible in one who professes to serve him.[104]

Another dreadful breach of this command is the sin of *perjury*, or false swearing. And we fear that heinous as this crimes is, there are many different modes in which it is committed among us, though differing in enormity. In taking a legal oath, we in substance invoke the all seeing God of truth as the *witness* of the truth of what we say. And we imply that we devote ourselves to his awful retributions as our judge and avenger, if we swear falsely. Legal oaths are also a most important means for securing fidelity in civil officers, and truth in witnesses. (Hebrews 6:16) If no dependence could be put in any oath, the benign bond of government would be sundered, it would be impossible to administer justice, to acquit the innocent, or punish the guilty, or to trust any officer or magistrate. Perjury therefore tends to plunge society into all the horrors of savage anarchy and mutual mistrust. Hence it is an atrocious crime against the community, and is justly punished as a felony by our criminal laws. But it is also a heinous act of profanity towards God. (Leviticus 19:12) It implies a thorough contempt for either God's knowledge or his judgments. It either says to God: 'I believe not that thou art the searcher of hearts'; or else, 'I brave thy wrath, and defy thy judgments.' It invokes the God of *truth* to witness the assertion of a falsehood. It drags down his sanctity and his majesty and degrades them into a cloak for the attempted deception. Can we wonder then that God abhors it, and condemns it in the sternest words of inspiration? (Zechariah 5:4, Malachi 3:5) An oath in the name of God should be ever regarded as a most sacred and awful bond: to be only taken with careful, circumspect truth and reverence: and when taken, to be more carefully preserved than life itself. Better to brave grisly death with all his terrors than the majesty of Jehovah insulted by dragging his name down to sanction a lie!

To swear heedlessly an oath binding ourselves to things beyond our power, profanes God's name. To take him to witness to a *sinful* vow is still more profane. To swear with a mental reservation, putting upon the terms of the oath a secret sense, and with the intention to break that sense in which it is administered and understood by others, is perjury. There is reason to fear that the same black crime is often committed in affairs of bankruptcy, where money or property is concealed by the bankrupt, or some artifice is used to vest in others a nominal right to that which should have been resigned to creditors. In the filing of the pleas in certain kinds of suits, the spirit of litigation, it is to be feared leads many to commit fearful perjuries. Many, in taking oaths of office, whose duties they heedlessly neglect, stain their consciences and their dignities with the same foul crime. And what shall we say of those honorable(!) legislators, who swear to maintain the constitution and laws, while at the very moment of taking the oath their ruling desire and purposes is to make everything bend to the interests of party: or the still baser interests of their own self advancement? And what of those *doubly* perjured men who not only swear thus, but then break in their own persons many of the laws which as legislators they enact? We fear that in the taking of all oaths of office, there is a grievous laxity of conscience, even among men otherwise honorable: that they have not weighed sensibly the requirements of their sacred vow; and that instead of serious purpose to attempt the fulfillment of them *all*, in their just and full sense, and in the fear of Him whose sanction they invoke: the highest intention formed in their minds is to imitate the imperfect conduct of those who are reckoned *decent* and respectable officers. How many a Grand Juror, Justice of the Peace, and legislator swears thus? Such swearing is not innocent. Well may we exclaim with the Hebrew Prophet, in view of the multitude of false or heedless oaths which pollute the name of the most High. (Jeremiah 23:10)

But the most important breach of this commandment, because the most awfully frequent, is profane conversation. By some the name of God, or some one of this titles or attributes is often mentioned as a mere expletive to their talk. Others again appeal to the Almighty for sanction to the most trivial assertions. Others imprecate the dreadful retributions of eternity upon themselves in certain contingencies, or upon others, when incensed by any trifle. While not a few seem to exert a diabolical ingenuity in inventing new and more blasphemous curses. The blackest extreme to which this sin can be carried is that of cursing or reviling God himself or his works.[105]

The exceeding wickedness of this vice appears from this: that it indicates a thorough irreverence for God himself. *Names* are spoken symbols of things and Beings. According to the habit and usage of all mankind, the name always suggests, more or less distinctly, the *idea* it represents. Hence an irreverent use of the *name* of God carries with it an irreverent use of the idea of God. It is vain for the man of profane language to attempt to disclaim the intention of disrespect towards God. A disrespectful use of his sacred names and titles betrays an indisputable disregard for the conception of *Him* whom the name necessarily suggests. No man can use, or permit others to use with levity the name of a parent whom he venerates and loves. There is not an ingenious son, whose cheek would not burn, and whose arm would not be nerved with resentment, if he heard the name of his Father used with that irreverence with which men employ the name of the Most High. In accordance with this, we find that God requires the same reverence to be paid to his name as himself. (Isaiah 29:23, Deuteronomy 28:58, Matthew 6:9)[106]

But what state of mind can be imagined, more wicked than irreverence or disrespect towards the Almighty? So acknowledge the existence of this Being, so awfully great, powerful and sovereign, on whom we depend at every moment, and to whom we must answer for every act, a being so holy and lovely in his character, so terrible in his eternal opposition to sin, and his zeal for his own glory: and yet to regard him with light and irreverent feelings is a moral absurdity, and an opposition to reason beyond the reach of human expression. Such a feeling may be regarded as the essential trait, the very core, of sin. For if we consider sin as a transgression of God's law, it may be resolved into a feeling of contempt and disrespect to the infinite majesty of the Lawgiver. The disposition of the profane man is then not merely one trait of a sinful man; it is the character of wickedness itself. It is to be wished that we could rid ourselves of the illusions produced by a dreadful familiarity with profanity: and apprehend the enormity of the practice as it appears to those who behold the unveiled glories of him whom sinful worms insult. We might see how unspeakably wicked a thing it is, that a creature so low and so puny and so vile as man, should select the name of him whom cherubim cannot behold without veiling their faces, whom all the heavenly principalities adore with profoundest awe, Him whose frown shakes creation, and whose anger sets Hell on fire, as the byword and scoff of their idlest and lowest hours.

Not less heaven-daring is the practice of cursing themselves or others, and invoking damnation upon those with whom the profane swearer is provoked. When God has proclaimed these awful, and eternal retributions, and surrounded the idea of them with all the terrors of his own offended majesty, in order to warn his creatures away from all sin; what shall we say of the reckless, God-defying contempt, with which they select those very terrors for their idle expletive and byword? Must not God regard it as studied defiance of his wrath; as a sneering at the very sword of his justice? When the swearer calls down damnation on his fellow sinner, we are to suppose either that he *is* in earnest, or that he *is not*. If he is in earnest: what fiendlike malice is this to invoke so dreadful a punishment as eternal perdition upon a fellow creature, perhaps a companion, or a friend? To pray that he may burn forever in torment, and all for some trivial offence that will be forgotten in a day?[107] But we are willing to take the more charitable supposition: that the swearer is *not in earnest* in his curses. Then if this be the case, if their imprecations are intended to have no real meaning, is not this more than to insinuate that, in their view, Damnation has no existence, and that the sanctions of divine law are an empty fable? Does it not imply that, in the swearer's view, Christianity is a dream, and its most awful doctrines, like the exploded fables of classic paganism, are only fit to embellish the eloquence of his invective? How could he who truly believed and felt that there is a dreadful hell for the disobedient, invoke its horrors on every trivial event, merely to clench and enforce the expression of his anger?

Nothing is more common than to hear the swearer invoke damnation upon himself, in case he should fail to carry out some unimportant assertion: or confirming such assertions by an oath. It is a sufficient objection to such a practice, that it ensures the commission of *perjury*. Where a person binds himself so heedlessly and so frequently by an oath, to the performance of various unimportant things, some of them must be omitted: and some of his oaths are sure to be broken. Every profane swearer is a perjurer. He has broken his oaths to God: and lies under the black guilt of calling upon Divine Truth and Majesty to attest a falsehood.

And let the swearer remember that in such cases, the condition on which his curse of himself was suspended, is fulfilled: and his imprecation stands as a prayer to God for his own damnation. He said, in substance: "if I fail to do this, or that: let this dreadful punishment come upon me": he has failed to do it, and his imprecation now descends upon his own head. Let us consider the true import of the *swearer's prayer*. What is it he has called down upon his own head, when he rolls the words 'damn' and 'damnation' so frequently from his guilty tongue? He has prayed that God would punish him in hell forever: that He would shut out every beam of mercy and of hope from his soul: that He would remember every sin he has ever committed, every Sabbath broken, every oath uttered, every unclean word or thought or deed, and avenge them to the utmost: that heaven may be shut forever against him: that Devils and lost souls may be his companions: that his body may be tortured forever in the bottomless pit with inconceivable agonies, and his soul be the eternal prey of remorse and despair. He has said to God: "Let my soul be blotted from the Lamb's book of life: let the blackness of darkness be my home: and do thou, infinite, almighty God pour out thy omnipotent fury upon me in hell forever, and ever and ever!" Such, profane swearer, is the prayer which you have offered up again and again to your Maker. Do not think that he will forget it. Every one of thy tremendous petitions is set down against thee, and unless thou repentest, will be answered to the full. And let the heaven and the earth wonder that the fearful answer has not fallen upon you already. And will you not fear to utter another curse, lest at last, the patience of God should fail, and your imprecations be at once hurled upon your head?

This is a useless and superfluous sin. It subserves no real purpose. Theft may put money into the pockets. Lying may secure a temporary advantage in business, avarice may secure riches, lewdness may gratify the appetites, gluttony and drunkenness may please the palate for a few minutes, though at the expense of subsequent nausea and disgust: but profanity answers no end and gratifies no appetite. It makes no one richer, or more powerful, or more respected. It is mere "superfluity of naughtiness."[108] It seems to be an empty badge worn by irreligious persons, to signify their allegiance to the enemy of souls to let the world see that they are not under the restraints of religion. We can assure such persons that they need not put themselves to this trouble to exonerate them from the suspicion of being fearers of God. There is no danger of their being mistaken for such, either here, or in the day of judgment.

It would seem that misguided young persons often use profane language, in order to give themselves an air of *manliness* and *courage*. What is it, which teaches them that to brave God's anger is a proof of courage, except the wicked ridicule of their ungodly associates, who scoff at religious restraints as a mark of weakness? Spare me from a courage which cowers at the *laugh of fools* more than it fears an almighty Judge, and an eternal Hell! And how a proficiency in this *language of hell* can conduce to *manliness*, it is hard to conceive, when those are most skillful in it whose baseness has sunk them farthest beneath the level of human beings: and the young aspirant to manhood will always find his highest superiors and best instructors in the art, among the most beastly outcasts who disgrace the human form. Profane swearing may make the youth devilish: It can never make him *manly*.

[Does any one excuse himself by saying that "the habit is already so strong that he cannot help swearing;" "that he does it unconsciously?" . . . You are mistaken: I will defend you against your own disgraceful admissions.][109] You can refrain before ladies. If you respected God as much, you could refrain before him.

[Some plead] your inferiors won't think you are in earnest, unless you clench your words with an oath: they have so long heard you swear. [I] answer: If you had behaved yourself as a gentleman should from the first, this difficulty would never have existed. But it is not true. You can easily show you are in earnest, by voice, countenance and acts.

[Some of you may excuse yourselves by saying that] you don't mean any thing by [swearing]. So much the worse: to use the most sacred and dreadful name entirely without meaning. What better definition could be given of the words, "take my name *in vain*"?[110]

"The Lord will not hold him guiltless that taketh his name in vain." This is the reason annexed for observing this commandment. However human laws may pass by your sin and man's rebuke may leave you untouched, God will take care that your guilt shall not go unpunished. All your curses will one day come rolling back upon your head freighted with the storm of God's wrath, unless you repent.

Then will you not repent, and seek forgiveness for these enormous sins, in Christ's blood? (Matthew 12:31) Oh come and seek pardon and *release* from the horrid practice. Grace alone can cure it.

The Sin of the Tempter[III]

A Sermon

on

Habakkuk 2:15

"Woe unto him that giveth his neighbor drink, that puttest thy bottle
to him, and makest him drunken also, that thou mayest look
on their nakedness."

Preached in the College Church, Hampden-Sydney, Va., February 1860.

About six hundred years before Christ, the great Chaldean or Babylonian empire reached the height of its powers. It rose rapidly in a few generations upon the ruins of the Assyrian or Ninevite kingdom by treacherous rebellion and violent wars, until it reached the zenith of its wickedness and success under Nebuchadnezzar. It is this triumphant power which forms the main subject of Habakkuk's prophecies. He foresees it founded in violence and revolt, ravaging its unoffending neighbors abroad, and building upon its splendor at home by domestic tyranny and exaction, until its iniquities are full; and it meets an overthrow as astounding as its successes. But it was in this short and rapid career of national crime that it was employed by God as a rod to scourge rebellious Judah. In like manner had Assyria been used to punish the kingdom of the Ten Tribes.

We learn that rapacity and violence were not the only crimes of the Babylonian kingdom. It appears that it was also notoriously guilty of propagating its false religion: a form of gross idolatry which was probably peculiarly arrogant and wicked. This people not only overthrew the altar and worship of the true God, and did what they could to suppress the very existence of his visible church, but profanely asserted the inferiority of Jehovah, and inculcated in the conquered nations the imitation of their own vices. Idolatry is as corrupting to man as it is dishonorable to God. It is the parent of all forms of moral depravity, and of all crimes. Hence the question between idolatry and the worship of the true God is always one between vice and virtue; so that, even if God's exclusive claim to the homage of his creatures be set aside, a most solid reason remains for his forbidding and punishing the worship of idols.

This intimate relation between false religions and gross morals may help to explain the fact that the symbolical language of prophecy has selected some of the more sensual vices to represent the complex guilt of idolatry. In many places (as Jeremiah 3:1, Ezekiel 16:15, and Revelation 19:12) it is represented by the sin of unchastity; in Revelation 17:2-5, the idolatry of Rome is symbolized by the combined figures of adultery and drunkenness; and in the text, the inculcation of false religion by the Chaldeans by enticing to the sin of drunkenness alone. When we give this general sense to the figure of one putting his bottle to his neighbor, we by no means exclude a particular reference to the literal sin of intoxication; for doubtless this was one of the abominations with which the orgies of their pagan worship were celebrated.

Now, as Babylon was the great persecutor and destroyer of the church under the Old Testament, so the Romish apostasy has been its great enemy and corrupter under the New. Hence it is, that in the Apocalypse, *Babylon* is the prophetic name for Rome and Popery. The symbol of Revelation 17:2-5, a pompous and licentious queen, as abandoned as splendid, seducing with the golden cup of her uncleanness and abominations the mighty ones of the earth, and drunk with the blood of saints, may assist us to explain the figure of the text. The crime of Rome was that she persecuted and slew a part and endeavored to corrupt the remainder of Christendom with her false religion and gross morals. Such, therefore, was the sin which the text denounces in Babylon: the teaching of irreligion and vice, and soliciting to its commission. The disgraceful exposure resulting from the seduction of the foolish victim represents the degradation and shame which the malignant tempter produces, and then scorns.

The principles of God's moral government are stable; the tremendous judgment of the Chaldean empire is but one instance of the righteous rule by which God has ever punished those who tempt their fellows to sin. The verses next to our text predict, in language of terrible power, the appropriate retribution which he poured out upon Babylon. The humiliation and ruin which this people had wrought upon so many of their innocent neighbors was speedily visited in its extremest form upon them; and the heaven-daring compound of impiety and sensuality, which they had gloried in inculcating, was the immediate occasion of their punishment. The proud kingdom of Nebuchadnezzar so speedily raised to the pinnacle of pomp and seeming strength, as speedily tottered to its fall. In the third generation from him the weak and impious Belshazzar held the throne, successful only in disorganizing his empire, provoking his enemies and distinguishing his own infamy. In the very night that he was celebrating an impious and disgusting revel, profaning the holy utensils of Jehovah's temple, and filling his palace with vile excess and lust, the hardy Medes and Persians forced the two-barred gates of brass, ravaged the pompous city, and slew the swinish king with his herd of parasites in the midst of their debauch. Here ended the haughty dynasty of Chaldea in ignominious and vile defeat, the victim rather of its own baseness than of its enemies' force. And the same God who directed this retributive drama sits in judgment upon sinners now, and pronounces the same "woe" against him who entices his neighbor to dishonor God by irreligion or himself by vice. Do not feel, my hearer, that we are enervating the majesty of this truth when we descend from the review of that grand assize of Providence in which nations and thrones were the culprits, and apply the principle to the conscience of the individual tempter of his fellow-man. Viewed in the light of eternity, the infliction of the disease of sin upon one soul is a more tremendous calamity than the overthrow of dominions and powers on this earth. No scenery of earthly crime and woe can form too grand a background for the suitable presentation of this sin and its punishment, though pertaining to the smallest sinner in this house.

My subject, then, is *the sin of tempting a fellow-man to transgression*. For the sake of brevity, I must classify the multifarious forms in which this sin is committed, under four heads.

The lowest class in guilt is that which unintentionally entices others to transgression by the mere force of evil example. These persons directly intend only their own sinful gratification in the breaking of God's law, and, therefore, their purpose is not intentionally malignant towards their fellows, nor their guilt so aggravated in this respect. But yet it is their duty to remember the obvious fact that man is an imitative and social creature, so that every deed performed by fellow-men exerts some influence to produce its imitation. The power of different habits and principles dictating opposite acts may not be in every case overcome by this influence, but it is always to some extent undermined by a process, it may be as slight and yet as sure as the "continual dropping which weareth away a stone." No evil action done in the knowledge of a fellow-creature is wholly devoid of the mischievous power of example, and no man is so obscure as to be without influence on others. Hence, while he who creates an unintentional evil example is not guilty of the malignant design of ruining the souls of others, he is guilty of a reckless indifference to their ruin. In carrying out the sinful and forbidden purpose of grasping unlawful pleasures, he incurs the further sinful result of misleading others. As he who accidentally takes life when he intended to commit an unlawful assault is guilty of murder, so these men are guilty of the blood of souls.

The second class is of those who provide for their fellow-men the means and appliances of vice from motives of gain or other selfish good to themselves. Their immediate object is not to ruin the virtue of others, but to secure for themselves advantage from the employment of the apparatus of transgression, while they well know, and coolly disregard the fact, that the use of the appliances they provide usually and surely results in sin, guilt, and injury to their victims. If it were equally convenient to secure from those victims the selfish advantages which they desire, by some more innocent expedient, they would have no objection to doing so; but as interest and convenience dictate it, they deliberately plan to make their ends out of the ruin of their neighbors' morality. To this class belong those who offer to the community the common means of drunkenness; to it belong all the varied troops of harpies, the gamesters, the thespians, the "singing men and singing women," who live by the dissipated and corrupting amusements of society. Here, likewise, must be classed all those literary caterers, whether the Grub-street hack who spins out of his sordid brain the penny fiction for the million or the towering genius who seeks readers and applause (objects as sordid, when prized as he prizes them, as the rusty shilling that is craved to relieve the hunger and purchase the dirty debauch of Grub-street) by painting vice or inflaming unholy emotions; whether the merchant prince at whose golden wand steam presses whirl to print the mental poison or the smaller dealer who scatters them for a penny profit through the land. We denounce the unfeeling man who for filthy lucre will offer his fellow-man the stupefying anodyne or the fiery draught which steals away the brain. By what argument do we judge him a less sinner who perverts the heavenly gifts of intellect in order to debauch the conscience or to burn in on the mind the images of lust and vice with the fires of eloquence or fancy till the brain is intoxicated with a worse frenzy than that of wine?

The guilt of all this class of tempters is far heavier than of the first, because the result is with them intentional and the motive selfish. In God's sight they are the deliberate producers of all the crime, guilt, and misery which may be reasonably foreseen as flowing from the vicious appliances which they provide and display. According to the Levitical law (Exodus 21:19), the man who reared an ox which slew a human being, if he knew that his ox was *wont to push* with his horns, was judged guilty of murder; he was held responsible for the whole result which he had selfishly contemplated for a paltry gain.

The third class exhibits a still more revolting grade of malignity. It is composed of those who inculcate vice and solicit transgression for the very pleasure of corrupting those who are less guilty than themselves. There are men, such is the fiendish malice to which human nature can sink, who, after they have degraded themselves to the abyss of corruption, delight to drag down as many others as they may into the same slough. Their superior experience in evil, their guilty skill in the commission of crime, are the merits on which they plume themselves; and the callousness with which they can tread on conscience, on vows, on all sanctities and restraints, where less hardy sinners blush to venture their foot, is the very glory of their position. It is on these super-eminent traits of depravity, and on the exploits of superior crime they base their proud pretensions to be the admired instructors of younger sinners than themselves. Does the fair earth bear on its indignant bosom a spectacle more abhorrent than that of one of these "oracles of profligacy," as he gathers around him his circle of younger sinners, less lost than himself, busies himself by every art of treacherous kindness or unfeeling ridicule to obliterate the last blush from the cheek of his victim, and encourages the dubious heart yet trembling with some sense of right to plunge into the debauch, or to roll forth the words of blasphemy, or to venture the approaches of her whose house is the way of hell? Other temptations win at least a selfish advantage by the ruin of their fellowmen. But this, like the gorged tiger, destroys for the gratification of a pure malignity, which draws its delight directly from the useless miseries of its victim.

The fourth species of this sin, doubtless, deserves the "bad preeminence" above all other forms. It is that usually designated by the term "seduction," when used in popular language in its special sense. If you will consider, you will decide that the honorable mind justly condemns it as the most loathsome combination of treachery, cruelty and selfishness which can be exhibited towards a fellow-creature. The victim is one whose feebler sex should have appealed to every manly instinct for honorable protection instead of wrong; and whose love, stronger than the instinct of life, creates of itself a sacred obligation to refrain from injury. But that very love, so generously and unsuspiciously bestowed, is the fatal weapon employed with meditated perfidy for her ruin. And then, the wiles by which virtue is disarmed; what are they but pretended tenderness and false vows of affection, in which the sacred bonds of truth and love, which are the foundation of all well-being, are prostituted by the traitor to his treacherous purpose. The baseness of the means can only be surpassed by the atrocity of the result; a result by which parents and relatives are wrung with a shame and anguish, beside which the emotions which would have followed the lost one to an early grave seem almost a joy; and the miserable victim herself, after becoming the sacrifice of ruthless selfishness, is "flung like a worthless weed away," and left either to a remorse, if enough of virtue survives a wrong so crushing to feel remorse, and a shame which court the grave as a coveted refuge; or else to a degradation and despairing depravity more lamentable than even a despairing death. Is there any symbol vile enough to body forth the seducer's wickedness? None but that serpent form which the satanic father of the brood assumes. Like a serpent he glides into the household he would ruin, hiding his sibilant malice and his fatal fangs under his burnished skin; displaying his perfidious graces with pretended innocence, until the moment is found to strike his remediless venom into the bosom which he has beguiled to cherish him. And yet there are men who, though foul with these treasons against all that is most holy and tender of human affections and social vows, dare to call themselves "men of honor!"—so honorable, forsooth, that the insinuation against their spotless fame must needs be washed out in blood! For such hypocritical iniquity there is no earthly infamy deep enough and no penalty heavy enough. The very cord that should stop their perjured breath would be dishonored to embrace their necks, and the gibbet would be defiled by the burden it had to sustain.

Having pointed out the leading forms in which the sin of tempting to evil may be committed, I proceed to that which is the main object of this discourse—to justify the "woe" which is pronounced against it—by some general considerations. And—

I. The sin of the tempter is enormous, because in enticing his neighbor to do wrong he has inflicted upon him the greatest mischief of which his nature is capable.

It has been said:

> "Who steals my purse steals trash,
> But he who filches from me my good name,
> Robs me of that which not enriches him,
> And leaves me poor indeed."[112]

With a more truthful emphasis may this be said of him who robs his fellow-man of his innocence; he strips him of that which adds no wealth except store of wrath to the plunderer, and leaves the victim beggared of happiness. Sin is the monster mischief of our world. He who brings it upon his neighbor has thereby helped to dash the image of God in which he was created, and to mar the health of his nature. He assists in spreading a moral leprosy which eats into the soul until the last lineament of virtue is effaced, and the corruption of spiritual death is spread over the whole being. He assists in opening a spring of perpetual misery in the victim's soul, from which the bitter floods of remorse must some day burst forth, with all their ingredients of selfishness, hatred, fear and despair. The transgression which he inculcates may for a season appear to sear the conscience in corrupting it, but just so surely as there is truth in Jehovah must man's "sin find him out," and avenge itself in the lashes of self-accusation. Nor does the tempter injure the object of his seductions alone: others suffer with him the pangs of shame and mortified affection, and those others perhaps virtuous, or at least innocent of wrong against the author of their calamity. But, above all, to entice into sin is to lead our brother under the wrath of the Almighty. It is to pluck down upon his head the penalty of eternal death. It is to thrust him into a quarrel with the omnipotent God, whose righteous wrath "burns to the lowest hell"; whose justice condemns the impenitent transgressor to make experiment of what infinite power can inflict through endless ages in recompense for the outrage of infinite attributes. This, sinful man, is what transgression accomplishes—that transgression which you so lightly commit—which you seek to thrust upon your comrade as though his fall into it were a merry jest. "Fools make a mock at sin!" That sin at which all else above the pit is solemn as eternity—"which brought death into our world and all our woe"—which hollowed out the abyss of hell and filled it with its torments and wails—which kills the soul with the second death. Had nature sense and feeling it would not be unreasonable to imagine the ground in mourning, and the skies dropping down their tears at every sin; as when the first tempter triumphed, Milton sang:

> "Earth felt the wound, and nature from her seat,
> Sighing through all her works, gave signs of woe
> That all was lost."[113]

II. The wrong done to our neighbor and to God in this sin is enormous, because it is irreparable by man. The creature can successfully solicit to evil, but God alone can efficiently recall the corrupted soul to good. Sin, when once committed, leaves its *virus* in the soul to spread and propagate itself in evil habits and dispositions, defying all stay by human power. Nor does he who tempts to evil intend to make any effort for its arrest. He puts forth his hand to begin or to accelerate the downward career, but he has not mind to trouble himself to stay it. No! when the irreparable injury is inflicted, he is done; his purpose is accomplished, and unless there is still some lower deep of ruin into which his victim may be plunged, he has no further concern with him than, like the Chaldean in the text, to ridicule or to despise the degradation which he has helped to produce.

Nor is the tempter either able or willing to bear the wrath of God which he has been the instrument of drawing down upon his fellow. Had he even magnanimity enough to offer it he would be refused; for it is written (Proverbs 9:12), "If thou be wise, thou shalt be wise for thyself; but if thou scornest, thou alone shalt bear it." The selfish cruelty which could inflict the mischief will not now awaken into disinterestedness when it has plucked down upon its comrade the mountainous load of Almighty vengeance, or put forth so much as a little finger to lighten it. And did it endeavor the rescue, it would find itself immovable beneath a still more tremendous burden—the judgments due to its own guilt.

So that, according to every rule of fellowship by which the men of this world combine, there is an element of mean treachery in the conduct of the tempter. When one invites his fellow to join him in some venture or enterprise of risk, it is well understood that he thereby makes an implied promise, in case his invitation is accepted, to stand by his comrade in any danger or disaster which may result. The associates are to be faithful to each other in sharing both the gains and the losses of their common undertaking; and the man who was not willing to be pledged to this, would refrain if he had one spark of magnanimity or honesty, from soliciting any one to join his enterprise. Thus, when the professed patriot summons his fellow-citizens to join him in the dangerous attempt to pluck their liberties by force from the grasp of the angry despot, and when they rally to his side, they expect him to share their risks and exposures—to share in the storm of battle, and if defeat and captivity must needs be, to share their bonds. When men who have any spirit combine to break the laws, when heedless youth associate to tempt the authority of their instructors, even they would think it foul shame that the very inventor of the offence should desert the friends whom he had inveigled into it, so soon as danger or exposure overtook them. Now, then, seeing that the tempter is neither willing nor able to do anything to remedy either the defilement or the guilt—either the shame and remorse of the polluted conscience, or the wrath of God incurred by the sin he is about to inculcate—if he has one spark of the honor of a man, one instinct of honesty or pity, he should refrain. If you must walk the dangerous road of transgression, if you must brave the power of the Almighty, we beseech you proceed on your way alone, and carry no comrade with you to your dreary fate. It will be horrible enough without being aggravated by the sight of their ruin, procured, in part, by your treachery, and without the torment of their just reproaches.

III. The work of the tempter has this farther element of treachery, that while the purpose is mischievous, and either directly or indirectly malignant, the pretense is always one of good fellowship and kindness. Whatever be the sin to which the inexperienced is allured, the seducer well knows, as it is his solemn duty to know, that it must in the end result in nothing but misery; and if his immediate purpose is not to inflict that misery, it is at best a purpose to gain some unholy, selfish, and often trivial end, by a reckless indifference to the terrible result. He is willing to help to murder a soul in order to gain the coveted companionship of an hour in forbidden indulgences! Were this repulsive atrocity of purpose candidly professed, who would not recoil from it with salutary horror? "In vain is the net spread in the sight of any bird." But it is always concealed under the veil of benevolence. The aggravated perfidy by which the destroyer, in the peculiar sin of seduction, employs the dearest and most sacred symbols of affection and vows of devotion to work his purpose, has been already noted. But all tempters are in this alike. Saith Solomon, "When sinners entice thee they plead, 'we shall find all precious substance, we shall fill our houses with spoil; cast in thy lot among us—let us all have one purse.'" Here is the language of a pretended generosity, of a genial, free-handed kindness. "But they lay wait for their blood; they lurk privily for their lives." In the case of all the classes who seek their selfish ends at the expense of their neighbor's moral injury, by offering the apparatus of dissipation, we find the same mask. Do they publish the cold selfishness of their purpose to batten on the sin and ruin of their fellow-man, to clear a shilling on a folly of his which will be to him more costly than all the jewels of an emperor's estate? Not they. Do they advertise thus, "The public is invited to come, that I may turn a penny by giving them to drink liquid damnation"? Or, "The young of both sexes are requested to attend, in order that I may give them the fires of remorse for their money"? Not they. Well would it be for their dupes if they did. But their guise before the public is always one of cheerful, benevolent alacrity, of polite attention, as though they delighted to confer true happiness. And the hardened reprobate who glories to extinguish the virtuous scruple from the heart, and the ingenuous blush from the cheek of the inexperienced, also assumes the suppleness of the serpent, and professes that his only motive is to confer enjoyment. So that in every form of the sin of the tempter, there is some degree of that TREASON, smaller or greater, which gave the satanic trait to the crime of Joab, the son of Zeruiah, when he took his comrade, Amasa, by the beard to salute him, while he smote him with his sword in the fifth rib; and to that blackest human act ever wrought on earth, in which Judas betrayed his Redeemer with a kiss.

IV. I have intimated that there is a satanic trait in all such enticements. Here, in truth, is the most startling view of their wickedness; that they do precisely the devil's work and carry out his cause. Consider the fearful analogy between the two. The cause which impelled Satan to attempt the ruin of the human race was that he had himself fallen; he desired to make his fellow-creatures as miserable as himself. So the seducer of his fellow-man endeavors to drag him down, because he cannot patiently endure the sight of a virtue superior to his own. The instrument by which Satan seeks to destroy is not the sword, or fire, or poison, but sin; so that his victim may be his own destroyer. It is thus with the human tempter. The guise under which the adversary appeared was one of innocence and amiability, and his plea was, "in the day ye eat thereof, then your eyes shall be opened, and ye shall be as gods, knowing good and evil." So the seducer pleads only the gratification which he pretends to offer. And last, the result in both cases is the same—the *death of the soul*—a misery irreparable, immeasurable and endless. To this whole class of sinners then may be justly applied those words of our Savior to the apostate scribes— words too full of dread severity for any other than the all-knowing to frame: "Ye are of your father the devil, and the lusts of your father ye will do, who was a murderer from the beginning."

Not seldom the dire results of temptation begin to manifest themselves on earth, so that the soul-murderer is enabled to look on his own work in its true lights. Pictures of those results are so frequent in human experience, dark as they are, that I shall not be justly liable to the charge of personal allusions, when I draw one or two in such a way as to represent what is, alas! too generally real. Who can live to old age in this evil world, and fail to know only too many of such scenes? There was the amiable and genial youth, who departed for college or some place of business freighted with sacred affections—-with a father's blessing, a mother's unutterable prayer, and pure sisterly yearnings. He went away innocent, and even ignorant of vice, gay and confident of well-doing. But he returns with the slime of the serpent upon him. His cheek is still red, but it is the flush of wine, not the rosy hue of health. His eye is no longer beaming with domestic love and cheerful animation, but is dull with the reaction of excess, or else fired with baleful passion. The simple pleasures and affections of his home are now all too mild to suit his palate, debauched with the fiery flavor of vice. Now let his tempter note the thrill of anguish which harrows the parents' hearts, as the suspicion of his change first shoots through them. Let him watch the long agony of the contest in which they strive against evidence, and are at last compelled to admit that he is lost, and the blight of the sister's bosom, as even she at last surrenders his cause and owns that she has no longer a brother. Let him follow the impetuous career of his ruin—it will not detain him long, for the fallen reprobate hastens to his catastrophe—until he is brought to his home the last time, slain, it may be, in drunken broil or dying of excess. And let him contemplate the hoary heads that are brought down in sorrow to the grave. There is his work: let him study it. There is "the beginning of the end."

Or, it may be, that the progress of the tempter's work in the early life of his victim is slower. He comes to man's estate with uncertain virtue, indeed, yet not wholly fallen; sometimes yielding far more from amiability and good fellowship than from actual love of vice, yet always restrained in part by his better instincts. His true friends tremble for him, while they love him for his generosity, and kindly conceal his danger from his own house. Thus he fares along until other destinies are linked with his own, so that when he falls he must carry a wider desolation. He has become a husband—a father. As the insidious seductions of his tempters and the folds of evil habits wind around him, he struggles against them sometimes even more manfully than before, for he is not dead to the gentle and potent pleas of love. But still his seducers return to the charge. The quick instincts of the wife have long divined, ah! too acutely, that all is not secure; and every absence from home is to her a torturing suspense, which yet she must conceal. But we will not attempt to detail this hidden warfare of fear and hope where each party in the strife is armed by love itself to rend her gentle breast and which embitters even the happiest days of her existence. At times his irregularities almost turn her fears into despair, and then the pleasing promise of permanent amendment is so prolonged that the agitating hope rises painfully towards peaceful confidence. It is at the end of some such season that his boon companions of former days meet him again. They are delighted to see him; they urge him to go with them to some festive resort, where they may drink again to the memories of "auld lang syne" and renew its wild enjoyments. But he demurs, and at first with apparent firmness. They press him again and again, and demand to know what ungenial change has come over him. Still he deprecates the proposal, and, it may be, alludes to the dangers which overhang his sobriety, explains in touching words the long and, he trusts, successful struggle he has made to save himself, and even suggests the sacred ties which draw him to self-denial. But what is all this in their profane eyes? They regard the compunctions of honor, principle, and love as no better than childishness; they rally him on his puritanism. He reminds them of what they well know, that with the first indulgence his self-command is liable to be overthrown, and begs them to spare him. They reply by jeering him for timidity, and assure him that he is in no danger; for where is the harm of a little jollity? At length he yields to their perseverance and his own false shame, and accompanies them "as an ox goeth to the slaughter, or as a fool to the correction of the stocks, till a dart strike through his liver; as a bird hasteth to the snare, and *knoweth not that it is for his life*." They drink; they jest; they laugh. There is one hour of vivid social enjoyment, while his false friends applaud him for his wit, and tell him that now he is himself again. But the slumbering demon appetite, which seemed long to be bound, and would soon have been starved to extinction by denial of its indulgence, has now awakened again in its fury, bursts the restraints of conscience and affection, and casts them wildly to the winds. He pours down the fiery floods with reckless hand; his late tempters now leave him, perhaps in genteel disgust at his excesses, and day after day he plunges on in a tempest of dissipation until brain and heart are stupefied.

But we turn from the scene of his debauch, where his boon companions now stand afar off from his shame, or sneer at the bestiality which they helped to produce, to his home and to the anxious heart that beats and watches there. Night after night has passed, and the failure of his promised return has held her eyes waking, and day after day her aching sight is strained to see whether he is coming, till hope deferred maketh the heart sick, and she now understands it all only too well. Shall we venture to lift the veil from the chamber of holy grief on one of those long night watches? See her pacing the floor with convulsive step, and then pressing her wet cheek to the window as though the poor eyes all dimmed with tears could pierce the pitch darkness of the stormy night,—a darkness yet not equal to the blackness that encloses her heart. Now she wrings her hands, and, in utter abandonment of misery, tears her fair hair and calls upon God, scarce knowing whether to invoke his vengeance with all the frenzy of a ruined wife and mother on the seducers of her husband or to implore his mercy on herself and her babes. And now those little ones awake from short slumber, frightened by the tempest of her grief, and cluster around her in strange alarm. Thus wears away the black, endless night, and with the sad, gray dawn there comes a step, a well-known step, that makes her throbbing heart stand still. But she does not fly to meet it, for it is heavy and unsteady, and announces the drunkard's stagger. He meets her, it may be with stupid petulance and brutality, or it may be with the maudlin tenderness of the sot; but either way, every word is a dagger that stabs her to the heart until the heavy sleep of the inebriate arrests his folly. Now, see that chaste couch polluted by the senseless frame that lies snoring—a human swine! At length he wakes up with a shudder; he glares at the wall with starting eye-balls, which see serpents and devils writhing about him; now he screams with fright, and now he babbles wild gibberish. It is *delirium tremens*! And now the drama hastens to its catastrophe. Parents and friends gather to him with their kindly offices and assist the wife as she ministers at his bed. But they venture no word of consolation, for her countenance is dreadful and rigid with self-contained agony, and shows a sorrow too deep to be intermeddled with. At length there is a bursting forth of the smothered anguish, and the wails that go up from the sick man's room tell that all is over. His ravings are now quiet, the inflamed cheeks are blanched, and the blood-shot eye has lost is speculation and its life and ceased to stare at the visions of the diseased brain. "He is dead, and gave no sign."

Shall we attempt to follow the guilty soul as it passes into the awful world of spirits and the presence of its God, from this scene of guilty pollution? No! we will not attempt to follow it; the heart recoils from an inquiry so dreadful. Let us turn rather, and look once more at the wife, as she sits a wan and woeful widow in her father's house, gathering her orphan children around her knees. They must henceforth bear a dishonored name, and study to forget the memory of him who gave them existence.

And now, what say the tempters to this, their handiwork? Perhaps they drop a word of hypocritical regret; or, more probably, they speak virtuously of the folly of the man who "makes a beast of himself, and thus destroys the happiness of his family!" And then they walk forth, defying the stars with their brazen front, as though they had done no wrong. Just heavens! is there no thunderbolt in your arsenal to strike such monsters dead? Look at their haughty impunity, and say, is it wrong to rejoice, with a stern and righteous joy, that there is a Judge who will know how to avenge, and a hell deep enough to give to such bottomless atrocity its full deserts? Yes, it is wrong, we will not rejoice, but rather pray to be enabled to say of them, as the Redeemer said of his murderers: "Father, forgive, them; they know not what they do."

No doubt they would be more ready than is just to avail themselves of this excuse, if taxed with the mischiefs they wrought, and to plead *thoughtlessness.* Yes, the palliation is, that these terrible consequences were neither intended nor foreseen; that they thought of nothing more than a little trivial amusement. It is to be hoped, for the credit of humanity, that this extenuation is true. But for what is forecast, understanding, memory, given to man, except to show him the well-established consequences of a given course of conduct? If men will disuse their faculties—will shut their eyes—will refuse to look at results which they could not but know lay just in the path they are wickedly pursuing, are they therefore innocent? Nay, verily! Inspiration hath decided this: "As a madman who casteth fire-brands, arrows and death, so is the man that *deceiveth his neighbor, and sayeth, am I not in sport?*"

There is another pretended justification which is often used by certain classes of the purveyors of the means of transgression. They plead, "Man will have such indulgences; if we forbear to provide them it will make no difference in the result, and we might as well enjoy the advantage of furnishing them as others." We need not dwell upon the obvious fact that this plea is always false in part, and that every addition thus made to the facilities for dissipation helps to swell the tide of temptations which bears increasing numbers to perdition. We rejoin: What is the plea itself, even if admitted to be true, but this: "Here are fellow-creatures who are bent on self-destruction, and, therefore, we are covetous, for the sake of a little filthy lucre, of a share in the horrible exploit of their damnation—of a part of the stain of the blood of souls, and of a portion in that unutterable woe which God denounces against those who give to their neighbors drink." If it is so certain that these misguided men will be corrupted by others, better leave to them the unenviable guilt and doom of that work.

Another excuse, raised frequently by other classes of tempters to evil is, that the subjects of their sinful allurements were already fallen: "They were corrupt before by the agency of themselves or others: we made them no worse." I reply, every repeated transgression makes the transgressor worse—more hardened and more guilty; and if ever these fallen fellow-creatures are to escape final perdition, must it not be by "ceasing to do evil and learning to do well?" Your plea, then, is this: Some previous hand thrust those wretched souls into the water: you found them in it, but alive, and only helped to hold them down until they were dead!

Sometimes a more defiant justification is pretended, and the tempters to evil say the men whom they helped to mislead were free agents; they had as good opportunities as others to know what was best for themselves, and to choose; they were not constrained to sin, and they went to it with their eyes open. "On their own heads be the consequences." I reply: just there is the refined malignity of the tempter's work, that it ruins his fellowman without taking from him his free agency. If the means which drew him to sin were constraining, then responsibility would be at an end, and his damnation would not result. But because the tempter acted freely and sinfully in soliciting, and the tempted in yielding, therefore, they both shall be punished for the common ruin of a soul. When one hires a bravo to strike the dagger into the heart of his neighbor whom he is too cowardly to attack alone, the hired assassin acts freely, but they both are guilty of murder. When the father of tempters seduced Eve she yielded freely, but his doom was none the less accursed.

In conclusion; standing as I do before so many of the young, the inexperienced, and the comparatively innocent, I must be permitted to apply this discussion as an enforcement of the advice of inspiration: "My son, if sinners entice thee consent thou not." When solicited to evil, I beseech you to look behind the deceitful veil of good fellowship and geniality which is worn, and consider the end, which is the death of the soul. Shun such associates, whatever their pretensions or their fascinations, as you would the scaly splendors and the serpentine grace of the venomous snake. Flee for your life.

And because we are told that, wheresoever the prey is, thither are the eagles gathered together, we fear that some of these classes of tempters to evil are here also, dogging the steps of intended victims.

To them I would say: See here the dread depravity of which the human heart is capable! When these malignant instances of cruelty present themselves in the persons of hoary sinners, whose habits are hardened and whose consciences are seared by a long course of sin, the spectacle is repulsive enough, though, alas! not unnatural. How much more monstrous and abhorrent, then, to see a young man so early in his career of transgression reach this bad preeminence in mischief? Hardened men, look into your own hearts and shudder at yourselves. Look up at the woe denounced by God, and tremble before his coming judgment. And fly, even you, with all your aggravated guilt, fly to the Lamb, that he may turn your stony hearts to flesh and purge away your dreadful guilt. "Though your sins be as scarlet, they shall be as white as snow; though they be red like crimson, they shall be as wool." (Isaiah 1:16)

The Christian's Best Motive for Patriotism[114]

"Because of the house of our Lord our God I will seek thy good."

The true Christian feels the claims of patriotism as sensibly as any other man, though he holds them subject to the limitations of justice and charity to others. Thus, King David resolves that he will seek the peace of Jerusalem, the capital city of the Hebrew commonwealth; not only as a patriotic king, but from an additional religious motive. So the Christian has a motive for patriotism far stronger and holier than those of all other men. Additional to theirs, he has this reason to pray for the peace of Jerusalem: for his brethren and companions' sakes, and because of the house of the Lord his God which is in it. The kingdom of Jesus Christ—that blessed kingdom whose scepter is peace, righteousness, meekness and truth, in whose prosperity the hopes of a suffering race are all involved, which alone can arrest the flood of sins and woes which now sweeps generation after generation into ruin—is committed by its Divine Head to human hands, and is partially dependent on the course of human events. This spiritual commonwealth among us, as it is proper, has no legal ties to the secular, and no other relations than those of mutual good-will and courtesy. But still, inasmuch as Christ is pleased to leave to second causes their natural influence over his church, it is largely dependent on our secular governments. Now, there are few things which can affect the interests of Zion so disastrously as political convulsions and war. Let the Christian weigh their influences.

First, we are taught, even by experience of customary party excitements, that a season of political agitation is most unfavorable to spiritual prosperity. Few experienced pastors expect revivals during excited presidential canvasses. The mind is absorbed by agitating secular topics, angry and unchristian emotions are provoked, and the tender dew of heavenly-mindedness is speedily evaporated by the hot and dusty turmoil of the popular meeting and the hustings. Few men who traffic habitually in such scenes exhibit much grace. We suspect that the Christian, returning from a day of such excitement, is little inclined to the place of secret prayer. But how much must all these evil influences be exasperated when the subjects of political strife assume a violent and convulsive aspect? When every mind is filled by eager, secular concerns—when angry passions rage in every heart, dividing brother against brother in Zion — when unscrupulous haste precipitates multitudes into words and acts of injustice and wrong, agitating and defiling their own consciences, and provoking the hot tumults of resentment on either side—what room is there for the quiet and sacred voice of the Holy Spirit? It has been remarked by wise historians that a time of political convulsions is a time of giant growth for all forms of vice. And just to that degree it is a time of barrenness for the Christian graces.

But when political strife proceeds to actual war, then, indeed, do "the ways of Zion mourn." War is the grand and favorite device of him who was a liar and murderer from the beginning, to obstruct all spiritual good, and to barbarize mankind. To all the above agitations, distractions and evil passions, raised now to actual frenzy, must be added the interruptions of the Sabbath rest and of public worship, while the sacred hours are profaned with the tumult of preparations, marchings, or actual combats. Domestic life, that most fruitful source of all wholesome restraints, is broken up by danger, fear, waste of property and separations. The youth hurry from that peaceful domain of humanizing and pious influences into the rude noise and gross corruptions of camps, whence they return, if they return at all, depraved by military license, unused to peaceful industry, and hardened to all evil, to poison society at home. Colleges and schools are scattered, the voice of science is silenced, the hopes of peaceful industry are violently destroyed, till recklessness and resentment turn the very husbandman into a bandit. And, above all, Death holds his cruel carnival, and not only by the sword, but yet more by destitution, by vice, by pestilence, hurries his myriads unprepared, from scenes of guilty woe on earth, into everlasting despair below. Need we wonder that the heavenly dove should spread its gentle wings, and fly far from such abhorrent scenes?

But civil feud has ever been known as the most bitter of all. "A brother offended is harder to be won than a strong city: and their contentions are like the bars of a castle." The very tenderness of brothers' love makes them more tender to the injury. The strength of the mutual obligations, which should have bound them to kindness, enhances the hot indignation at mutual outrage. When the twin lands which now lie so intimately side by side, parted by a line so long, so faint, so invisible, that it does not separate, begin to strike each other, the very nearness and intimacy make each more naked to the other's blows. How dire, then, would be the conflagration of battle which would range along this narrow line across the whole breadth of a continent. How deadly the struggle, when the republican hardihood and chivalry, the young giant strength and teeming wealth, which begin to make the mightiest despots respectful, are turned against each other. Some seem to delight in placing the relative prowess of the North and South in odious comparison. Should we not, my brethren, rather weep tears of blood at the wretched and wicked thought, that the common prowess with which North and South have so often side by side carried dismay and rout into the ranks of common enemies — that terrible prowess which, in North and South alike, withstood the force of the British lion, while we were yet in the gristle of our youth, and which, ever since, has overthrown and broken every enemy, with the lion's force and the eagle's swiftness combined — should hereafter be expended in fratricidal blows? And, then, this vast frontier must be forted and guarded. This hostile neighborhood, so dangerous because so intimate, must be watched on either hand by armies; and these armies become, as among the unhappy and suspicious nations of Europe, as much the machines of internal oppression as of outward defense. Our future growth of men and wealth would be swallowed up by the devouring maw of strife. These teeming fields, whose increase fills the granaries of the famishing nations, and makes their owners' bosoms to overflow with wealth, must go to feed the barren waste of warlike preparation and labor. The source of half the missionary activities which now gladden the waste places of the earth would be dried up. Farewell to the benign career of imperial *Peace*, by which we had hoped the Empire Republic would teach the angry nations nobler triumphs than those of war. A long farewell to that dream we had indulged—dream not unworthy surely to have been inspired by the *Prince of Peace*—that here a nation was to grow up on this soil, which God had kept till "the fulness of time was come," wrapped in the mysteries of pathless seas, and untainted by the steps of civilized despots or organized crime; a nation composed of the strong, the free, the bold, the oppressed of every people, and, like the Corinthian brass, more precious than any that composed it; which should come, by the righteous arts of peace, to a greatness such as at last to shame and frighten war away from the family of kingdoms; which should work out the great experiment of equal laws and a free conscience, for the first time for the imitation of the world; and from whose bosom a free church, unstained by the guilt of persecution and unburdened by the leaden protection of the state, should send forth her light and salvation to the ends of the earth to bring the millennial morning. This cunning machine of law, which now regulates our rights, would be wrecked amidst the storms of revolution. The stern exigencies of danger would compel both the rivals, perhaps, to substitute the strong, but harsh will of the soldier for the mild protection of constitutions. And the oppressors of soul and body, from every stronghold of absolutism throughout the earth, would utter their jubilant and scornful triumph: "Lo! the vain experiment of man's self-government has drowned itself in its own blood and ruin!" The movement of the world's redemption might be put back for ages, and the enthroning of the Prince of Peace over his promised dominion, so long ravaged by sin and woe, would be postponed, while eternal death preyed upon yet more of the teeming generations.

Now, in view of this picture of possible crime and misery, would to God that I could reach the ear of every professed servant of Jesus Christ in the whole land! I would cry to them: Christians of America—brothers—shall all this be? Shall this church of thirty thousand evangelical ministers, and four millions of Christian adults—this church, so boastful of its influence and power; so respected and reverenced by nearly all; so crowned with the honors of literature, of station, of secular office, of riches; this church, which molds the thought of three-fourths of our educated men through her schools, and of all, by her pulpit and her press; this church, which glories in having just received a fresh baptism of the Spirit of heaven in a national revival—permit the tremendous picture to become reality? Nay, shall they aid in precipitating the dreaded consummation, by traitorously inflaming the animosities which they should have allayed, and thus leave the work of their Master to do the devil's? Then, how burning the sarcasm which this result will contain upon your Christianity in the eyes of posterity! Why, they will say, was there not enough of the majesty of moral weight in these four millions of Christians to say to the angry waves, "Peace be still"? Why did not these four millions rise, with a LOVE so Christ-like, so beautiful, so strong, that strife should be paralyzed by it into reverential admiration? Why did they not speak for their country, and for the house of the Lord their God which was in it, with a wisdom before whose firm moderation, righteousness, and clear light, passion and folly should scatter like the mist? Were not all these strong enough to throw the arms of their loving mediation around their fellow citizens, and keep down the weapons that sought each other's hearts; or rather to receive them into their own bosoms than permit their mother-country to be slain? Did this mighty church stand idly by, and see frenzy immolate so many of the dearest hopes of man, and of the rights of the Redeemer, on her hellish altar? And this church knew, too, that the fiend had borrowed the torch of discord from the altar of Christianity, and that therefore Christians were bound, by a peculiar tie, to arrest her insane hand before the precious sacrifice was wrapped in flames. Then shame on the boasted Christianity of America, and of the nineteenth century! With all its parade of evangelism, power, and light, wherein has it been less impotent and spurious than the effete religion of declining Rome, which betrayed Christendom into the dark ages; or than the baptized superstitions which in those ages sanctioned the Crusades and the Inquisition? In the sight of heaven's righteous Judge, I believe that if the Christianity of America now betrays the interests of men and God to the criminal hands which threaten them, its guilt will be second only to that of the apostate church which betrayed the Savior of the world; and its judgment will be rendered in calamities second only to those which avenged the divine blood invoked by Jerusalem on herself and her children.

How, then, shall Christians seek the good of their country for the church's sake? This raises the more practical question of present duty, and introduces the more practical part of my discourse.

And first, Christians should everywhere begin to pray for their country. "Because of the house of the Lord our God, let us seek its good." The guilty churches of all our land should humble themselves before a holy God for their Christian backslidings and our national sins. "Blow the trumpet in Zion, sanctify a fast, call a solemn assembly; gather the people, sanctify the congregation, assemble the elders, gather the children, and those that suck the breasts; let the bridegroom go forth of his chamber, and the bride out of her closet. Let the priests, the ministers of the Lord, weep between the porch and the altar; and let them say, Spare thy people, O Lord, and give not thy heritage to reproach."

And along with this should go humble confessions of our sins, individual and social. And here let me distinctly warn you, that I am not about to point your attention to sins of fellow-citizens of another quarter of the Confederacy, from whose faults some may suppose the present fear arises. Whether they have committed faults, or how great, it is not my present concern to say. Our business is today with our own sins. It will do our hearts no good to confess to God the sins of our fellow-men; He already knows them, and estimates them more fairly than perhaps our prejudice will permit us to do. It is for our own sins alone that we are responsible to God. It is our own sins alone that we have the means of reforming, by the help of his grace. Let each man, then, consider and forsake his personal transgressions; for as your persons help to swell the aggregate of this great people, so your individual sins have gone to form that black cloud of guilt which threatens to hide from us the favorable light of our heavenly Father's face. But let us remember, and confess also, our social sins: that general worldliness which hath set up the high places of its covetous idolatries all over the good land God hath given us; that selfish profusion and luxury which have squandered on the pride of life so much of the goods of our stewardship; that heaven-daring profanity and blasphemy by reason of which the land mourneth. And let me not forget faithfully to protest, on such a day as this, against that peculiar sin of the southern country, the passion for bloody retaliation of personal wrong, which has been so often professed and indulged among us, un-whipped of justice. You have allowed too often the man of violence, the duelist, professing his pretended "code of honor"—most hateful and deceitful pretense of that father of lies, who was a murderer from the beginning—to stalk through the land with wrongs upon his angry tongue and blood upon his hand, while his crime was winked at by justice, and almost applauded by a corrupt public opinion. "So ye have polluted the land wherein ye are; for blood, it defileth the land, and the land cannot be cleansed of the blood that is shed therein, but by the blood of him that shed it." Let us remember, also, that our innocence or rightfulness in the particular point of present differences and anticipated collisions gives no assurance that God may not chas-tise us for our sins by those very events. Often has his manifold, wise, and righteous providence permitted an unjust aggressor to make him-self the instrument wherewith to lash his sinning people, even when he afterwards punished the invader himself.

Second, we would say, with all the earnestness and emphasis which the most solemn feeling can inspire, let each individual Christian in our land, whether he sits in our halls of legislature or rules as a mag-istrate, or guides public opinion through the press, or merely fills the station of the private citizen, consider his own personal concern in this matter. We would affectionately individualize each man, and say to him, "My brother, thou art the man. Consider what would God have *you* to do?" Every Christian man, whether law-maker or law executor or voter, should carry his Christian conscience, enlightened by God's word, into his political duty in another manner than we have been accustomed to do. We must ask less what party caucuses and leaders dictate, and more what duty dictates; for the day is at hand when we shall be brought to an awful judgment for the thoughtless manner in which we exercise our civic function. My brethren, the Christians of this land are able to control the selection of reckless and wicked men for places of trust, if they please, and will do their duty. Here are four millions of men and women, chiefly adults, among a people of twen-ty-six millions of men, women, children, and slaves—four millions who profess to be supremely ruled by principles of righteousness, peace, and love, and to be united to each other in the brotherhood of a heavenly birth. If even the voters among these would go together to the polls to uphold the cause of peace they would turn the scale of every election. Where is the community in all our land where the male citizens, who are professors of Christianity, would not give the victory to that party to which they gave their united support? But alas! how often have we gone on Monday to the hustings, after having appeared on Sabbath as the servants of the Prince of Peace, and brethren of all his servants, and, in our political heats speedily forgotten that we were Christians? Let each Christian citizen have his independent political predilections, and support them with decision, if you please. Let them, if need be, render that enlightened and moderate allegiance to the party of their choice which is supposed to be essential in free governments. But when their party demands of them that they shall sustain men of corrupt private morals or reckless passions, because of their supposed party orthodoxy, let all Christians say: "Nay, verily, we would fain yield all reasonable party fidelity; but we are also partisans in the commonwealth of King Jesus, and our allegiance to him transcends all others. Unless you will present us a man who to party orthodoxy unites private virtues, we cannot sustain him." Then would their reasonable demand be potential in every party, and the abuse would be crushed. And this stand, if taken by Christian citizens, we affirm, would infringe no personal or associated rights; for is there any party who would admit that it had not a single member respectable, virtuous, and sober enough to deserve the suffrages of Christian men? If there is surely it is time it should slink away from the arena of political competition and hide itself in oblivion! Here, then, is a prominent duty, if we would save our country, that we shall carry our citizenship in the kingdom of heaven everywhere, and make it dominate over every public act. We must obey the law of God rather than the unrighteous behests of party, to "choose out of all the people *able men, such as fear God, men of truth, hating covetousness, and place such over them to be rulers,*"[116] or God will assuredly avenge himself for our violated allegiance to him. The Christians of this country must sternly claim that wicked or reckless men shall no longer hold the helm of state; that political orthodoxy shall no longer atone for the worst offence against citizenship, a wicked life. And along with rulers I would include the directors of the public press as being of the general class of "leaders of the people." Even while you boast of the potency of this engine of the nineteenth century, you have allowed it to fall, in many cases, into most incompetent and dangerous hands. See who have held this responsible lever in our land in these latter days! Some are honorable and patriotic, but more are unreliable; some mere half-educated youths, without any stake of family, estate, or reputation in the community; some fiery denouncers; some touching the springs of public affairs with a drunken hand; and many the open advocates and practitioners of the duelist's murderous code—these men you have permitted, and even upheld and salaried, in your easy thoughtlessness, to misrepresent, misdirect, and inflame the public sentiment of the nation!

There are many reasons which demand of every God-fearing citizen that he shall sustain, directly or indirectly, none but honest and prudent men in places of influence. When you elevate a bad man, you give to him a hundred-fold more power of example to corrupt your sons, and your neighbors' sons, by his evil acts. Those acts are a hundred-fold more conspicuous and more weighty to attract notice and imitation than if you had left him in his deserved obscurity. When you delegate your money, influence or civic power to a bad man, you make his wicked official acts and influence your own; he is your chosen agent, and acts for you, and be assured a jealous God will not forget to visit the people for the guilt thus contracted.

But especially should you remember, at such a period as this, the boundless mischief wrought by the habit of reckless vituperation and the political violence in which bad and foolish or inexperienced men indulge to further political ends. It is this which chiefly has created our present unhappy dangers, by misrepresenting each section to the other. You have heard descriptions of the *reign of terror* in the first French Revolution, and perhaps as you saw the frightful and murderous violence of political factions there displayed, you have exclaimed, "Were these men or devils?" They were men, my brethren; "men of like passions with us." Read the narrative of the philosophic [Adolphe] Thiers, and you will learn the source of these rivers of blood. Unscrupulous leaders of parties and presses, in order to carry their favorite projects and overpower political rivals, resorted to the trick of imputing odious and malignant motives to all adversaries; democrats denouncing Girondists and royalists as traitorous plotters of foreign invasion and national sack; royalists denouncing democrats as agrarians and robbers, till by dint of bandying the outrageous charges backwards and forwards, all minds were gradually embittered and prepared to believe the worst. Hence the bloody political proscriptions; hence the frightful butcheries of the *Septembriseurs*; because misguided men were taught to believe that no less trenchant remedy would anticipate the treason designed against the country.

Now, I say to you in all faithfulness, that the reckless and incapable men whom you have weakly trusted with power or influence, have already led us far on towards similar calamities. They have bandied violent words, those cheap weapons of petulant feebleness; they have justified aggression; they have misrepresented our tempers and principles; answered, alas, by equal misrepresentations and violence in other quarters, until multitudes of honest men, who sincerely suppose themselves as patriotic as you think yourselves, are really persuaded that in resisting your claims they are but rearing a necessary bulwark against lawless and arrogant aggressions. Four years ago an instance of unjust and wicked insolence was avenged on the floor of the Senate of the United States, by an act of ill-judged violence.[117] And now, not so much that rash and sinful act of retaliation, but the insane, wicked and insulting justification of it generally made by Southern secular prints, directed by reckless boys or professed duelists, a justification abhorred and condemned by almost all decent men in our section, is this day carrying myriads of votes, of men who, if not thus outraged, might have remained calm and just towards us, for the cause whose triumph you deprecate. Thus the miserable games goes on, until, at last, blood breaks out, and the exhausted combatants are taught in the end, by mutually inflicted miseries, to pause and consider, that they are contending mainly for a misunderstanding of each other.

Now, I well know, my brethren and fellow-citizens, that if I should speak to you in private, you would all concur in my honest reprobation of this folly and injustice; I know that I have but expressed the common sentiments of all good men among us. Yet, in your dislike to be troubled, in your easy good nature, you let things take their course, under the wretched mismanagement of the hands into which they have fallen; you even permit your money and your influence to go, indirectly, in support of these agents of mischief and misrule, who thus misrepresent your characters, and aims, and rights. If the public interests cannot arouse you from this good-natured sin, let me see if I cannot touch you more nearly. Whereunto can all this mutual violence grow? Do not the increasing anger and prejudice, which seem so fast ripening on both sides for fatal collision, tell you too plainly? And when these rash representatives of yours in our halls of legislation and our newspapers shall have sown the wind, who will reap the whirlwind? When they have scattered the dragon's teeth, who must meet the horrent crop which they will produce? Not they alone; but you, your sons, your friends and their sons. So that these misleaders of the people, while you so weakly connive at their indiscretions, may be indirectly preparing the weapon which is to pierce the bosom of your fair-haired boy, and summoning the birds of prey, which are to pick out those eyes whose joy is not the light of your happy homes, as he lies stark on some lost battlefield. For God's sake, then, for your own sakes, for your children's sake, arise, declare that from this day no money, no vote, no influence of yours shall go to the maintenance of any other counsels than those of moderation, righteousness and manly forbearance.

Last: Every Christian must study the things which make for peace. All must resolve that they will demand of others nothing more than their necessary rights, and that in the tone of moderation and forbearance. Yea, that they will generously forego all except what duty forbids them to forego, rather than have strife with brethren. We must all be magnanimous enough to forbear the language of threatening and reproach, language which evinces no courage, to acknowledge the excesses of ourselves and our friends, and to make reparation for it, whether such reparation be offered on the other side or not. Instead of complaining in vindictive and bitter spirit of the extravagances of misguided men on the opposite side, each man should inquire whether there are not sinful extravagances on his own side; and when it is necessary to remonstrate, do it in the tone of wounded love, rather than of insane threatening. In one word, let each party resolve to grant all that is right, and ask nothing else, "and lo, there will be great calm."[118]

The Christian Philosopher

An Expository Sermon

on

Philippians 4:4-7

"Rejoice in the Lord always: and again I say, Rejoice. Let you moderation be known unto all men. The Lord is at hand. Be careful for nothing; but in every thing by prayer and supplication with thanksgiving let your requests be made known unto God."

Preached at Camp Lee, near Richmond, Va., by moonlight;[119] to a number of volunteers, May 1861.[120]

The Christian religion is singular, my Brethren, in that it makes religious joy not only a privilege, but a duty. Its exercise is commanded more than once in the Bible. Psalm 33:1: "Rejoice in the *Lord*, O ye righteous: for praise is comely for the upright." In the text, the obligation is enforced with an emphatic repetition: "Rejoice in the Lord always; and again I say: Rejoice." Had the Philippian Christians possessed no more fortitude than we, they would possibly have demurred from this command, as ill-suited to their dangerous and afflicted circumstances. They would perhaps have reminded the Apostle, that their church was planted by him amidst a storm of persecutions; (see Acts 16:22) and had grown up under its peltings: and that he had himself taught them (ch. 1:29) that suffering under their adversaries was one of the regular allotments of the servant of Christ. 'How can we rejoice,' they might have said, 'who live with the sword at our throats, and who only serve our Redeemer at the cost of exciting a jealousy, which may burst out at any time into murder, and which makes us feel its bitterness daily in exactions and revilings?'

But the Apostle could, at least, rejoin, by asking whether he was in more cheering circumstances, an obscene prisoner in the vast capital of Pagan Rome, with powerful accusers, without friends. Yet he was able to be "exceedingly joyful in all his tribulations." They could not charge him then, with enjoining upon them a higher rule than he observed for himself. If this holy Apostle's spiritual joy sustained him in his gloomy captivity, surely, my brethren, we should be ashamed to bear our lighter lot less cheerfully.

For, the joy of the Lord is independent of outward circumstances. It consists of the inward peace and sunshine of a conscience cleansed from evil works, of the sweet assurance of God's friendship, of delight in his perfect and admirable attributes, and of the triumphant hope of heavenly glory in reserve for us. It has been said that the Apostle not only invites, but commands us to feel it. And is not this just? A voluntary profession of faith in Christ involves an obligation to act in consistency with the creed professed. Now, your creed is, that all your sins are reconciled, that the ruins of the fall are surely repairing in your soul, that this glorious, infinite God is your friend and portion, that a heaven of bliss is your destined home; in a word, that as an heir of God you are journeying to an inheritance, in comparison with whose glories the scantiness of your *viaticum*, and the toils of the way, are trivial evils. Nothing can be more inconsistent than such a profession, and a murmuring, melancholy spirit. Your Redeemer has a right, my brethren, to ask that you shall not seem to contradict his gospel, and to belie his assurance, that his "yoke is easy and his burden light," and to malign that celestial city to which he is inviting men, by your discontented air. He may justly complain of those who defraud themselves of that happiness during their pilgrimage, which he purchased for them by his pangs.

There are many men, who have been persuaded by the "Father of Lies," that Christianity is a gloomy thing. They believe that its practice will suffuse their whole lives with somber melancholy. So dark and repulsive does the Christian life appear to them, they deliberately purchase a postponement of its hated restraints at the cost of hazarding the immortal soul. But lo! Christianity is not gloom: solid joy is one of its constituent parts! "Its ways are ways of pleasantness, and all its paths are peace." So false is that guilty fear, at the prompting of which you are now postponing duty, and risking your everlasting welfare.

But, returning to Christ's people, we are taught that the joy of the Lord should supersede all inordinate emotions concerning lower things. "Let your moderation be known unto all men." Here is inculcated that continued and self-governed spirit, which refuses to be keenly agitated by earthly desire, or by earthly wrong and loss. It pursues even lawful good without overweening cravings: it submits to its privation without excessive grief or indignation. It refuses to allow the steady balance of its equal mind, filled with better things, to be greatly disturbed by any thing below the skies. The Apostle points us to the fact that "the Lord," Christ, "is at hand"; as the ground of this Christian philosophy. Does he mean to suggest the nearness of the Divine Redeemer, as ubiquitous God: with his power, and readiness to succor and to vindicate his own people? If we accept this as his meaning, surely his reasoning is excellent. Omnipotent, redeeming love is at hand, as a resource. Is not this truth enough to breathe composure in every trial? How can that soul be agitated, which reposes in contact with the 'Rock of Ages' beneath it? Or if we attribute to the Apostle another meaning which is consonant to his usage of the phrase, then his argument is equally just. (Indeed it will scarcely seem erroneous to receive the words with a sort of happy ambiguity, and draw from them both senses.) The second idea which they will bear, is the rapid approach of the end, which brings to everyone the final consummation of this earthly scene, and of all its interests. Time is short. The hour is near when Christ will call you away from sublunary fears and joys, to more substantial realities. [Therefore][121] then, it is not reasonable that the heir of immortal riches should be overmuch occupied either by the gains or losses which are soon to be forgotten amidst vaster joys.

Notice too, the Apostle says: "Let your moderation *be known* unto all men." You must not only cultivate, but exhibit this spirit, to all who behold your life. This is a tribute which we are, brethren, to the truth of the Gospel, to the reality of heaven, to the superior moment of eternity. Shall we seek with as querulous anxiety, what we shall eat, and what we shall drink, and wherewithal we shall be clothed, as the poor idolaters of earthly good around us, who have no superior hope? "After all these things do the Gentiles seek"! If the worshippers of this world see us jostling them in their race, with a covetousness as keen as their own, or retorting the loss of temporary things with as hot an indignation as theirs, will they not be likely to conclude that we believe in our hearts, in no better prize? Conscious as they are of the infinite superiority of our inheritance, over the beggarly object of their idolatry, they will find it difficult to believe that we could confound the two, if we truly possessed both. But if we exhibit a noble indifference to all these objects which so engross their desires, they will feel, that "they who say such things declare plainly that they seek a better country, even a heavenly."

Let us therefore "be careful for nothing." We are not taught here, indeed, to forswear a reasonable forecast and industry in providing for temporal wants. We may safely assume that St. Paul does not mean to contradict himself, when he says, (Romans 12:11, 17) that we must "not be slothful in business," and that we must "provide things honest in the sight of all men"; and when he commands (II Thessalonians 3:10) "that if any will not work, neither shall they eat." But the term 'careful' in the intent of the venerable translation of our version, bore the sense (which is a correct representation of the meaning of the word which they render by it) of gnawing anxiety. We are here forbidden to indulge inordinate care for any terrestrial concern. The Apostle echoes the precept of Christ in the Sermon on the Mount, in which he commands us to take no thought, no over-anxious thought, "what we shall eat, or what we shall drink, or wherewithal we shall be clothed"; but to commit these smaller interests to our Heavenly Father, and seek first the kingdom of God and his righteousness. Our inability to secure the objects of our desire, and the inutility of our strivings without a favoring Providence; our reliance on a present God and Savior, who knows our real wants: the superior moment of heavenly good; all these argue against excessive earthly cares.

But what Christian heart has not experienced the rebellion of these inordinate anxieties against the soundest argument? They will not be charmed down by logic, let it charm ever so wisely. These obstinate cares cleave to the heart, infest the most sacred seasons and exercises, and throng between our souls and their Redeemer, even when we seek him on his Mercy seat. The Apostle therefore shows us a more excellent way. He proposes a holy art, by which these enemies of our heavenly-mindedness may be disarmed, and even enlisted to assist in our approaches to God. This method is, instead of making them subjects for an ineffectual and consuming anxiety, to make them *subjects of prayer*. "But," as another and better alternative than sinful care, "in every thing, by prayer and supplication with thanksgiving, let your requests be made known unto God." Let all our wants be carried to Him in earnest, humble prayer: and that accompanied with thanks for mercies already received. For what attitude is more inconsistent, than that of an ungrateful petitioner? And what consideration could more properly arrest the future bounties of our Heavenly Father, than the discovery that we were thankless for the good already bestowed?

But do you ask: 'Shall I carry every want thus to the throne of grace: the trivial as well as the grave: the temporal as well as the spiritual? Would not the obtruding of the former be derogatory to the majesty of God; and of the latter, to his sanctity? Shall I be so presumptuous as to ask the sovereign Ruler of angels and worlds to repair the lesser inconveniences, and to remedy the petty arrogances which are the daily worry of my existence? If I went to him for the life of a child languishing with mortal disease, or for the soul of one wandering in devious paths of sin, I should feel that there was a proportion in the gravity of the petition to the grandeur of the King. But how can I ask the Majesty of heaven to stoop to the healing of the fleeting indisposition which is the vexation of a day: how request Him whose infinite mind is filled with designs for the redemption of immortal souls, to turn aside for the bestowal of some little corporeal good?'

It is by such fallacies as these, perhaps only half-uttered in the heart, that many a Christian defrauds himself of the larger part of his Savior's legacy of peace. And here is to be found one solution of that strange blemish, which has been so often observed in God's people: that while, in the grave emergencies of life, they are calm, and in its heavy calamities, nobly submissive; they have no philosophy to sustain the smaller annoyances, but yield with a petulance unworthy of their heavenly birth. This occurs, because the weighty events drive them to the throne of grace; whence they receive strength to endure: but the light ones are met in their strength alone, which is weakness.

Now, in opposition to all his error, St. Paul says: "in *every thing*, let your requests be made known unto God." In large things, and in small things: in spiritual, and in secular things: in those which move the world's sympathy, and in those which evoke its sneer. If there is any want, which you do not make known to God by prayer and supplication, that is a want not disarmed of its sting of inordinate care. If there is anything which it is right for you to desire; then it is right for you to ask it of God. If there is any annoyance which men call trivial, that is sufficient to disturb the Christian integrity of God's child, then it is important enough to claim the attention of the Redeemer who died for him. If it is large enough, my brother, to be a temptation to you, then it is large enough for the reasonable notice of God; for in his eye, sin in you is the most momentous occurrence of which your being can be the subject.

But the illusion which has been described is effectually dispelled by two thoughts. One is, that relatively to God, human affairs are not large and small, as they appear to our limited capacities. If we compare the grandest transactions of earth with his infinitude, they are inexpressibly minute beside Him. He counteth "the nations as the small dust of the balance: behold he taketh up the isles as a very little thing." If, on the other hand, we regard his omniscience, we see that no fatigue can arise in the divine mind, from multiplicity or minuteness of details. There is a sense in which nothing earthy is great, nothing is small to God. The other truth is, that he has already proved his concern in the most trivial events which befall His own people. We believe in a special Providence: we hold that, to God, there is nothing which comes by chance: we read that the very hairs of our heads are all numbered. As every thing which exists was created by Him, so every event which occurs is superintended and directed by His design. Remember, my brother, when you taste an evanescent or unimportant pleasure, that you would not have enjoyed it, but for the purpose and care, and power of God. This is true, even though that pleasure is merely corporeal, and wholly unessential to the good of your nobler part, the soul. Your eye is delighted with the beauty of a landscape? Who spread the field with verdure, swelled the hills into forms of grace, and arched them over with the azure sky? Who directed your steps to it just when the scene was refreshed with showers and illuminated with the mellowest light of morn or evening? You regale your senses with the tint and the perfume of an ephemeral rose. Who dyed its leaves with those pure colors, and imbued them with that sweetness? It was your Heavenly Father: and he did it, in part, that he might prepare for you, his child, this fleeting joy beside your pathway. So, when we receive those supplies of the commonplace wants of every day, the failure of which would so soon plunge us into heavy trouble, we see in every gift the detailed watchfulness, the paternal care of our omnipresent Father. He who has taught us to pray: "Give us this day our daily bread," does not disdain to provide the homely gift. We have in our own experience, the most complete proof that our God condescends to provide for the smallest wants of his creatures. Let us then, "in everything, by prayer and supplication, with thanksgiving, make known our requests unto God." Nothing will be so great as to overtask his power: nothing so minute as to elude his omniscience.

In thus calling us, with all our wants, to the throne of grace, the Apostle tacitly encourages us with the warrant of the sacred Scriptures, that all earnest, believing prayer of Christians is surely answered. God has pledged his own power and faithfulness to this, in many great and precious promises, such as these: "God will give grace and glory: no good thing will he withhold from them that walk uprightly." (Psalm 85:11) "Shall not God avenge his own elect which cry day and night unto him, though he bear long with them? I tell you that he will avenge them speedily." (Luke 18:7-8) "He that spared not his own Son, but delivered him up for us all; how shall he not with him also freely give us all things?" (Romans 8:32) God has not indeed found himself here, to gratify every specific desire for unessential, earthly good, in spite of his wiser knowledge on our time interests; but he has done what is better: he has engaged to watch over our all, for time and eternity, with an omniscient love, which secures us whatever is for our honest good, and which, where it withholds, makes the privation a more real blessing than the bestowal would have been. Thus it is plain, that he who reposes, by a habitual life of prayer, upon his God, has enlisted the resources of his infinite attributes in his own cause. He has the Almighty pledged to his security, for time and eternity.

Now let us notice the blessed consequence which follows from this life of prayer. "The peace of God, which passeth all understanding, shall keep his heart and mind through Christ Jesus." This peace is surely some great thing, seeing the Apostle dignifies it with so majestic a term. Shall we, with some, receive this as meaning no more than a phrase of amplitude, an instance of a Hebrew mode of speech, which expresses superlative excellence or greatness of created things, by attributing them to God as their immediate possessor? Thus, the lofty cedars of Lebanon were called "trees of God," grandest of God's vegetable creation; and the plain of Jordan is compared to the "Garden of God," for its fruitfulness and beauty. Nay, I am persuaded that these blessed words signify far more, that the peace which they assure to the praying Christians is God's own peace; the peace which God himself enjoys, communicated by his own Spirit in that measure which befits the created soul. And I rest this conviction not only on the grounds that this meaning is more simple and obvious, and more accordant with the usual expressions of the Apostle Paul, but especially upon the words of our Savior to his disciples: (John 14:27) "Peace I leave with you: my peace I give unto you." It is his own peace: It is the same serene composure and assumed blessedness which reigned in the soul of the God-man: and which constitutes the eternal sunshine of the Divine Spirit. Sublime, audacious thought! Yea, impious for a poor sinner to think: were he not invited to it by the gracious words of his master. But, brethren, splendid as is the conception, it is not extravagant; for we have it in the very words of God and of Christ, that they invite us to share their own peace. "The eternal God is our refuge, and underneath are the everlasting arms." (Deuteronomy 33:27) He has taught us, that "he that toucheth his people, toucheth the apple of his eye." (Zechariah 2:8). He authorizes us to say: (Psalm 46:1-2) "God is our refuge and strength, a very present help in trouble. Therefore will not we fear, though the earth be removed, and though the mountains be carried into the midst of the sea." How much nobler and truer thy Lyric, believer, than the vain boast of the classic heathen, who vaunts a fortitude amidst the most appalling calamities, built upon the strength of his own virtue and stability of his own will!

> "If man be just, and to his purpose true,
> The rage malign of urgent populace
> And willful despots' angry face
> Shall not his steadfast will subdue,
> Nor stormy South-wind, restless Hadria's king,
> Nor yet the mighty hand of thundering Jove,
> His fearless soul shall never move,
> If worlds their ruins round him fling."[122]

Be our fortitude, brethren reared on a more stable foundation; the strength of God-Almighty, pledged to us! To him who lives the life of believing prayer, our God has engaged himself, to withhold no good thing, and to give grace and glory. The covenant is ordered in all things and sure. It is fortified by two immutable things in which it is impossible for God to lie, his word and oath. Thus all the perfections of Jehovah are enlisted for us, with the fidelity and zeal of redeeming love. When the Divine mind regards the future interests of its own unchangeable blessedness, and sees the kings of earth and hell taking counsel against his throne, what is the thought which fills the heart of God with his ineffable and changeless composure? We infer, with, reverence, that it is the recollection of his own immense resources of wisdom, knowledge and power, and of his own immutable rectitude; of an omniscience which no cunning of human or Satanic malice can elude; of an omnipotence which no created power can successfully assail . . . [123][T]he same attributes are engaged for our protection, by a love which was strong enough to die for us, so that the security of our souls reposes on the same foundations, which support the honor of Jehovah's throne. "Our lives are hid with Christ in God." Is it not with justice then, that the Apostle calls the repose of that faith, which embraces the promises of redemption, of *the peace of God*?

This peace, he declares, "passeth all understanding." It is indeed, most obviously incomprehensible to the unbeliever. Conscious that his soul possesses no such foundation, and that it will shiver with helpless fright before the stroke of fate, he looks on with wonder, and almost with incredulity, when he sees the man of faith composed, or even joyful, in the presence of calamity and death. But more than this, it passeth *all* understanding, even that of believers themselves. There is a breadth and length, and height and depth in it, which passeth knowledge. No trials to which Christians have yet been subjects have fully tested or exhausted its resources. No soul has yet drawn all the sweetness which is contained in the ineffable truth that this God is our God, and our portion forever. To Zion He said: "Behold, I will extend peace to her like a river." (Isaiah 66:12) On this blessed flood the child of God is sustained and borne: He is immersed in its waves; they embrace him all around with a full and satisfying volume: he feels no boundary to his joy around him, beneath him. But he is not able to fathom and measure the generous flood: all he knows is, that it is more than large enough for his largest desires.

This abounding peace, saith St. Paul, "shall keep your hearts and minds through Christ Jesus." The verb he uses is of peculiar strength: It shall *garrison* your souls, to keep out every assailant, as the detachment of soldiers guards and watches a besieged fortress. And this, the Christians' peace effects, whether the temptation is armed at the affections of the heart, in the form of seductive passions, or at the understanding, in the form of sophisms and heresies. Spiritual joy garrisons the heart against corrupt desires, chiefly by filling and satisfying it with its own purer blessedness. Has not your experience taught you, my brethren, that these temptations have power over you only when your souls have lost the savor of divine things? When your heart is no longer filled with this peace, its native craving for happiness, rising in your emptiness into a consuming hunger, impels you to feed upon the baser food of forbidden pleasures. Like the prodigal, estranged from his Father's house, and famished for good, you feed upon the husks which the swine did eat, which none gave unto you. But when the prodigal has returned, and has been embraced by his reconciled father, when he has satisfied his soul with the meat and wines of the feast of rejoicing, do those husks again tempt him? No: they have no longer any allurement for him: he is secure from their seductions: his nature is satiated with better things. Even so vile, brethren, do impure joys seem to your hearts, when they are solaced and fed with the joys of your salvation.

It is true, although less obvious, that peace in believing is the best defense against all erroneous dogmas in religion. And here a remark may be made parallel to one just uttered, which deserves the special reflection of all who are, or may become guides of other souls; that the great inlet to speculative errors concerning Christianity, is spiritual declension. When Christians fall into the domain of "Doubting Castle," or under the frightful clutches of "Giant Despair," it is always found that the misfortune has begun by turning aside into the bypaths of transgression and forfeiting their peace. When professed religious teachers are betrayed into heresies or damnable errors, it will always be found that 'prayer and supplication with thanksgiving' had first declined, and the peace which passeth all understanding had been lost. When that blessed peace is felt, the mind finds in self-evident holiness and reality of the gift, the best argument for the correctness of that system of redeeming truth by which the happy state of the soul has been propagated. The sanctified heart is teacher to the enlightened head. And this, instead of dethroning reason, is the order which is supremely rational. Will you go and tell the man who is basking in the light, that there *is no sun* shining in his strength? It will be vain: he will say, even though blind: 'Nay verily: I know there is a Sun in the heavens, and that he shines on me: For do I not feel his blessed beams, filling every fiber of these limbs but now frozen, with his vivifying warmth?' "He that believeth, hath the witness in himself."

It is through Jesus Christ the soul is thus defended; for it is through him this peace is derived to us. The prayers and supplications, which are the means for its descent, must all be offered through him. His intercession must obtain the gift, as his death purchased it. His Spirit must infuse it in our hearts.

And now, I end this exposition, by asking you, by Brother: Is not this peace of God worth the pains of gaining it? Oh, is it not well worth the surrender of those deceitful, beggarly pleasures of sin, which are but for a season, that defraud us of the blessed endowment, and worth the diligence in Christian duties and prayer, by which it is attained?

I ask you, in turn, Unbeliever: What think you of this peace? Is it not worth having? Contrast it with your present condition and future destiny. What have you here, to set against it? A few treacherous, hollow joys, clashed with satiety, and evil conscience, and disappointment: with the miserable license of your darling self-will; the whole speedily terminated by death; and then – the blackness of darkness forever! Poor, beggared soul: Is it nothing to have peace between yourself and your Almighty Judge: to have a mercy seat thrown open to your every want: to have the infinite powers of God all engaged, by the most faithful love, for the presentation of your highest welfare, and transmuting apparent evils into occasions of blessing: to have wounds, calamities death itself, disarmed of all their real sting: to have a home in heaven pledged as the end of your toils here below? Surely, even your heart avows that this is worth the winning. But is it for you too? Yea, for all, who come through Jesus Christ, by prayer and supplication, with thanksgiving. Bring your spiritual wants then, to God (and they are many): he will meet them all: your sins, to be covered with Christ's atonement: your self-will, to be subdued by his Spirit: your darkness to be illuminated by his light: your weakness of purpose as to all good: to be upheld by his strength: your misery to be enriched by his love. "And the peace of God which passeth all understanding, shall keep your heart and mind, likewise, through Jesus Christ."[124]

Encouragements to Prayer[125]

A Sermon

on

Luke 18:7-8

"And shall not God avenge his own elect, which cry
day and night unto him, though he bear long with them?
I tell you that he will avenge them speedily."

Preached to the 18th Regiment. Va. Volunteers in their camp, within the Entrenchments of Manassas Junction. June, 1861[126]

Of the most of us it may probably be said, that we are more deficient in a proper value for spiritual blessings, than in confidence in God's generosity and faithfulness. There is danger that we shall supinely recline on an indolent assurance of God's willingness to bless, while we seek his blessings with no true earnestness and desire. And perhaps, the language of rebuke would be more appropriate to the present state of the church, for its sinful indifference to spiritual good, than the language of encouragement. But kindness often touches the heart more than severity. It may be, that a consideration of the loving assurances which our Father has given us, of his willingness to answer prayer, may affect us with a tender and ingenuous compunction for our lack of faith and desire. Shame! that these have so straitened our spiritual gifts,[127] while God has been so ready to communicate! Let us dwell for a time upon his assurances; until we are filled with a generous contrition for the scantiness and languor of our prayers, and until we feel "boldness to come to the throne of grace, to obtain mercy, and find grace to help us in time of need."

The text contains the moral of the preceding parable; and its language is obviously formed upon that of the story. "And he spake a parable unto them to this end, that men ought always to pray; and not to faint: saying, There was in a city a judge which feared not God, neither regarded man. And there was a widow in that city; and she came unto him saying: Avenge me of mine adversary. And he would not for a while; but afterward he said within himself: Though I fear not God, nor regard man; yet because this widow troubleth me, I will avenge her, lest by her continual coming, she weary me."

"And the Lord said: Hear what the unjust judge saith! And shall not God avenge his own elect, which cry day and night unto him, though he bear long with them! I tell you that he will avenge them speedily."

It is clearly implied that the widow, by the phrase, "Avenge me of my adversary," intended, not malicious revenge, but a claim for her just rights. We shall best apprehend our Savior's meaning, by looking only at this simple idea, that the widow had a suit to urge. Hence, when it is said, in drawing out the instruction of the parable in the text: "Shall not God avenge his own elect?" we are to find no more meaning in the words, than simply this: Shall he not grant their suit? To illustrate the strength of this gracious assurance, our Savior presents this picture. The petitioner is a widow, a name in Oriental society, synonymous with that of a person friendless and unprotected. She could bring no social influence or patronage, to allure, or to overawe the judge. On the other hand, his character was at once so ruthless, and so godless, that nothing was to be hoped from an appeal to his benevolence, his regard for reputation, or his religious fears. The poor, helpless applicant had nothing on which to rely, but pertinacity. And by the mere force of pertinacity, she was successful! How much more then, may not God's own, chosen people be assured of success, when they persevere day and night in prayer; seeing they come, not friendless, but with the powerful advocacy of Jesus Christ; and not to a ruthless judge, but a faithful and pitying Father?

Such is the argument involved by our Redeemer, in this beautiful parable. Of course, we are not to wrest it to the preposterous and impious idea, that God, like this judge, will yield unwillingly to our prayers, from a selfish fear of being "wearied." We are to limit ourselves to the one idea; see here, the force of mere perseverance! And is it not a strange and touching thing, my Brethren, that it is God, the Giver, who here uses the importunity, which among men, is usually found on the side of the beggar? It is evidence of inexpressible graciousness in God: of lamentable blindness and hardness in us! Let us pursue farther, the proofs of God's willingness to answer prayer.[128]

But that our faith may be firm, it should be intelligent. Let us therefore understand how far God's warrant for prayer extends. When Christ says (Matthew 21:22) "All things whatsoever ye shall ask in prayer, believing, ye shall receive;" or when similar promises are given elsewhere, we understand, of course, that there is a limitation – God has not bound himself to bestow literally every thing which a pious heart may ask, in the exercise of Christian affections. For there are many things; many innocent things, even, which the Christian might very piously desire; which would be disastrous to his welfare. If God had bound himself to give every such request, with literal exactness, he would have made his omnipotence the slave of our ignorance. The believer would be deprived of the advantages of having the Divine omniscience for his guide; and would have no better direction than his own pious but often misjudging desires. If God had given such a promise, he would have given us the greatest curse. According; we find instances in Holy Writ, where the pious requests of pious men were refused by the Hearer of prayer. – II. Samuel 12. We find that David earnestly besought God to spare the life of his child by Bathsheba; and yet the child died. This too, was after his penitence induced by the rebuke of Nathan, and recorded in the 51st Psalm; and we may therefore conclude, that the prayer was offered with the right spirit. In II Corinthians 12, Paul tells us that, when a thorn in the flesh, a messenger of Satan, was sent to buffet him, lest he should be exalted above measure through the abundance of the revelations, "he besought the Lord for this thing thrice, that it might depart from him." But God's answer was: "My grace is sufficient for thee; for my strength is made perfect in weakness" – We cannot suspect that Paul's request, thrice repeated, was rejected because it was offered in an improper spirit.

There is therefore, a limitation implied in these promises. To see the extent of this limitation, we must draw a necessary distinction. There is a large class of objects, in themselves innocent and proper, concerning which we have no certainty whether they will be best for us or not. For all these, we must pray conditionally. Thus: we may submissively ask God to rescue us from temporal afflictions, or to exempt us from them in the future. But we do not know whether he may not see it best for us to afflict us farther; because we have no light by which to read the designs of his providence in this matter. And yet it may be lawful and right for us to offer this prayer. It is even made our *duty* to pray: "Give us day by day our daily bread." And yet we have no warrant that God may not see it to be best for us to suffer actual want. How many a poor saint, who has meekly offered this petition, has suffered for the lack of daily food? To the same class belong all such objects as health, competence, long life, good name, ease. We may ask for these objects; but it must be with entire submission; and all must be suspended on the proviso: "If it be agreeable to thy will." And yet, even with regard to these, we have the explicit warrant to ask this, which is the most important concern respecting them; that, whether given or withheld. God will make them all subserve our highest good – Is not this enough for the meek soul?

But there is a higher and nobler class of objects concerning which we should pray with far different boldness and assurance. These may be described in general as being the gifts that pertain to redemption; or spiritual good things. Concerning all these we know, when we pray for them, that they are agreeable to God's will: for he has told us so – "This is the will of God; even our sanctification." When praying for any spiritual good, we may rely with undoubting confidence on God's literal engagement to give the answer. "This is the confidence that we have in him, (says the Apostle John) that if we ask any thing *according to his* will, he heareth us: whatsoever we ask, we know that we *have* the petition that we desired of him." The *when*, the *how*, the *where-with* of the answer, may be far other than we expected. The desired gift may be so long delayed that we begin to fear God has forgotten us; for the times and seasons are in his own hands. The blessing may come in a shape so different from our foolish expectations, that we scarcely recognize it. It may be brought to us by means which, to us, had seemed most unlikely. But we believe that for all objects of spiritual good, the words of the promises are literally and universally exact; that *every* scriptural prayer for such objects is answered.

But now, let us to the proofs. And first, is not evidence to be found that we may[129] expect an answer to prayers for any of the gifts accompanying redemption, in God's very nature? He is intrinsically a holy being. He loves and delights in holiness with ineffable intensity. He delights in holy beings with an infinite delight. "The righteous Lord loveth righteousness." "Such as are upright in their way are his delight." Now, the tendency of all these spiritual gifts is to make the soul holy; in other words, to make it that in which God delights. We may say, therefore, that the native inclinations of the Divine mind are on the side of such petitions. He who prays for any grace, prays that he become just what God loves. In going to a fellow man, how strong an assurance of an affirmative answer would we feel, when we knew that we were inviting him to do something to which he was of himself inclined: and that we should have a warm prompter in his own breast, seconding our request? If there is not some external obstacle which forbids it, we feel certain that he will gratify himself and us at once, by assenting to our petition. In the case of God, all obstacles to the bestowal of grace, have been removed by the work of Christ. He may now lavish all the stores of redemption on any penitent and believing soul, without injury to his justice, majesty, or authority. And when our prayers fall in exactly with God's own inclinations, and no obstacle forbids him to indulge that inclination, may we not confidently expect a favorable answer?

Again we may say that God's own interests are too strongly on the side of an answer to all such prayers, to permit us to fear that they will be rejected. God is himself glorified in the redemption, and in all the graces and services of his children. And although he is independent and perfectly glorious and blessed in himself, and sufficient for himself, yet it is certain that the promotion of his own declarative glory in the acts and events of his creation, is a grand motive of his determinations. His purposes are formed by him, "to be to the praise of the glory of his grace." We believe that there is no event which occurs on this globe, which so glorifies God, as the redemption and perfection of a soul. There is no work by which so many of the divine attributes are so illustriously displayed. To form out of a fallen, debased and rebel sinner, a glorified saint, a mate for angels, and a possessor of eternal glory, is a work more splendid than would be the conversion of a clod into a star. Every acquisition of Christians in holiness, and every good work, is also a tribute to God's glory. "So is my Father glorified, that ye bear much fruit." "The fruits of righteousness which are by Jesus Christ, are unto the glory and praise of God." Will God begrudge the gifts of redemption, when they all redound to his own advantage? When the Christian prays for larger measures of the Spirit, for more wisdom, for more spiritual comfort, for victory over indwelling sin, for warmer zeal, or for stronger faith, he only prays for what will enable him to promote God's glory better. When the servant comes to the wise master, and asks for better implements,[130] only in order that he may be able to earn more for that master, will he be refused? So when the Christian prays for any spiritual good, what is it, but asking that he may be equipped for serving his God better? God's own self-interest and wisdom are on the side of the answer of such prayers.

There is a third fact which is yet more conclusive. All believing prayer for spiritual good is itself the fruit of the Holy Spirit. He himself has evoked it: therefore it is offered up. "The preparations of the heart of man, and the answer of the lips are from the Lord." "Likewise the Spirit also helpeth our infirmities; for we know not what we should pray for as we ought; but the Spirit itself maketh intercession for us with groanings which cannot be uttered." In man's natural heart, there is no good desire. Now, does the Spirit of truth prompt these desires for spiritual good, in order to disappoint them? Does he thus make a mock and sport of believing souls? It is impious to suppose it. When we feel a spiritual desire, why did he inspire it? It was a part of the eternal plan of his grace to us; that, through asking we might receive. He does not put petitions into our mouths and send us with them to his own footstool, in order that he may reject them. The fact that we feel a true and believing desire for any spiritual good is, therefore, the evidence and earnest of the Divine intention to bestow that good; in his own good time and way. Just so far as we are assured that our desires are sincere and pious, we may argue, with pleasing awe, and humble joy, that God himself has inspired them; inspired, because he intends to gratify them. We may spread the words of our requests before him, and urge that they are the Holy Spirit's own words. Thus the Spirit makes intercession for us. We may plead with God that he disappoint us not: because he himself hath taught us to hope.

There is, what may perhaps be called, another view of the same truth, derived from the doctrine of our *union with Christ*. He is the head of which Christians are the limbs, receiving spiritual sensation, vitality and volition from him. He is the vine stock, and they are the branches, blooming, and bearing fruit by his sap, which circulates in a common flow through him and them. Wherever a believer possesses gracious exercises or qualities, it is in virtue of this vital union to

Christ. Our gracious affections are therefore to be all regarded as the evidences of the existence, in full glory and perfection, of similar graces and affections in Christ our Head. As the drop of sap trickling from the twig is evidence of the strong flow of the[131] same sap throughout the generous vine-stock, so the existence of a pious affection in the breast of a believer, is evidence that the same affection is glowing, in full purity and perfection, in the breast of the Savior. As we pass along, with our eyes fixed upon the ground, we suddenly behold a flush of splendor which dazzles the sight, thrown from the surface of a pool, to whose margin we have come. Whence that blaze of light? Not from the pool, which is in its own nature rayless, and perhaps sordid! We know at once, that it is reflected light; descending first from the king of day, and that therefore he is now shining in his strength from the sky. So, every gracious desire in our poor breasts, is reflected from the heart of the Sun of Righteousness. In like manner, when we have a good[132] desire to offer to God, we have the unspeakable encouragement of believing that the same desire burns, in far superior strength, in the breast of him who is "our Advocate with the Father" and "Head over all things to the church." If Christ, into whose hand "all power in Heaven and in earth is given," desires the same things which we desire; if this is so true, that the *reason why* we felt the desire, was that he felt it first and communicated it to us, how can we be disappointed? Such gracious desires for spiritual good are as certain of an answer in Christ's own time and way, as it is certain that Christ is King in Zion.

In our desires and zeal for Christ's cause and church, especially, does not our forgetfulness of this sometimes amount to an impertinence towards Him? When we go, with ardent zeal for the revival of religion, to plead before Him, is not this the implied language of our temper and feeling: "that God and Christ are too cold and inattentive to the interest of Zion; and that we must arouse and warm them?" My brother; if that zeal is pure, which sends you to your knees, interceding for Zion, whence comes it, except from the infinitely purer and stronger zeal for the Church, which ever glows in the breast of him who gave his blood for it? Let us remember this for our rebuke: for what an impertinence is it, that when *our* remissness, and follies, and faults, have brought the cause of Christ into an evil case, (the only causes of the church's reverses,) we should go querulously to him who loves the church with a perpetual and intense love, as though he were not zealous enough for his own cause? Let us remember it also for our encouragement. It is our privilege to pray always for Zion in the strain of Asaph, in the 74th Psalm. "Arise, Oh God, plead *thine own* cause." If we feel that it is dear to us, herein we have the evidence that it is infinitely dearer to Christ. If the opposition of the wicked grieves our hearts, we know thereby that it grieves Christ far more. His care and concern for his cause are infinitely more tender than ours; for ours are only a faint reflection of his. And while we are living a life of purity, consistency, and faithful effort for Zion, we should offer all our intercessions for her, and commit all her concerns to her Head, with a blessed composure and peacefulness, which would fill our souls with heavenly assurance and courage, amidst all delays, discouragements and oppositions.

To be further strengthened in encouragement, let the Believer ask himself, for what purpose he has been redeemed, and what was the expense at which the work of his redemption has been set on foot. Both these questions are answered in Titus 2:14. "Christ gave himself for us, that he might redeem us from all iniquity, and purify unto himself a peculiar people zealous of good works." Now, we have an assurance of God's sincerity in tending our complete redemption, in the immense expense he has already incurred to begin the work: and it is the strongest of all inferences, that a wise Being, having gone to this expense, will not begrudge any thing else which is necessary to perfect the undertaking. When the Christian prays for any gift accompanying redemption; he prays for just the object for which God has already made this great expenditure. And when he prays for the largest measures of grace, he does not pray for more than is embraced in God's object, for that object is his *perfect* sanctification.

But more; since Christ has been given for us, all other gifts are, to God, inexpressibly easy. Not only are they vastly less precious and costly than this first, great gift: but the giving of this has smoothed the way for the prompt and easy bestowal of all the rest. To God's almighty power, it is, and always has been an effort perfectly easy[133] to put forth any exertion of strength or wisdom, which may be needed for our complete redemption. How slight[134] are the works of renewing our hearts, of conquering our indwelling sins, of foiling our enemies, human and spiritual, of enlightening our minds, and of moving the wheels of providence for our highest welfare, to that God whose understanding is infinite, whose word made the worlds, "who spake and it was done; who commanded, and it stood fast?" The only obstacles which ever existed to our receiving all spiritual blessings, were those arising from our guilt and God's truth, holiness, and justice. By the gift of Christ, these have been all so thoroughly removed, that God is actually more glorified in giving than in withholding. All the rest then, which pertains to our redemption, however precious and necessary to us, is to God, in comparison with his first gift, unspeakably easy and light. Is it conceivable that God, after having proved the earnestness and reality of his purpose to save us, by so great a gift, will begrudge the less? Would a wise man who had expended great treasures, to purchase a pearl of great price, then begrudge the additional expense of a trifling sum to secure the gem from being lost? Could there be any doubt, after Abraham had bound his only son, the son of promise, as a sacrifice to God, whether this pastoral Prince would spare a lamb out of his countless flocks, as an offering to him? So argues, the Holy Spirit for our encouragement: "He that spared not his own Son, but delivered him up for us all, how shall he not with him also freely give us all things?" (Romans 8:32) To taste the richness of these words, we must try to conceive something of the divine and eternal love for the coequal Son. We must remember how freely he was bestowed. We must consider to what he was surrendered for our redemption; to how cruel and bitter, and humiliating a destiny. Can a love so unspeakable as that which gave Christ to die for us, stint us in any of those slighter gifts which we now need? (slighter for God to give, though still invaluable to us.) If he so love, must he not now delight to lavish these gifts of his grace upon his people?

But the Apostle Paul raises this argument to a delightful climax, when he says, Romans 5:8, 10: "God commendeth his love toward us, in that while we were yet sinners, Christ died for us: – For if when were enemies, we were reconciled to God by the death of his Son, much more being reconciled, we shall be saved by his life." This love, and this gift, so unspeakably great, were bestowed upon us while as yet we were in a state of heinous rebellion, and loathsome guilt. It is impossible for us to express or conceive the abhorrence and indignation, with which God regards the character of an impenitent sinner. He averts his eyes from him, as a loathsome object. "He is angry with the wicked every day." If we have been truly convinced of sin, we can recall the impressions of our own guilt and hatefulness which we then had; and we may remember that these were but a little glimpse of the character which we then bore in God's eyes. It was in that hateful condition, that he thus loved us, and gave this unspeakable gift for us. But now, we hope we are reconciled. We are, "accepted in the Beloved." "Like as a father pitieth his children, so the Lord pitieth them that fear him." All our sins are covered with the precious atonement, and the robe of Christ's obedience, so lovely in the Father's eyes, is thrown all around us. And although there is not and[135] will not be, anything, in our personal characters or conduct, meritorious in such a sense as to purchase the justification of a holy, perfect, and absolute law; yet there is a change here, which must render believers very different objects to God's eye. In place of obduracy there is repentance. In place of insolent rebellion, there is imperfect, but affectionate obedience. None of this personal change can be presented by us, to satisfy the law; for it is all imperfect, while the law is perfect; and it is all the inwrought gift of God to us: as a price to purchase anything from Him of our own right? But the fact that all this conversion is God's work, surely does not render it less interesting in his eyes. Doubtless, He is pleased with His own holy and excellent handiwork in us, although He still disapproves that evil which our indwelling sin mingles with it. Here then, is St. Paul's argument: if in our old estate of guilt and enmity, God loved so much, and did so much for us, will He not now, when we are reconciled, when we are clothed, with Christ's glorious righteousness, when our souls begin to show some of the results of His gracious handiwork, give us all that our souls need? How can words strengthen the blessed assurance?

The answer of prayer is farther ensured to believers, by the Advocate who presents it. His merits are complete: he is the "beloved Son in who God is well pleased." His mediation has never been unsuccessful; he could say to his Father when asking of him that the bonds of death should be broken from the limbs of his friend, Lazarus, "I knew that thou hearest me always." "He is able to save to the uttermost them that come unto God by him." God the Father stands pledged to grant all his mediatorial petitions; having engaged: "He shall see of the travail of his soul, and be satisfied." Yea, he exercises the authority of a regal advocate; for "God hath set him at his own right-hand in the heavenly places, . . . and hath put all things under his feet, and made him to be head over all things to the church." This Christ is also, even ready to undertake for believers. He declared: "Him that cometh to me I will in no wise cast out." Let us recall his tenderness, compassion, and liberality when upon earth, and remember that he is "Jesus Christ the same yesterday, today, and forever." It is to be noted, that there is not a single instance, in all the biographies of Christ by the Evangelists, where any applicant was turned away with neglect or refusal. Even though it was but a corporeal evil which brought the petitioner to him, and the evidence was lacking of any true gracious desire for the better gifts of redemption, even though it was the Canaanitish woman, daughter of an unclean and doomed race, none ever found an ear inattentive to their woe. The God-man wears the same tender heart upon the throne of the universe. Come, then, brethren, with all your wants and sorrows, to the mercy-seat, and you will not be disappointed.

To conclude the proof, let us recite a few of the promises so thickly strewn over the Bible. "The Lord God is a sun and shield: the Lord will give grace and glory: no good thing will he withhold from them that walk uprightly."[136] "But they that wait upon the Lord shall renew their strength: they shall mount up with wings as eagles; they shall run and not be weary: they shall walk and not faint."[137] "I said not unto the seed of Jacob, Seek ye me in vain."[138] "I am the Lord thy God, which brought thee up out of the land of Egypt: open thy mouth wide, and I will fill it."[139] "Hitherto ye have asked nothing in my name; ask, and ye shall receive, that your joy may be full."[140] He repudiates the blame of our leanness. It is we, who have straitened ourselves, with a suicidal folly and indolence. Let us not pervert the truth of the sovereignty of grace; and tacitly assign our shortcoming to God's disposing purpose; for He has assured us that he purposes a full and liberal answer to our prayers. We deceive ourselves here: we argue that the higher measures of holiness and zeal are not within our power. When we compare our barren and sluggish lives with that of a Paul we say, 'it is God who maketh us to differ.' True, such grace, the least true grace, is not within our natural power: but it is within the promises; those same promises which were given to the great Apostle. We are, indeed, not responsible that a disposing Providence has refused to us the genius, and the opportunity, of a Paul. But we are blameworthy if we fail to pray so that equal measures of love, fidelity, faith, and zeal are granted to our more lowly capacities. It is our duty to ask great endowments of grace, and to labor for them, and to expect them.

But I am reminded, that the Christian heart is often vehemently concerned for other gifts than those pertaining to redemption, to which alone, as I have today taught you, the express and literal warrant of answer extends. Many of these things, though not essential to your glorification as ransomed souls, are very dear, you say, to your affections: the life, the comfort of beloved ones at home, your health, your life, your good name. And especially is there one desire, belonging to this class, which lies near the heart of every Christian patriot among us, today – the deliverance of the bleeding country for which we contend. What are we entitled to claim, and to expect of God, concerning these dear objects? Perhaps, my brethren, it becomes us to conclude that one reason these precious interests are permitted to be jeopardized today, is, that our God sees our innocent attachments to them are becoming inordinate, and so are no longer innocent. Perhaps we have suffered them to intrude into that supreme place in our hearts, which should be reserved for God and for heaven alone; and therefore he is constrained to cast the anxious shadow of fear across them, to remind us that they should not be our chief good.

With regard to this class of objects, the warrant of God's word may be expressed in these propositions: That is our petitions for them are offered in a believing, submissive spirit, they are graciously entertained by our Father, even though they cannot be expressly granted: That they will not be granted, unless a loving omniscience sees that to refuse them is a truer kindness, in view of the whole interests of an immortality, and of his glory: And that in any event, all these things shall be made to work together for your truest-good. Ought not this to suffice for a Christian heart? Is it not sufficient for the servant, that he be as his master? When our Redeemer in Gethsemane, cried: "Father, if it be possible, let this cup pass from me," his holiness caused him to add: "Nevertheless, not my will, but thine be done." And the cup did not pass! But a gift was bestowed, in answer to this earnest cry, (for, saith the Apostle, "he was heard in that he feared.") fuller of glory and blessing than immediate deliverance could have been; strength to endure, and thus, to achieve man's redemption and his own infinite exaltation. Look, then, unto Him, who is the "author and finisher of our faith": there is your model at once, of importunity, and of submission.

It may be added, that the tender compassion of our Advocate and king prompt him to give every innocent gift which affects the happiness of his people, unless their higher good, or his higher glory, forbids. And perhaps, if we attempt to prognosticate whether a lawful secular object of our desire, such as the independence of our beloved country, will be formed accordant with the higher spiritual interests; no safer rule can be given, to guide our surmises in so uncertain a question, than this: That we may probably encourage ourselves to expect its bestowal, if we find that the motives of our request are not only innocent, but godly. Why do we beseech God to crown our land with independence, liberty, and just civil government? Is it that pride and resentment, ambition and animosity may be gratified in such a triumph? If our hearts be so, then we certainly have little to encourage us in the hope that the king of Zion smiles on our prayer: and if the boon be given, we may fear that it will rather be in righteous anger, than in love. But if the church in these Confederate States can say, in the presence of the Searcher of Hearts, that its desire is prompted by zeal for righteousness, and the hope and purpose that all the fruits of our new prosperity shall be sanctified to the honour of Christ, then she may probably conclude that the wish was inspired by the Holy Ghost, the only author of holy aspirations in man: and is therefore to be fulfilled.

In conclusion, let me remind you of our Savior's description of the successful petitioner. He is one who "cries day and night unto him": one who "prays always, and faints not." We must "ask in faith, nothing wavering." "For he that wavereth, is like a wave of the sea, driven with the wind and tossed. Let not that man think that he shall receive anything of the Lord."

But I hear some anxious sinner, some feeble, doubting Christian say: 'Ah me: this great and precious promise is for the elect: it is to them the Savior limits it. How shall I know whether I am of that mysterious number? This question, I answer, my brother, in the words of the Holy Spirit! "Give diligence to make your calling and election sure." And this you are instructed by the Apostle Peter to do: by believing on Christ; and then, "adding to your faith virtue."[141] God's elect are those who truly go to him as the Publican went, saying, "God be merciful to me a sinner." Are you willing to go thus? Then you, oh sinner, may claim and appropriate all the blessings of the throne of grace, as fully, as triumphantly, as a Paul. Are you unwilling to go thus? Then that is your fault alone.

Spurious and Genuine Repentance Contrasted

A Sermon

on

II Corinthians 7:10

"For godly sorrow worketh repentance to salvation, not to be repented of; but the sorrow of the world worketh death."

Preached within the Entrenchments at Manassas Junction, to the 18th Regiment of Va. Volunteers, June or July 1861[142]

The word used by the Holy Spirit for the grace of repentance, has undergone, my brethren, a strange fortune, in its translation into the languages of Western Europe. Its proper meaning is *a change of the principles of the soul as to the evil conduct.* The Latin language, inferior to the Greek in its adaptation to the expression of abstract and spiritual truths, offered no ready word to express this elevated idea. The early Christians of the Roman world therefore adopted another word, also derived from the Greek, approaching the desired meaning in its popular use, but suggesting by its origin a totally foreign idea;[143] that of *ransom price paid for guilt.* It is curious to trace this radical and primitive idea, which the ancient Greek attached to the root, reappearing in the religious phrases and creeds in modern Europe, in spite of the clear sense of God's word. Because the Latin words, *penitence, repentance,* contain this allusion to the penal suffering which is the established price of transgression, the way was prepared for the admission of that most unscriptural and deplorable delusion, which mingles the ideas of penance and evangelical repentance, and assigns to the former an atoning virtue as to the guilt of sin. The *penalty* of the ancient Greek was, indeed, the atonement of guilt, the price of sin: the repentance of the Gospel is not: it is the new inward principle of soul which hates sinning. If we use this word, we must understand that it is to be employed with no reference to the ancient sense. The godly sorrow which sin awakens in the believer's heart is no atonement for his guilt: the only ransom-price of this is the death of Christ.

"Repentance unto life is an evangelical grace, the doctrine whereof is to be preached by every minister of the gospel, as well as that of faith in Christ."[144] The Scriptures are very full of repentance: much fuller, it is to be feared, than the sermons of ministers, or the hearts of Christians. It was the burden of the preaching of the new dispensation, at its introduction: for we read that the language of John [the] Baptist and of Christ alike was: "Repent ye, for the kingdom of heaven is at hand." This grace is everywhere urged as essential to redemption. Often it is joined with the mother-grace, faith: and sometimes it is even mentioned without it, leaving faith to be implied. We are nowhere taught indeed, that repentance shares the peculiar instrumental function of faith, that of embracing the righteousness by which we are justified; but we are expressly told, that except we repent, we must all likewise perish. Do I need any apology then, for requiring your earnest attention to the teachings of God's word concerning the doctrine of repentance? I say: the teachings of God's word. The speculations of man are of no worth here. For it is to God we have to look, as sovereign, for pardon and salvation: whence it is plain that it is for him alone to define the terms of salvation.

It is reasonable to ask your anxious study of this doctrine, farther, because, as the text intimates, there is a spurious repentance which imitates the genuine; and yet it only worketh death. There is a counterfeit coin current here, my brother: if you take it for the pure gold, you are bankrupt forever. Look out, then! Examine the tests of the King's "image and superscription," by which you may discriminate. It is my business to teach them to you, out of the King's own book of directions. It is yours, to listen and learn, for your lives.

The separation between the sorrow of the world, which worketh death, and godly repentance, is rendered very distinct by this fact: that in the New Testament, there are two words, unlike in etymology and origin, which are always used separately to express the two exercises, and never interchanged. Our version fails entirely to express this distinction, and translates them both, "repent," "repentance." But one may see how significant God intended to make the distinction, when he finds that out of sixty-five cases, in which the New Testament use the two families of words, the difference of their meaning is accurately observed in every instance. Some critics do indeed say, that in two or three of these passages, there is an interchange of meanings; but I am confident that a correct understanding of the sense will show, in these likewise, that there is none. The one family of words, corresponding to "the sorrow of the world," means simply, *natural regret for one's conduct.* The other, corresponding to "godly sorrow," means a *change of principles of soul,* as to wrong doing. Let it be agreed between us, in the remainder of this discourse, that we will call the former *regret,* and the latter *repentance.* In the passage from which the text is taken, the Apostle Paul observes this distinction with a curious accuracy. The occasion of his language here was this: His first Epistle had contained a stern rebuke of the Church, for immoralities which they had permitted among some of their members. Having sent that Epistle, the Apostle felt his generous soul moved with anxiety concerning its effect. When Titus returned, who had visited the Church on his behalf, he learned that the rebuke had caused the Christians at Corinth great distress; and also, that it had led to a thorough repentance and reform of their irregularities. Thereupon, the tender heart of Paul was agitated by two contending emotions: first regret at the pain he had inflicted on his dear spiritual children: and then, joy at the wholesome effect of his action upon their souls. And, he says, upon the whole, he was glad that the letter was written: not because their distress was pleasing to him; but because it had done them good! Notice now, how accurately he observes the distinction between natural regret, and gracious repentance for sin. "For, though I grieved you by the epistle, I do not *regret* it: (yet I did *regret* it at one time.) for I perceive that this epistle grieved you, but only for a time. Now, I am glad, not that you were grieved, but that you were grieved unto repentance; for you were grieved in a godly manner, that you might receive damage by us in nothing. For the grief which is according to God; worketh *repentance* unto salvation, not to be *regretted.* But the grief of the world worketh death." Godly sorrow cannot with propriety be spoken of as the object of *repentance:* for this means a gracious turning from sin. Hence, the apostle, in speaking its praises, is particular to say that it is *"not to be regretted."* He does not say, *not to be repented;* for, while men sometimes *regret* having done right, they cannot *repent* of it. Would that all other religious teachers had been as careful as St. Paul, in their use of terms!

First, let us describe this sorrow of the world. By calling it sorrow of the world, the Apostle teaches us, that its origin is natural, and not gracious. It is, in a word the kind of sorrow which the world of unconverted men feels for its conduct. To ascertain its elements clearly, we must remember the doctrine of the Scriptures touching man's native ungodliness. He has a conscience, and an understanding: he is made by nature capable of feeling the obligation of the right. He has a heart susceptible of sundry ingenuous affections towards his fellow creatures. Hence, we find him, in his natural estate practicing some disinterested virtues relative to them; and spontaneously preferring those virtues. Yet, even here, the perversion of the soul from rectitude has introduced confusion, selfishness and sin, in different degrees, in different men. But as to God, the natural state of the soul is perfectly decided, and this, whether the degree of its secular virtues is greater or smaller. To God's holiness and authority, man's heart is originally and radically opposed: though his conscience shows him clearly God's right over him, his will is inexorably set against it. The purpose to disobey God in such things as the sinner's social principles may allow him to pursue, is full, and absolute. In a word self-will reigns supreme, so far as God is concerned; and reigns by nature. "The carnal mind is enmity against God." God say "that every imagination of the thoughts of man's heart was only evil, continually." (Romans 8:7. Genesis 6:5) But why need we appeal to any other evidence for the correctness of this statement, than your own consciousness? You know perfectly well, that, naturally. 'God was not in all your thoughts.' (Psalm 10:4)

Hence it is plain, that in the regret of the worldly man for his conduct, ingenuous sorrow for the injustice done God can have [no] place: the very principle of such a feeling is radically wanting. So far as the will and rights of God are concerned, this unconverted heart would still neglect them, if it dared. If it does not continue to do so, it is not restrained by a righteous regard to God's will: for self will is fully set in that heart to resist it. But it is restrained by other influences. One of these is the reproach of fellow men. The love of applause is a powerful propensity of the heart: and it knows that its fellows are naturally prompted by the force of reason and conscience to applaud that which is right. Hence the apprehension of the reproach of man is always painful: and is sometimes a pungent anguish. But the sensibility to it argues nothing spiritually good towards God, because the native appetite for applause is only a form of self-love.

Another element of the pain of natural regret is fear. Self-will would always fain resist God's will, if it dared. But it knows that He is almighty, and hence it unwillingly trembles at his wrath. When reason speaks clearly, she pronounces a sure connection between sin and penalty: and it is in view of that price of guilt, the natural heart selfishly quakes.

The third element is the instinctive pain of remorse; which is usually, much quickened by the other two, shame and fear. Our Maker hath so established [the] conscience within us, as the intuitive law of our reason, that its condemning voice cannot be wholly silenced when we do wrong: and its verdict is inseparably attended with an instinctive pain. It is wholly involuntary. The heart would fain silence it: but it cannot. The sinning will may still prefer to transgression for the sake of the natural pleasure to which its indulgence leads: but in spite of all this, the testimony of conscience against it is only bitter. Indeed, this great fact of conscience is, of itself, conclusive proof that man's soul is in a state of ruin; for it shows us his will in invincible opposition to his moral judgments, which should be the regulative power of the whole man. This pain of conscience is not prompted by a selfish sense of danger, as is the fear we have just described; but it arises directly in view of the moral evil of one's own conduct. Yet, while it has this trait of truth and fidelity, it does not prove the existence of any right intention, or spiritual good, in the heart. For it is involuntary: the sinner only feels it because he cannot help it: he usually fights against it with all his power of will: and could he have his choice, he would banish it forever. Hence, it is fairly to be regarded only as God's testimony echoing in his unwilling breast.

These, then, are the elements of this sorrow of the world for sin: shame, selfish fear, and unwilling remorse. There is not a spark of love for the God and Savior offended, nor a trace of righteous regard for the rightfulness of his authority. There is no diminution, but rather an increase, of the guilty enmity: for this grief sets God only in the attitude of a hated and dreaded avenger, who would be still openly resisted if the sinner dared. It does not draw his soul towards his Maker, but repels it. It prompts no honest and permanent reformation of conduct: but only results in the servile repression of the particular sins by which the remorse has been awakened, until such time as the anguish is allayed by sinful diversion, or habit, or the searing of the conscience.

You will find this description verified in every lineament, if you will consider the worldly sorrow of Judas Iscariot for his sin. (Matthew 27:3-5) "Then Judas, which had betrayed him, when he saw that he was condemned, repented himself." (i.e. regretted) "and brought again the thirty pieces of silver to the chief priests and elders, saying, I have sinned, in that I have betrayed the innocent blood. And they said: What is that to us? see thou to that. And he cast down the pieces of silver in the temple, and departed, and went and hanged himself."

This sorrow of the world, saith the text, worketh the spiritual death. That is to say: its tendency is to confirm and establish the death of the soul in trespasses and sins. This it does, because its nature is not gracious, but carnal. It includes not one holy motion of the will: but is only a new expression of the same selfishness and rebellion, which impelled the sinner, in his more thoughtless moments, to his transgression. Must it not then cultivate these ungodly principles, instead of expelling them? But more: this sorrow of the world worketh death, because it separates the soul still farther from the God whom it dreads. But communion with him is the only fountain of holiness. Thus, instead of softening, it hardens. Instead of hope it begets despair. In place of love it plants fear and hatred. But the clearest proof of the justice of the Apostle's verdict upon it is seen when we ask ourselves what are the elements of that anguish of the lost in hell, which constitutes the second death? Are they not obviously the very shame, fear, remorse, despair, which we have found in the regret of the conscience-struck sinner here? As heaven is but the consummation of the grace which here works in the penitent child of God, so perdition is but the maturity of this sorrow of the world, unmitigated by hope, sensual pleasure, or social restraints. So true to facts is the Apostle's description of this spurious repentance; the instances are not rare, in which it has driven the miserable men exercised by it, like Ahithophel and Judas, to literal suicide. The fullest completion of its tendencies are thus seen, in this life, in the crime of self-murder, which is the stepping stone from earth to hell.

Let me pause here, my hearers, to set in the light which we have now reached, that seductive notion of the awakened, or uneasy sinner, that he must postpone coming to Christ, in order to foster serious feelings, as a preparation for embracing him. Doubtless there are many here, who, if I should urge Christ, upon them in their present hardness of heart, would resist my proposal as preposterous. They are persuaded that they must feel more, must be convicted and awakened, must go through some mysterious and hitherto unexperienced routine of seekings, strivings, and sorrows, must reform many things, and begin many duties, before it can be proper for them to close with a Savior. To the proposal that they shall embrace the redemption and the service of this Christ, as they are, all unprepared, unsoftened, and unreformed, they turn an ear absolutely incredulous. But I ask: why? This sorrow of the world is no preparation: it "worketh death"! Do you retort the question: 'Is not conviction of sin a necessary stepping-stone, at least, to conversion?' I answer: yes: a condition precedent, but not a procuring cause of it: just such a condition as the sense of the agony produced by bodily disease is, to the invoking of the physician's aid. They that believe themselves whole do not call the physician, but they that feel themselves sick. But is the anguish, with which the mortal disease thrills the frame, itself a producing cause of restoration, of health? Will a man nurse it, and propagate it, as a means of recovery? Nay: he knows that it is at once [a] sign and partial cause of the deadly ravages which are wasting the very springs of life. Yet, even this is less terrible than the insensibility which shows that death has already overmastered the body! But why need the diseased man crave, or wait for any more conscious pain, if he knows himself diseased? If he but knows this, let him call the physician at one. So hearer: if thou only knowest thyself a lost sinner, this is all that conviction can do for thee: call now for the Physician of Souls. "He is exalted as a Prince and a Saviour, to give unto Israel repentance, and remission of sins." (Acts 5:31) The only emotions which the natural heart can have, away from Christ, are the pains of this sorrow of the world. And these are not salutary, but deadly. Their completion is found in the pains of the lost: if they constituted a beneficial preparation for the work of Christ in the heart, damned souls would be ripest for the gospel message, of all others: and hell would be the most proper and hopeful place for its proclamation. Yea: it is precisely this worldly sorrow for sin, which the devils feel, when they "believe and tremble."

Let us turn then, in the second place to the contrasted exercise, that "godly sorrow which worketh repentance unto life, not to be regretted." This is that saving grace, "whereby a sinner, out of a true sense of his sin, and apprehension of the mercy of God in Christ, doth, with grief and hatred of his sin, turn from it unto God, with full purpose of, and endeavor after new obedience."

The true penitent is not insensible to shame, nor indifferent to the tremendous danger incurred by transgression, nor unconscious of the natural pains of remorse. For he is still a man, and not an abnormal monster: he feels that regard for the applause of the good, and for his own welfare, and that sensibility of conscience, which are proper for a rational creature. But these emotions are not inordinate in him, nor are they, any longer, expressions of an idolatrous selfishness. They are exercised in subordination to a nobler and purer principle. That principle is *love for God and the right*. This gives him a better, higher, and more immediate motive for lamenting his own sin, than that it is dangerous, or than that it incurs the reproach of creatures; it is because it is wrong. Disobedience of God, before, the souls determined preference, is now odious for itself, and not merely for its painful consequences. The penitent soul eschews it with abhorrence, though no penalty now threatens him for it. His enmity to the great lawgiver is now turned to hearty love: love inspired not only by his mercy, but by his divine excellence. Transgression is no longer cherished with a secret preference of the will, as resistance to a hated authority: (thus the sinner cherishes it even in the most anxious moments of his guilty terror) but sin is lamented with a tender and generous grief, because it is a wound aimed at a beloved Father. The holy law is no longer regarded as an abhorred restraint: but is approved as reasonable and excellent, with a righteous delight: the only sorrow is, that the soul is not able to conform to it in all things, because of remaining infirmity. Hope is born in the breast: because the same gospel which inculcates this repentance, also holds out a blessed way of pardon: and thus, the penitent soul is led sweetly up to a forgiving God, instead of being driven to a more guilty distance. Above all, does the doctrine of the Cross become the argument of repentance: because it manifests at once the heinousness of sin, displays the unspeakable love of God and Christ, and melts the obdurate heart with the thought of a dying friend pierced by its transgressions.

The results of this godly sorrow are as excellent as its nature: it "worketh repentance unto life." It reforms the conduct radically and permanently, turning the will by its inward energy, to a full purpose of, and endeavor after, new obedience. And that obedience, though still irregular in extent, is now pure in motive, prompted not merely by selfish fear, but by righteous preference, and by love. It is universal, attempting all known duty, and forsaking all known sin, and not merely the few glaring crimes by which a galled conscience has been awakened. It is abiding; for it flows, not from panic and remorse, but from an inward principle of soul. Worldly sorrow, like the sluggish beast of burden, begins to lag, just as soon as the goad of present fear is withdrawn: godly sorrow endureth to the end, and ceases not to run in all the ways of holiness: because it is willing, and self-prompted.

I beseech you now, brethren, hearken, while I substantiate this description of the true repentance from the Scriptures: 'that your faith may not stand in the wisdom of men, but in the power of God.' And let me beg you to read for yourselves the exercises of the penitent, as the Holy Ghost hath portrayed them, for instance, in the 51st Psalm, and the parable of the Prodigal, Luke 15. But hear now: "For I acknowledge my transgression, and my sin is ever before me. Against thee, and thee only, have I sinned, and done this evil in thy sight, that thou mightiest be justified when thou speakest, and be clear when thou judgest."[145] "Create in me a clean heart, O God: and renew a right spirit within me."[146] "Then shall ye remember your evil ways, and your doings that were not good, and shall loathe yourselves in your own sight, for your iniquities, and for your abominations."[147] "Repent, and turn yourselves from all your transgressions: so iniquity shall not be your ruin."[148] "And they shall look upon me whom they have pierced, and they shall mourn."[149] "For I delight in the law of God after the inward man: But I see another law in my members, warring against the law of my mind. . . . O wretched man that I am! who shall deliver me from the body of this death?"[150] "For behold this self-same thing, that ye sorrowed after a godly sort, what carefulness it wrought in you," (that is to say, what watchfulness against sin.) "yea, what clearing of yourselves," (purging out the evil.) "yea, what indignation," (a holy anger against their own folly.) "yea what fear" (fear of God.) "yea, what vehement desire" (after conformity to Him.) "yea what zeal" (for holy living.) "yea, what revenge!" (against their sins.) "In all things ye have approved yourselves to be clear in this matter."[151]

The difference between worldly and godly sorrow may be justly displayed by that which is often seen in domestic life. There are two children of the same tender and righteous mother. The first is cold, obdurate, selfish, and rebellious in temper: the second, though not seldom heedless, is docile, generous, and affectionate. Both have been betrayed into the same act of disobedience. Both, of course, dread the threatened chastisement, and listen to the sound of their mother's approaching steps, with anxious and downcast countenances. The first trembles with servile panic, as he seems to himself to feel already the smarting lash upon his back: and perhaps he persuades himself that he is resolved to commit the folly no more. At least, he is ready to deprecate the dreaded pain, by any amount of fair promises. The second is frightened too, and dreads the lash: but other elements of sorrow, which he can scarcely analyze to himself, swell his heart, and make him dumb before his mother. But she declares her pity, and her purpose to pass by the punishment. She describes the evil of their fault, pleads with them by her love and forbearance to disobey no more, and beseeches them to remember all her benefits, her tenderness, and her sacrifices for them. The first boy, just so soon as his impunity is announced, is wholly relieved of his pain, and he is now ready, with obdurate heart, to repeat his sin, whenever there appears due promise of concealment. Here is the sorrow of the world! But how is it with the second? This display of the evil of his fault, with the love of his forbearing mother, makes him hate himself, as he had not done before. The knowledge of his impunity is no sufficient solace to his grief: but the unworthiness of his behavior wounds him now, with a tender smart, to which the mere pain of the punishment would be almost a relief. And as he weeps upon his mother's knee, he confesses his fault, and vows obedience, with a sincere purpose, because it is the purpose of love and duty. Here is the illustration of the godly sorrow, working repentance unto life.

In like manner, to the gospel penitent, the pardoning love of Christ, protecting from the penalty of his sin, is not an encouragement, but the strongest possible barrier, to transgression. The more clearly he reads the freeness of that love, the glorious power of the atonement, and his own title to an interest in it, the more strongly does he feel that it is impossible he can now consent to sin against such a Savior. "The love of Christ constraineth him." But as the root of the sinner's grief for his sin was in his selfish fear; just in proposition as this is allayed by any delusive or dead faith, or by returning deadness of conscience, he is prepared to sin again with greediness. And this, my brethren, is the most scriptural test of the character of your repentance. Does your comfort of hope make your consciences more tender, and your godly obedience more diligent? Then you may hope your sorrow for sin is according to God, and worketh unto life. But if the love of sin and power of temptation return, in proportion as your fears of wrath are appeased, be sure, it is the sorrow of the world, that worketh death.

From this description of true repentance, it must be inferred that, if the picture given of the unconverted heart is correct, it will never exercise this grace of its own motion. Resistance of God's will is its native preference: How then can it prefer subjection for its own sake? The indulgence of self-will is its native food: how then can it heartily abhor and bewail it? Just as the sick child may be frightened by the terrible approach of death, to forego the food which his natural palate prefers, so the conscience-struck sinner may forego sin for a time. But will the child loathe, as well as forego, the food in which he delighted? Will he not only submit to swallow, but love and prefer the nauseous potions, to which the urgent fear of death reconciles him? Can he love the medicines for their own taste? Now, true repentance is that grace, which not only consents to forego beloved sins, for fear of the second death: but hates them: which not only consents to holiness as a bitter medicine to which he is driven by danger, but loves and chooses it for its own sake. Before you can feel this, you must cease to be a sinner in heart: you must be born again. That is to say, no man truly repents, save he that is regenerated. It is not meant that there is an appreciable interval of time, in every sinner's experience, between the moment of the new birth, and the first exercises of true repentance; but that regeneration must be the cause, and repentance the effect. The new-born infant may move and breathe from the instant of its birth: but it must be born in order to breathe: and it is by these two signs we know that it lives. So the exercise of repentance and faith are the immediate consequences, and appointed signs of regeneration. It is the uniform teaching of the Scriptures, that Repentance is not the effect of the sinner's own will, but of sovereign grace. In Jeremiah 31:18, penitent Ephraim is heard saying to God: "Turn thou me, and I shall be turned; for thou art the Lord my God. Surely, after that I was turned, I repented." The same Prince of Peace who gives remission unto Israel, in Acts 5:31, also gives repentance. The disciples glorified God saying: "Then hath God also to the Gentiles granted repentance unto life." (Acts 11:18) And in II Timothy 2:25, St. Paul instructs the Christian minister, "in meekness to instruct those that oppose themselves, if God peradventure will give them repentance, to the acknowledging of the truth." Thus, my hearer, you are brought face to face with a solemn fact, which has ever been the subject of cavil to unbelievers. "Except ye repent, ye shall all likewise perish." And no man can repent, without almighty grace to renew him. Do you say this is a paradox? It is a fearful difficulty. But what has caused it? God? Or your sin? How can he who avows that he is a sinner, deny the reasonableness of sorrow for his fault? It is self-evident that he cannot. Then if you find that your heart is so obstinately in love with sin, that it will not be moved to eschew it, by all the attractions of heaven and terrors of hell, and convincing light of truth and duty, and love and mercy of the cross: is it not time for you to cease caviling, and in despair of your own goodness, to cry?: "O wretched man that I am, who shall deliver me from the body of this death"!

The Immediate Decision[152]

A Sermon

on

I Kings 18:21

"And Elijah came unto all the people and said, How long halt ye between two opinions? if the Lord be God, follow him: but if Baal, then follow him. And the people answered him not a word."

Preached in the camp of the 18th Regiment, Va. Volunteers, in their encampment at Centreville, Fairfax County, July 1861[153]

Decision of character has ever been esteemed a valuable trait. It is the strongest evidence of littleness and triviality of soul, to hang undecided although all the facts and truths on which a decision should be based are fully before the mind. This temper is the sure occasion of disaster. Indecision lets slip the golden opportunity, and forfeits the tide in the affairs of men, "which, taken at the flood, leads on to fortune."[154] Efforts weakly made in inconsistent directions, neutralize each other, and waste their labor. While the double-minded man is hesitating, the man of decision has viewed his ground, has formed his conclusion, and has half accomplished it. Without decision of character, no man, was ever successful in any secular undertaking, except by accident, and for a short season.

If indecision is so disastrous in temporal affairs, what must not be its mischief, in the more momentous concerns of the soul? Here its folly is enhanced by the critical nature of the interest, the plainness of the duty to every clear mind, the vastness of the stake, and the uncertainty of the time.

It is on this fault the venerable prophet Elijah remonstrates with those Israelites, who were hesitating between the service of Jehovah, and the seductions of idolatry, under the reign of Ahab and his Phoenician wife, Jezebel. God's messenger seeks to terminate their indecision, by a miraculous demonstration of the claims of his Master. The sacred narrative of his proposal and its issue is one of the grandest pictures of moral sublimity in all history. Elijah seems to have overawed the mind of the vacillating king for a time, by the majestic authority of truth, and his moral courage: and he thus gains his assent to a test so fair, that the pretext for objection could not be found. He caused the whole nation to assemble by its representatives, on the side of Mount Carmel, and near the great Sea. This is a lofty range in the west of Palestine, which running straight from the plains of Galilee, terminates in a grand promontory, overlooking the boundless waves of the Mediterranean, and the sinuous coast. At its base runs the River of Kishon, "that ancient river," celebrated in the song of Deborah and Barak, which swept away the slaughtered hosts of Sisera; and beyond it extends the great plain, which from this hoary antiquity to our own century, has been the battle ground of contending nations. On this promontory, overlooking the waste of waters, and a range of country equally boundless, and now equally barren with a three years' drought, are assembled the wicked king, and a great throng of the elders of Israel. On the one side are the priests of Baal and of the groves, nine hundred men, arrogant with royal patronage, gorgeous with all that the favor of their superstitious queen could confer, and drunk with persecution. On the other side is the solitary prophet, worn with fasting and hermitage, clad in his rude robe of camel's hair, but instinct with the severe, rugged majesty of the desert mountains which were his sanctuary. He repeats his challenge: Let the priests of Baal select their victim, and let him choose another: Let each party rear their altar, arrange their sacrifice, but put no fire under: and then let them invoke their divinity: and let Him that answereth by fire from heaven, be God. The prophet has now gotten his cunning adversaries away from their temples, on the bare mountain side, where none of the apparatus existed for these pseudo-miracles in which the priests of superstition have ever been such adepts. He intends moreover, to keep up a sharp watch upon their maneuvers: and he compels them to undergo the test in open day, and with hundreds of curious eyes fixed upon them. But in everything he gives them the precedence: in the hour, in the choice of the bullock. They slay the animal: they build their altar: they dispose the wood: they place the flesh upon it: they cry to their idol to interpose: "Oh Baal, hear us." Thus, from morning until noonday, did they supplicate their imaginary god, dancing with frantic, superstitious fury around their altar: "But there was no voice: nor any that answered." Then it was, that the prophet, expressing in righteous sarcasm, his scorn for their hypocrisy and delusion, mocked them, saying "Cry aloud: for he is a god: either he is talking, or he is pursuing, or he is on a journey, or peradventure he sleepeth, and must be awakened!" At these biting words, their frenzy was redoubled and to their wild cries they added the more sanguinary rites with which, like modern pagans, they were wont to propitiate their savage idols in extremity; and wounded themselves until the blood gushed out upon them.

But it was all in vain: and after their failure was manifest to the most obstinate, Elijah began at length to bestir himself. Inviting the people to draw near and inspect every motion, he repaired the prostrate altar of Jehovah, building it of twelve unhewn stones, one for each of the holy tribes. He slew his sacrifice: he arranged it on the wood: and then, to silence forever the charge that fire was secreted beneath it by some artifice, he caused the victim, the wood, the altar, and the very soul around its base, to be thrice drenched with water. And now, the sacred hour of the evening sacrifice at Jerusalem had arrived: so dear to every reverent Hebrew's heart, that hour at which, for so many centuries, the smoke of the fire kindled from the Shekinah of glory, had ascended from the sanctuary to the sky, freighted with the penitence and prayers of the people of God: the prophet spread forth his hands towards heaven, and without pomp or frenzy, with all the simplicity and calmness of conscious truth, uttered his brief prayer: "Lord God of Abraham, Isaac, and of Israel, let it be known this day, that thou art God in Israel, and that I am thy servant: and that I have done all these things at thy word. Hear me, O Lord, hear me, that this people may know that thou art the Lord God, and that thou hast turned their heart back again." The people stood in silent, awful expectation: while the holy man looked upward with confident faith: For had not the inspiration of the Holy Spirit already warranted his appeal? When lo: like a flash of lightening from a cloudless sky, the fire of the Lord fell, and consumed the victim, and the wood, and the incombustible stones and dust, and licked up the water around the altar! Well might the people, at this sight, prostrate themselves, and cry: "The Lord, he is the God." But did they, for this reason, cease to halt between the two opinions, and follow him? Alas no: the subsequent history shows that they, like so many of you, satisfied their consciences with a barren recognition of God, and then continued to postpone his serious service.

The minister of the Gospel does not profess to offer you, at this time, such a visible, miraculous demonstration of the claims of the God of the Bible. It is not necessary. To the honest inquirer, the evidences of its authority are as solid as those arising from a miracle, if less impressive to the sensibilities. The Scriptures possess an unbroken chain of historical testimony for their genuineness, such as no other ancient record can claim. They present us daily, a miracle of foreknowledge, in their prophecies, unfolding and fulfilling under our eyes. Their signs and wonders which they record are attested by eyewitnesses, competent and honest, who had nothing to gain, but everything to lose by attesting an imposture. They commend themselves to us by an internal excellence, which commands the assent of every conscience. And the results which follow their track, of souls redeemed, and nations blessed witness to their origin in the skies. But this argument is not pursued, because it is supposed that the indecision of more here is produced by the disbelief of the God of the Bible.

Let me however, introduce the farther appeal to your consciences, by an inquiry into a popular opinion, as to the proper influence of real doubts. Many seem to suppose that if these are sincerely entertained, they relieve them from all obligation, until they are dissipated. They act as though one, because he really doubts, may dismiss all practical concern in his own duties towards God. But is this correct? I argue, that he who doubts a proposition, has some probable evidence that it is true (counterbalanced, indeed by, by seeming objections). For if there is a total absence of evidence, we do not doubt: we say nothing. Would you profess doubts of this assertion: that there are red men on the planet Jupiter? But now consider, that man is often bound to act on evidence which is merely probable, and sometimes, on that which is slight. Yea, he may be impelled by the most sacred sanctions to act, and that immediately, by this uncertain light. It may be true, that you are thus bound to act in doubt concerning duty to God. But to doubt implies a probability that Christianity may be true. Now, a possibility of its truth begets an immediate obligation. If you admit even a possibility, you are bound to forbear all action, and all opposition, which would be found unwarrantable, should the truth of Christianity ever become certain to you. Moreover, you are sacredly bound to pursue, at the earliest practicable hour, the most thorough inquiry into its claims, and never to rest, until you have either ascertained its certain falsity, or the impossibility of a decisive conclusion. For, if it is indeed true, then you undoubtedly owe it your allegiance, and he who loves his duty must desire to remove that ignorance which, he suspects, obstructs its performance. This may be evidenced by a simple parallel. You have had a settlement of intricate transactions with your neighbor. After he has paid you your claims, new evidence reaches you, making it probable that the settlement has been unjust to him; and that certain parts of the sum paid you are his property. Will any man say, that because it is only suspected, and not certain, therefore you may retain the money, and refuse all inquiry? He who is capable of this, has the heart of a thief. If the suspicion should turn out truth, you would be found depriving your neighbor of his goods: the doubt, as soon as it is awakened, originates as obligation, which every honest mind will admit, to a new and faithful inquiry. So: if there is a suspicion that the Gospel may have claims upon you, you are under obligation to dispassionate and thorough inquiry: in order that if this debt of faith and love is indeed due, you may pay it at once.

But doubt is all that the skeptic can honestly profess. *Skeptic* is his proper name. He is one who is not convinced: who sees some proof, and who is considering. He would be a rash man, indeed, who should presume to demonstrate that the Gospel cannot possibly be true! But how different is the temper which unbelievers usually exhibit, from that honest anxiety to have their doubt happily solved, and this dispassionate readiness to discover and fulfill their duty? The petulance, the prejudice, the hatred of the light, the industrious care to evade every fair solution, and to magnify every cavil, which usually characterize them, betray the enmity of the heart to God.

But in those who do not even profess a doubt of the truth of revelation, hesitation is yet more inexcusable. They fully admit that "the Lord is God": yet they refuse to follow him, and still "halt between two opinions." Among those who profess respect for the claims of the Bible, all those Christians are guilty of this halting, who consciously neglect any of that effort which is involved in 'following the Lord fully,' and 'making their calling and election sure.' All worldly men are guilty of it, who, while they admit the necessity of repentance, faith, and holy living, postpone the day of giving themselves to Christ. To all these, the message of the prophet comes: If the Lord be God, serve Him: but if Baal, then follow him.

The idol which divides your convictions with Jehovah, is not, indeed a pagan image. It is that universal object of the worship of unconverted men, this world, with its pleasures, riches, honors. For that to which you look for your prime happiness, which you seek with supreme devotion, and in which you rely as your chief good, is practically your God. And now I remonstrate with you: if this world is a sufficient god, if it can satisfy the instincts of a rational soul, and confer solid happiness; if it can minister relief to a diseased conscience; if it can be your unfailing solace in the hour of desolation; if it can sustain you against the king of terrors; if it can endow your immortality with everlasting sources of bliss; then follow the world; follow it at once, and decisively, and exclusively. Halt no longer between it and God. But if it is manifestly insufficient for these ends, then turn at once from it, and follow God. This I urge:

First, because a hesitating and divided service of the two masters is useless and impracticable. Such a life is but time and labor thrown away. Consider who God is; how sovereign, how majestic, how righteous, how jealous. Will he accept a divided heart? a heart divided with such a rival? Remember what the Christian life is: a race, a wrestle, a labor, a warfare. Can the halting man win this race? Can the maimed soul fight this battle successfully? When the righteous scarcely are saved, with all their zeal, where shall the hesitating sinner appear? Be sure of this: that such a prize as heaven will never be won by these feeble strivings.

But the world also is an exacting master, and refuses to dispense his favors to any but those who give him the whole heart. If then this is to be your God, why mar his service with this abortive religiousness? It is but an uncompensated loss of those "pleasures of sin which are but for a season." It only hinders your enjoyment of the world. It only troubles you with importunate thoughts of the future. And yet, it effects nothing towards the salvation of the soul. If therefore you will not follow God in earnest, it will be much more rational to say, with the atheist: "Let us eat and drink, for tomorrow we die," than to continue your halting. It will be better for you to make the utmost of your sinful joys, and then, for the rest, enter into covenant with death, and into agreement with hell.

For, second, this must be the natural end of your hesitation, if its proper tendencies are allowed their course. Let this startling proposition be tried by the homely conclusions of our daily experience. There is a man, whose interests imperatively demand a given conclusion and a decided course of conduct. He has before his mind all the facts which are necessary to determine the case: he has long had them: and yet, he is never able to make up his mind. Months, years roll by, and still the man is not yet decided, but ever going to decide. With what contemptuous positiveness does every practical man say of him: 'Oh, he will never do any thing: he must be ruined.' There is, as we shall see, excellent reason for this conclusion. Or, let us state the matter thus: our friend employs our intervention to dissuade his reckless son from some manifest imprudence: we use all our skill: we array arguments perfectly decisive of the case, and facts of which ought to be absolutely commanding over any sane judgment. We throw all the earnestness of our souls into our persuasion: and all is unavailing. You repeat the effort again and again: but it avails nothing. Still your friend begs you to make another trial. Do you not say, al last: "There is no use: I have no new arguments to use: If reasoning could move his mind, he would have been long ago convinced: therefore in his case it is ineffectual. Shall I repeat the same hackneyed topics? They have already been resisted several times; and if I advance then again, the habit of neglect now formed in his breast, can but ensure their more certain neglect. There is no hope." And you would have most excellent reason for your conclusion.

For you would know that this man, a reasoning creature, could not thus violate the dictates of his own understanding, unless some active cause was swaying his will. Passion, ungoverned desire for the mischievous object, was resisting reason successfully. So, the reason you halt between two opinions, in the presence of motives for godliness as vast as eternity, and as solemn as the miracle of Elijah, is that you are swayed by your repugnance to the hated service of God. But, I pray you, consider, whether this passionate enmity to Him remains without increase, while it is thus causing you to halt? Was there ever a passion of man's soul, that did not grow by its indulgence? Can man repeat the same acts again and again, and not experience that universal law of habit, that what is often done becomes more likely to be done, and more facile to do? Can Gospel motives be thus presented to your moral sensibility, and again and again, repelled, without an inevitable blunting of the capacity for impression? No: the smallest experience of the laws of human nature gives the answer to these questions. While you halt, then, the arrows of divine truth, which with their best[155] force could but make you hesitate in your career of sin, are blunted by every ineffectual blow upon your heart. While you halt, every sinful habit grows upon you: every good sensibility is worn and hardened: every ungodly propensity is fastened by its indulgence into more rampant strength: your enmity to God is confirmed in its sway: the tide of worldly cares and occupations absorbs you more and more in its current. Then, the truth which is today too weak to decide you effectually for God, must, by the stronger reason, fail still more completely and certainly in any future application. As you conclude today, to postpone: so will you conclude, still more surely, the next Sabbath, and the next, and every Sabbath: until at length, death will come, and find you still procrastinating.

Some one may say: 'This reasoning cannot be just: for if it were, it would teach that the[156] men who have resisted lights of duty as clear and numerous as ours, are already in a desperate condition of soul; and their doom is practically sealed. But, the preacher himself does not believe this: for if he did, he would no more continue to urge the gospel on us, than on men already dead, or on devils.'

We reply: true: so far as your own action or the preacher's power is concerned, your doom would be practically sealed by your present choice. Were there not an Almighty Spirit, "which bloweth where he listeth," whose saving influences you are now doing your utmost to alienate by your halting, your condition would be hopeless: and I, for one, would no more preach the gospel to you, than to those already dead and damned. Surely you are not entitled to count upon those gracious influences to interpose, when you are willfully rejecting them in your present act! I repeat then: so far as the tendency of your own hesitation is concerned, your purpose to continue it today may be virtually regarded as equivalent to the purpose to die in your sins. But now: if the enemy of your soul stood revealed at your side (as he may possibly be there invisibly), with all his gloomy terrors, and urged you with all his fiendish malignity, today to make a final rejection of the grace of God, and to seal his title to your soul forever, and to bid a last farewell to hope, and to embrace everlasting despair, with what horror would you recoil from the ghastly proposal? With equal dread should you flee this day from the tempting plea[157] of procrastination: it is but the same Devil masked and counterfeiting his traitor voice: and if he gains this point with you,[158] he will fly to the pit, to regale his subjects with mocking laughter, assured that the same temptations which have deceived you today will yet more surely deceive you tomorrow.

How long then, will you halt between two opinions? How long will you play the part of the sick man, who knows that his disease is unto death without this remedy, and who yet hesitates and dallies because of the bitterness of the potion? Does the draught grow any the less bitter while you boggle[159] at it? Is not your disease meantime making its steady progress? Up then: before it is too late: and play the man! If you are a reasonable being, you will seize the cup and drain it, as eagerly as though it were nectar.

What think you of the merchant who finds the ship freighted with his wealth overtaken by a storm, leaking and crippled, and about to founder in the sea. The master has told him that except she be lightened of her cargo, she must in a little while go to the bottom with all on board: already she is slowly settling: and the pumps fall steadily behind their task. But he cannot resolve to sacrifice his beloved riches: he hesitates, and while they argue that time presses: that if he gives up his treasures he may save his life: but if he cleaves to them he must lose both, he stands wringing his hands, and halting between the two opinions. Is this the conduct of a man, or of an imbecile?[160] The man of true decision will have already resolved upon the necessary loss: and you shall see him heaving over his precious bales[161] into the deep, as industriously as though he were glad to see them swallowed by the remorseless waves. Thus, O perishing man, cast out of thy heart thy self-will, thy besetting sins, and thy delays, before they sink thee in the burning lake.

And remember, that while thou haltest between the two opinions, time halts not! No: it bears thee with its ceaseless roll towards that eternity where hesitation will be forever ended. The rise of your accumulated provocations tarries not, mount ever to a more threatening height, until they fall and overwhelm you in perdition. Death halts not, whose inexorable[162] tread is ever advancing alike upon the waiting saint and the befooled sinner. Judgment halts not, but moves forward its appointed day, close in the rear of the last enemy. Up,[163] then, soul, and flee today from these advancing enemies: or else, while thou haltest, time, and judgment[164] and death, and hell will overtake thee.

I beseech you to tell me, literally, 'how long halt ye between two opinions?' What is to be the duration of your hesitancy? I would require of you, to fix for yourselves a date, for terminating this irrational delay. You are not willing, you say, to accept despair as your deliberate portion. You purpose and expect to make the needed preparation for eternity, some time this side of death. I pray you, *when*? Select the proper measure of time for the continuance of your present state: and be pleased to announce it to us. Shall it be five years? One year? One month? Are you sure that you may venture the infinite stake of a soul upon the uncertainties of time, for ever one month, without an insane rashness? Will it be safe for you to bring upon your soul the added sins, and obstacles, and evil habitudes, of another month, when you feel it already so obdurate? And dare you insult the holiness and majesty of that infinite god, on whose good pleasure your helpless soul must hang for life and grace, by telling Him that you will outrage his law, and vex His Spirit, and trample on his Son's cross and blood, one month more, before you begin to turn to him? Will you venture to invoke His converting grace, with[165] such a proposal as this? No: there is no answer to the question but "today," "now." Your own reason refuses to sanction any delay, and tells you, that the only reply she can make to the prophet's challenge, is that of the Scriptures: "Behold now is the accepted time: behold now is the day of salvation."

The sacred historian adds: "And the people answered him not a word." The irresistible force of the prophet's appeal left them not a word to say in justification of their halting: so they were silenced. How justly does this incident describe your condition today, in the presence of God's majestic truth, and your own consciences. There is no venerable here, to awe you by the sanctity of his aspect, or by astonishing signs and wonders with which he was armed by omnipotence. There is nobody but a sinner like yourselves, (saved by grace). But the same message is here, given from the skies, and the same Holy Spirit is here to write it upon your hearts. I take you to witness, that like the men of Israel, you find it impossible to dissent from these doctrines. You know the importance of an immediate decision of your duty: you know that it has unspeakable, infinite arguments. It has not been necessary that a preacher of the gospel should come, and reason with you, in order for you to know, that it is not right to postpone present duty, to prefer the temporal to the eternal, to tamper with perdition for the sake of a few sinful and deceitful pleasures. Every dictate of your own reason and conscience is on the side of my message.

And yet, you purpose to disregard it! I leave you then, with this final question to ponder: Are you willing to dethrone reason, to abdicate the crowning attributes of your humanity, and whereas God gave you reason, and conscience for your guides to immortality, to assimilate yourselves to the brutes, in this most important of all concerns? Will you throw away your own understanding in this one vastest of all affairs, for which above all others, understanding was given to you? Will you be so unwise as obstinately to pursue a course of conduct for which, as you admit, no apology can be uttered? Should God, in his righteous displeasure allow you to go on, until you have reached your doom, how bitter will be your remorse, as you remember that you had not only to resist the ministers of the gospel, the expostulations of your friends, the Spirit of God, but to trample upon your own understanding, and outrage every law of your own better nature, in order to destroy yourself?

"How long, then, halt ye between two opinions? If the Lord be God, follow him: but if Baal, then follow him." "Today, if ye will hear his voice, harden not your hearts."[166]

The Happy Service[167]

AN EXPOSITORY SERMON

ON

MATTHEW 11:28-30

"Come unto me, all ye that labor and are heavy laden, and I will give
you rest. Take my yoke upon you, and learn of me; for I am meek and
lowly in heart; and ye shall find rest unto your souls.
For my yoke is easy, and my burden is light."

PREACHED IN THE CAMP OF THE 18TH REGIMENT, VA. VOLUNTEERS, AT CENTREVILLE,
FAIRFAX CO. VA. AUGUST, 1861[168]

This world, my brethren, is a weary one. If any of you think not
so, I can but liken you to inexperienced youths, who are sum-
moned in the morning to set out on a toilsome journey, and in their
ignorance of its real character, suppose it to be a pastime, because
the adjuncts of the hour of setting forth are pleasant. They are in
raptures with the free motion, and the exercise of their own exuber-
ant energies, with the perfumed heath of dewy morn, with the fields
glittering with liquid pearls, with the eastern sky bathed in crimson
and gold, and with the beams of the rising sun. They bound along
the way in sport, wasting the vigor which they will sorely need ere
nightfall. They forget the sultry hours of the afternoon, when this
cheering sun shall have put on his fervid heats, the dusty, lengthening
miles, the thirst, and hunger, the aching limbs, with which they must
drag themselves at evening towards a goal which seems ever to recede.

But no man lives long enough to learn what life truly is, without
reaching the conviction, that this is a weary world. We "labor and are
heavy laden." How precious and timely, then is the promise of rest
to such beings? Many of you are weary and burdened with the impossible endeavor to feed an immortal mind with earthly food. Some
perhaps are heavy laden with their toils of self-righteousness, while
they go about to establish their own acceptance with God, grievously

galled by an uneasy, disapproving conscience. A few, I trust, are laboring with the salutary burden of conviction for sin, and conscious guilt. Some of you are wearying yourselves in vain, with the effort to break your bondage under sin in your own strength. God's people among you are oppressed with the "heat and burden of the day," while they strive, painfully, yet with better heart and hope, "to make their calling and election sure." Many are crushed with sorrows and bereavements, or with anxieties and fears. All these are invited by the benevolent Redeemer, to come and find rest in him. Whatever may be their burden, he promises a gracious relief. How general then, ought the interest in these divine words to be; and how eager?

When we are invited, "come unto me," we understand, of course, that this coming is not a corporeal approach to Christ's local habitation, which is not possible for us, in the flesh, nor necessary; but the embracing of his redemption by faith. This usage of the word is too well established in our Savior's preaching, to need much illustration. When, for instance, he says, (John 6:35) "he that cometh to me shall never hunger, and he that believeth on me shall never thirst," the coming is manifestly faith. The yoke which we are to take up, is the service of Christ. And when rest is promised to those who believe, and who obey, it is not bodily indolences, or sensual ease, which the Savior offers, but inward peace. He himself defines it in the subsequent words, as "rest to our souls." He may call us to stormy trials for his sake; he assuredly will call us to diligent, persevering labors for his cause: but he guarantees to us that sweet repose of soul, with which outward toils are light, and without which the ease and prosperity of sin is but a mocking torture. The main doctrine taught us, then, in this passage is, that,

[First,] Our Peace is to be found in embracing Christ and his service, by faith.[169]

At the threshold of the subject, we are met by this inquiry: Who is it, that makes this generous offer of rest, to all the weary and heavy laden, of earth? Consider how much is implied in it. To fulfill the obligation which is thus assumed, will require no small resources of wealth, power, and love. To succor the multitudinous evils of humanity is, indeed a mighty undertaking. Let us suppose that the mightiest emperor of earth, or the most powerful angel in heaven, had ventured such an invitation as this: and that it had been universally accepted.

Before this vast aggregate of the wants and woes of men, his resources would seem to shrink into a mite, and the greatest finite mind would reel and stagger in the mere attempt to comprehend, as all created riches would be absorbed a thousand times in relieving the mighty mass. Who is this then, that calmly stands up, and announces to his dying race the audacious proposal? 'Come one, come all, to *me*; and I will give you rest.' Is this the Nazarene, the carpenter's son: the man who "had not where to lay his head"? How dares he pledge to suffering mankind, he, in his beggary, a relief which Caesar, upon the throne of imperial Rome, with all the legions of her armies bowing to his scepter, and all the nations of the civilized globe pouring their tributes into his royal treasury, would not presume to undertake? If he is only what he seems, well may scribe and Pharisee resent with hot indignation, the insolence of such imposture; and say, this man at once blasphemes God, in assuming a prerogative of compassion, which belongs to Him alone, and mocks the miseries of man, by vainly offering to take them all upon his puny arm.

Be assured, my brethren, that the holy Jesus would have been incapable of using this language, had he not been conscious that he was not only man, but God. It was because he could claim: "I and my Father are one." "It pleases the Father that in him should all fullness dwell." "He hath set him at his own right hand in heavenly places, and hath put all things under his feet, and gave him to be head over all things to the Church."[170] Unless the Son of Man hath power on earth to forgive sins, and infinite attributes of omniscience and omnipotence, he cannot give peace to mankind. But he is both God and man. Unless the charge of insincerity and imposture can be brought against his character, this promise compels us to receive his proper divinity. And here, my brethren, is the foundation of our trust in him. Because he hath in himself all the fullness of the Godhead, therefore we can rely upon his love, power, wisdom and faithfulness, to make us happy in our dedication to him. Thus, the apparent paradox at the outset of his invitation is turned into a noble support of its solidity.

Second: we read assurance of our peace and blessedness in Christ, in the nature of the yoke which we are invited to receive. "Take my yoke upon you and learn of me; for I am meek and lowly in heart: and ye shall find rest unto your souls."

Here again there appears to the unbeliever a still greater paradox; he is invited to look for rest in assuming a yoke! It is when the yoke is unbound and the wearied ox is released to follow his own will pasture-ward, that he finds rest. So, the perpetual delusion of the unbeliever is, that he can find his preferred happiness in the emancipation of his soul from the dreaded restraints of Christianity, and in this alone. This error, we trust, may be dissolved, by reminding you of a few plain facts. The first is, that there is no such possible alternative for you, as you vainly dream, between the bearing of Christ's yoke, and entire immunity. No: the only real choice, within your reach, is that between the yoke of Christ, and the yoke of sin; of which Satan is the master. Now, if this is so, manifestly, one may be reasonably invited to seek the relief of his toil by exchanging a cruel and unrighteous bondage, for a mild and righteous service. But I repeat: no man is free; or can be; all who do not bear the yoke of Christ, groan under that of sin and Satan. Such is the testimony of the Scriptures. "Jesus answered them, Verily, verily, I say unto you, Whosoever committeth sin, is the servant of sin." "Thou art in the gall of bitterness, and the bond of iniquity." They are "taken captive by the devil at his will."[171] I appeal to your own experience: Is the most reckless sinner in this army really free from constraint! I speak not of the bonds of discipline and military duty. But in other respects, is he at liberty to regulate his actions by his own preferences? Nay: how often does his own passion and sin lay him under the most cruel constraint and self-denial? His delusive enjoyments in transgression are often purchased at a heavy cost, and then concealed at the expense of irksome sacrifices of inclination. These are but instances of the pinching of Satan's yoke. Here, then, is the choice which you have to make, transgressor; not whether you may repudiate every yoke and go free as the wild ass of the desert described by Job: but, whether it will most conduce to the repose of your soul to bear the yoke of Christ, your loving Redeemer, or of Satan, the soul-murderer. The first is right and reasonable: (your own conscience avouches it) and your heavenly Master deals honestly, and graciously with you. He lays it upon your shoulder: but he assists you with his loving and almighty hand to bear it; he solaces your labor with the sweetest foretastes of an approving conscience and heavenly hope: he makes it grow perpetually lighter by the growth of holy habitudes of soul; and at the end, he converts it into a crown of glory.

But Satan, a "liar from the beginning," brings his foul, unrighteous yoke to you, concealed with frippery, and persuades you that it is but a toy. Thus he binds it upon your neck, and when he has befooled you effectually, leaves you to bear it unaided, or mocks you with sardonic malice, while it grows ever more weighty, and having galled you like iron here, crushes your miserable soul at last into perdition. Under which now, of these yokes, will you find rest to your souls?

The second fact is, that it is no apathetic indolence, or sensual ease, which Christ promises, but rest for the soul. It consists of peace of conscience, harmony of the affections, and the enjoyment of legitimate and ennobling exercise for all the powers. Man's true well-being requires activity. Even an ancient pagan sage learned enough of this truth, to define happiness as 'virtuous energy.' This definition we may accept, if we be permitted to take it in the sense of the normal and healthy exercise of the soul's powers. He who has no rule of life, no worthy aim, no duty, can never be happy, because he puts forth no virtuous energy. He who bears the right yoke, or in other words, has assigned to him the proper activities, is the man who truly enjoys his existence.

Third; we may expect rest under the yoke of Christ, because of the character of our Master. "He is meek and lowly in heart: and we shall find rest unto our souls." He is a gentle, kindly, tender master. A merciful master makes an easy service. His benevolence makes him watchful of the welfare of his servants, and considerate in dealing with their infirmities. His lowliness of heart ensures that he will never sacrifice the happiness and lives of his subjects in reckless and ambitious enterprises. He is not a tyrant, to drag his wretched subjects, like an Alexander [the Great], or a Tamerlane, through frozen wilds and burning wastes, and to pour out their blood as a libation to the idol of his fame. He is the prince of peace, whose scepter is truth, and meekness, and righteousness, and whose law is love. To his own people, he is the "Lamb of God," who loved them and gave himself for them. How then is it possible that he, in regulating the lives and services of his ransomed ones, should impose on them any other law than one which conduces to their truest well-being? To dread the yoke of Christ is guilty mistrust and unbelief.

But we shall not acquire the richest meaning of the passage, unless we include the connection of the clause, "learn of me," with the rest of the verse. Saith the Savior: "Take my yoke upon you, and learn of me." What shall we learn of him? Obviously, we learn of his meekness and lowliness of heart, how to take the yoke and how to wear it. Thus shall we find true repose of soul. This is but teaching us, my brethren, that if we would have true peace, we must imitate the spirit with which our Redeemer fulfilled the will of His Father, and love his cross. No more complete and ready method of proof appears, to establish this assertion, than to ask you to form to yourselves a conception of the inward life of such a man as the man Jesus. Suppose a servant of God endued with just his affection and benevolence, with his unselfish disinterestedness, with his purity, with his forgiving temper, with his magnanimity, with his elevated devotion, and moving among us in the fulfillment of the duties of the Christian life, under the impulse of these lovely sentiments, combined with the social ties appropriate to our nature sanctified: Does not this, at once, constitute a picture of a life, than which none can be conceived more imbued with the sweetness and sunshine of true happiness? Would not such a life glow with the very light of heaven's own bliss, amidst the gloom of our sorrows and sins? Some one may say, perhaps: Such was the temper of Jesus: yet he was "the man of sorrows." True: but it was because he "bore our griefs, and carried our sorrows." It was the burden of our guilt which pressed upon that pure and holy heart. Let us suppose that he had borne no load of obloquy, of death, and of divine desertion for us; that he had enjoyed the friends and outward blessings with which our lot is crowned; and had experienced no heavier chastisements, than God's fatherly mercy appoints to his adopted children here, sustained by the consolations of his grace. Then indeed would his life have been one of heavenly peace within. And such would ours be, if we learned of him, his heavenly temper. Reproach and opposition might still befall us, for we should still be in a wicked world; but the serene spirit of conscious rectitude and of forgiveness would sustain our souls in a loftier atmosphere, high above the flights of all the embittered shafts of malice. Pain, fatigue, sickness, would still visit us: but the spirit baptized in peace would sustain our infirmity. Our hearts would sometimes bleed with bereavements: for we should still be sinners, although pardoned: yet there would be no poison in the wound, for the assurance of the love of the hand which directed the stroke, would medicate our pain. If, then, we would find rest to our souls, let us learn to imbibe the temper of the meek and lowly Jesus, and to bear his yoke with that devoted spirit with which he fulfilled his Father's will in living and dying for us.

Fourth: In the concluding verse, our Savior gives this crowning argument: "For my yoke is easy, and my burden is light; and ye shall find rest to your souls." But this reasoning the unbeliever repels with more incredulity than any thing that has preceded it. The yoke easy; and the burden light! he exclaims? How can this be? Has not Christ himself said? "Straight is the gate, and narrow is the way." Is not the commandment declared to be "exceeding broad"? "The righteous scarcely are saved." How then can it be argued, that we shall find our true repose of soul in the service of Jesus Christ, because the burden of it is easy?

The unconverted man has often a worse ground of incredulity than this; that of his own experience and consciousness. He says to himself: 'I *have* endeavored to bear that yoke: I was earnest in my attempt; for was I not impelled to it by the infinite moment of the worth of an immortal soul, the sense of dreadful guilt, the terrors of an endless hell? I strove hard to live the Christian life; often I renewed my struggle, even with almost despairing bitterness; but the task was too great. I have relinquished it, and again I am living the life of careless impenitence, conscious that the danger of perdition is not removed, but only veiled partially for my own eyes by my insensibility, well aware that my conscience is not cleansed, but only seared. So well have I learned, by my own miserable experiments, that this grievous yoke of Christianity would crush out every enjoyment of life for me, if borne in earnest, that I am now stubbornly braving the appalling risks of our unprepared death, and a lost immortality, rather than face the burden again at present. And after all this, would the preacher persuade me that "the yoke is easy and the burden light"? Alas: I know better!'

Such is the skepticism, and such its ground which most adult transgressors read in their own hearts, when they scan their contents honestly. Say, Unbeliever: Have I not given correct form to your inmost thought? And your most intimate conviction is at points with the express declaration of your Savior. How shall I attempt to solve this crowning paradox for you, and to reconcile your unbelief to this gracious truth? This is a task which the Holy Spirit can alone accomplish with efficacy: and, thanks to Him, he does not require the execution of it from his ministers. Nothing but a true conversion by His power, experienced in the heart, can enable the sinner to appreciate the nature of Christ's service. The blind man cannot be taught precisely what are the beauties of the Spring, before his eyes are opened. But yet, something may be said to obviate your incredulity; something which, though it will not make you comprehend how this yoke becomes light, may yet enable you to apprehend that it is not unreasonable it should become so to the believer.

Remember then, that the declarations which the Scriptures make of the straightness and difficulty of the Christian's way, refer always to man's native and unassisted strength. Relatively to that strength, the way is indeed arduous. It is impossible to exaggerate its difficulty: if we should persuade the unconverted heart that it is absolutely certain his unaided strength and resolution will fail before it, we should be strictly true. And now, I appeal to your own consciousness: Were not those illstarred efforts to serve Christ, whose failure now so discourages you made in your own poor strength? Did you not begin then unconvinced of your impotency? Was not this the thought of your heart: 'Seeing the danger of my soul, *I*, as a rational being, will resolve: and *I* will fulfill what I resolve. I shall not be an inconsistent, half-way Christian, like these despised ones whose blemishes have so often been the butt of my contempt. I shall reform my life truly, and keep the law, and thus prepare and recommend myself for gospel forgiveness.' Did you form those purposes of piety, and make those efforts, in explicit, full dependence on a spiritual ability to be communicated to you by Christ of free grace; so that your sole encouragement to attempt them was his faithful word of promise? Alas, no! And therefore your service of him was a mortifying failure. Now I beg you to weigh the real statement of your Savior in the text. He has never said that the yoke would be easy, or the burden light to a soul which attempted to lift it apart from him. What he taught was this: that he who 'cometh' to him, he who 'learns of him' shall find the yoke easy. This you refused to do: you have never really tested the correctness of Christ's declaration: you have, in fact, no experience whatever upon the subject.

"But when we were yet without strength, in due time Christ died for the ungodly."[172] And one chief portion of his purchase for us was enabling grace; which is offered to our faith on the same terms with remission of sin. Hear now, some of the blessed assurances of this fact. "If any man be in Christ Jesus, he is a new creature: old things have passed away: behold all things have become new: and all things are of God."[173] "I am crucified with Christ: nevertheless I live: yet not I, but Christ liveth in me: and the life which I now live in the flesh, I live by the faith of the Son of God, who loved me, and gave himself for me."[174] "And he said unto me, My grace is sufficient for thee: for my strength is made perfect in weakness."[175] "A new heart also will I give you, and a new spirit will I put within you: and I will take away the stony heart out of your flesh, and I will give you a[n] heart of flesh. And I will put my [s]pirit within you, and cause you to walk in my statutes, and ye shall keep my judgments, and do them."[176]

If these precious promises are true, is it not clear that he who has them fulfilled in his soul may reasonably expect a wholly different experience from yours, in bearing the yoke? Here new views of truth are given: a spiritual ability is awakened in the faculties hitherto misdirected to sin and sense: man's impotence of will for spiritual good is renovated by the almighty will of the Spirit. If indeed Christ does all this in him who comes, and learns of him, and takes his yoke, plainly that service may be easy and pleasant to him, which before was intolerable. Sometimes the curious child, straying where the laborers have laid down their implements, takes up the axe or scythe adapted to a man's strength, and undertakes to use it. But his youthful limbs are unequal to the task: his toil is excessive: his breast[177] heaves with panting, his heart throbs, and his joints quiver with fatigue. As he lays it down, he concludes perhaps thus: "How burdensome and repulsive must the life of the laborer be! Surely every pleasure of existence is crushed out by their excessive toil!" Yet he is mistaken; he has judged their tasks by his measure of strength. They have the muscles of men: and when they come forth into the breezy fields or fragrant wood, refreshed with food, and their veins rich with lusty blood, there is a positive joy in the vigorous swing of these weapons of sturdy and honest labor. Similar is the error which you have made, when you have attempted to bear Christ's yoke in your own strength, which is weakness; and overpowered by the burden, have inferred that Christ cannot make it light by his grace.

But there is another solution, which is, if possible, more important. It is found in the difference of motive and affection by which the service of the believer and that of the unbeliever are prompted. Those labors are easy and pleasant, which are inspired by love, however absorbing they may be of time and strength. But if they are compelled by reluctant fear, and rendered with hatred, the lightest exertions gall the heart. The man who is incapable of domestic love looks on the toils of the laborious father with disgust: he thinks his life that of a galley slave: and says to himself that no power nor price on earth shall ever bend him to so irksome a bondage. But does that careful parent think so? Nay: his labors, his crops, the glebe watered with the honest sweat of his brow, are dear to him: he cherishes them with all the affectionate interest of heart's treasures: they feed those whom he loves. As he pursues his busy tillage through the sultry hours, although he does feel the heat and burden of the day, he is happy in his endurance: because he has before him the peaceful home which is blessed with the fruits of these labors, the board spread with bounty by the work of his sturdy hand, with the smiling faces around it, the welcome of pattering feet, and gleeful voices, and childish arms about his neck, which he expects to meet him as he returns at eve, heavy perhaps of limb, but light of heart, from his daily tasks, and the loving smile of the thoughtful mate, who keeps the hearth bright for his coming. Go now, to that man, and tempt him to leave his fields for some scene of sinful amusement: tell him that his daily labor is nothing but a miserable drudgery, and that it is time for him to seek enjoyment abroad. Will he hearken? No: his labor is his enjoyment: those guilty and mischievous scenes have no allurement for him, because love makes him happy enough in his industry.

Or, if this instance is not enough, we may find a more conclusive one in that which is the strongest and purest of all affections formed among sinful men, the love of a mother for her babe. And this also imposes the severest toils which any of the duties of common life require. As the young female, a stranger as yet to this devoted love, witnesses the sacrifices of some mother lately her comrade, amidst the perpetual watchings and sleepless cares of the nursery, it may be that she looks on with disgust and dread: and she says to herself, "not for all the world would I submit to such an abhorred burden." But the time comes when the fountain of maternal love is opened in her heart also. Now see the recent votaress of fashion! How zealously does she forsake the admiration of society, and sacrifice the bloom of her beauty, lately so much prized, amidst the vigils of her domestic tasks. These cares are no longer repulsive. Propose to her to resign her tender charge wholly to some hireling, whose well paid skill will probably far surpass her inexperience, in providing for its welfare, and to return to the delights of the ballroom. She will reject it: and as she presses her infant to her bosom, will declare that no joy of earth is so sweet as the care of this darling object. Whence this change? It is because a new love has been born along with her offspring. The yoke of love is ever easy, and its burden is light.

In like manner, if he who comes to Christ and learns of him, learns thereby to love, this new motive abundantly explains the fact, to you, Sinner, so incredible, that His yoke becomes easy. For I take your own heart to witness, that in your former efforts to live a religious life, no love animated your resolve. The world and self-will were still sweet to you intrinsically. If you felt the sting and bitterness of any of your sins, it was only because self-love was terrified by the looming of the danger they incurred. The Christian life was abhorrent to your secret heart; and the language of your inner thought was, that this Divine Master was an austere man whose service you would defy, if you dared. Poor, unwilling captive! No wonder your service, wrung by fear from a bitter, reluctant[178] heart, was a galling bondage.

But now remember the blessed truth already established from the Scriptures: that when a believing soul embraces the cross, Christ "crucifies the enmity thereby": that he engages to take away the stony heart out of our flesh, and give us a heart of flesh: that when he reconciles us to God by our effectual calling, and sheds abroad his love upon our hearts. Then, as the regenerated sinner considers the amazing love and condescension of a Redeemer God, stooping to death to rescue him from unutterable ruin, a new-born gratitude conspires with adoration for his excellences, and he begins to say: "I love him, because he first loved us." Then the love of Christ constraining him becomes the spring of a joyful obedience; and he sings with devout delight, in the language of David: "O Lord, truly I am thy servant: I am thy servant and the son of thy handmaid: Thou hast loosed my bonds." This is the way, O Sinner, the yoke is made easy, and the burden light! Cannot you apprehend it?

Perhaps such a glimpse of the beauty and glory of the Cross hath penetrated your heart, (which may God grant!) that you are almost ready to say: 'Ah, if I could only claim that wondrous Savior as mine, if I could believe that the divine blood was indeed shed for my sins: that the burning throne, whose just wrath now blights every look, which my wretched soul turns towards God, with fear and enmity was changed for me into a throne of grace; that this dreadful God was indeed reconciled, and was become a tender father, I too, could love: I too could serve with hope, and cheerful obedience. But how shall I know this? How read the secret verdict of heaven, which acquits and adopts the object of almighty grace?'

I will tell you how. But first, let me warn you, not to mistake obstinacy of your own native opposition to God. If you think that the mere apprehension of your own interest in the cross, and of the excellence and love displayed therein towards you, will be enough of itself, without the inworking of the sovereign Spirit, to renovate your obdurate heart, you will be disappointed. No doctrine, no moral suasion alone, not even that of dying love, will melt that flinty thing: nothing but the power divine which first created it. But if you feel that you could indeed love Christ, if only you were assured that he had first loved you, then it is my delightful commission to tell you that you may claim that privilege of loving. Christ invites you. His own words are: "Whosoever will: let him come." He tells us that the man upon whom God's secret verdict of the heavenly justification and adoption is passed, is he who is truly willing to embrace, and to serve Christ. Are you willing? Then you are one of those for whom the invitation is sent. Come then, thou weary, heavy laden soul. "Come to Jesus, and He will give you rest. Take his yoke upon you and learn of Him; for he is meek and lowly in heart; and ye shall find rest to your souls. For his yoke is easy, and his burden is light."

Permit me, in closing this discourse, to point out two instructive lessons, which are contained in these words of the Savior.

One is: that faith always includes an immediate assumption of all known duty. Christ here explains "coming to him" in v. 28th, (which is his customary expression for believing) by taking up the yoke and learning of him in v. 29th. The true believer, although of all men most impressed with his own impotency sets about that very thing. It is because the gospel promise pledges Christ's strength to make the yoke easy; and the function of faith is, to embrace the promise just as it is. Now, there is somebody here, whose failure and distress are all explained by this remark. My brother: you think you comprehend and approve the plan for sinner's pardon through Christ, and that you can trust it: But you have not found rest for your soul? It is because there is some yoke, some duty, which you have not assumed. What is it? You know: I do not: God does. Take it upon like a man: do it now: not self-righteously, but believingly: and you will find the blessed rest.

Second: there is somebody else here, who thinks he sees and craves the blessedness of the soul which has received the conscious assurance, it its own exercises, of being saved in Christ. He says: 'Oh, if I could only feel in my heart those new-born affections, and thus known my interest in Him; how joyfully would I flee to Him, and embrace Him with his service; and no toils nor sacrifices should tempt my happy heart for one moment to forsake his yoke. But alas! when I look within, all is cold and dark. How can I venture, with this unrenewed heart?'

The answer which Christ here implies is this: The conscious inward experience of his grace is bestowed by your coming, and when you come; not before. Hear him. "Take my yoke upon you and learn of me," . . . "and ye shall find rest to your souls." You must find it by taking the yoke, not before you take it. You must venture on his divine word, trusting that alone, and committing yourself to his fidelity, in advance of your own experience. And does not He deserve this, who died for you? Cannot you trust him? If he saved you by the method you desire, your trust would be, after all, not on Him, but on your own experiences. How sandy a foundation!

But there is a more offensive form of this mistrust. Some anxious, convinced souls would fain have the peace; but they are loath to commit themselves irrevocably to Christ's yoke, until they have made a sort of conditional experiment for themselves, of the comfort and ease with which they may bear it. They cannot trust the word and oath of the Savior who is very[179] God, and who so loved them as to lay down his life for their souls. No: they must be allowed to finger the yoke, to weigh it in their hands, to judge how it will wear; and then, if they like it, perhaps Christ will be permitted to bind it on permanently. Deluded soul! Of course the yoke, thus tried, will not wear lightly. And what is such mistrust, but an insult to the majesty, the love, the faithfulness of Christ? He will not traffic with you for your deliverance on such terms as these. You must trust yourself without reserve to his fidelity; or he will turn with holy scorn from your insolent proposal, and leave your miserable soul to perish in its doubts. "The fearful," (they who are too timid to trust themselves to the faithfulness of their God and Savior) "and unbelieving and abominable . . . shall have their part in the lake which burneth with fire and brimstone, which is the second death." (Revelation 21:9)

Our Comfort in Dying[180]

A Sermon

on

Acts 7:59

"Lord Jesus receive my spirit."

Preached August 25th 1861 on a wooded ridge east of Centreville, Fairfax Co., Va., to the 27th Va. Regiment[181] of the Stonewall Brigade[182]

It is proper that the minds of Christians should be familiar with thoughts of death. This seems to be the object of the prayer of Moses in Psalm 90:12: "So teach us to number our days, that we may apply our hearts unto wisdom." It is inculcated by our Savior, in Matthew 24:42: "Watch, therefore, for ye know not what hour your Lord doth come." In the season of health and prosperity it will be wholesome for us to remember that it is appointed unto men once to die. It will sober our inordinate desires and restrain us from abusing our abundance. And to the mind accustomed to look its destiny in the face, the sorrows of old age, of sickness and of death, will not come with the bitterness of surprise.

It is somewhat remarkable that under each dispensation the first believer's death which is recorded was that of a martyr. In the Old Testament it was that of Abel; in the New that of Stephen. Let us endeavor to conceive the awe and dreadful curiosity with which the first human beings witnessed the first execution upon one of their fellows of the threatened doom, death for sin. Hitherto, the visage of death had never been seen; man only knew that it was something irresistible and terrible, which terminated the existence of the body and restored it to the dust from which it was taken. But now they beheld it; they saw the glazed eye, the sunken and pallid countenance, the marble rigidity, and above all the ghostly aspect of the corpse. How much was the terror of the spectacle enhanced by the fact that the death of their brother was by violence: that his blood was poured out in murder, and the image of humanity in him foully marred before he became food for worms!

There is also a peculiar interest in the death of the first Christian of the new dispensation; for the grave and the world of spirits had now received a new illustration. The saints of the Old Testament had, indeed, good hope that "their souls should not be left in Hades." But the instructions and the resurrection of Christ had now illuminated the tomb with a new flood of light and hope.

> "There the dear flesh of Jesus lay,
> And left a long perfume."[183]

His death had now conquered the king of terrors, disarmed him of his sting, and led captivity captive. Believers, with such an example, must surely learn a new lesson of submission and courage. Accordingly, the death of the proto-martyr, although accompanied with every outward circumstance of cruelty and horror, was full of consolation and peace. Persecuted upon the unjust charge of perverting the religion of Moses, he had defended himself and rebuked his accusers' sins with a faithful boldness by which they were cut to the heart, insomuch that they gnashed upon him with their teeth. His justification of himself and his charges against them were unanswerable; but the tyrant's argument remained to them, and they resolved at once to silence his voice and to gratify their malignity by his death. He was condemned to that ghastly mode of execution, stoning to death with stones. Surrounded with a raging multitude, who were rather wild beasts than men, he was dragged out of the city; and while a young Pharisee named Saul, afterwards the great apostle of the Gentiles, kept the clothes of the executioners, they stoned Stephen, calling upon *God*, and saying, "Lord Jesus, receive my spirit."

But his Redeemer, who had so recently passed to his throne through a similar ordeal, did not forsake him. By the power of the Holy Ghost he vouchsafed to his dying servant a vision of the glory of God, and of Christ standing on his right hand, which was sufficient to repay for the agonies of a violent death. How amazing, my brethren, was the contrast between that scene, which was obvious to the eye of sense, and that different one which disclosed itself to the eye of faith at the same time? The one presents us with a solitary, helpless sufferer, the center of a group of murderous assailants, prostrate, crushed with innumerable blows, his dying countenance begrimed with dust and blood, and his palpitating form mangled almost beyond the semblance of humanity. But oh! behold the other! Look up! There opens before us that heavenly court, which violence, sin and death can never enter, radiant with light ineffable, displaying the throne of Almighty justice, now newly occupied by the God-man, who rises up at his martyr's cry, and with a countenance combining unutterable human love and pity with the terrible glories of deity, stretches forth his hand, lately bleeding for us on the cross, now armed with the scepter of the universe. At his beck the liberated soul leaps from its poor, dishonored tenement, leaving it all insensible to its wrongs, and mounts, beaming with love and triumph, to the inviting arms! Blessed compensation. What are the pains of dying compared with such a reward?

Could we see invisible things we should often witness similar contrasts at the bedsides of the departing people of God. That which our senses make known to us is a gloomy, shaded room, a couch, a circle of tearful, solemn watchers and a gasping, pallid mortal, in what men call the agonies of death. But could we see in the light of the upper sanctuary, we should more correctly call them the agonies of birth. One moment the sufferer is hovering in insensibility upon the faint line which separates life and death, or wrestling with the strong throes of his last struggle. The next, the body lies a corpse, and the suppressed wail of bereavement from the survivors fills the chamber of death. But could we follow the ransomed spirit, as it soars to its home, how different would be the world of glory which bursts upon its sight, and the shout of joy with which it enters in?

But I have proposed, my brethren, to consider especially the proto-martyr's dying prayer, "Lord Jesus, receive my spirit."

First. This seems to teach us that Stephen regarded Jesus Christ as very God. There are sundry places in the Scriptures where this prime doctrine is not so much dogmatically asserted as unintentionally, though clearly implied. These evidences of our Savior's divinity are, in one aspect, even more satisfactory to the mind than the set and formal assertions, because so obviously sincere expressions of the sacred writer's inmost heart, and because they show how this cardinal truth is interwoven with the believer's whole experience. We are told by Scripture that Stephen was an eminent saint and an inspired man. The heavens had just been opened to him, and the celestial realities had been disclosed, with the position of Jesus at the right hand of the Father. And now, immediately after this vision, and amidst the solemn emotions of the last hour, he prays to Jesus Christ, addressing to him the most momentous petition which the creature can raise to deity. Your English bibles read: "They stoned Stephen, calling upon *God* and saying, Lord Jesus, receive my spirit." You will notice that the word *God* is printed in italic letters; by which our translators would signify that there is nothing in the original answering to it, but they have judged it better to supply it in order to complete the sense. In my judgment it would have been more correct to have it as it stands in the Greek: "They stoned Stephen, invoking and saying, Lord Jesus, receive my spirit." Thus the intention of the evangelist, which was to state that Christ was the object of his prayers, is made clear. But even though his meaning be lost in this point, the petition which is raised to Jesus Christ in the last clause is one which no scriptural believer could address to any other than God. He alone is the proper object of religious worship; and the man is blind, indeed, who would entrust his everlasting all in the article of death to any other than an omnipotent arm.

In every office of the Redeemer the enlightened Christian feels that he could not properly rely upon him for salvation unless he is very God. It is "because he is God, and there is none else," that Isaiah invites "all the ends of the earth to look unto him and be saved." But in the hour of death especially, the Christian needs a Savior who is no less than God. An angel could not sympathize with our trial, for they cannot feel the pangs of dissolution. A human friend cannot travel with us the path through the dark valley; for the creature who yields to the stroke of death is overwhelmed, and returns no more to guide his fellow. The God-man alone can sustain us; he has felt the mortal blow, for he is man; he has survived it, and returns triumphing to succor us, for he is God. Unless this divine guide be with us we must fight the battle with the last enemy alone and unaided. Just when the struggle becomes most fearful to the soul, the veil of approaching dissolution descending between it and all this world shuts it off in the outer darkness; and then, in vast solitary night, must the king of terrors be met, with no human arm to succor and no ear to hear the cry of despair that is lost in the infinite silence. So must you die, my friend, and I. Though wife and children, and officious comrades be crowding around your bed, and loved ones be stooping to receive your last sigh to their very hearts, and your dying head be pillowed upon the bosom which was the dearest resting place of your sorrows while living, the last approach of death will separate you from them all, and you will meet him alone. The icy shadow of his dart, as it comes near your heart, will obstruct all the avenues of sense by which their sympathy can reach you. Even then, practically, you will die alone; as truly alone as the last wanderer in some vast wilderness, who falls exhausted on the plain, and sees nothing above but the burning sky, or around save the boundless waste; as truly alone as the mariner who, when the ship is rushing before a gale through the midnight sea, drops from the mast-head, and buffets vainly with the innumerable billows amidst the pitchy darkness, while his despairing shriek is drowned by the tumult of the deep.

But then it is that Jesus Christ draws near as an omnipotent Savior. He alone of all the universe has fathomed the deepest abysses of death, has explored all its caverns of despair, and has returned from them a conqueror. He is not only sympathizing man, but omnipresent God, who can go with us into the *penetralia* of the court of death. When our last hour comes, then let us say, brethren, "Lord Jesus, receive my spirit." "When I pass through the valley of the shadow of death, be thou with me; let thy rod and thy staff comfort me."

Second. I am taught by this prayer of the martyr to expect an immediate entrance into the blessed presence of Jesus Christ. I see here that Stephen believed that "the souls of believers are, at their death, made perfect in holiness, and do immediately pass into glory."[184] He evidently did not expect that the grave would absorb his spirit into a state of unconscious sleep, to last until the final consummation; or that any *limbus*, or purgatory,[185] was to swallow him for a time in its fiery bosom. His faith aspired directly to the arms of Christ, and to that blessed world where his glorified humanity now dwells.

Some would persuade us that death is an unconscious sleep; that the soul is not a distinct substance, possessed of its own being and powers of thought independent of the body, but a mere *phenomenon*, the result of the body's organic action, as sound is of the vibration of the musical chord; and that so there is an absolute suspension of the soul's conscious existence until such time as the body is reared from the dust in the resurrection. So thought not the inspired martyr. He manifestly regarded his spirit as separable from the body, and therefore as true, independent substance. The latter he relinquishes to the insults of his enemies; the former he commits to Jesus Christ. So taught not that Savior and his two favored disciples when they showed us Moses and Elijah in glory. So promised not the dying Redeemer to the penitent thief, when he said, "This day thou shalt be with me in Paradise." His body was left upon the tree a prey to the brutality of his executioners, and probably to ravenous birds. Yet his soul, the true being, passed with his dying Redeemer into immediate blessedness. So believed not Paul when he said that "to him to live was Christ and to die was gain," and that "to be absent from the body was to be present with the Lord." And would he ever have been in a strait betwixt the two desires, to live and labor for his converts and to die, had the latter been a sleep of dreary ages in the dust? Surely this zealous laborer for Christ could not have hesitated between the choice of such a useless, unconscious blank on the one hand, and a life of praise and of happy activity on earth on the other hand, albeit it was checkered with toils and persecutions.

How much more dreary would not the tomb be if the sentient, thinking soul were engulphed in it along with the body? Nor is there an answer in the saying that its loss will virtually be no loss, because the soul will be totally unconscious of it at the time. But it would not be unconscious of it before and after. Man is a being of forecast and of retrospection; and it is impossible that he should not recoil with dread from the absorption of his own active, thinking being by this realm of annihilation, and the dedication of so many ages which might have been filled with usefulness and enjoyment to fruitless non-existence. Such is not our creed, my brother. If only we are in Christ by true faith, the grave will have naught to do with that which is the true, conscious being. Is the tomb dark and doleful and chill, and loathsome with the worm and the dust? "What is that to me? I shall never lie there; I shall never feel the gnawing worm. The coffin lid will never confine me! The spirit, the conscious, spontaneous, thinking, knowing, feeling thing, which constitutes the true man, the *I*, which alone can hope or fear, or experience the tooth of pain, which will have soared away to a brighter realm before these abhorred scenes overtake it. Only the poor, disused tenement, the unconscious clay, will be their victim.

It is with equal comfort that the believer's mind is emancipated from the fears of a purgatory beyond death. The efficacy of Christ's vicarious righteousness is asserted in terms which forbid the thought that any retribution will ever be exacted of one who by a true faith has become interested in Him. "There is now no condemnation to them which are in Christ Jesus." "Who shall lay any thing to the charge of God's elect? It is God that justifieth; who is he that condemneth"?[186] "For by one offering he hath perfected for ever them that are sanctified. . . . And their sins and iniquities will I remember no more. Now, where remission of these is, there is no more offering for sin."[187] I will not detain you uselessly by following all the thorny sophisms by which this most potent engine of superstition and priestcraft supported. One conclusive view will show you that it cannot be true. The passages cited teach, beyond a peradventure, that no other penal retribution exists or is required for the guilt of the believer's sins than that of Christ's sacrifice. I now add: neither is it possible that any purifying chastisement, sent in love and not in judgment, by purgatorial fires after death, can be inflicted upon believers, for the reason that *when they die they are at once made perfectly holy*. How can that be purged which is already absolutely clean? But that justified sinners are at death immediately made perfect in holiness is taught beyond dispute, where we are told that they go directly from death to heaven, and that heaven is a place of perfect purity. "Lazarus died and was carried by angels to Abraham's bosom." To the thief it was said, "This day thou shalt be with me in Paradise." Stephen, looking up from the bloody ground which was about to be his death-bed, said to a present Savior, "Lord Jesus, receive my spirit." "If our earthly house be dissolved, we have a building of God in the heavens." "To be absent from the body" is "to be present with the Lord." But "corruption doth not inherit incorruption." That upper sanctuary is the assembly of "the spirits of just men made perfect," "and there shall in no wise enter into it anything that defileth."[188]

On these impregnable foundations rests the blessed assurance of our immediate glory after death. "And I heard a voice from heaven saying unto me, Write, Blessed are the dead which die in the *Lord* from henceforth: Yea, saith the Spirit, that they may rest from their labors; and their works do follow them."[189] Dreary would be the Christian's death-bed, indeed, if the best prospect which could be offered him amidst the decays of nature were but this: that he must pass from the toils of life and the pangs of dying to fiercer pains beyond the grave, of uncertain duration, which could only be abridged by the piety and doubtful care of survivors. Blessed be God, such is not our hope; but when once life's pilgrimage is ended, if we live in faith and love towards God, the eternal peace begins. The pains of our last struggle are the last experience of evil to which the ransomed spirit is called forever.

Third. We learn from the text to what guidance the Christian may commit his soul during its unknown journey into the world of spirits. Let us endeavor, my brethren, to obtain a practical and palpable conception of that world. I believe that heaven is as truly a place as was that paradise of the primeval world where the holy Adam dwelt. When we first arrive there we shall be disembodied spirits. But finite spirits have their locality. The clearer evidence, however, that heaven is a literal place is, that it now contains the glorified, material bodies of Enoch, of Elijah, of Christ, and probably of the saints who rose with their Redeemer. But where is this place? In what quarter of this vast universe? In what sphere do the Man Jesus and his ransomed ones now dwell? When death batters down the walls of the earthly tabernacle, whither shall the dispossessed soul set out? To what direction shall it turn in beginning its mysterious journey? It knows not; it needs a skillful, powerful and friendly guide.

But more; it is a journey into a spiritual world, and this thought makes it awful to the apprehensions of man. The presence of one disembodied spirit in the solitude of night would shake us with a thrill of dread. How, then, could we endure to be launched out into this untried ocean of space, peopled by, we know not what, mysterious beings? How would we shrink with fear at the meeting of some heavenly or infernal principality, rushing with lightning speed through the void, upon some mighty errand of mercy or malice, clothed with un-imagined splendors of angelic attributes, and attended by the hosts of his spiritual comrades? How could we be assured that we should not fall a prey to the superior power of some of these evil angels? How [could we] be certain that we might not lose our way in the pathless vacancy, and wander up and down forever, a bewildered, solitary rover, amidst the wilderness of worlds? This journey into the unknown world must, else, issue in our introduction to a scene whose awful novelties will overpower our faculties; for even the very thought of them, when they are permitted to dwell upon our hearts, fills us with a sense of dreadful suspense. Truly will the trembling soul need some one on whom to lean, some mighty, experienced and tender guardian, who will point the way to the prepared mansions, and cheer and sustain its fainting courage. That guide is Christ: therefore let us say, in dying: "Lord Jesus, receive my spirit."

It is a delightful belief, to which the gospel seems to give most solid support, that our Redeemer is accustomed to employ in this mission his holy angels. What Christian has failed to derive sublime satisfaction as he has read the allegorical description in the *Pilgrims Progress* of Christian and Hopeful crossing the river of death, and ascending with a rejoicing company of angels to the gate of the celestial city. It is, indeed, but an allegory, which likens death to a river. But it is no allegory—it is a literal and blessed truth—that angels receive and assist the departing souls which Christ redeems. "Are they not all ministering spirits, sent forth to minister to them who shall be heirs of salvation?" When Lazarus died "he was carried by angels to Abraham's bosom." They are our destined companions in the upper world to which we go. With what tender sympathy will not these pure spirits assist the dying moments of their ransomed brethren of earth; and with what loving joy will they not welcome them to their home? When we were brought by repentance out of our guilt and enmity, there was joy among them. During all the long and wavering contest of the saint on this earth these ministering angels are his watchful assistants. And now that the victory is won, the culture of the soul for heaven completed, and the fruit which first budded in his repentance is matured for glory, with what glad songs will not the angels shout the harvest home? We cannot distinguish by our gross senses the presence and agency of these incorporeal assistants. Even while they minister to us they are unknown to us, by name, as in nature. But none the less are they present.

> "There are more things in heaven and earth
> Than are dreamed of in our philosophy."[190]

And when the walls of the flesh are battered away by death, the vision of the spiritual world will flow in upon us unobstructed. Not seldom does the death-bed of Christ's people present instances which seem as though some gleams of that celestial light, and some glimpses of the beings who inhabit it, begin to reach the dying saint before he quite leaves the clay, through the rents which are made in his frail tabernacle by the strokes of the last enemy. What is it that sometimes makes the sunken countenance light up in the article of death with a sudden glory, and the eye, but now devoid of speculation, beam with one more expiring flash of heaven's light? Has the soul seen through the torn veil already the angels' faces bending over its agony, and heard their tender call, unheard by ears of flesh, wooing it out of the crumbling body:

> "Hark! They whisper; angels say,
> Sister spirit, come away!"[191]

But perhaps these questions are not authorized by the revelation God has vouchsafed to give us of the secrets of the other world. Yet there is one more truth which is revealed, even more glorious than this. It is that ransomed souls are the actual companions, not only of angels, but of the "God manifest in the flesh." When the martyr uttered the prayer of the text he manifestly looked to the arms of Christ as his final home. We are authorized by his example to say, "Lord Jesus, receive my spirit, not only that thou mayest sustain it in the pangs of dying and guide it to its heavenly home, and clothe it in thy own robe of righteousness and answer for it in the great day of accounts, but that it may dwell with thee in a world without end. Thou didst pray, 'Father, I will that they also whom thou hast given me be with me where I am, that they may behold my glory;'[192] and thee the Father heareth always. Thou didst show the holy apostle that, after thou comest with the voice of the archangel and the trump of God, 'we shall ever be with the Lord.'[193] Thou has taught us that, 'when thou shalt appear, we shall be like thee; for we shall see thee as thou art.'"[194] Oh! blessed resting place! "In thy presence is fulness of joy; at thy right hand are pleasures for evermore."[195] Let us, brethren, live and die like believing Stephen, and our spirits will be received to the place where the God-man holds his regal court, to go out thence no more forever. We shall see him on his throne, so gloriously earned; we shall see the same face which beamed love upon the sisters of Bethany and upon the beloved disciple, and which wept at the grave of his friend; not, as then, marred with our griefs and pensive with the burden of our sorrows, but shining as the sun. Yet that splendor will not sear our vision; it will be the light of love. We shall see the very hands which were pierced for us; not then bleeding, but reaching forth to us the scepter of universal dominion to guide and protect us. We shall hear the very voice which once said, "Come unto me all ye that labor and are heavy laden," bidding our worthless souls welcome to his glory. And as we gaze and adore and praise, we shall be changed by his Spirit into the same image of holiness. "This honor have all his saints."

But, alas! all whom I address have not the faith and holiness of Stephen. They live in willful impenitence, and call not on the name of Christ. Yet they too must pass through this iron gate of death! On whom will you call, you who have neglected your Savior, when you pass down into this valley of great darkness; when the inexorable veil begins to descend, shutting out human help and sympathy from your despairing eyes; when death thrusts out your wretched soul from its abused tenement; when you launch forth into the void immense, a naked, shivering ghost; when you stand before the great white throne? Can you face these horrors alone? How will you endure a beggared, undone eternity?

It may be that you will seek in vain this terrible, helpless solitude, rather than the worse alternative which the justice of God may assign you. The devils who now tempt you may then become your captors, beset your dying bed and seize your wretched soul, as it is cast out from the body, to bind it in everlasting chains under darkness against the judgment of the last day.

Call on Christ, then, today, in repentance and faith, in order that you may be entitled to call upon him in the hour of your extremity. Own him now as your Lord, that he may confess you then as his people.[196]

Procrastination

A Sermon

on

Proverbs 27:1

"Boast not thyself of tomorrow; for thou knowest not
what a day may bring forth."

Preached to the 2nd Va. Brigade, Jackson's Division, Sabbath, April 27th 1862
near Swift Run Gap. Rockingham, Va.[197]

Brethren: We "know not what a day may bring forth." Man's ignorance of the future is, to the meditative mind, a most solemn and touching thought. Experience projects some light forward into it, by virtue of our confidence in the stability of the laws of nature and causation. That there will be a morrow we believe; and can surmise some of its attendants: we are very sure that it will bring us duties and temptations, and we expect that it will also be marked by some blessings, and by our sins. That the seasons will run their rounds, bring seed-time and harvest, we confidently anticipate. That vice will sooner or later produce misery, we can predict, as safely as though we had the spirit of prophecy.

But a true foreknowledge belongs to none but the Almighty. It is only because there is a God, by whose wisdom and power the regularity of natural laws is maintained, that there is room for the creature's forecast. Were there no divine providence, there could be no rational prognostication among men: for blind chance furnishes no basis for it. But God, the almighty, foreknows because he has foreordained. That which He wills to pass out of the realm of the possible into the actual, is what makes up the events of time. An event is in the future, solely because it is in God's purpose and will. Thus His foreknowledge is as complete as man's is partial.

This text contains two parts: a fact, and an inference therefrom. That which is first in logical order, is last in the order of its mention.

The fact is, that man has no complete foreknowledge, even of a single day. The inference is, that therefore he should not boast himself of the morrow. Let us examine each of these in turn.

I. "Thou knowest not what a day may bring forth." Your journey through life, my hearer, is like that of a traveller in some foreign labyrinth, where the very next turn may bring him face to face with destruction, or some unexpected bliss. Yet in this dread path he must ever move. He would fain pause: he would fain recoil from the unknown terrors which may people the darkness before him, but inexorable time propels him. He must advance, not knowing but that as he turns the next curve of the thicket, he may meet his fate. He is like the man journeying in Egyptian darkness over a rugged mountain path. An irresistible impulse compels him to advance, but he is conscious that he moves amidst beetling precipices and pitfalls, and unseen torrents, whose roar comes up from the mysterious blackness, informing his ear of nothing but their nearness, and his danger. How anxiously do his sightless [eye]balls glare after the light, and his trembling hands grope in the thick darkness? But, neither sight nor touch gives them any guidance.

It is not strange therefore, that it should ever be one of the wildest yearnings of the human soul, to be able to pierce this darkness, and to foresee the future. Witness the popularity of all the pretended arts of prophecy, oracles, witchcraft, necromancy, palmistry, astrology, and divination. Nor is this passion limited to barbarians, nor to ancient ages. The most civilized races in this century betray the same passion, as strongly as their savage ancestors, wherever it is not checked by the influence of the only true revelation. Indeed, men justify this craving, and persuade themselves that a fuller insight into futurity would be exceedingly beneficial: because, as they imagine, that which was foreknown could be better provided for. But the craving for foreknowledge is erroneous: it is better that man should not have it, unless he had also omnipotence. The prospect of coming evils which he could not evade, would only harrow his soul with unavailing fears. Or, if the danger were evitable, the knowledge of its certain approach, and of its date, would scarcely avail to stimulate him who was inert under the keener spur of the truth which the text teaches us. He who now procrastinates, while the very uncertainty of the time when danger may befall should be the most reasonable argument for preparation, would be very sure to practice the same folly, when he knew the actual amount of the interval which he possessed.

To realize the truth of the proposition that we know not what a day may bring forth, we need only to ask ourselves this question: What may not the possibilities of the next day be imagined to include, without any strained or unnatural supposition? Possibly it may bring to us the news of some national disaster, which may cause all faces to gather blackness. It may inform us of the illness or death of some whom we love best. It may bring battle, bodily wounds or death to some of those here. It may initiate some fatal sickness in our frames, which, after a few short days of progressive suffering, may terminate in dissolution. It may possibly bring sudden temptation and sin, even such sin as may finally vex the Holy Spirit, and thus seal our impenitency even before life is ended. Is there anything improbably in either of these? Or else, the morrow may bring some glad tidings of the prosperity of those we love, of their souls newly born unto God, of some splendid military success, of the salvation of our beloved country. These things also are possible, so far as our shortsighted knowledge can foresee.

II. From this uncertainty of the future, we may learn not to boast ourselves of the morrow. This caution I understand as teaching us several connected truths. One is, that since our earthly future is so obscure to us, no temporal possession can be the portion and happiness of a rational creature. For the spirit of man will persist in running forward: foresight and hope are its essential attributes. Man must cease to be man, in order to divest himself of them. Hence, how necessary to his happiness, that he shall have some certain good in the morrow, of which he can 'boast himself'? That good must be found in something above this unstable earth. "There is nothing true by Heaven." How blessed then, to have heaven for our inheritance, and God for our guide through this intricate and dangerous journey! Without Him, we are blind men, staggering along amidst pitfalls and precipices, yet compelled to advance. "Our way is dark and slippery, and the angel of the Lord pursues us." "Surely we are set in slippery places." (Psalm 38:6, 73:18) But he who has his treasure in heaven, has heaven's King for his guide. He indeed is blind, but his divine Leader is omniscient: and so he may reasonably boast himself in an immortal future of security and glory.

Another lesson which God teaches us from the uncertainty of the future is, that of moderation in all earthly attachments. "But this I say, brethren: The time is short: It remaineth that both they that have wives be as though they had none: and they that weep as though they wept not: and they that rejoice, as though they rejoiced not: and they that use this world as not abusing it: for the fashion of this world passeth away." (I Corinthians 7:29-31) But foolish man persists in the opposite. He wraps himself in the turmoil of business and pleasure, seeking to veil from himself by the confusion which he creates, the obstinate fact that all to which he attaches his idolatrous affections, is deceitful. Thus he ensures that every sudden stroke which rends these perishable goods shall tear his own heartstring[s] with anguish.

But some one may ask: Are we to cultivate a perpetual fear which poisons the enjoyment of the present? Is hope, the solace of disappointed hearts, and great spring of human energies, to be cast away, because it may perchance be disappointed? Are we to be ever borrowing trouble from the future, by imagining evils which may never befall us? I reply: No. This is a caricature of that temper, which the Apostle inculcates. The text enjoins, not a thankless, morose, and querulous spirit; not a proneness to look ever upon the darker side: not a refusal of present innocent good because there is no guarantee of the future. This is the very result of the inordinate affections which it discourages. It is at one with our Savior when he says, "Let the morrow take thought for the things of itself." But it enjoins the subordination of earthly good to spiritual, the wise diffidence of the temporal, and the hearty embracing and preference of those treasures which "moth and rust do not corrupt, and which thieves do not break through and steal." It is that chastened spirit of Christian moderation, which is born only of renewing grace.

Now, the advantages of this diffidence of temporal good are manifold. It delivers from much of the pain of disappointment. The greater the *momentum* with which you pursue the uncertain good, the more violent must be the shock of disappointment with which you impinge against an unforeseen obstacle. There is a cheerfully disciplined temper, (the Christian knows how to exercise it) which enjoys innocent earthly good, as sweetly as though its possession were secure, and yet surrenders it as meekly as though its loss were foreseen. This temper again, if it diminishes the joys of anticipation, (How often deceitful!) will enhance the pleasure of possession by an agreeable surprise. Thus, they who go of set purpose pleasure seeking, are very likely to find little except disappointment. They who make duty their chief object, and thankfully accept such lawful pleasures as fall incidentally along their way, often enjoy much more than they anticipated. But the great mischief of an overweening confidence in the earthly future is this: It tempts to neglect the provision for the eternal future. The child, in the sports of summer, forgets to provide for winter. The reckless sailor, intoxicated with the pleasures of the sea-port, makes no preparation for the voyage and the storm. Then boast not thyself too much of the morrow.

But third: the most glaring and mischievous instance of this vice is procrastination. He who promises himself that he will do tomorrow what he should do today, does most flagrantly disregard this heavenly wisdom. Whatsoever thy hand findeth to do today, do it with thy might: for thou knowest not what a day may bring forth.

There are three sure results which follow every instance of the postponement of present duty: and these are additional to whatever evil the neglect of the task directly entails. One of these consequences is the waste of present time. Such delays are never practiced for the purpose of gaining time, to be diligently expended in some competing duty. This would not be the vice of procrastination: it would be prudent discretion. No: as the motive of procrastination is indolence, so, the leisure of today, thus unlawfully purchased, is very surely wasted upon some unnecessary occupation, or amusement. A second consequence is, that the duty, postponed to tomorrow, will not be done then: for will not the same disinclination which today rejected it, being thus fostered and humored by indulgence, be still more likely to refuse it tomorrow? And the third result is a self-condemned, restless, unhappy mind. The stolen leisure is never much enjoyed.

But the chief instance of the vice of procrastination, with which the Christian minister has to do, is the delay of the duty of immediate repentance. And on no subject should the warning by lifted up with so loud a voice as this: 'Boast not thyself of tomorrow' for making thy peace with God: 'for thou knowest not what a day may bring forth.' Each of the three remarks just made upon the folly of procrastination, has its most emphatic application to the delay of repentance. It results in a waste of precious time in earthly pursuits, where all was too short to make the calling and election sure. Each delay fosters and strengthens the guilty repugnance to duty. It dashes every enjoyment with the pains of an uneasy conscience; or, what is worse, sears the heart into a deadly indifference.

But none of these reasons for immediate repentance equal the one contained in the text, in urgency. "Thou knowest not what a day may bring forth." Thou knowest not whether it may bring the preoccupation and confusion of pressing events, which will enhance tenfold the difficulties of action for heaven, and give a yet more dangerous plausibility to the pleas of the heart for a future convenient season: whether it may bring sickness or delirium such as to deprive you of the power of thought and prayer, and repentance: whether it may bring a sudden death, to remove you to that world where repentance is forever too late: or whether it may introduce a catastrophe no less terrible: the termination of your day of grace, and the secret withdrawal of the Holy Ghost forever. "Except ye repent, ye shall all likewise perish." And there is no repentance nor remission in the grave to which ye haste. Whatever risk there is of your death, oh sinner, in your present state, there is the same risk of your irreparable perdition. And whatever probability there is, of our incurring either of these consequences, by which your repentance will be prevented, in the lapse of one day, that probability of everlasting ruin do you run, in postponing your repentance even to tomorrow. Do you say, that within the limits of a single day the risk is slight? God grant that it may be so! Yet in some cases it may not be slight. Were you certain of living through your three-score years and ten, and were you sure that nothing would happen, to their close, to aggravate your hardness and danger progressively, you might ascertain by a process of subordination, your chance of damnation incurred by each day's delay. I use the word chance: because to you, sudden death has all the [u]ncertainty of chance although to God there is no chance nor contingency. The first day of your three score years and ten, which you thus cast upon the chance of continued life, the risks were largely in your favor: but every time the die was thrown one element was passed over to the other side of the calculation. Thus the probabilities of safety in even one day's delay are continually diminishing, and turning against you with every day's venture. At length, the day will come, (not distinguished by any note of warning or dread from the previous days) when those probabilities will be violent against you: and yet another day, when the probability in your favor will be finally extinguished; and you will drop into hell, finding that you have run that little risk once too often. Practically then, the risk of one day's procrastination may not be small: it may be terribly great: and the season when it becomes so, is known to none but that almighty God, to whom there is no contingency or chance, but all is clear foreknowledge and providence.

Perhaps this reasoning has grated on some pious ear, as though it savored too much of the profane calculations of the gamester. Well: what is this delay of repentance till tomorrow, but a gambling with your everlasting all, upon the chances of uncertain life? The stake which you risk, oh Sinner, is an immortal soul: the price which Satan matches against it is but the beggarly "pleasures of sin for a season," and this most unequal wager is cast upon that most hazardous of all uncertainties, the continuance of the brittle thread of life. Such is the madness of delay in the soul's concerns! But is it only until tomorrow that you are delaying? Or until next year? Until middle life? Until old age? Then the danger which you incur is the more tremendous. And who is it, that so insanely dares this hazard? A soldier, a man whose very profession it is to face danger and wounds; whose daily tasks all point to the field of battle, where death holds high revel! Of all men, the soldier can with least reason be thoughtless of his soul.

Would that I could reproduce, with all the graphic power of a [George] Whitefield, that fearful picture, by which he represented the rashness of the sinner, venturing impenitent into the thick darkness of the future. He is like the blind man, traveling over a champaign, which though smooth of surface, is seamed here and there with bottomless chasms. He has advanced a number of steps, cautiously feeling his way with his staff over the level turf, until its evenness reassures his uneasiness, and he begins to proceed with confidence. But he is unconsciously nearing a frightful precipice, which heaps sheer down from the sharp brink; and there is nothing to give warning to the sightless man, of the diminishing distance between himself and it. Every step, so securely taken, diminishes that distance, even as it diminishes his caution: and when only one more separates him from it, his confidence is strongest. That one step is passed over, and his foot is upon the very edge: But he knows it not! He heedlessly descends his staff, thinking assuredly that it will touch the same even plain. It slips from his hand, so deep down into the abyss, that no sound comes up from its fall, where it strikes the sharp crags beneath. Believing that it has fallen noiselessly upon the soft turf, the blind man advances one more step to regain it; but ah: it is just one step too much. His foot is one instant poised over the empty void, the next, he seeks to plant it, as though on solid ground; he bends, he topples over: and is gone: having time only to turn to the spectators one look, ghastly with the flash of a horrible surprise! Such is the course of him who boasts himself of the morrow, postponing his preparation for eternity, though he knows not what a day may bring forth.

Is there, now, one unbeliever here, who says to himself: "Yes, I have been unwise: I must no longer tamper with an uncertain future: I must do something at once"? I ask, awakened soul: What is it that you will do? You answer, "I will read by Bible. I will reflect: I will reform: I will pray: I will begin to obey." I reply: all this is right, provided it be prefaced and accomplished with faith in the Lord Jesus Christ. When Jesus Christ was asked: "What must we do that we may work the works of God"? He replied: "This is the work of God, that ye believe on him whom He hath sent." If you essay prayer: let that prayer be the utterance of faith, from the first. If you attempt to reform and obey, see to it that your compliance is the obedience of faith. If you endeavor to feel repentance, let it be that repentance, which is the sister-grace to faith, and which Christ bestows to faith along with remission of sins. Otherwise, your beginning is all wrong: and is but a more refined form of procrastination. Until faith is exercised, nothing is done. For, it is by faith alone that you are united to Christ: and "without him you can do nothing." (John 15:5)

Christian: boast not *thyself* of the morrow. Think not that this exhortation has no application to you. As long as you are in the flesh, and not wholly purged from the stain of sin, this subtle vice of procrastination will beset you likewise. You have perhaps, applauded the warning which has now been applied to unbelievers, and as an impartial spectator, devoid of personal concern in the matter, have said well-done to the minister. Well: I claim this as your admission: by which you are sacredly bound to apply this message to your own conscience. Is there nothing that remains for you to do, for you own salvation, or that of others? Is your calling and election made sure? Is there no indwelling sin to conquer? Are you sure that you are meet for the inheritance of the saints in light? Is there no neglected duty to others to be repaired? Is there no labor for souls which you would fain complete, before you go hence? Then, boast not thyself of tomorrow; for thou knowest not what a day may bring forth. "Let your loins be girded about, and your lights burning; and ye yourselves like unto men that wait for their lord, when he will return from the wedding, that when he cometh and knocketh, they may open unto him immediately." (Luke 12:35-36)[198]

Public Calamities Caused by Public Sins

A Sermon

on

Isaiah 9:12-13

"For all this his anger is not turned away, but his hand is stretched out
still. For the people turneth not unto him that smiteth them,
neither do they seek the Lord of hosts."

Preached May 12th 1862[199] in the meadows near Franklin, Pendleton Co. Va, to
Poague's Battery of Artillery[200]

Men ask anxiously, 'When will the war end?' I reply, when God
has gained those purposes, which he proposes to himself in it.
It is not we, nor our enemies, who began this war, or who can end it;
but God. That it is his agency, is proved by this fact: that the struggle
has notoriously been precipitated against the purposes and expectations of both parties. I shall then attempt to give an answer to this
anxious question, from Sacred Scriptures. But do not fear that I propose to inflict upon you that nuisance, so justly hateful to all Christian souls, a political sermon. Far be it from me to make the sacred
pulpit a partisan in any secular debate, or an advocate of any social
plan or advantage. But the attempt will be made to apply God's own
truth to the explanation of his providences towards us. Were this
oftener done, we should see more life and interest in the Sacred Scriptures, and should derive more profit from the lessons of our Father's
chastisements.

To learn the instructions of this passage, we must [return][201] to the
eighth verse. "The Lord sent a word into Jacob and it hath lighted
upon Israel." Of this word of warning we have examples in the 28th
chapter of Deuteronomy, for instance. There God has most solemnly
declared that public and social sins should be followed by calamities.
This threat had already begun to take effect upon Israel, the kingdom
of the ten tribes, more notably than upon Judah. Its fulfillment was

plainly seen in the disasters inflicted upon them by their pagan neighbors and their own wicked kings. But the people of the kingdoms of Samaria, and especially Ephraim, the leading tribe, arrogantly refused to learn the lesson of reproof: they persisted in tracing their calamities to the wrong source, and in disregarding the hand of God in theirs. They boasted in their own ability to repair, and more than repair all their losses. "Have our enemies," said they, "ravaged our cities, leveling our dwellings of brick? We will rebuild with marble. Have they cut down our groves of sycamore fruit? We will replace them with nobler and more valuable groves of cedars." No wonder then, that a righteous God, thus despised in his awful judgments, resolves that these proud rebels shall be made to recognize his hand. He determines that he will redouble his providential blows upon them; and to this end, he causes the Assyrians, lately the enemies of Rezin king of Syria and Damascus, to join with him in an alliance against Samaria, so that the two powers, instead of hindering each others' aggressive designs against Israel, should now cooperate in ravaging him. And the Philistines, the traditiona[l] enemies of the Hebrews, were to assail him in the rear, while the Syrians and Assyrians invaded him from the East and Northeast. Between the three, Israel would be devoured, as by the gaping jaws of some wild beast.

But for all this, adds the prophet, after all this extremity of disaster, God's hand would still be stretched out to punish: and this, because the culprits refused to repent and reform. And the result of this obduracy would be, that the Lord would be provoked to proceed to their final and summary destruction: so that the heads of the commonwealth, the princes and rulers, represented by the boughs of the lofty and precious palm tree; and the rabble, represented by the lowly and worthless rushes or sedge of the open fields, should be swept away together by massacre and captivity. Thus, the very name and existence of the kingdoms of the ten tribes would be extinguished, for their impertinence.

Our text then, my brethren, is a very clear declaration of the connection between the sins of a people, and their calamities. It teaches us that when men come under God's chastening hand for their sins, his strokes will be continued until they repent and reform, or else will be repeated for their destruction. Here then, we have a divine answer to the anxious inquiry with which we began. The scourge of this war will cease, when 'we turn unto him that smiteth us, and seek the Lord of hosts.'

War is a grievous scourge, however victorious it may be. Do not we feel it to be such, in our separation from the homes and households which we love; in our hardships, cares, and dangers; in our exposure to wounds and death? Our country feels it to be a grievous calamity, by the ravaging of her teeming fields, the wasting of her wealth, the banishment and beggary of once peaceful families, and the slaughter of her sons. Surely, "God's hand is stretched out on us."

To evince farther the truth of the text, I shall attempt to establish the following propositions:

I. Public calamities are always God's chastisements upon communities for their sins. If there is anything emphatically revealed in the Bible, it is there taught that Jehovah is King of kings, and that the affairs of commonwealths are under his providential government. "Shall there be evil in a city, and the Lord hath not done it?" (Amos 3:6) Now a state is a corporate personality, possessing as such a common will, a public morality, and an organic activity, and bearing duties and moral responsibilities towards God and its neighbors. But it has no immortality: where its citizens appear before God in the other world, they stand only as individuals, and the state is resolved into its integral elements. Hence, the manifestation of the glory of God in the righteousness of his government prompts him to visit the marks of his displeasure upon them in this world, in the shape of national evils. This outward display of His righteous anger, in time, which is irregular in the case of single human beings, because His final and complete dealings with them are reserved for eternity, must be uniform and sure in the case of commonwealths, because they have no future. While therefore the individual sinner may be permitted to prosper here in his sin, the guilty state must, sooner or later, pay its penalty, in the shape of temporal calamities.

Does not universal history show this to be true? National crimes have ever been followed by national disaster and ultimate ruin. The whole drama of Assyrian, Persian, Macedonian, Roman, and modern empire, has been but a commentary upon this law – that "righteousness exalteth a nation, but sin is a reproach to any people." Does anyone reply that this is but a national law, and that the causative connection can regularly be traced between public vice and public disaster? True, and this fact is precisely to my hand. For what is natural law? Whose is the power in those regular links of causations, to which you point? That law is not in itself a force; it is but the method which we observe as characterizing the operations of Providence; and the powers which operate under the law are just those providential forces, which God at first deposited in these natural causes, and which he perpetually sustains and regulates. So that this great law of history is but one phase of the revelation of God's judgments against public sins.

I urge, next, that this is confirmed by God's express announcement of the same rule of government, in his dealings towards the commonwealth of Israel. There, obedience and public prosperity, disobedience and disaster are uniformly bound together. The whole history of Judges, Kings, and prophets is but the detailing of the execution of this law, as, for instance, it is laid down in Deuteronomy 28:1-2, 15-16. "All these blessings shall come on thee and overtake thee, if thou shalt hearken unto the voice of the Lord thy God." "But it shall come to pass, if thou will not hearken unto the voice of the Lord thy God, that all these curses shall come upon thee and overtake thee." &c. Here, again, it may be objected that this rule was peculiar, because God had separated the Hebrews to be his peculiar people, and had entered into a unique relation with them under the theocratic covenant, to be their civil ruler or king. But I reply, it is the same unchangeable and righteous God who rules, as providential Lord, over us; and since he is immutable, there cannot be any essential difference between the principles of his government there and here.

See also, the uniform declarations of the prophets against the pagan nations of the old world. Of these we have a fair specimen in Isaiah 14:4-23. There, destruction is denounced against Chaldea, even in the height of its prosperity, as the penalty of its crimes. "Prepare slaughter against his children for the iniquity of their fathers," (v. 21) is the language of the divine judgments. "This," adds the Prophet, (v. 26) "is the purpose that is proposed upon the whole earth: and this is the hand that is stretched out upon the nations." So, in every minatory message of Isaiah, of Jeremiah, of Ezekiel, of Jonah, against Assyria, Egypt, Moab, Tyrus, Edom, the doom is pronounced upon them for their sins. Will any one be hardy enough to assent, that God bore more intimate relations to these pagan nations of the old world, than to us, a Christian people nominally devoted to his service? The law is, then proved beyond dispute. Our calamities are, beyond a peradventure, God's testimony against our social and public sins as a people.

He is employing our present enemies as the rod of our correction. Here let me pointedly call your attention to this scriptural truth: that God may righteously employ them for our punishment, although they be greater sinners before him than we, and although we may be wholly in the right as to them, in this quarrel. Whether we be less sinners before God than they, it may not be appropriate for us to assent, in this hour and place, where we stand before Him as penitent supplicants: and whether we, or our adversaries are the aggressors in this war, it may not be proper for the minister of the gospel to decide; for it is not his business, when speaking as God's herald, to adjust political rights and obligations. But the decision of those points is unnecessary to my doctrine. It is painful to hear many men say, that God must be on our side, because ours is the righteous cause. I solemnly warn you, my brethren, that this does not follow. To have God surely on our side we must also be a righteous people. However innocent as to our assailants, we are miserable sinners against Him; and he often employs the more guilty as a rod to scourge, or a sword to hew, the less guilty; reserving the subsequent punishment of the more criminal instrument to some future day, which seems to his sovereignty suitable. Hear the prophet: Isaiah 10:5-6, 12&c. "O Assyrian, the rod of mine anger, and the staff in their hand is mine indignation. I will send him against an hypocritical nation, and against the people of my wrath will I give him a charge, to take the spoil and to take the prey, and to tread them down like the mire of the streets . . . Wherefore, it shall come to pass, that when the Lord hath performed his whole work upon mount Zion and on Jerusalem, I will punish the fruit of the stout heart of the king of Assyria, and the glory of his high looks," &c. Babylon had no quarrel with the little kingdom of Judah. Their territories were not coterminous; they had no relations whatever with each other. In the war between them, the Chaldean was wholly the aggressor. Nor was Judea more idolatrous or guilty than the pagan nation. But God permitted the aggression; he righteously employed the nefarious and arrogant instrument, to chasten his disobedient children for a time, by defeat and captivity. Yet did blood-stained Babylon escape her appropriate doom? Nay verily. When the secret and sovereign purposes of God were served with her, in due time she also was punished for all her crimes, inclusive of this unprovoked invasion and ravage of Judea; punished, not with a captivity of seventy years, but with a vengeance which blotted her forever from the face of the earth, and made her palaces the abodes of owls and satyrs.[202]

II. What then are the sins which provoke public calamities? In one sense, it may be answered, that as the individuals make up the nation, so the aggregate guilt is made up of the numberless sins of single persons. It is conceivable that a nation which committed no organized crimes, might yet become exceedingly guilty, and pluck down on itself the curse of God, if the individuals composing it were generally criminal. But probably no such instance can ever occur in fact, because as are the people, such are the governments. But it is clearly taught in the sacred Scriptures, that some sins are far more momentous in God's sight than the ordinary transgressions of private persons. And among these are, unquestionably, the overt sins of kings, rulers, commanders, and representative men. So saith Isaiah [9]:16, "For the leaders of this people cause them to err; and they that are led of them are destroyed." The pagans even had perspicuity enough to see this truth: Virgil, following Homer, represents the Greeks at Troy as scourged by the anger of the gods for the follies of their commanders.[203] The same truth is apparent in the very arrangements of Providence. The people actually suffer for the faults of their rulers; the sins of parents bring obloquy and poverty upon their children; and the acts of leaders have a representative power, with both God and man. These heads, in their official acts, impersonate the commonwealth; for they act in its name: indeed it is through them that the commonwealth acts. In their private and personal character they are representative exemplars. And as God's purposes in his national judgments are so largely declarative, it is appropriate that He should judge the people by the acts and characters of those by whom they are represented. Especially is this just in the case of a people like us, who boast of being republicans, and select our own rulers by vote, according to our own option. The acts and characters of our rulers and legislators are still more strictly ours; since it is by our choice they are clothed with their representative functions.

Have we then delegated power to bad men, as chief magistrates, commanders of armies, legislators? Do these representatives of our public morality despise God's laws, profane his name and his Sabbath, set to the younger citizens an example of profligacy, and pervert their sacred position as executors of justice, to work wrong and oppression upon God's people? If this is so: we may easily understand why his hand is stretched out still, and his anger is not turned away from us.

Again; the army of a people may be justly regarded as a representative body. It is composed of a selection of its most active citizens. It is the nation's organ of defense. It is, in a certain sense, the nation's right hand, and the executioner of its will against its enemies. God may therefore be reasonably expected to judge a people according to the guilt of its army. If this public organ is lewd, profane, drunken, lawless; if this sword of a nation's justice, which should be a terror to evildoers, and a praise to them that do well, makes itself the implement of oppression and violence against the innocent and peaceful, what more natural than that God's indignation should rise against it, and that he should make the guilty agent a means of calamity and overthrow to the people it was appointed to protect? If our people, in the very act of appealing to the Lord of Hosts by the ordeal of battle, is found lifting up to him a hand foul with crime, will not He blight and wither it with his righteous curse? Our army may be called our people's shield; if now when we hold up this buckler of our defense in the face of mankind and the heavens, to meet the assaults of our enemies, it be found all over defiled with names of blasphemy, what may we expect; but that an insulted God will shiver it with the lightning of his wrath?

As the leaders of a people are representative men, so its capital city may be regarded as their representative place. So this agrees [with] the prophet. (ch. 7:8-9) "For the head of Syria is Damascus, and the head of Damascus is Rezin . . . and the head of Ephraim is Samaria, and the head of Samaria is Remaliah's son." (Pekah) The metropolis of a country is a miniature of the nation. It is the habitation of its rulers and men of chief influence. Its customs and manners are exemplars for every other community in the nation. Thither repair the strangers who visit the country, and from what they see there, they take their impressions of the whole. If now that capital is the chief seat of disorder; if the evil example of the selected rulers and representatives of the people make it the Sodom of the whole land, if its halls are fowl with bribery and venality, if its streets echo with the din of violence and the cry of riot and murder, if while the guilty nation bleeds and groans under the rod of the Lord, its mansions reel with sensual joys, it will not be strange that an offended God surrenders it to capture and sack. It was thus that guilty Jerusalem, more than once, sealed her own overthrow.

III. The purposes of God in his judgments are either to punish, or to amend; they are either for vengeance or for paternal correction. The Scriptures reveal no other object in his afflictive dispensations than these two. Now whichsoever of these may be his secret purpose, it will assuredly be accomplished. Hath not God said, "My purpose shall stand, and I will do all my pleasure"? The men of Sodom and righteous Lot behold the same fiery tempest sweeping over their dwelling: to the former it meant extermination; to the latter, wholesome correction. Of his erring children God says, (Psalm 89:30-33) "If they forsake my law and walk not in my judgments; if they break my statutes and keep not my commandments; then will I visit their transgression with the rod, and their iniquity with stripes. Nevertheless my lovingkindness will I not utterly take from him, nor suffer faithfulness to fail."

If the purpose of God in national judgments is only vindicatory, and he designs the extermination of the guilty subjects, then I can understand how He may arrest them while they are still impenitent. I can comprehend that it is His fearful but righteous purpose to make the criminals without excuse by these impressive warnings of coming vengeance, and summons to repentance; and then, after they are slighted He leaves them to ripen for their doom in an accurse and treacherous prosperity. This is just the solution which was given to the Psalmist Asaph (Psalm 73:12-19) in the sanctuary of God, concerning the prosperity of the wicked. "Behold these are the ungodly who prosper in the world; they increase in riches . . . I went into the sanctuary of God; then understood I their end. Surely thou didst set them in slippery places; thou castest them down into destruction . . . As a dream when one awaketh, so, O Lord, when thou awakest, thou shalt despise their image." God placed before Abraham in prophetic vision the contrasted career of his posterity, and of the Amorites, among whom he was sojourning. The chosen people were to be chastened with a long pilgrimage, and a bondage for four generations in Egypt, while the idolatrous Canaanites reveled in the prosperous enjoyment of cities walled up to the skies, and of land flowing with milk and honey. It was because "the iniquity of the Amorites was not yet full." (Genesis 15:16) Because God had purposes of mercy towards Israel, therefore he must needs correct his backslidings until he repented. But from the Amorites, his partial judgments were withdrawn, leaving them obdurate and progressively impious; because the secret purpose of God towards them was extermination. So when I see the disciplinary strokes of God upon a people suspended (as upon the great unchristian nation of the French),[204] leaving them unreformed and impenitent, I can only explain it by the supposition, that He purposes to leave them for a time, after thus uttering his testimony against their impiety in the presence of their cotemporaries, to ripen for some fiercer wrath in the future.

But if the design of God's discipline is paternal, then I see not how it is possible that it can be happily suspended, until the subjects of it are brought to sincere repentance. "For all this his anger is not turned away, but his hand is stretched out still. For the people turneth not unto him that smiteth them, neither do they seek the Lord of hosts." Because penitence is not produced, therefore the correction must continue. The majesty, the wisdom, the very goodness of God require it. Shall God take up the rod for the purpose of turning his children thereby away from their folly, and lay it down again with the purpose unfulfilled? Where would be His wisdom? Shall the Almighty contend thus with his puny creature, and cease, leaving the victory in his vile hand? When the parent is impelled by his fidelity to his child's welfare, to chasten him for his good, his very love urges him not to cease until hearty submission is produced. For if he does, the ruinous insubordination of the child is only hardened, the incomplete discipline results in unmingled mischief, and every pang uselessly inflicted on the child becomes a gratuitous cruelty. Thus the wise parent is constrained by his very love, to go on, although it may be with a bleeding heart, and to continue the stripes until his authority is acknowledged.

Now then, brethren; do you wish to claim this chastising God as your heavenly Father, or your avenging Judge? If he is to be found the former, the war will not end, until 'this people turneth unto him that smiteth them, and seeketh the Lord of hosts,' by a genuine repentance and reform. If the calamity ends otherwise, short of our extermination, its meaning must be the following: that God's secret purposes in it were not paternal, but vindicatory; that having seen our sins outrage his holiness and beneficence until his honour demands a vindication before the world, he has poured out upon us this vial of wrath, as a sufficient prelibation of destruction to warn this generation of mankind, in our example, that he hath not forgotten his judgments; and that then, he leaves us in righteous anger, to mature our impenitency for some still more condign retribution. Oh! shall the scourge be arrested thus? Shall so fearful and ghastly a victory be won by us? Far better for us, that we, a sinning people, should lie groaning under the rod for as many generations as Israel served in Egypt; if thereby we are taught to avouch the Lord as our God indeed.

IV. And now, that we may ascertain whether a happy end of our calamities is near, all we have to learn is, whether our people are turning unto Him that smiteth them, and are seeking the Lord of Hosts. Perhaps it is not best for me to undertake to answer this question. It will be better that each one of you shall decide it for yourself, as to your own heart and life; it is these for which you are primarily responsible. And as we are taught that the kingdom of heaven is within us, and cometh not with observation, it does not befit a fallible creature to say, Lo here! or Lo there! too confidently, concerning the sinfulness or repentance of his fellow men. But alas! There are signs of reckless impenitence so alarming, as to compel every thoughtful patriot to harbor conscious fears. When I look at the slumberous condition of many of the churches, at the avarice and extortion which absorb the hearts of so many at home, at the profanity which echoes through our camps and through many of our high places, at the boastful self-reliance which inflates so many minds, at the loathsome drunkenness, whose streams, once partially restrained, are now breaking out again with such volume, at the sins of violence which defy the skies, I am compelled to fear, that God's angry hand is not soon to be withdrawn from us.

And these are the things which frighten me, with reference to the issue of our contest. It is not the countless levies, and mammoth armies of our foes; it is not their determined malignity or obstinate rage; it is not their hundreds of cannon nor myriads of bayonets pointed at our breasts; it is the sins of our people and soldiers. Hear that oath! (A loud and profane oath heard in the distance.) Such an insult to the Almighty God to whom we have made our appeal in drawing the sword, appalls my heart far more than the loudest thunders of our enemies' artillery. And such sinners, however bold in the day of battle, are the worst foes of the country for which they profess to fight.

The conclusion of the whole matter, my brethren, is this: There is one way, and only one, by which our people may ensure a happy issue out of our struggle beyond a peradventure. This is by hearty reform. I do not say that God is pledged to reward it with precisely that form of deliverance on which our hearts are set: we are too blind to be allowed by our Heavenly Father to elect the particular forms of our own well-being. But if we turn to Him that smiteth us, He will assuredly restore to us a time [of] prosperity and honour. Not only are we assured of this by the scriptural truths now established; but in the midst of his readiness to forgive and bless, does he not exhibit? We have been, thus far, sustained against our gigantic foe beyond our own expectations. Again and again has success against the most fearful odds been granted, at the critical hour. We should regard each of these interpositions as a species of overture from God to us, encouraging us to claim his paternal shelter against our foes, by repenting and serving Him. By these mercies God is making proof to us, whether we are suitable objects for his favor. Hear Him say, O my brethren, by these events: "If ye be willing and obedient, ye shall eat the good of the land; but if ye refuse and rebel, ye shall be devoured with the sword; for the mouth of the Lord hath spoken it." (Isaiah 1:18-19) Bear with the entreaty of one who would willingly die for this cause and country, that you will turn from sin, and walk in the fear of God. This, believe me; this, which is your Christian duty, is your truest patriotism! "And may the Lord bless you and keep you. The Lord make his face shine upon you, and be gracious unto you: The Lord lift up his countenance upon you, and give you peace."[205]

Our Ineffectual Prayers[206]

A Sermon

on

James 4:3

"Ye ask, and receive not, because ye ask amiss."

Preached near Mossy Creek, Augusta, Va. on the afternoon of May 18, 1862,[207] to the 44th Va. Regiment[208]

Brethren.

The subject of *our ineffectual prayers* should be one of lively interest to all of us. There has been, apparently, much 'asking' among us. Often the Sabbath witnesses four formal prayers, in which we all profess to unite our voices and hearts, in a general concert. Many praying circles weekly, or perhaps daily, offer up their social petitions to God with less publicity. Every Christian waits before his God in secret, every day. Many large and varied requests are urged with him habitually, and with every form of repetition. But, alas; there has been much less 'receiving' than asking. Our prayers are, in seeming, abundant, and our answers scanty. Do you say, it is unsafe for short-sighted man to judge positively in this matter; because many of the prayers of Christians may be graciously accepted by their Father, and yet not specifically granted, for the reason that omniscient love has seen it was more merciful to withhold than to give: or because our God may purpose a full answer, but he may have seen that the fullness of time has not yet come; or because he is bestowing the gift, but in a way so different from our expectations, that we scarcely recognize it? I grant it all: but, after making allowance for such explanations, in every case to which they can be fairly applied, we must admit that a multitude of our requests remain wholly unanswered. We have prayer for growth in grace: Are we indeed advancing to the measure of the stature of perfect men in Christ Jesus? We have invoked the witness of the Spirit with our spirits: Are we rejoicing in hope of the glory of

God? We have prayed for revival, and for the redemption of the souls of our heedless comrades. But alas: the ways of Zion still mourn, and our fellows are even now falling around us, unprepared, by battle and disease. We supplicate God to deliver our beloved country from the destroying sword: but enemies throng around her in increasing numbers, and assail her with more determined ferocity. Surely, we ask, and we receive not.

But see, how positive is the connection established by the promises of God, between believing prayer, and the answer. "For every one that asketh receiveth: and he that seeketh findeth: and to him that knocketh it shall be opened."[209] "And all things whatsoever ye shall ask in prayer, believing, ye shall receive."[210] "Verily, verily, I say unto you, whatsoever ye shall ask the Father in my name, he will give it you."[211] Are these pledges abrogated? Is prayer now an unmeaning and fruitless form? Of old, it was not so: when holy men prayed in faith, heaven was moved, and God stooped to earth. There was a time, when the saints "through faith subdued kingdoms, wrought righteousness, obtained promises, stopped the mouths of lions, quenched the violence of fire, escaped the edge of the sword, out of weakness were made strong, waxed valiant in fight, turned to flight the armies of the aliens."[212] "Elias was a man subject to like passions as we are, and he prayed earnestly that it might not rain: and it rained not on the earth by the space of three years and six months. And he prayer again, and the heavens gave rain, and the earth brought forth her fruit."[213] It was true in those days, at least, that "the effectual, fervent prayer of a righteous man availed much."

But He to whom we pray is "the Father of lights, in whom is no variableness, neither shadow of turning." How then, can we suspect that God is no longer true to his promises? Nay: "Let Him be true, but every man a liar." The solution of our ineffectual prayers is to be found not in God's unfaithfulness, but in our unbelief: "We ask, and receive not: because we ask amiss." Let us then, examine the nature of our prayers, in order that we may both justify our God, and amend what is amiss in ourselves.

First, may not one reason of our disappointment be suggested by the words following the text? We "ask amiss that we may consume it upon our lusts." This word, lusts, usually bears, to our apprehension, the meaning of sensual appetites and desires; of something both unlawful, and gross. We misapprehend the sense of the sacred writers in it. True, in the New Testament, it usually signifies the bodily desires; but desires are not therefore unlawful, merely because they are bodily. The word which signifies *evil concupiscence*, whether of body or spirit, is a different one: and this word, "lusts," suggests no more by its proper meaning, than man's natural desires for natural enjoyment. Perhaps, when you heard the Apostle James rebuke his readers for offering to God, prayers prompted by their own lusts, you had before your mind a picture of some soul so besotted in superstition and gross ignorance, as to insult the holiness of God, by asking of him only material good, for the purpose of lavishing it in foul and criminal orgies of sensual excess. And it is not strange that you felt, this picture was too monstrous to be verified in your petitions to God. But you limit the charge of the Apostle unwarrantably. He brings this general accusation; that if any man is prompted chiefly by the wish to expend God's gifts in natural gratification, legitimate, or illegitimate: that man asks amiss. If the propensity you thus seek to gratify be unlawful, then plainly, your request is an insult to both the righteousness and purity of God. But if it be innocent, still it may not be proper for you to make it your predominant motive. This is inordinate: it savors of the sin of idolatry: its tendency is to dethrone God, and exalt self as the chief end: it is inconsistent with that supreme love for God, and zeal for his glory, which are the very essence of Christianity. Need we be surprised that even a merciful and pardoning God, who receives the petitions of sinners through their Advocate, Christ, should consider himself constrained by his own honor, to refuse such prayers as these?

Now then: when you ask for the salvation of comrades, of children, are you moved only by natural affection for them? Natural affection is right in its place. But if you give it the supreme place, what is this but saying to the Searcher of Hearts, that you greatly desire that his attributes and mercies shall be made to subserve the advantage of those creatures whom you love; but care not whether they shall subserve the glory of their Creator and rightful proprietor, and Redeemer? When you ask independence and just government, and prosperity, for our beloved country, is it merely from pride: from anger: from the desire that you, and those dear to you by natural ties, may enjoy the material good of a prosperous commonwealth? Or is it chiefly because you desire to see the righteousness of God's providential rule over nations manifested, and the resources of a free and happy people consecrated to his glory? You pray for the prosperity of Zion: Is it, that party spirit may be gratified: or, that Zion's Redeemer may "see of the travail of his soul, and be satisfied"? I beseech you, examine in this manner, all your prayers: and see whether you do not 'ask amiss, that you may consumer it upon your lusts.'

Second. It may be that we err in allowing some other dependence than Christ's righteousness and intercession to insinuate itself into our prayers. Do not be too confident. I beseech you, in rejecting this surmise. I know that you are all members of the great Protestant communions, which hold the doctrine of gracious justification as "the article of a standing or falling Church"[214]: and that you are all familiar with your Bibles, where they say that 'no man cometh unto the Father but by Christ.' I know how you have been taught to recite in your catechisms the very definition of prayer, as "the offering up of our desires unto God, in the name of Christ."[215] I know that you have been instructed in the things of God, far beyond that gross ignorance, which avows the vain expectation of procuring his favor by alms, or mortifications, or fastings or idle repetitions. I hear you begin and end your prayers with the orthodox formularies, which make due mention of the name of Jesus Christ as your only plea.

But, brethren: our hearts are deceitful. Self-righteousness is a potent, cunning, treacherous enemy. Be not so certain that it is expelled, merely by the use of correct form of words. "Leviathan is not so tamed." Thrust out self-righteousness by the door: and it will return by the window. Pride, like a Proteus, when evicted in one form, will assume another, and re-enter unobserved. You have approached the mercy-seat with heartfelt confession of guilt: and have expressly repudiated all dependence on your works and almsgivings. But may it not be, that after this, a lingering hope is harbored, that now God must hear you, because of the merit of you contrition, or of your self-abnegation; or of your strong faith; or of your perseverance in prayer? What is this but self-dependence? You must not only say, but feel, that your contrition, however genuine, your faith itself, however scriptural, constitute no claim of merit whatsoever in themselves; and that the only reason God may not justly reject your prayer, notwithstanding the truest faith, is, that He has condescended, of his own free grace, to promise to Jesus Christ the reception of all who come in his name. The only merit is that of our Redeemer's righteousness and intercession. If any other trust intrudes, you ask amiss.

Third. It is more probable, that there is a lack of earnestness and fervency in our prayers. This lamentable defect betrays itself in our lack of expectation and pointed desire, and in the absence of watchfulness. We do not "watch unto prayer." We do not anxiously wait for God, and stand looking to see whether the answer to our request be coming. How often do we remember at night, what it was, for which we prayed in the morning? Would it not often tax the recollection of a Christian congregation, to state the main points of the prayer offered by the minister, before they had left the house of worship? And this shameful forgetfulness is not wholly the fault of the people: but the minister also not seldom, shows, by the aimless, and pointless language which flows at random from his mouth, that he is professedly praying, not because either he or the people have any heartfelt errand to press at the throne of grace, but because they feel it incumbent on them, to comply with the customary form of prayer. Now, true desire is always definite. If a man wants, he wants something: and he will be very sure not to forget that thing. But so little in earnest are we, that the answer to many of our prayers would probably take us by surprise, if it were granted.

Now praying thus, can we wonder that we do not receive? Such petitions are an insult to the kindness of the benefactor to whom they are addressed. We go to a human friend, and tell him of some great exigency which threatens our happiness, or perhaps, our very existence. We tell him that he alone has the means of our deliverance; and we beseech him, of his compassion, to extend to us the aid which is for our very lives. He replies by reminding us that it is no small thing which we ask, but we are in substance requiring him to sacrifice for us his own dearest interests. We reply: "Yea, we know this: but we thought that our extremity, and your love would combine, to make you feel that even such a request was not too presumptuous." He then, moved with compassion, decides that he will give our request favorable consideration: and that his answer shall be made known when the day of our necessity is fully come. Well: the season passes by: and our friend has generously determined with himself, moved by his magnanimous and tender heart, that he will even make the sacrifices necessary to grant us relief. He comes: he begins to announce his noble purpose: when lo! he finds us oblivious of the whole transaction, of the pretended exigency, and of our own request. What must he conclude? but that our anxiety and danger were a mockery, and that his compassion has been shamefully abused. He will turn away in honest indignation, saying: "Henceforth, if these hypocrites fall into trouble, let them help themselves, if they can"!

But if such righteous anger is natural in a fellow creature, what should we not expect, when we mock, with a similar heedlessness, the majestic King of Kings? We, who are guilty worms in his sight, thrust ourselves through all the shining ranks of the angels, and ask that the Almighty shall turn to us, and divide his attention between the vast affairs of his universal empire, and the worthy praises of the heavenly principalities, and our little woes and sins! We claim of him assistance purchased for us by the blood of his own Son. And when he stoops with infinite condescension to bestow it, he finds that we have forgotten our own petitions and his mercy and majesty, amidst the trivial, and perhaps, sinful toys of the hour! Well is it for us, that God's ways are as high above ours as the heavens above the earth: otherwise, such prayers would not only fail of answers, but bring down on us the swift lightening of His wrath.

In seeking such gifts as those of redemption, from such a God, it is reasonable that we should be not only honest and sincere in our petitions, but fervent. God and his grace deserve such homage at our hands. You may object that fervor of emotion is a thing to which it is difficult to affix an exact measure. Perhaps you ask, whether I require that your heads should conceive, and your hearts feel the full moment of heavenly things, in order that God may recognize you as coming "in spirit and it truth." No: The man lives not who does, nor can appreciate, either with head or heart, the blessings of redemption and the woes of the second death. They are unutterable: we are finite. Nor do I require that the believer of feeble soul shall feel as large a flood of sacred emotion, as the great and blazing spirit; nor that he who is naturally phlegmatic should burn with the same warmth, as the ardent, impulsive nature: nor that the same believer shall feel, in every hour of lassitude, of distraction, of depression, the same liveliness of emotion, which attended his first espousal to Christ, and the seasons of greatest elasticity of animal spirits. But is it not reasonable, that whether we be calm or passionate, light of spirit, or heavy, we shall be at least *in thorough earnest*, whenever we ask the attention of our God to our wants? It is entirely conceivable that a man may be terribly in earnest, and yet very deliberate. No such measure is proposed for the efficacy of our prayers, as that they shall be uttered with strong crying and tears, or that they must be warmed by so many degrees of conscious emotion, in order to be acceptable. But it is conceived that God exacts of us this standard: that whether our emotion be much or little, our practical estimate of his gifts at the time shall truly place them above all earthly gifts. He demands of us, that we shall at least, not give the world our preference over him, in our desires and efforts. You go to your closet, my brother, at morning, and there ask God that you may "grow in grace, and in the knowledge of the Lord." Do you then go to your place of business, and demonstrate by your conduct, that your soul is more thoroughly set upon growing in wealth? This earthly object may be very soberly and calmly pursued; and yet, it may be the dominant object of your heart. Or did you go to your closet to pray that a beloved child might become an heir of heaven, and then go forth and exhibit more practical zeal that he might be fashionable or distinguished? What I claim for God is, that, though the temper in which you pursue his gifts be sober, calm, deliberate, it shall be your dominant temper: it must give Him and His redemption the sincere preference over all created good. Otherwise you ask amiss.

For, it would not be proper, that God should bestow Himself upon a soul which thus treats him with comparative depreciation: All the vicarious merit of Christ's righteousness wrought in place of the sinner cannot make it proper. What: shall man thus tacitly inform God, in his very prayers, that he idolatrously prefers self, and selfish good, to those pure and heavenly gifts, which Christ died to purchase for him with his precious blood: to dispense which he now sits upon the throne of the Universe, governing all things for the Church's sake: to minister which mighty angels fly on their zealous errands: which all heaven admires and studies: and shall such a petitioner expect success? Should the Almighty answer such prayers, he would seem to make Himself an accomplice in our degrading estimate of his blessings; and to assent to the dishonor done himself. He will not do it. Surely it is little enough to demand of a beggar, that he shall not disparage the boon which he receives gratuitously.

Fourth. We ask amiss, because we do not enough follow up our petitions by our labors. We pray for many excellent things: but we fail to second our prayers by the appointed exertions for receiving them. Thus we at once evince our unfitness to receive them, and betray our lack of earnestness. Do not tell me: that man is wholly dependent for spiritual good, upon Divine Grace. I know it. Yet this hearty exertion in the use of means is regarded by God as an expression of pious desire, just as essential as prayer itself. And this, for two reasons. One is, that God has established the connection between means and results as regularly in the kingdom of grace, as of nature. The fact that he alone can give, does not destroy the fact that we receive only through the appointed instruments. Hence, if we have truly prayed, we shall be rationally impelled to work for our object, as truly as though prayer were naught, and our efforts the only efficient cause. The other reason is, that God knows we are active beings; and the law of our nature simply forbids our inactivity, where our souls are profoundly interested. Where we desire, there we must strive: it is our nature. Here is a mother, whose darling child is writhing in pain from disease. She is told that she neither needs to do, nor can do, any thing more than others have done: that a professional physician, and hireling nurse are administering all the practicable remedies: that she must know her skill cannot equal theirs: and therefore, the reasonable thing for her, is to sit perfectly still, and confine herself to mental aspirations for the relief of her child. She admits all your facts: but will she sit passive? Can she? It is not possible: reasonable or not, efforts she must make, for her loved one's deliverance; if from no other cause, from the uncontrollable prompting to seek relief for her own longing of soul, in exertions.

So, God properly judges, that where there is no persevering effort for the good sought, there is no true earnestness in our seeking. Do you not find sufficient solution for the failure of answer, my brother, in your neglect and indolence in religious labors? You prayed last Sabbath for growth in grace. Now it is by the knowledge and practice of God's will revealed in the gospel, that one grows in grace. Did you, then, after uttering that prayer, devote your leisure to the study of the Scriptures, and the regulation of your own heart and conduct, in that business-like way, in which you would use the means for any secular end? You prayed for self-acquaintance: Did you then dedicate your efforts to that painstaking self-examination, which is the appointed way to self-knowledge? Or were your leisure hours spent in unnecessary talk, or useless lounging? You who are parents, have prayed for the conversion of your children. Have you also been as diligent to teach them that saving knowledge of the truth, by which the soul is renewed? Let us ask ourselves all these questions: and we shall see, why we ask and receive not.

Fifth: A farther explanation may be found in these words of [the] 66th Psalm: "If I regard iniquity in my heart, the *Lord* will not hear me." He who lives in secret sin, whose heart goes, unrestrained, after his unlawful desires, cannot be received at a propitious throne of grace. And this is not because a true repentance, and a sincere evangelical obedience, have merit in themselves to purchase the answer: their imperfection, and their own dependence on communicated grace, forbid this. But they are the tests of that faith in the soul, by which Christ's merit, our soul propitiation, is embraced. Faith without works is dead. Moreover: the honor and purity of God cannot permit him, (not even through the virtue of the glorious righteousness of our Substitute) to communicate Himself to the rebel who is outraging his law and holiness by intentional sin. Even the omnipotence of the Almighty cannot separate the inevitable connection between sin and death, and make an immortal soul truly, and permanently blessed, in its disobedience. Hence, allowed sin, and successful prayer are incompatible. Let us search, then, my brethren, whether some plain duty neglected, some known sin entertained, be not between us and our God. So long as it is there, it must be a black cloud to keep out every ray of his spiritual blessings.

And now that we have made this short and partial inquiry into the nature of our prayers: now that we have seen the selfishness of their motives, the self-righteousness of their dependences, the lukewarmness of their desires, the lack of seconding diligence in effort, and the sinfulness of our lives: is there any longer any wonder that we ask, and receive not? Is not God's faithfulness abundantly justified? I protest unto you, that when I estimate the poverty of the prayers which we offer up to God, instead of finding any remaining evidence of a failure of His promises, instead of seeing him any longer in a reluctant or grudging attitude, I wonder that the Church receives as many answers to prayer, as we actually experience: I seem to behold God bending over his unworthy children, with both hands full of generous gifts for them, and a heart anxiously yearning for the joy of bestowing them, watching eagerly on every side for the first sign of such true desire as his own honor will permit Him to bless, that he may at once answer it with a shower of mercies. Brethren: our God is not unfaithful: "we ask, and we receive not, because we ask amiss." Let us prove him now, with true, scriptural prayer, and see if he will not pour us out a blessing, such, that there shall not be room to contain it.

He who only offers ineffectual prayers, virtually does not pray at all. How many, by this rule, are living prayerless lives! A Christian without prayer! Sorrowful anomaly! He is separated from the only fountain of life. He is a branch severed from the vine-stock. Brethren: we must pray, with "the effectual, fervent prayer of the righteous," or we perish.

God's Eminent Mercy

A Sermon

on

Psalm 108:4

"For thy mercy is great above the heavens."

Preached in the Stonewall Brigade, on the morning of June 15th 1862[216] near Mt. Meridian, Augusta County, Va.[217]

Brethren.

There are a few facts, simple and indisputable, that show man to be in a melancholy condition, which he seems very little to apprehend.

The punishment of everlasting death is threatened against all sin, by inflexible truth and justice. "The wages of sin is death." (Romans 6:23) God is one who "will by no means clear the guilty." (Exodus 34:7)

All of us have sinned: yea we were born sinners, "being by nature children of wrath, even as others." (Ephesians 2:3) Conviction has taken place, under the joint testimony of God and our own consciences.

Sentence of condemnation is already passed: "He that believeth not, is condemned already." (John 3:18) Hence, escape is impossible: unless the supreme magistrate of the universe may be induced to pardon.

We have no guarantee that the execution of this sentence may not take place any day. "The God in whose hand our breath is, and whose are all our ways, we have not glorified." (Deuteronomy 5:23) We are warned: "Boast not thyself of tomorrow; for thou knowest not what a day may bring forth." (Proverbs 27:1)

Is it not a correct simile, then, to compare the world of sinners to a prison, occupied by condemned criminals? There is this aggravation of the state; that these convicted culprits of God's government may be executed without a moment's warning; whereas, in man's government, a distant day is fixed, and the wretch's fate does not take him by surprise. And on the other hand, there is this alleviation; that sinners are allowed sundry temporal comforts, while detained as 'prisoners of hope.'

How little do thoughtless men behave as such creatures should? What indifference to their doom! What levity! The face of society wears far more the appearance of a festival, where men are celebrating their secure triumphs, than of a doleful prison, where they are awaiting their death with no hope except that of reprieve.

There have, indeed, been cases in actual history, when feasts were held in dungeons of despair. They tell us that during the reign of terror in Paris, under the terrible rule of the Committee of Public Safety, as it was called by a species of bitter irony, and of the Revolutionary Tribunal, a multitude of pretended political offenders were confined in the state prisons, awaiting trial. Few escaped sentence of death in that ferocious court; and execution followed swift upon the heels of judgment. Daily the public prosecutor came to knock at the doors of the prisons, and read a list of the names of those who were ordered for trial. None knew on what day their turns would come. At the time of these daily visits of death, we are told, a momentary chill of dread seemed to fall upon all spirits. But as soon as the doomed persons were separated from their company, the tide of gaiety rolled back again; luxurious meals were spread in the prisons: music resounded: and the hours were hastened with amusements, amours, and private theatricals.

Such, you exclaim, was the ghastly recklessness of atheist France! But is not this shocking picture a fair illustration of the behavior of the world of unpardoned sinners? They too are shut up, prisoners, awaiting the dreaded summons: the chief point of difference is, that it is not unjust. Death makes his frequent rounds, and calls out some, no one can predict whom, for execution. Yet how are you, meantime, spending your hours?

Let us return now, to the subterraneous vaults of those prisons of state; let us suppose that the news of pardon, release, acquittal, were rumored through them. Would not the hardened inmates have gathered in breathless interest, to hear the terms? But can I hope for so much attention from you, condemned sinners, while I speak of the mercy of God to you? Shall I arrest the tide of indifference or levity, while I tell of a pardon bought with blood, from a worse death than that of the reeking scaffold, offered to you with a generous compassion which towers above the skies? Listen, for once, O brethren, while I explain the greatness of this transcendent mercy of God.

It is not unusual with the sacred writers, to exalt the divine superiority, by comparing it to the elevation of the heavens above the earth. In this strain God says by Isaiah, "As the heavens are higher than the earth, so are my ways higher than your ways, and my thoughts than your thoughts." (55:9) In many things are His ways and character in splendid contrast with man's: in their stability, in their wisdom, in their power, in their vast range. But in nothing is the superiority of God to man so admirable, as in his exercise of mercy towards the guilty. The Psalmist seems to behold the conception of this attribute rising and expanding like a vision, as vast as lovely, until it towers above the heavens, and fills the whole firmament, and floods all the earth, with its mild glory. Let it be my delightful task today to justify this encomium, by unfolding so much as I am able of the traits of God's mercy to sinners. In doing this, I shall at once explain and commend them.

1. The foundation for the excellency of God's mercy is laid in this, that He exercises it without any expense to His law. The understanding of this important truth must be gained, my hearers, in order that you may apprehend all the rest of His mercy. When other rulers pardon those justly condemned, it is at the expense of the law's inflexibility, of its claims, and of its threats. The ordained penalty is disappointed: 'mercy boasteth itself against judgment.' Law and justice must be violated, in order that the criminal may enjoy his impunity. But with God alone it is not so: because his infinite wisdom has found a way to satisfy both justice and mercy, in the same transaction. This he does, by both punishing and pardoning the same sins. Is this a paradox? It is one of those seeming paradoxes, which is true: yea, a blessed truth. And this is the scriptural solution: that God, having appointed his Divine Son as smited to humanity, our Substitute, laid the guilt of our sins to his account: and fully punished it in Christ Jesus; while we, the doers of the sins, are freely pardoned in believing on him. Thus, when eternal rectitude and truth prohibited the proper and beneficial pardon of sin without a penal substitute, and none could be found

adequate beneath the throne of God, His mercy was so great above the heavens, that He freely gave His own, co-equal Son as the victim, so that our sins might be punished in him, and pardoned to us.

It is this which renders the mercy of God so secure and precious. When man pardons at the expense of the law, the forgiven criminal feels that he owes his impunity to the disregard of justice, which requires, and of truth, which threatens, his punishment. Should these resume their rightful sway, he must fall again under the curse of his sin, and perish. But our pardon is as much founded on justice as compassion. "Mercy and truth have met together: righteousness and peace have kissed each other." (Psalm 85:10) The same unchangeable attributes which must, else, have stood inflexibly opposed to our escape, now array themselves beside us, and defend the rectitude of our release, when we penitently plead the sacrifice of Christ in our stead.

2. Because among men, mercy is exercised at the expense of law, only a few of the justly condemned can be safely pardoned. And these favored instances must be selected among the offenders whose intention was least malignant, and whose crimes admitted the most palliation. Should forgiveness be promiscuously offered to all, and should the most hardened and flagrant offenders be pardoned along with the rest, then all order and justice are overthrown: lawless anarchy, riots over everything valued in the commonwealth.

But God's mercy, more extensive than man's, can be safely offered to all, and to "the chief of sinners." For Christ hath so fulfilled and honored the law, both in its precept and penalty, that justice herself, as well as her sister, mercy, is more glorified in the substitution, than she would be in the sinner's own destruction. The more offenders are pardoned, the more is the law magnified. Thus no fear holds mercy back, lest too many should escape: no question need be asked concerning degrees of aggravation. God can remit the blackest crime, without relinquishing in the least his abhorrence of crime. None are excepted, but those who exclude themselves. The herald of mercy is authorized to go forth, as I am now, and proclaim forgiveness to every creature, and to the blackest criminal; even though he be foul with murder. "The blood of Christ cleanseth from all sin." (I John 1:7)

3. God pardons many and repeated offences of the same person. Men talk of mercy as possible towards the first offence, or perhaps the second. But a few repetitions makes forgiveness with them impossi-

ble. When they are able to point to the repetitions of the offence, this is with them the sternest count in their accusation, and the strongest ground for refusing farther mercy. When Christ's disciples, not yet fully enlightened by His example and Spirit, asked him how far their mercy should reach over repeated offences from their brother, they said: 'Shall we forgive until seven times?' Doubtless they thought they had strained mercy far, in saying, 'until seven times'; for they desired to seem to imitate the tender forbearance of their master. How must they have been astounded by his answer: "I say not unto you, until seven times, but until seventy times seven." But this measure of mercy, so astonishing to them, He immeasurably transcends, in His own dealings towards us. For how countless are our offences? And yet he forgives. 'He forgiveth all our iniquities.' 'As far as the east is from the west, so far hath He removed our transgressions from us." (Psalm 103:3, 12) "Thou wilt cast all their sins into the depths of the sea." (Micah 7:19)

4. Men seldom pardon without upbraiding. Often they say: "I may forgive, but I cannot forget": meaning, not only that the injuries of which they speak will remain as involuntary marks upon the tablets of memory: but that they are to be carefully cherished, and willfully kept rambling in their hearts, while they only forgo the acts of outward revenge. Not so with God: the generosity with which He casts our sins behind his back, has just been stated in the words of inspiration. When earthly authorities remit guilt, they usually do no more than place the criminal upon a sort of probation. They hold out to him an opportunity to retrieve his position before the law by a painful and watchful obedience. The old load of wrath is not finally and decisively removed, it is only held in suspense, over his anxious head; and if he fails in the slightest point of obedience, the whole incubus of guilt rolls back, increased by the aggravation of this new lapse, and the last state of the man is worse than the first.

But God, when he pardons, also adopts. So boundless is his mercy, that the criminal is not only released, by virtue of a sacrifice which was provided wholly at God's expense, and not his own, from all the penal debt: but he is graciously received into the number of God's beloved children, selected as the object of His tender favor, and crowned with all the benefits of redemption. The reconciled Father does not hold him suspiciously to his good behavior, awaiting the opportunity of some new lapse into transgression, to hurl back all the mountain-ous curse of sin, temporarily suspended from him. No: He takes him into His bosom; and that the erring child may not again compel di-vine justice to array itself against him, by his relapse into rebellion, God tenderly guides him, and watches and sustains his steps in all the paths of new obedience. "He puts His Spirit within them, and causes them to walk in his statutes, and they shall keep his judgments and do them." (Ezekiel 36:27) He says: "I will make an everlasting covenant with them, that I will not turn away from them to do them good: but I will put my fear in their hearts that they shall not depart from me." (Jeremiah 32:40) "They are kept by the power of God, through faith, unto salvation." (I Peter 1:5) Thus the mercy of God in the gospel not only restores the guilty sinners out of the consequences of his sin, but raises him to a state of adoption, more secure than the innocence of paradise from which Adam fell, and as gloriously stable as that which Gabriel has won by his holiness.

5. It has been already intimated that the mercy of God is so great, it forgives the sinner without requiring any costly conditions on his part. Indeed, the only meritorious conditions in the transaction, are those which God himself, in Christ, provides and fulfills, in order that he may consistently pardon. He pays the sinner's debt. He works out the meritorious righteousness for the sinner's reconciliation. He earns not only that pardon for which the sinner is perishing, but all those provisions of wisdom and strength which must needs be admin-istered to him, for his perseverance in his restored state. How high is this above the mercy of this earth? The offended man, when mercy is asked for the offender, arrogantly requires that every sacrifice shall be made upon the culprit's side. If he, on his part, sacrifices some pique, or some fancied dignity of his resentment, if he makes some cheap advance towards condescension, he thinks that he had done enough. And then, he takes great praise to himself, that he is merciful! But God, in his forgiveness, although most majestic and infinite Sovereign, bears the whole expense of the reconciliation, and requires none of the pardoned sinner, who receives all the gain. And this expense is, the bitter, shameful death of His Son, Jesus Christ, who, in his divine nature, was in His bosom from eternity.

Consequently, His pardon is perfectly free. He requires no price, and establishes no terms, except those simple ones which are as imperatively demanded by the welfare of the beneficiary, as by the honor of Him who pardons. Does he exact faith? This is inevitable; for how can the returning sinner be reconciled to a Father in whom he does not trust? How can the beggar receive the benefaction, except he shall, at the least, reach out his hand to accept it when it is offered to him? And faith is no more than this trusting, this receiving. Hence, too it follows, that it can never claim the office of a price to purchase the gift, which it merely receives. Does God require a penitent obedience of him whom his mercy pardons? This also is as necessary for the sinner, as for God's holiness. For sin is misery: and even omnipotence cannot make that creature truly happy, who continues to love transgression.

But so free is the pardon, that the ability to comply with even these light terms is supplied by God, as it is purchased by Christ. "He is exalted, as a Prince and a Savior, to give unto Israel repentance, as well as remission of sins." (Acts 5:31) "For unto you it is given in the behalf of Christ to believe on him." &c. (Philippians 1:29) He causes the pardoned to love his law. He enables them to keep their vows of future obedience and submission. All this he does in, and for every sinner, who permits himself to be blessed. Was ever mercy as great as this seen under the heavens?

6. The mercy of God is magnified in this: that it forgives that offence which, with all other rulers, is held to be necessarily unpardonable: the offence against itself. Men reason thus: that an outrage against justice or authority may possibly be forgiven with propriety: but not an assault committed upon offered mercy: because this betrays an utter malignity of opposition, which should be at once accepted as irreconcilable: and because he who assails this attribute in its mission of benevolence, shows himself an enemy of goodness, outside the pale of humanity. Does not even the loving parent argue against the son that has insulted his very forbearance: "any resistance to my mere authority, I might have forgiven: but this, never! When compassion herself is outraged, then the cup of patience ought to be full."

But God has mercy on the sin against his mercy. Men may blaspheme the Father, and yet be forgiven: they may speak against the Son who died for them, and be forgiven. (Matthew 12:32) Indeed, all sinners who hear and intelligently reject the gospel, or postpone its claims for self-will and sin, experience this forbearance of God; and if they escape perdition, must obtain the pardon of the sin of resisting mercy. They have "made light of Christ." They "have done despite to the spirit of his grace." But cherishing the sins which slew him, they "crucify the Son of God afresh, and put him to an open shame." So that the mercy of God to you obstinate unbelievers, will, henceforth, be like the forgiveness of a righteous king towards armed rebels, who have fired on his flag of truce. You have broken his laws, defied his authority, introduced anarchy and ruin into his peaceful dominions, and injured his law-abiding citizens. The righteous sovereign has been compelled to muster his forces against you: and you have retired before his irresistible might. He has surrounded you on every side, and his angelic hosts stand ready to let loose upon you the arrows of destruction, which will overwhelm you with perdition. But the merciful king bade them withhold their fury yet longer, that he might try one more experiment with your infatuated souls. His pity persuaded him to offer one more overture of forgiveness, before his angry hosts were let loose to sweep you from the earth. But who will volunteer to bear this flag of truce, and face the truculent obstinacy of these desperate men? Lo! His Son advances, the tender and lovely image of his Father's virtues, heir of his throne, and sole sharer of his bosom: he exclaims: "I will go: I share the noble impulses of thy compassion, my Father. Surely they will reverence thy Son: they will reverence the divine Pity, whose messenger I shall be. I will entreat them not to destroy themselves, by all the tenderness of thy compassion, and by the terrors of thy royal wrath: and they will hearken. Thus shall their blood be spared, thy kingdom shall regain a host of devoted subjects; and all thy dominions lovingly admire thy wisdom and goodness." Hereupon, the Father smiled upon the Son with ineffable pride and love: and answered: "Go, my only Begotten, my joy and my heir: Let my subjects see thee first exercising those kingly functions which are thy inheritance, in this act of royal clemency. Go, and by thy love woo back those misguided criminals to duty and happiness." Thus the Son set out upon his errand of mercy to you: He laid aside his glittering armor, the helm that waved with horrors dark as the wings of death, the shield whose bosses shot devouring fire against you, and the sword whose edge could devour whole ranks at every blow: and taking the snowy banner, emblem of Peace, in his hands, he advanced to you, down from the heights of heaven which were crowned with his embattled hosts of angels, into the vale of despair where you had pitched: while every eye was intent to watch his reception. They saw him draw nigh to you, gently wave his flag of truce, and reach forth his warmed hand in entreaty: when lo! you, miserable culprits, instead of falling upon your knees, and casting guilty weapons away, lifted them and shot him dead: dead by the hands of those he was endeavoring to save! and the sacred, inviolable emblem of peace is trailed in the bloody dust!

Then, did not the Father lift his hand with a grief and wrath too vast for utterance, swear with an oath which made the very depths to quake, that there should be no more truce for you, but vengeance that should burn to the lowest hell; and speak the instant word to his indignant hosts, to let lose upon you all the volleys of their might? No: O wonder, no. There came back to his ear, as a sigh borne upon the breeze, these dying words from his murdered Son: "Father forgive them: they know not what they do": and at that word, his righteous fury was all calmed, and his hand was only lifted up to restrain his impatient followers. O wonder! he dispatches new messengers to you, to entreat you, by the love of the Prince whom you have slain, yet to him, and be forgiven! Was there ever mercy like this? Is it not "great above the heavens"? But such is God's mercy to you, by me, this day.

The news of forgiveness should be a moving, melting sound. He who 'knoweth what is in man' has taught us: "If thine enemy hunger, feed him: if he thirst, give him drink: for in so doing, thou shalt heap coals of fire upon his head." He knew that there was a gentle power in mercy, to melt the angry and obdurate heart, which would only harden itself against threats, even righteous threats. And that policy which He enjoins upon us, He pursues himself towards you, his enemies. Mistaken souls: how can you resist it? Relent, relent before the attractions of Jesus' cross. Ye hearts, that shake not at the wrath and terrors of God Almighty, melt beneath the beams of this mercy, which is above the heavens.

But alas! Are not God's compassions as peculiar in the reception which befalls them in this world, as they are eminent in themselves? In all this world, there is nothing that can equal the mercies of God in Christ to sinners, save the hardness of those sinners' hearts against Him.

And shall I now stay, to show you how unutterably your doom must needs be embittered by the recollection of this obstinacy, when God's mercy shall at length have given place to judgment? (And if you reject constantly the atoning sacrifice of Christ, be assured, judgment must some day awake: for God is a perfect God.) Shall I remind you how your awful sentence must be aggravated by the weight of this rejected love: and how your remorse will tear your souls, as you reflect how much mercy you had to slight in order to fright your way down to perdition? No: I will not dwell on these dread truths: I wish to leave you, to send you to your solitude, with the sweet voice of divine mercy lingering in your ears, and wooing your souls to the Prince of Peace. "God commendeth his love towards you, in that while you were yet sinners, Christ died for you." "Turn you to the strong hold, ye prisoners of hope." (Romans 5:8, Zechariah 9:12) "Come now, and let us reason together, saith the Lord: Though your sins be as scarlet, they shall be as white as snow: though they be red like crimson, they shall be as wool." (Isaiah 1:18) [218]

The Believer Born of Almighty Grace[219]

A Sermon

on

Ephesians 1:19-20

"And what is the exceeding greatness of his power to usward who
believe, according to the working of his mighty power, which he
wrought in Christ, when he raised him from the dead,
and set him at his right hand in the heavenly places."

Preached at Frederick's Hall, Va., in John Bell Hood's (4th) Texas Brigade,
June 22, 1862, and published in tract form at the request of Gen. "Stonewall"
Jackson.[220]

The saving belief of the gospel, my brethren, is the first and most
uniform action of the new-born soul. Hence, when the Apostle Paul here speaks of himself and brethren as "us who believe," he
refers directly to their new-birth or regeneration. "God's power to
usward who believe" means his "power by which we are made believers," or in other words, are born again. And this is the power whose
greatness he so exalts. Other wondrous displays of divine might were
made in connection with the mission of Christ and his apostles; but
of these Paul is not speaking here. Let him explain his own meaning.
Two verses below he resumes the comparison of the text and says
(2:1), "You hath he quickened who were dead in trespasses and sins."
And in the fifth and sixth verses still more clearly, "Even when we
were dead in sins he hath quickened us together with Christ, and hath
raised us up together, and made us to sit together in heavenly places in
Christ Jesus." The thing which is compared to Christ's resurrection
in the text is then beyond doubt the renewal of the souls of sinners.

This passage, therefore, exhausts the strongest expressions of human language, to assert the divinity and omnipotence of the power by
which the sinful soul is changed. It is God's work, not man's. "They

are born, not of blood, nor of the will of the flesh, nor of the will of man, but of God." (John 1:13) It is effected by "the greatness of his power." Nay, more, it is "the exceeding greatness of his power." And, as though to exalt the work to the utmost, it is likened to the most illustrious miracles which demonstrated the gospel, the resurrection and ascension of the Lord Jesus Christ. It is "according to the working of his mighty power, which he wrought in Christ, when he raised him from the dead, and set him at his own right hand in the heavenly places."

We are all in substance agreed, that a miracle was such a manifest suspension of the laws of nature as only God can work. Miracles were usually rare in their times; for had they become customary, their end would have been disappointed. Blessed be God, this divine work, the new birth, is frequent and customary wherever his gospel is faithfully taught. It is not palpable to the senses save by its effects. But neither could you have seen the subtle essence of Lazarus' soul reenter his corpse had you been present at that tomb of Bethany; you would only have known its return by its effects, when you saw the dead man come forth. Let us consider, and we shall see that the change of a godless, self-willed, worldly soul into a sincere, believing, joyful Christian, is as truly above the laws of his natural heart as the living again of a corpse is above the powers of matter. This text teaches us, then,

That the saving change of the soul is God's own almighty work, and is, in that sense, supernatural.

What is this change? Some, from shallow observation, answer: It is only the sinner's *change of purpose* concerning his duty to God. But the Scriptures answer, that it is a *change of the dispositions of heart*, which prompt and regulate man's purposes concerning this duty. Note, I pray you, my words, and apprehend the difference, for it is that between light and darkness. And this I promise to show before I am done, if you will give me your attention. That new birth, I repeat, which is necessary to salvation, is some deeper thing than the mere making of a new resolution by the sinner. It is the fundamental revolution of the very dispositions of soul, out of which his purposes were all prompted. Hence, it is not the work merely of reasonings and inducements presented to the mind, but of God's almighty power, through his Holy Ghost, quickening the soul to feel those reasonings and inducements.

Having explained my meaning, I present some probable proof of it from this fact: that human efforts have by themselves done so little to remedy the moral evils which curse the hearts of mankind. In the world of matter, men's exploits have been marvelous, especially when they have combined their industry. They have bridged mighty floods, traversed the pathless oceans, pierced the entrails of the earth for her treasures, bent the winds and even the lightnings to serve them, and modified the face of continents. But how fleeting and scanty are man's moral exploits, where God, in the gospel of his Son, has not wrought through him? Where are his drunkards reformed? Where his vices abolished? Where his races civilized and redeemed, without Christianity?

Every instance of the permanent change of a hardened sinner to godliness bears, to the experienced eye, the appearance of a power above man's, because we see so few men make otherwise a radical change of habits and principles after these are fully formed. The wise observer of the world will tell you that few men, except under this peculiar power of Christianity, change their course after they pass the age of thirty years. Those who are then indolent do not become systematically industrious. Those who are then intemperate rarely become sober. The radically dishonest never become trustworthy. It is also happily true, that good principles and habits then well established usually prove permanent to the end of life. But, as it is easier for feeble man to degenerate than to improve, the few instances in which this rule does not hold are cases of changes from the better to the worse. When, therefore, I see, under the gospel, a permanent change of a hardened sinner for the better, my experience inclines me to believe that he has felt some power above that of mere nature.

But third: when we consider what the change in the new birth is, and what the heart to be changed is, we plainly see that the work is above nature. The soul of man has its natural laws as truly as the world of matter. In both worlds we learn these laws by the uniformity of our experience. Because all men have ever seen water run down hill, therefore we say that this is the law of its gravitation. And, therefore, when the waters of Jordan stood on a heap while the ark of God and Israel passed through its channel, men knew it was a miracle. The sun and the moon have always proceeded regularly from their rising to their setting. Hence, when their motion ceased at the word of Joshua, it was plainly a miracle.

Now universal observation proves that *ungodliness* is the natural law of man's soul, as the holy Scriptures declare. Let me explain. By this bad word, *ungodliness*, I do not mean some series of sins peculiarly degrading in man's eyes, or some peculiar degree of enormous criminality. I mean that natural alienation from God, that obstinate reluctance to submit your wills to his righteous will, that native preference for the good things of this world over God and his service and favor, which you all feel in your breasts, and which, in the best of you, show themselves in the fixed purpose to break, for the present, some commands of your Maker, and to neglect at least some known duties. There may be much difference in the sinfulness of different men here. Some of you have no leaning to certain sins, which others pursue with greediness; social principles may make you despise them. But I know that I may make *this* charge against the most decent impenitent man here: you prefer the world to God; he "is not in all your thoughts;" you are alienated from him; you are determined not at this time to surrender your will entirely to his holy will; and you are resolved, with full purpose of heart, not to do at this time the whole of what you know to be your duty to your God. I have read you aright, have I not?

Well, this heart is, in different degrees and phases, universal among natural men, in all races and ages, under all religions and forms of civilization, whatever religious instincts men may have, and to whatever pious observances they may be driven by remorse, or self-righteousness, or spiritual pride. We perceive that this disposition of soul begins to reveal itself in all children as early as any intelligent moral purpose is disclosed. We observe that while it is sometimes concealed, or turned into new directions by the force of circumstances, it is always latent, and is a universal and controlling principle of conduct towards God. We find that it holds its evil sway in spite of all light and rational conviction in men's own minds, and of inducements drawn from conscience and heaven and hell, which ought to be omnipotent. Such is every man's inward history, until *grace* reverses his career.

Now I claim that these facts of experience authorize me in regarding this ungodly disposition in man as natural and fundamental. How do we learn more certainly that any other native trait or affection belongs to the constitution of his soul? It is plain that, since Adam's fall, ungodliness is as radically a native disposition of man's soul as the desire of happiness or the fear of pain. (John 3:6)

But here I remind you, that no man ever reverses or totally eradicates or revolutionizes any material or fundamental disposition of soul by his own purpose or choice; nor can any mere inducement persuade him to do so. Look and see. These principles may be bent, they may be concealed, they may be turned into new channels by self-interest, or by education, or by restraint. The same selfishness which in the season of heady youth prompted to prodigality, may in thrifty age inspire avarice, but it is never eradicated by natural means. Again I say, look and see. Hunger is a natural appetite. Should a physician tell you that he had a patient with a morbid appetite, but that by his eloquent pictures of the dangers of relapse and death from the imprudent indulgence in food, he had actually caused the man no longer to be hungry, you would tell him, "Sir, you deceived yourself; you have only persuaded him to curb his hunger; he feels it just as before." Suppose this physician told you that he had plied his patient's mind with such arguments for the utility of a certain nauseous drug that it had actually become sweet to his palate? Your good sense would answer, "No, sir; it is in itself bitter to him as before; you have only induced him by the fear of death — a more bitter thing — to swallow it in spite of its odiousness."

Try my assertion again by some of the instinctive propensities of the mind, instead of these animal appetites, and you will find it equally true. The distinction of *meum* and *tuum* is universal in human minds, and the love of one's own possessions is instinctive in men's hearts. Can you then argue or persuade a man into a genuine and absolute indifference to his own? This was one of the things which monasticism professed to do: monks were required to take the three vows of "obedience, chastity and poverty." Many devout and superstitious persons upon entering monasteries reduced themselves to absolute and perpetual poverty, by giving their goods to the church or the poor, and foreswore forever the pursuits by which money is acquired. But was the natural love of possession really eradicated? The notorious answer was, No. Every one of these monks was as ready as any other man to contest the possession of his own cell, his own pallet, his own gown and cowl, his own meager food. And for the commonwealth of their monastery and order they uniformly contended with a cunning and greediness which surpassed all others, until they engrossed to themselves half the wealth of Europe.

The love of applause is native to man. Can reasoning or persuasion truly extinguish it? These may correct, direct, or conceal this passion; they can do no more. The hermit professed to have extinguished it. He hid himself in deserts and mountains from the society of men, and pretended that he was dead to their praise and their attractions, dead to all but heaven. But he who sought out this hermit and conversed with him soon detected in him an arrogance and spiritual pride above those of all others; and the chief reason why he was content to dwell in savage solitudes was that the voice of fancy brought to his soul across the wastes which sundered him from the haunts of men, their applause for his sanctity, in strains sweeter to his pride than the blare of bugles and the shouts of the multitude.

I return, then, to my point. There is, there can be, no case in which mere inducements work in man a permanent purpose contrary to the natural dispositions of his soul. But ungodliness is a native, a universal, a radical propensity. Hence, when we see such a revolution in this as the gospel requires in the new birth, we must believe that it is above nature. This great change not only reforms particular vices; it revolutionizes their original source, ungodliness. It not only causes the renewed sinner to submit to obedience, as the bitter, yet necessary medicine of an endangered soul; it makes him prefer it for itself as his daily bread. It not only refrains from sin, which is still craved, as the dyspeptic refuses to himself the dainties for which he longs, lest his indulgence should be punished with the agonies of sickness; it hates sin for its own sake. The holy and thorough submission to God's will, which the convert before dreaded and resisted, he now loves and approves. Nothing less than this is a saving change; for God's command is, "My son, give me thine heart." He requireth truth in the inward parts, and in the hidden parts he shall make us to know wisdom. Saith the Savior, "Either make the tree good and its fruits good, or else the tree evil and its fruits evil." Such is the change which makes the real Christian. It is a spiritual resurrection; it is the working of that "mighty power of God which he wrought in Christ when he raised him from the dead."

Indeed, a little plain reflection, of which any thinking man should be capable, will convince you that this conclusion of our experience could not be otherwise. It is unreasonable to expect any inducements you can offer from without to make a thorough change of the natural propensities of the heart of your hearer; and this because the natural propensities are the causes which decide already whether any objects you may propose to his mind and heart shall be to him inducements or repulsions. Is it reasonable to expect nature to work against or above nature? Surely not. Can a thing by its power determine or change that prior force which gives or deprives it of all the power that is in it? Can the effect change its own cause? Can the quality of the child determine what shall be the nature of the father who begat him? Just so reasonable is it for you to hope that gospel truth and inducements will suffice by their natural influence to change the moral nature of a sinner radically, when that evil nature determines already that the gospel is to his heart no natural inducement at all, but, on the contrary, intrinsically hateful. You see an engaging child playing in some place of danger; you wish to draw it away; and you crave to caress it and please yourself with its beauty and grace. Would you call to it, "Come hither, pretty child, and I will give you *aloes* and *quinine* to eat?" Will such an inducement fetch it to you? I trow not. Suppose, then, you exhibit the lure in more force; increase its quantity, intensify its odor and bitterness; cause the child to smell of it near at hand, and receive a more correct perception of its nature. Try whether by this means you can attract it to your arms. Do you not know that the more you press the bitter drug the more the child will recoil? And your good sense gives the explanation. You know that the child has beforehand a natural palate, whose laws determine that these drugs are intrinsically unpleasant and can only repel instead of attracting. If you had presented sweetmeats and ripe fruits, you might have succeeded in attracting. You see clearly enough here that it is preposterous to expect that the offer of bitter things will attract the palate to a change, because the nature of the palate has determined in advance that they shall be only nauseous and repulsive to it. If there is any superior medical agent which will revolutionize the very law of this child's palate, so that the bitter shall now be sweet, and the sweet bitter, then you may present your drugs where that agent works, and they will attract. So holiness and submission of the inward heart to the sovereign will of God are now bitter to the taste of the sinner's soul; the more they are displayed the more will he recoil from salvation, until the same Divine Physician who healed the stroke of death in Jesus' body heals the perversity of his heart by his sovereign touch.

I argue, fourth, that the new birth is the exceeding greatness of God's power, because of the different effects which accompany the preaching of the gospel to different men, and to the same men at different times. Were the power only the natural influence of the truth, these diverse effects could not be explained consistently with the maxim that like causes produce like effects. The same gospel inducements are offered to a congregation of sinners, and "some believe the things which are spoken and some believe not." It is not always the most docile, amiable or serious mind that yields; such unbelievers often remain callous to its appeals, while some ignorant, stubborn and hardened sinner is subdued. How is this? If the whole influence were in the truth preached, should not the effects show some regular relation to the cause? Should not the truth prevail where the natural obstacles are least, if it prevailed at all? Why do we see cases in which it fails before the weaker and triumphs over the stronger resistance? It is because, in one case, "the exceeding greatness of God's power" is behind that truth, and in the other case, is absent.

But if you deny the sovereign agency of the Holy Ghost in the new birth, you have a more impracticable case to explain. It is the case of him who had resisted this gospel for twenty, thirty, or fifty years, and has yet been subdued by it at last. If the truth had natural power within itself to persuade this soul, why did it not effect it at first? If it lacked that power, how does it come to effect the work at last, after so many failures? This mystery is enhanced for you by two great facts: the one is, that the futile presentation of this gospel-truth for so many years must, in accordance with the well know the law of habit, have blunted the sensibilities of the soul, and rendered the story of redemption trite and stale. If you know anything of human nature, you cannot but admit this result. Repetition must make any neglected story dull. That which at first somewhat excited the attention and sensibilities, urged so often in vain, must become as

"Irksome as a twice told tale,
Vexing the dull ear of a drowsy man."[221]

Familiarity and inattention must blunt the feelings toward such a story. The man who first approaches Niagara [Falls] has his whole ear filled with that mighty, sullen roar of the waters, which shakes the very ground beneath his feet. The dwellers at the spot are so habituated to it by use that they forget to hear it at all! The ingenuous boy almost shudders at the first sight of blood, though it be only that of the bird he has brought down in his sport. See that person, when hardened by frequent scenes of carnage and death into the rugged soldier, insensible to the fall of his comrade by his side, and planting his foot with a jest upon human corpses, as he mounts to the "imminent, deadly breach."

The other fact which you must take into the account is, that while this sinner is growing more callous to sacred truth by its neglect, every active principle of ungodliness within him must be growing by its indulgence. Is any one ignorant of this law, that a propensity indulged is thereby strengthened? Need I bring instances to prove or illustrate it? How else does any man grow from bad to worse; how does the temperate drinker grow into a drunkard, the card-player into a gambler, save by the force of this law? It must be then that, while the sinner is neglecting the gospel, at the bidding of ungodliness, the love of the world, avarice, sensual lusts, self-will, pride, ambition, false shame, with every evil outward habit, are growing into giant strength.

This, then, is the case which you have to solve. Here is an influence, the natural force of sacred truth, which was fully plied to overcome the unbelief of the young heart, with every advantage of fresh interest. The tenderness of maternal love, the gentle and venerable authority of a father amidst the sweet sanctities of home, plied when the soul was still unformed, and in the plastic gristle of its childhood. But even in this tender heart the inborn power of ungodliness was too strong, the application utterly failed. But now, after this truth has been exhausted of its power by twenty, thirty, or it may be, fifty years of useless presentation; and after this native ungodliness, too strong in its infancy, has been hardened by as many years of sin into the rugged bone of manhood, lo! the powerless truth suddenly becomes powerful! The stubborn sinner listens, feels and submits. Natural agencies cannot account for this. The finger of God is there. Let me suppose a parallel case. Years ago, suppose, when the trees which embower this forest sanctuary were lithe saplings, and I in the vigor of my first prime, you saw me lay hold of one of them with my hands, and attempt to tear it from its seat. But, though a sapling, it was too strong for me. Now years have rolled around, that tree has grown to a giant of the forest, and I return, no longer in the pride of youth, but a worn and tottering old man; and you, the same spectators, are here again. You see me go to that very tree, and attempt to wrench it from its place. You laugh scornfully; you say, "Does the old fool think he can pull up that sturdy oak? He was unable to do it before, when it was a sapling, and he was strong." Yes, but suppose the tree came up in his feeble hand? You would not laugh then. You would stand awestruck, and say, "Something greater than nature is here."

And so say I, when I see the sturdy old sinner, hardened by half a century of sins and struggles against the truth, bow before that same old gospel story, which he had so often spurned. When I see the soul which was by nature dead in trespasses and sins, and which has been stiffening and growing more chill, under all the appliances of human instruction and persuasion, at the last, when the zeal and hope and strength of man are almost spent, suddenly quickened under our hands, I know that it is "the exceeding greatness of God's power (not ours) according to the working of his mighty power which he wrought in Christ when he raised him from the dead."

Does any one attempt to escape this conclusion by saying that the new efficacy of the truth may have been derived from the superior force or eloquence of the orator who preached it on this occasion, or from the advantage of some such circumstance? I have two answers. One is, that there are no circumstances so auspicious, and no eloquence so persuasive as those which this soul has already resisted as an impenitent child. What eloquence is equal to that of the Christian mother, as she draws her beloved son to her knee, and tells him the history of Jesus' love in accents tremulous with unutterable tenderness? Would that I could imitate it, while I beseech you to seek the new heart! The other answer is, that the plain facts and persuasives of the gospel are, in themselves, too infinite to receive any appreciable weight from the trivial incidents of a perspicuous statement and an eloquent tongue. In the simple story of the cross, with divine love there dying a shameful and bitter death for its guilty enemies, in the offer of a heaven of everlasting and unspeakable bliss, and the threat of an eternal and remediless hell, even if they be but intelligibly lisped in the feeble voice of a child, there should be a weight so immense that beside it all the enlargements of human rhetoric would be as naught.

Ah, my brethren, man's skill of speech cannot weigh where Christ and eternity prove too light. It is as though that mighty mountain, whose ridges we scaled a few days ago, had been put in the balance against the mightier strength of your ungodliness, but could not counterpoise it. And then I come, and with my puny hand cast one little stone at the mountain's base, and say, "There, I have added to its weight; it will no longer prove too light." Such folly is it to expect that man can convert. Where the story of the cross has been resisted, naught can do it "save the exceeding greatness of his power."

Once more I argue, in the fifth place, from the uniform representations of the Scriptures. The picture which they give of man's spiritual state by nature proves the text. Your souls, before the new birth, are blind, "having the understanding darkened, because of the blindness of your heart" (Ephesians 4:18). They are "enmity to God" (Romans 8:7). They are "stony" (Ezekiel 36:26). They are "dead in trespasses and sins" (Ephesians 2:1). Do you object that these are tropes? Yes; but I suppose that the Spirit of all truth does not select tropes such that the figurative resemblance to the truths contained under them would be false. Now, then, can the blind eyes so admit the light as to open themselves thereby? Does obstinate enmity beget love out of itself? Does the stone imbue itself with softness? Does the dead corpse prepare its own resurrection?

Again: the images by which the Scriptures describe the great change are obviously chosen so as to teach that it is directly of God. It is a "new birth" of the Holy Ghost (John 3:5). It is an "opening of blind eyes" (Psalm 119:18). It is a "new creation unto good works" (Ephesians 2:10). It is a "quickening of the dead" (Ephesians 2:5). Again I ask, Does the infant generate itself? Does the wood shape itself for the artisan into the form of utility he desires? Does the corpse raise itself to life? Then must the infant work before it existed; the wood exercise intelligence and will, and the dead body perform the prime action of life before it is alive!

And to this agree the express testimonies of the Word in other forms: "I have planted, Apollos watered; *but God gave the increase*" (I Corinthians 3:6). They "that believe on his name are born, not of blood, nor of the will of the flesh, nor of the will of man, but of God" (John 1:13).

Every genuine conversion, then, reveals the quickening power of

God's almighty Spirit; it is a supernatural work. But if it is according to the working of God's mighty power, which he wrought in Christ when he raised him from the dead, then it is as valid a proof that "the kingdom of God is come unto you" as though you witnessed a sensible miracle; it carries the same high responsibility to believe and love and obey the word of that kingdom.

But I pass by this corollary, to urge upon you, in conclusion, this one solemn thought: "Except ye be born again, ye cannot see the kingdom of God." You will never work this new birth of yourselves; you are absolutely dependent on the sovereign inworking of that God against whom you sin hourly. Unless he condescends to stoop and touch your stubborn heart, it will remain ungodly, just as surely as the corpse remains dead. All the zeal of religious teachers, all your own self-righteous resolutions and vows, will be assuredly vain. But your whole life, your every act now tends to alienate that almighty hand, on whose touch your salvation depends. How complete is this dependence! How mad your rebellion! Will you not now cease fighting against your only deliverer, and begin to cry, "Create in me a clean heart, O God; and renew a right spirit within me?" (Psalm 51:10)

I know the cavil with which impenitence excuses itself, and I know its emptiness. Will you object that my exhortation is contradictory to my doctrine? Will you tell me that if you are dependent on sovereign grace, and will never change your own hearts, then the only consistent effect of the teaching must be to make you to fold your hands, and await in absolute apathy the almighty touch?

"Fold your hands," I reply, while you passively await God's help? Nay, your hand is stretched out every moment in active resistance to God's will and grace. Talk not to me of passivity, when the very nature of your soul is active, and that activity is ceaselessly directed by a rebellious will against God and duty. I would that you could become passive from sinning. Nor is it true that the Bible doctrine herein chills or represses your exertions after redemption; for, in truth, you do not believe in your real dependence. Would God that you did; would that you knew it as well as I do, for then we should see you, instead of coldly caviling against facts and duty and grace, crying mightily unto God for his aid. It is not according to reason or nature that your clear knowledge of your coming ruin, and of your absolute dependence on help from above for deliverance, should paralyze effort or produce apathy. Here is a man whose house is hopelessly involved in flames. He is within, in an upper chamber, busily collecting his treasures, and he supposes that he has the means of escape wholly at his own command, to resort to them whenever he deemed it imprudent to venture farther. This notion, as you well know, will tempt him to postpone his escape, to venture near the utmost moment, to listen to the attractions of his wealth which he would fain rescue.

And this is just your delusion now. But meantime the man casually looks at the stairway without, by which he expected to escape, and finds to his surprise that it is wrapped in flames. He sees that he has no means of egress at his own command; unless assistance comes from without he is lost. Now, what does nature or reason prompt this man to do? That moment there is an end of his rash delays. No longer does he tamper with the rescue; his dearest treasures drop from his hands, and he runs to a window and shouts, "Help, help, or I am gone!"

So do you cry to God. It is the very thing, the only thing, which a helpless sinner, who is guilty for his very helplessness, should do. "Save, Lord, or I perish!"

The Christian Soldier[222]

A Sermon

on

II Samuel 10:12

"Be of good courage and let us play the man for our people, and for
the cities of our God; and the Lord do that which seemeth him good."

Commemorative of the death of Abraham C. Carrington. Preached in College
Church, Va., Dec. 14th, 1862.[223]

The duties of patriotism are not prominently urged in sacred
Scripture. This we account for, not by supposing, with a certain
sickly school of moralists, that this sentiment is selfish, narrow or
inconsistent with the broadest philanthropy; but by the facts, that the
obligations of the citizens are not directly religious, and that they are
so natural as to require little inculcation. The Hebrew Scriptures do
indeed say enough, as in the text, to justify an intense love of native
land and its institutions. Civil government is God's ordinance, and
if it be just, one of his greatest temporal blessings. The diversity of
tongues, characters, races and interests among mankind forbids their
union in one universal commonwealth. The aggregation of men into
separate nations is therefore necessary; and the authority of the governments instituted over them, to maintain internal order and external defense against aggression, is of divine appointment. Hence, to
sustain our government with *heart* and *hand* is not only made by God
our privilege, but our duty. Our best way to advance the well-being of
the race is to advance that of the portion of our race associated with
us in the same society. He who extends his philanthropy so broadly as
to refuse a special attachment to the interests of his own people, will
probably make it so thin as to be of no account to any people.

I therefore believe that there is nothing opposed to an enlightened
Christianity in a warm patriotism for our particular country. This

feeling is made up of several elements: a legitimate regard for our own welfare and worldly estate, interest in that of our families, and a wider benevolence towards our fellow-citizens; together with an honest pride in the glories of our history, and in the justice of our institutions, with the attachments of local affection to the very scenery and soil of our native land.

The text expresses this sentiment in action against the unrighteous assailant of our country. It was uttered by one who was very far from being a friend of God at heart, the haughty and violent Joab, the murderer of Abner, the patron of the dissolute Absalom, the chieftain who closed his stormy career by bringing his hoary head at last to the block for treason against his master's chosen successor. But Joab was now the lawfully appointed general of Israel. Although not a child of God, he was probably a sincere patriot; and his unsanctified lips, like those of Balaam, were now employed by God to utter words of truth and duty. We regard the text, then, as God's command, not because it was spoken by Joab, but because his language is virtually sanctioned by the Holy Ghost in the general tenor of the narrative and the issue of the transaction. The Ammonites, after publicly affronting King David's ambassadors without provocation, had hired a multitude of pagan Syrians, and were threatening to desolate the land of the Hebrews. Joab went to meet them, and after making the most prudent disposition of his forces, exhorted them, "Be of good courage," etc.

Unprovoked war is the most monstrous secular crime that can be committed; it is at once the greatest of evils, and includes the worst forms of robbery and murder. Wherever war is prompted by mere pique or lust of aggrandizement, or ambition for fame and power, it deserves all that can be said of its mischiefs and criminality by the most zealous advocates of peace. And nothing can rescue a people waging war from this guilt except the fact that their appeal to arms is necessary for the defense of just and vital rights. But while the Scriptures teach this, they give no countenance to the weak fanaticism which commands governments to practice a passive non-resistance in such a world as this. Nations are usually unjust and unscrupulous. The very fact that they are politically sovereign implies that there is no umpire between them, except divine providence. A passive attitude would usually only provoke, instead of disarming, attack. Hence its only effect would be to bring all the horrors and desolations of invasion upon the innocent people, while the guilty went free. God has, therefore, both permitted and instructed rulers, when thus unjustly assailed, to retort these miseries upon the assailants who introduce them. The very fact that all war is so terrific a scourge, and that aggressive war is such an enormous crime, only makes it more clear that the injured party are entitled to their redress, and are justified in inflicting on the injurers such chastisement as will compel their return to justice, even including the death and ruin which they were preparing against their inoffensive neighbors.

It is perfectly clear that sacred Scripture legalizes such defensive war. Abram, Moses, Joshua, Samuel, David, Josiah, the Maccabees, were such warriors; and they were God's chosen saints. It was "*through faith* they waxed valiant in fight, turned to flight the armies of the aliens." (Hebrews 11:34) God fought for and with them, by giving, in their battles, answers to their prayers and miraculous assistance to their arms. Under the New Testament, when Christ's forerunner was preaching the baptism of repentance, he did not enjoin on soldiers the surrender of their profession as sinful, but only the restricting of themselves to its lawful duties. The New Testament tells us of a centurion affectionately commended by our Redeemer as possessed of "great faith;" and of a Cornelius, who was "accepted with God, as fearing him and working righteousness." (Luke 3:14; 7:9; Acts 10:33) The Apostle Paul (Romans 13:4) tells us that the magistrate "beareth not the sword in vain; for he is the minister of God, a revenger to execute wrath upon him that doeth evil." It would be strange indeed if the ruler who is armed by God with the power of capital punishment against the domestic murderer could not justly inflict the same doom on the foreign criminal who invades our soil, unprovoked, for the purpose of shedding blood. The security of life and property which the magistrate is intended to provide by his power of punishing would be illusory, indeed, if it could only be used against individual criminals, while the more mischievous and widespread crimes of organized multitudes must go unpunished. Aggressive war is wholesale murder; and when the government sends out its army to repel and chastise the invader, it does but inflict summary execution on the murderer caught in the act.

I have briefly stated this truth in order to ground firmly your belief in the righteousness of the calling of the Christian soldier. God has authorized him. The objects for which he contends are excellent, noble, yea of supreme temporal value "for our people and for the cities of our God." Our homes and the shelter of our families, the rights bequeathed to us by our ancestors, the whole earthly welfare of us and all our fellow-citizens, every thing which is included as valuable in the words, *my country*, is committed to his protection. And how much that phrase includes he can appreciate who, as a conquered exile, has no country. We could understand in part lately, when we began to fear that this fate might be ours. The godly soldier is called to defend also the far dearer interests of the church of God, involved in so many ways with those of the country in which it is planted. He protects all these precious objects by the exercise of the noblest attributes of manhood, courage, self-devotion, faith in God.

The glory of the soldier's prowess has always inflamed the admiration and dazzled the fancy of mankind above all other greatness. To the warrior who has done acts of high emprise on the bloody field, have ever belonged the loudest shouts of popular applause. The multitudes throng his chariot wheels as those of no other benefactor. His name is written highest on the monumental marble. The heart of ingenuous youth thrills more warmly as he reads his exploits than at all the other marvels of history, and even tender woman reserves for him her sweetest smiles, "and loves him for the dangers he has passed." Let not the pseudo-philanthropist say that this universal, this resistless impulse of the popular heart is merely an irrational remnant of the more bloody and ruthless ideas of Paganism, or a gust of the fancy fevered by the romance

> "Of moving accidents by flood and field,
> Of hairbreadth 'scapes i' the' imminent deadly breach;"[224]

that it is unworthy of the benevolence and knowledge of a Christian age; that the admiration of men should rather be bestowed on those who bless by the gifts of science and the exertions of our nobler part, the mind, than on those who are eminent only for their power to destroy; that he who has "made two blades of grass to grow where but one grew before," or who has helped to civilize his fellows by invention in the arts of peace or the lessons of high philosophy, should be the true hero, and not he who exhibits the might of a mere animal rage to devastate and degrade.

It is true that, if this admiration of the military virtues is bestowed on the hireling, the mere soldier of fortune or the scourge of nations, who, like "Macedonia's madman or the Swede,"[225] fights from the lust of fame and power; it is a monstrous perversion. But the great instincts of the human heart and reason never go totally astray. These perverted instances would not occur unless there were a *true* military glory, to blind men as to the black deformity of its counterfeit. This universal applause of the martial virtues is the instinctive testimony of man's heart to the fact, that they require the exercise of the noblest sentiments of the human soul. He who cultivates the arts of peace does, indeed, make a worthy contribution to the well-being of his fellow-men; but he who defends them with his life makes the contribution of supreme value. He maintains that peace and security which are the necessary conditions for enjoying all other acquisitions. But for his protection it would be of no avail to the citizens that the two blades of grass grew for every one that grew before, when all were trampled down by the ruthless invader. Nor is it true that the exploits of the soldier are merely those of the brute muscle and sinew, and of animal courage. War, and especially modern war, is not an unreasoning art; but it is a profession requiring, especially in its leaders, the widest combinations of the elements of thought, the most sleepless reflection and most rapid sagacity.

But the true glory of the Christian soldier is in this: that he is called to the noblest exertions of the emotions and the will. And even if his occupation were contrasted with those of the civilian and the philosopher, as being non-intellectual, which we have denied, the moral sentiments which actuate his exertions justify the exalted admiration of his fellow-men. For the heart is nobler, wiser, greater than the head. The speculations of the head are cold and devoid of moral trait. It is the impulses of the heart which characterize man as a moral being. To love is better than to analyze. To will magnanimously is more noble than to invent. Disinterestedness is more excellent than ingenuity, and courage for the right is grander than talent. If a man go upon the battlefield in foolish forgetfulness of his duty and danger; if he is bold merely because he refuses to think; if he rushes forward only with the senseless fury of the bull maddened by the trumpet, and

"His courage dwells but in a troubled flood
Of mounting spirits and fermenting blood;"[226]

if he is moved by no moral appreciation of the cause for which he stakes his life, he is not brave; his frenzy is not true courage; he is not the man of whom we speak, however he may sometimes intrude himself into his honor.

But let us suppose the Christian man, who wholly prefers peace and its joys to the turmoil of war, who considers all his risk, and weighs well the preciousness of the home, the life and the love, from which a violent death would tear him, but who yet foregoes those dear delights of peace, and deserts that home and its loves, for a time, and jeopards life itself, reluctantly, yet with determination, because he finds that *duty*, dearer than peace and home and life, demands the sacrifice. This is he who "is of good courage and plays the man for his people and for the city of his God." And I assert this Christian courage is but another name for self-sacrifice. It does but postpone self to duty, and to the good of others. Its spirit is precisely that of the martyr, who yields up his life rather than be recreant to duty, to his church and to his God. It expresses the same disinterestedness, the same consecration to the sentiment of obligation, the same faith in God. I believe that in many a soldier who is now baring his breast as a bulwark for our rights, this determination is as true a work of the grace of God as was ever fulfilled in the Christian martyr when he embraced the stake rather than deny his Lord. Yes, this courage, I assert it with reverence, is, in the true Christian soldier, but the reflection in his humbler measure of the spirit with which his divine Master set his face steadfastly towards Jerusalem and calmly braved the baptism of fire which awaited him there. He is the vine; they, the branches. He is the noblest exemplar of true moral courage; they, the feebler reflectors of his spirit in their lower spheres. It was this magnanimous sacrifice of Christ which purchased for him the throne of universal dominion, and filled all heaven with the acclaim of angels and ransomed saints. Shall we not, then, pay to his followers, when, for their humbler imitation of his self-devotion, they die for their people and the city of their God, the best tributes of our earthly affections? Such, I believe, was the courage of our brother, prompted, indeed, by a chivalrous and honorable nature, but regulated and sustained by the grace of God derived from the example and spirit of Christ his head.

The temper of the Christian soldier is also one of high faith and profound submission to God. While he plays the man for his people and the cities of his God, he adds, "And the Lord do that which seemeth him good." Here is a recognition of the overruling providence of God in the fate of commonwealths and the decision of battles. Here is expressed a hearty confidence in the wisdom, goodness and justice of the event which God may ordain, and acquiescence in his decisions. There is here no senseless fatalism, dissevering the appointed means from the desired end, and reposing in vain confidence or supine despair. But the truth is recognized that "duty is ours, events are God's."[227] Every nerve is strained to perform the task allotted by the providence of the hour, manfully, and if in its performance death or defeat is met, it is well. The Christian accepts this result as a revelation of the fact that this was the hour and this the place appointed by God for his end, and that, therefore, no other hour and place can be so suitable. He feels that if duty be courageously done all else will be secure. He may die, but the cause of his country is immortal; the blood with which he enriches her soil becomes to his fellow-citizens a new argument of the preciousness of the cause in which it was shed, and a sacred pledge to persevere in it to the end. Thus the blood of our country's martyrs becomes the seed of our new armies. The dying patriot achieves more for her by his death than by all his life, and lays down his sword at the gates of the tomb in the triumphant assurance that a people contending for their right in the fear of God will be made invincible by his aid. He leaves the family for whose home he was fighting; but his God and a grateful country become their guardians in his place. "I have been young," says the Psalmist, "and now am old, yet have I not seen the righteous forsaken, nor his seed begging bread." Life is ended; but it is to begin a better life in heaven. Matthew 10:39: "He that loseth his life for Christ's sake, shall find it."

Death, and especially what men call a premature death, must ever be regarded by us as a natural evil. If I should profess to be, myself, or should demand of you, to be insensible to it, you would justly consider me as guilty of cant. The very instincts of man's animal nature abhor it, and his earthly affections shudder at the severance which it effects between them and their dear objects. So, the death of friends cannot but be a felt bereavement to survivors, be its circumstances what they may. But it has ever appeared to me that, in the fall of the Christian soldier in battle, there was more to mitigate the stroke and to overcome death by the victory of triumphant consolation than in any other by which the good man meets his fate. The unreflecting may be startled by this assertion. They think of all the externals of a death on a battlefield; of the ghastly forms in which the destroyer comes; of the corpse prone upon its mother earth, begrimed perhaps with the sweat and dust of the conflict; of the burial to which he is taken fresh and gory from the field, his breast unconfined by coffin or winding-sheet, and shrouded only in his martial cloak; and of the nameless grave where he sleeps alone in his blood. All this is pictured in contrast with the solemn decencies of those funeral rites which affection renders, in more peaceful seasons, with a sort of mournful delight. They afflict themselves with the thought that no friend was near to minister to his pangs, no saintly man of God to calm the agitation of his soul by his prayers, no mother or wife to receive his last farewell; that his dying groans found no echo but the thunders of the receding battle.

Well, all these things are true; too often, alas, have I seen them verified; but they are true as elements of pain only to the survivors. The dying hero feels them not. Here is our illusion: that we cheat our sorrow into the belief that these ministrations of affection reach the insensible clay when in truth they only solace our own bereaved affection. Death is always a solitary struggle; however we may be surrounded by friends, when the shadow of the great agony falls upon us it shuts us out like a dark veil from their aid, and we must meet the last enemy alone. And however the neglect of the beloved's remains may harrow the feelings of those who loved him, the departed is all unconscious of it. On the other hand, is it nothing that he is translated to his reward by a sudden and painless stroke? He feels one electric shock as the deadly missile smites him, and then the very capacity for pain is benumbed, and he awakes no more till he awakes in that world where pain is unknown. He has no share in the long tortures of wearing sickness or the mortifying decay of age; he feels none of the anxious forebodings, the hope deferred waning into sickening despair, by which the more peaceful bed of disease is haunted. Death casts none of its shadows before. But in place of all this there is the calm testimony of a good conscience, the elation of the manly soul nerving its noblest powers for duty, the tumultuous rapture of those powers in highest action, the generous emulation, the hope of triumph, the joy of victory. And in the midst of this exaltation of soul comes the sudden stroke, and death is finished almost before it is felt. Such an end is not a death; it is a translation. Shall the bereaved count it no compensation for their loss, too, that the warmest instincts of every man's soul declare the glory of the soldier's death? There is solace in this; yea, more than consolation, there is proud triumph in it. And it is a triumph not unworthy of the Christian heart. It is even more appropriate to us than it was to the Greek to sing:

> "Glorious his fate, and envied is his lot,
> Who for his country fights, and for it dies;"[228]

for we contend, not only for the lawful interests of home and country, but for the more precious and sacred cause of God and of souls. I am not one of those who hold that these sentiments are the birth only of pagan ferocity, or unholy pride. The principles of personal honor and the love of glory have been perverted among us into a code of wickedness and bloody retaliation, for which we now doubtless suffer the chastisement of an offended God.[229] From this abuse the professors of a spurious and debased puritanism have taken occasion to decry all such sentiments until they seem to be vanished from among them; and the vileness of public morals, which is the consequence of this extreme, has become as loathsome as the other was violent. But there is a true glory and a true honor, that which cometh from God and not from man: the glory of duty done, of obstacles overcome, of fears resisted, and of generous sacrifices made to a worthy cause, the honor of an integrity of principle stronger than the sense of pain or the fear of death. He deserves most of this honor who from pure motives braves the direst evils and pays the costliest sacrifice for the noblest object. What fear can be darker than that of death? What more precious than life? What object more worthy than the cause of our country and our God? In attuning our souls so as to make them thrill at the applause of our fellows, our Creator doubtless assigned to this affection some legitimate scope. Its lawful exercise is found when we seek the approbation of the good and wise, which is but the echo of the divine verdict, "Well done, good and faithful servant." Such applause, when nobly won, is valuable; it is ennobling. It is an inheritance of honor to the children who emulate the virtues that won it. Is there one who "hath the stomach and mettle of a man" that would not rather leave his sons freemen, enriched only with this heritage, won for them by a father's blood, than wealthy slaves? And is there a true woman who would not elect, heart-rending as it might be to make the election, to be the widow of such a Christian hero than to live in the embraces of a dishonored and abject man, the serf of despots?

The doctrine which I have now drawn, as I believe from the word of God, finds strong illustration in the death of Lieutenant Carrington. My conception of the proper objects of funeral discourses has usually forbidden all eulogistic reference to the dead. If its purpose were to gratify or benefit the departed, it would be superstitious folly. Not only are they forever removed beyond the reach of our applause or blame, but beside the solemnities of that bar before which they have been arraigned, our verdict would seem to them infinitely trivial and impertinent. If the purpose of funeral encomiums is to compliment bereaved survivors, it might be admitted to be socially amiable; but to employ the pulpit for such a purpose is a perversion. God has appointed him who stands here to be the herald of his truth alone. No other message is allowed to proceed from his mouth. The only lawful purpose of these services is to commend that truth to the living.

But God sometimes teaches us by example; and when his grace has given to the church an instance peculiarly bright, it should be improved to impress the lessons of Christianity by the aid of the affections and memories which cluster around it upon the hearts of survivors. To pass over such a Christian character as that of our brother, and let his memory drop in silence without thanksgiving to him who formed him to holiness, would be ingratitude to God and neglect of the instruction of his church; for never have I known a man in whom grace bore more excellent fruit in its short summer time than in him. Under the ministry of the late venerable pastor, Doctor [Benjamin Holt] Rice, the sacred instructions of his childhood ripened into faith, and he devoted his early manhood to God. From the very first his modest, brave, and honorable nature displayed the refining influence of grace, and he assumed at once the standing of a thorough Christian. His religion was of that type which, like Joshua's and Caleb's, "followed the Lord fully." The result was that, after two years, he was introduced into the eldership, with the unanimous approval of the church. In that office he was a model of fidelity, ever postponing his private convenience to the calls and duties of the elder, firm in discipline, in purity of life an "ensample to the flock," and ready to assume any burden of labor or responsibility to which duty called him; so that, though of all men most modest and least pragmatical, he soon found the largest share of the church's work resting on his shoulders. It was thus that I came, first as stated supply and then as pastor of this church, to know and love him. If I did not know that my estimate is warmly sustained by all who knew him best, I should suspect myself of a too partial affection, and put a constraint upon my heart and lips; for truly can I say that my soul was knit to his as the souls of David and Jonathan. And now that I have lost him, I can find no words to express my personal bereavement better than those of David in the requiem of his princely friend: "How are the mighty fallen in the midst of battle! O Jonathan, thou wast slain in thy high places; I am distressed for thee, my brother Jonathan; very pleasant hast thou been unto me." (II Samuel 1:25- 26)

Need I commend his kindness as a neighbor when I see so many glistening eyes before me attest it? Need I remind you of his public spirit, his inflexible integrity, his courage for the right in this community? On the graces of his character as son, brother, husband, father, in the interior circles of his home, the sacredness of the grief which his loss has left behind it almost forbid me to enlarge. Abram C. Carrington was the *truest man* with whose friendship it was ever my lot to be blest. Let him but be convinced in his clear and honest judgment of the call of duty, and his effort to accomplish it was as certain as the rising of the sun; and it was made at once, without a pause to consider whether the task was easy and pleasant or arduous and repulsive. Let him once bestow his friendship upon you, and he was yours in every trial, with fortune, and hand, and heart, and, if need be, life blood.

As a soldier, his courage was the truest temper. His comrades whom I see before me will remember how his body was prostrate with disease at the first battle of Manassas, but the energy of a determinate will seemed to be medicine for his weakness; so that, instead of making it an excuse for going to the rear, as so many did, his spirit invigorated his failing strength.[230] In the battle of Gaines Mill, where his regiment had one man of every three struck, his gallantry was conspicuous; and on Monday, June 30th, at Frazier's Farm, he was encouraging and cheering on his men, when he fell, with a bullet through his breast. His was the courage of the Christian. It was as truly exhibited by his steady Christian example in the camp as on the field. In a letter written on the morning of the day he died, while describing the carnage through which his company passed the Friday before, he modestly says of himself: "Amidst it all, I lifted up my heart to God in prayer for safety, and, thanks to his holy name, he was pleased to hear me." In the same calm spirit, he again commits himself to God in prayer and well doing with reference to the bloody day before him.

And now, my hearers, of what use shall this symmetrical and lovely example be to us? Let me exhort the young men of this community to be "followers of him as he also was of Jesus Christ."[231] Let me also commend the example of our brother to my co-presbyters, the elders of his church. How many of us, my brethren, how many of you who have instructed me to preach this sermon and display the lessons of the life we have reviewed, will come up to the measure of his fidelity, of his manly and vigorous piety, of his industry in the concerns of God's house? Who will fill the breach we now feel? Happy would that people be whose pastors were always actuated by his steady zeal! And I will add, boldly bidding away every thought of personal offence by the awful solemnities of that bourne whence our dead colleague's example preaches to us, happy would those pastors be whose sessions all sustained them like other Abram Carringtons!

True Courage[232]

A SERMON

ON

LUKE 12:4-5

"Be not afraid of them that kill the body, and after that, have no more
than they can do. But I will forewarn you whom ye shall fear: Fear
him which, after he hath killed, hath power to cast into hell:
yea, I say unto you, fear him."

A DISCOURSE COMMEMORATIVE OF LIEUT.-GENERAL THOMAS J. JACKSON[233]

A little wisdom and experience will teach us to be very modest, in
interpreting God's purposes by his providences. "It is the glory
of the Lord to conceal a thing." His designs are too vast and complex
for our puny minds to infer them, from the fragments of his ways
which fall under our eyes. Yet, it is evident, that He intends us to
learn instruction from the events which occur before us under the regulation of his holy will. The profane are more than once rebuked by
him (as Isaiah 5:12) because "they regard not the work of the Lord,
neither consider the operation of his hands." And our Savior sharply
chides the Jewish Pharisees: "O ye hypocrites! ye can discern the face
of the sky; but can ye not discern the signs of the times?" (Matthew
16:3) We are not therefore to refuse the lessons of those events which
Providence evolves, because caution and humility are required in
learning them. We have a guide, which will conduct us securely to the
understanding of so much of them as God intends us to study: That
guide is the Holy Scriptures. Among the several principles which they
lay down for the explanation of God's dealings, it is sufficient for
our present task, to declare this one: That the characters of his children, which exhibit the scriptural model, are given as examples, to be
studied and imitated by us. He would thus teach us more than those
abstract conceptions of Christian excellence, which are conveyed by
general definitions of duty; he would give us a living picture and con-

crete idea. He thus aims to stimulate our aspirations and efforts, by showing us that the attainments of holiness are within human reach. He enstamps the moral likeness on the imitative soul by the warmth of admiration and love. That such is the use God intends us to make of noble examples, the Apostle James teaches us (5:10) — "Take, my brethren, the prophets, who have spoken in the name of the Lord, for an example of suffering affliction and of patience"; and the Epistle to the Hebrews (6:12) when it desires us to "be followers of them who, through faith and patience, inherit the promises."

Common sense teaches us then, from these texts, that the lesson is important and impressive, in proportion as the example given us was illustrious. By this rule, God addresses to us instruction of solemn emphasis, in the character, and the death, which we have now met to commemorate. Our dead hero is God's sermon to us, his embodied admonition, his incorporate discourse, to inculcate upon us the virtues with which he was adorned by the Holy Ghost; and especially those traits of the citizen, the Christian, and the soldier, now most essential to the times. He calls us, not to exhaust the occasion in useless sensibilities, but to come and learn the beauty of holiness, by the light of a shining example; and to let our passionate love and grief burn in upon the plastic heart, the impress of his principles. Happy shall I be, if I can so conceive and execute my humble task, as to permit this character to speak its own high lesson to your hearts. The only reason which makes you think this task appropriate to me, is doubtless this: that I had the privilege of his friendship, and an opportunity for intimately observing his character, during the most brilliant part of his career. The expectations which you form from this fact, must be my justification from the charge of egotism, if I should allude to my own observations of him, in exemplifying these instructions. But I must also forewarn you, that should there be any expectation of mere anecdote to gratify an idle curiosity, or of any disclosures of confidential intercourse, now doubly sanctified by the seal of the tomb, it will not be gratified. And let it be added, that however the heart may prompt encomiums on the departed, these are not the direct object, but only the incidental result, of this discourse. I stand here, as God's herald, in God's sanctuary, on his holy day, by his authority. My business is, not to praise any man, however beloved and bewailed, but only to unfold God's message through his life and death. Among that circle of virtues which his symmetrical character displayed, since time would fail me to do justice to all, I propose more especially, to select one, for our consideration, his Christian courage.

Courage is the opposite of fear. But fear may be described either as a feeling and appreciation of existing danger, or an undue yielding to that feeling. It is in the latter sense, that it is unworthy. In the former, it is the necessary result of the natural desire for well-being, in a creature endued with reflection and forecast. Hence, a true courage implies the existence of fear, in the form of a sense, that is, of a feeling of danger. For courage is but the overcoming of that feeling by a worthier motive. A danger unfelt is as though it did not exist. No man could be called brave for advancing coolly upon a risk of which he was totally unconscious. It is only where there is an exertion of fortitude in bearing up against the consciousness of peril, that true courage has place. If there is any man who can literally say that "he knows no fear," then he deserves no credit for his composure. True, a generous fortitude, in resisting the consciousness of danger, will partly extinguish it; so that a sensibility to it, over-sensitive and prominent among the emotions, is an indication of a mean self-love.

There are three emotions which claim the name of courage. The first is animal courage. This is but the ferment of animal passions and blind sympathies, combined with an irrational thoughtlessness. The man is courageous, only because he refuses to reflect: bold because he is blind. This animal hardihood, according to the obvious truths explained above, does not deserve the name of true courage; because there is no rational fortitude in resisting the consciousness of danger. And it is little worthy of trust; for having no foundation in a reasoning self-command, a sudden, vivid perception of the evil hitherto unnoted, may, at any moment, supplant it with a panic, as unreasoning and intense as the previous fury. The second species of courage is that prompted by the spirit of personal honor. There is a consciousness of risk; but it is manfully controlled by the sentiment of pride, the keener fear of reproach, and the desire of applause. This kind of fortitude is more worthy of the name of courage, because it exhibits self-command. But after all, the motive is personal and selfish; and therefore the sentiment does not rise to the level of a virtue. The third species is the moral courage of him who fears God, and, for that reason, fears nothing else. There is an intelligent apprehension of danger; there is the natural instinct of self-love desiring to preserve its own well-being; but it is curbed and governed by the sense of duty, and desire for the approbation of God. This alone is true courage; true virtue; for it is rational, and its motive is moral and unselfish. It is a true Christian grace, when found in its purest forms, a grace whose highest exemplar, and whose source, is the Divine Redeemer; whose principle is that parent grace of the soul, *faith*. "David, and Samuel, and the prophets, *through faith* subdued kingdoms, * * * waxed valiant in fight, turned to flight the armies of the aliens." (Hebrews 11:33, 34) Trust in God, in his faithfulness, his approbation, his reward, his command to brave the risks allotted to them, was their motive. But "Christ dwelleth in our hearts by faith." (Ephesians 3:17) This is the principle by which the soul of the believer is brought into living union with Christ; and the heart, otherwise sapless and withered, is penetrated by the vital sap of his holy Spirit. He is the head; men of faith his members; he the stock; they the branches; his divine principles circulate from him into their souls, and assimilate them to him. But the whole mission of Jesus Christ on earth is a divine exemplification of moral courage. What was it, save the unselfish sentiment of duty, overruling the anticipations of personal evil, which made him declare, in prospect of all the woes of his incarnation, "Lo I come, in the volume of the book it is written of me; I delight to do thy will Oh my God?" What else caused him to press forward with eager, hungering haste, through the toils and obloquy of his persecuted life, to that baptism of blood, which awaited him in Jerusalem? What else nerved him, when deserted, betrayed, and destined to death, desolate, and fainting, amidst a pitiless flood of enemies, one word of disclaimer might have rescued him, to refuse that word, and assert his rightful kingship over Zion, with a tenacity more indomitable than the grave? Jesus Christ is the divine pattern and fountain of heroism. Earth's true heroes are they who derive their courage from him.

Yet it is true, the three kinds of bravery which have been defined, may be mixed in many breasts. Some who have true moral courage may also have animal hardihood; and others of the truly brave may lack it. No Christian courage, perhaps, exists without a union of that which the spirit of personal honor, in its innocent phase, inspires; and many men of honor have perhaps some shade of the pure sentiment of duty, mingled with the pride and self-glorifying, which, chiefly nerve their fortitude. *But he is the bravest man who is the best Christian. It is he who truly fears God, who is entitled to fear nothing else.*

I. He whose conduct is governed by the fear of God, is brave, because the powers of his soul are in harmony. There is no mutiny or war within, of fear against shame, of duty against safety, of conscience and evil desire, by which the bad man has his heart unnerved. All the nobler capacities of the soul combine their strength, and especially, that master power, of which the wicked are compelled to sing: "It is conscience that makes cowards of us all," invigorates the soul with her plaudits. In conscious rectitude there is strength.

This strength General Jackson eminently possessed. He walked in the fear of God, with a perfect heart, keeping all his commandments and ordinances, blameless. Never has it been my happiness to know one of greater purity of life, or more regular and devout habits of prayer. As ever in his great taskmaster's eye, he seemed to devote every hour to the sentiment of duty, and only to live to fulfill his charge as a servant of God. Of this be assured, that all his eminence and success as a great and brave soldier, were based on his eminence and sanctity as a Christian. Thus, every power of his soul was brought to move in sweet accord, under the guidance of an enlightened and honest conscience. How could such a soul fail to be courageous for the right?

But especially did he derive firmness and decision, from the peculiar strength of his conviction concerning the righteousness and necessity of this war. Had he not sought the light of the Holy Scriptures, in thorough examination and prayer, had his pure and honest conscience not justified the act, even in the eye of that Searcher of hearts, whose fear was his ever-present, ruling principle, never would he have drawn his sword in this great quarrel, at the prompting of any sectional pride, or ambition, or interest, or anger, or dread of obloquy. But having judged for himself, in all sincerity, he decided, with a force of conviction as fixed as the everlasting hills, that our enemies were the aggressors, that they assailed vital, essential rights, and that resistance unto death was our right and duty. On the correctness of that decision, reached through fervent prayer, under the teachings of the sure word of Scripture, through the light of the Holy Spirit, which he was assured God vouchsafed to him, he stood prepared to risk, not only earthly prospects and estate, but an immortal soul; and to venture, without one quiver of doubt or fear, before the irrevocable bar of God the Judge. The great question: "What if I die in this quarrel," was deliberately settled; so deliberately, so maturely, that he was ready to venture his everlasting all upon the belief that this was the path of duty.[234]

II. The second reason which makes the man of faith brave, is stated in the context: "Are not five sparrows sold for two farthings, and not one of them is forgotten before God? But even the very hairs of your head are all numbered: Fear not therefore; ye are of more value than many sparrows." God's special providence is over all his creatures, and all their actions; it is over them that fear him; for their good only. By that almighty and omniscient providence, all events are either produced; or at least permitted, limited, and overruled. There is no creature so great as to resist its power, none so minute as to evade its wisdom. Each particular act among the most multitudinous which confound our attention by their number, or the most fortuitous, which entirely baffle our inquiry into their cause, is regulated by this intelligent purpose of God. Even when the thousand missiles of death, invisible to mortal sight, and sent forth aimless by those who launched them, shoot in inexplicable confusion over the battlefield, his eye gives each one an aim and a purpose, according to the plan of his wisdom.[235] Thus teacheth our Savior.

Now, the child of God is not taught what is the special will of God as to himself; he has no revelation as to the security of his person. Nor does he presume to predict what particular dispensation God will grant to the cause in which he is embarked. But he knows that, be it what it may, it will be wise, and right, and good. Whether the arrows of death shall smite him or pass him by, he knows no more than the unbelieving sinner; but he knows that neither event can happen [to] him without the purpose and will of his Heavenly Father. And that will, be it whichever it may, is guided by divine wisdom and love. Should the event prove a revelation of God's decision, and this was the place, and this the hour, for life to end; then he accepts it with calm submission; for are not the time and place chosen for him by the All-wise, who loves him from eternity? Him who walks in the true fear of God, God loves. He hath adopted him as his son forever, through his faith on the righteousness of the Redeemer. The divine anger is forever extinguished by the atonement of the Lamb of God, and the unchangeable love of God is conciliated to him by the spotless righteousness of his substitute. The preciousness of the unspeakable gift which God gave for his redemption, even the life of the Only-begotten, and the earnest of the Holy Ghost, bestowed upon him at first while a guilty sinner, are the arguments to this believer, of the richness and strength of God's love to him. He knows that a love so eternal, so free, so strong, in the breast of such a God and Savior, can leave nothing unbestowed, which divine wisdom perceives to be for his true good. "He that spared not his own Son, but delivered him up for us all, how shall he not with him also freely give us all things." (Romans 8:32) And this love has enlisted for his safeguard, all the attributes of God, which are the security of his own blessedness. Why dwelleth the divine mind in ineffable, perpetual peace? Not because there are none to assail it; but because God is conscious in himself of infinite resources, for defense and victory; of a knowledge which no cunning can deceive; of a power which no combination can fatigue. Well, these same attributes, which support the stability of Jehovah's throne, surround the weakest child of God, with all the zeal of redeeming love. "The eternal God is his refuge; and underneath him are the everlasting arms." (Deuteronomy 33:27) Therefore saith the Apostle, that the believer hath "his heart and mind garrisoned by the peace of God which passeth all understanding." (Philippians 4:7) And therefore our Savior saith, with a literal emphasis of which our faint hearts are slow to take in the full glory: "Peace I leave with you; *my* peace I give unto you." (John 14:27) In proportion as God's children have faith to embrace the love of God to them, are they lifted in spirit to his very throne, and can look down upon the rage of battle, and the tumult of the people, with some of the holy disdain, the ineffable security, which constitute the blessedness of God. "Their life is hid with Christ in God."

It has been said that General Jackson was a fatalist, by those who knew not whereof they affirmed. He was a strong believer in the special providence of God. The doctrine of a Fate is, that all events are fixed by an immanent, physical necessity in the series of causes and effects themselves; a necessity as blind and unreasoning as the tendency of the stone towards the earth, when unsupported from beneath; a necessity as much controlling the intelligence and will of God as of creatures; a necessity which admits no modification of results through the agency of second causes, but renders them inoperative and non-essential, save as the mere, passive stepping stones in the inevitable progression. The doctrine of a Providence teaches that the regular, natural agency of second causes is sustained, preserved, and regulated by the power and intelligence of God; and that in and through that agency, every event is directed by his most wise and holy will, according to his plan, and the laws of nature which he has ordained. Fatalism tends to apathy, to absolute inaction: a belief in the providence of the Scriptures, to intelligent and hopeful effort. It does not overthrow, but rather establish the agency of second causes, because it teaches us that God's purpose to effectuate events only through them (save in the case of miracles) is as steadfast, as his purpose to carry out his eternal plan. Hence it produces a combination of courageous serenity – with cheerful diligence in the use of means. My illustrious leader was as laborious as he was trustful; and laborious precisely because he was trustful. Every thing that self-sacrificing care, and preparation, and forecast, and toil, could do, to prepare and to earn success, he did. And therefore it was, that God, without whom "the watchman waketh but in vain," usually bestowed success. So likewise, his belief in the superintendence of the Almighty was a most strong and living conviction. In every order, or dispatch, announcing a victory, he was prompt to ascribe the result to the Lord of Hosts; and those simple, emphatic, devout ascriptions were with him no unmeaning formalities. In the very flush of triumph, he has been known to seize the juncture for the earnest inculcation of this truth upon the minds of his subordinates. On the momentous morning of Friday, June 27th, 1862, as the different corps of the patriot army were moving to their respective posts, to fill their parts in the mighty combination of their chief, after Jackson had held his final interview with him, and resumed his march for his position at Cold Harbor, his command was misled, by a misconception of his guides, and seemed about to mingle with, and confuse, another part of our forces. More than an hour of seemingly precious time was expended in rectifying this mistake; while the booming of cannon in the front told us that the struggle had begun, and made our breasts thrill with an agony of suspense, lest the irreparable hour should be lost by our delay; for we had still many miles to march. When this anxious fear was suggested privately to Jackson, he answered, with a calm and assured countenance: "No; let us trust that the providence of our God will so overrule it, that no mischief shall result." And verily; no mischief did result. Providence brought us precisely into conjunction with the bodies with which we were to co-operate; the battle was joined at the right juncture and by the time the stars appeared, the right wing of the enemy, with which he was appointed to deal, was hurled in utter rout, across the river. More than once, when sent to bring one of his old fighting brigades into action, I had noticed him sitting motionless upon his horse with his right hand uplifted, while the war worn column poured in stern silence close by his side. At first it did not appear whether it was mere abstraction of thought, or a posture to relieve his fatigue. But at Port Republic, I saw it again; and watching him more narrowly, was convinced by his closed eyes and moving lips, that he was wrestling in silent prayer. I thought that I could surmise what was then passing through his fervent soul: the sovereignty of that Providence which worketh all things after the counsel of his own will, and giveth the battle not to the strong, nor the race to the swift; his own fearful responsibility, and need of that counsel and sound wisdom, which God alone can give; the crisis of his beloved country, and the balance trembling between defeat and victory; the precious lives of his veterans, which the inexorable necessities of war compelled him to jeopardize; the immortal souls passing to their account, perhaps unprepared; the widowhood and orphanage which might result from the orders he had just been compelled to issue. And as his beloved men swept by him to the front, into the storm of shot, doubtless his great heart, as tender as it was resolute, yearned over them in unutterable longings and intercessions, that "the Almighty would cover them with his feathers, and that his truth might be their shield and buckler." Surely the moral grandeur of this scene was akin to that, when Moses stood upon the Mount of God, and lifted up his hands, while Israel prevailed against Amalek! And what soldier would not desire to have the shield of such prayers, under which to fight? Were they not a more powerful element of success than the artillery, or the bayonets of the Stonewall Brigade?

III. The true fear of God ensures the safety of the immortal soul. United to Christ by faith, adopted into the unchanging favor of God, and heir of an inheritance in the skies which is as secure as the throne of God, the believing soul, is lifted above the reach of bodily dangers.

But the soul is the true man, the true self, the part which alone feels or knows, desires or fears, sorrows or rejoices, and which lives forever. It is its fate which is irrevocable. If it be lost, all is lost; and finally lost; if it be secure, all other losses are secondary, yea, in comparison, trivial. To the child of God, the rage of enemies, mortal weapons, and pestilence are impotent. True, he has no assurance that they may not reach his body, but they reach his body only, and,

> "If the plague come nigh,
> And sweep the wicked down to hell,
> Twill raise the saints on high."[236]

This is our Savior's argument, "Be not afraid of them that kill the body; and after that *have no more that they can do.*" Pagan fable perhaps intended to foreshadow this glorious truth, when it described its hero with a body made invulnerable by its bath in the divine river, and therefore insensible to fear, and indifferent to the weapons of death. But the spiritual reality of the allegory is found only in the Christian, who has washed his soul from the stain of sin (which alone causes its death), in the Redeemer's blood. He is the invulnerable man. "The arrow cannot make him flee; darts are counted as stubble; he laugheth at the shaking of a spear." He shares, indeed the natural affections and instincts which make life sweet to every man, and bodily pain and death formidable. But these emotions of his sensuous being are counteracted by his faith, which gives to his soul a substantial, inward sense of heavenly life, as more real and satisfying than the carnal. The clearer the faith of the Christian, the more complete is this victory over natural fears. To the mere unbeliever, this mortal life is his all-in-all, bodily death is utter extinction, pain is the master evil, and the grave is covered by a horror of great darkness unrelieved by one ray of hope or light. And Christians of a weaker type, in their weaker moments, cannot shake off the shuddering of nature in the presence of these, the supreme evils of the natural man. But as faith brightens, that tremor is quieted; the more substantial the grasp of faith on eternal realities, the more does the giant death dwindle in his proportions, the less mortal does his sword appear, the narrower and more trivial seems the gap which he makes between this life and the higher; because that better life is brought nearer to the apprehension of the soul. Does the eagle lament to see the wolf ravage its deserted nest, as it betakes itself to its destined skies, and nerves its young pinions and fires its eyes in the beam of the king of day? The believer knows also, that should his body be smitten into the grave, the resurrection day will repair all the ravages of the sword, and restore the poor tenement to his occupancy, "fashioned like unto Christ's glorious body." He can adopt the boast of inspiration: "God is our refuge and strength; a very present help in trouble. Therefore will not we fear though the earth be removed, and though the mountains be carried into the midst of the sea." (Psalm 46:1-2) Amidst the storm of battle, and even the wreck of defeat, his steadfast heart knows not fear.

But that the enemy of God should have courage in battle, is incomprehensible to me. It can only be explained by thoughtlessness. When the danger which assails the body reaches the soul also, when the weapon that lays the body in the dust, will plunge the soul into everlasting and intolerable torments, by what philosophy can a reasoning being brace himself to meet it? He who has not God for his friend, has no right to be brave. But we should be far from inferring thence, that the citizen who is conscious of his enmity to God, is therefore justified in shunning the exposure to this risk, at the expense of duty and honor. This would be but to add sin to sin, and folly to folly. If safety is not found in the path of duty, still more surely it will not be found, when out of it. He is in the greatest danger, who is disobeying God; and infinite wisdom and power can never be at a loss for means to strike their enemy, however far removed wounds and weapons of war may be. To refuse a recognized duty is the surest way to alienate the mercy of God, and to grieve that Holy Ghost, on whom we depend for faith and repentance. The only safe or rational course therefore, for the ungodly soldier, is to make his peace with God at once; and thus advance with well-grounded confidence in the path of his duty, and of all men, the soldier has the strongest reasons to become a Christian!

Such was the foundation of the courage of Jackson. He walked with God, in conscious integrity; and he embraced with all his heart "the righteousness of God which is by the faith of Jesus Christ." His soul, I believe, dwelt habitually in the full assurance that God was his God, and his portion forever. His manly and vigorous faith brought heaven so near, that death had slight terrors for him. While it would be unjust to charge him with rashness in exposure to danger, yet whenever his sense of duty prompted it, he seemed to risk his person with an absolute indifference to fear. The sense of his responsibilities to his country, and the heat of his mighty spirit in the crisis of battle, might sometimes agitate him vehemently; but never was the most imminent personal peril seen to disturb his equanimity for one moment. It is a striking trait of the impression which he has made upon his countrymen, that while no man could possibly be farther from boasting, it always became the first article of the belief of those subject to his command, that he was, of course, a man of perfect courage.

But courage alone does not explain the position which he held in the hearts of his people. In this land of heroic memories and brave men, others besides Jackson have displayed true courage. God did not endow him with several of those native gifts which are supposed to allure the idolatry of mankind towards their heroes. He affected no kingly mien nor martial pomp; but always bore himself with the modest propriety of the Christian. Nor did he ever study or practice those arts, by which a [Napoleon] Bonaparte or an Alexander [the Great] kindled the enthusiasm of their followers. The only manifestation which he ever made of himself was in the simple and diligent performance of the duties of his office. His part on the battlefield was usually rather suggestive of the zeal and industry of the faithful servant, than of the contagious exaltation of a master-spirit. Nature had not given to him even the corporeal gift of the trumpet tones, with which other leaders are said to have roused the divine frenzy in their followers. It was only at times that his modest and feeble voice was lifted up to his hosts; and then, as he shouted his favorite call: "Press forward," the fiery energy of his will, thrilled through his rapid utterance, rather like the deadly clang of the rifle, than the sonorous peal of the clarion. His was a master-spirit; but it was too simply grand to study dramatic sensations. It impressed its might upon the souls of his countrymen, not through deportment, but through deeds. Its discourses were toilsome marches and battles joined, its perorations were the thunder-claps of defeat hurled upon the enemies of his country. It revealed itself to us only through the purity and force of his action; and therefore the intensity of the effect he has produced.

This may help to explain the enigma of his reputation. How is it that this man, of all others least accustomed to exercise his own fancy, or address that of others, has stimulated the imagination, not only of his countrymen, but of the civilized world, above all the sons of genius among us? How has he, the most unromantic of great men, become the hero of a living romance, the ideal of an inflamed fancy in every mind, even before his life had passed into history! How did that calm eye kindle the fire of so passionate a love and admiration in the heart of his people? He was brave, but not the only brave. He revealed transcendent military talent; but the diadem of his country now glows with a galaxy of such talent. He was successful; but we have more than one captain, whose banner never trailed before an enemy. I will tell you the solution. It was, chiefly, the singleness, purity, and elevation of his aims. Every one who observed him was as thoroughly convinced of his unselfish devotion to duty as of his courage; as certain that no thought of personal advancement, of ambition or applause, ever for one instant divided the homage of his heart with his great cause, and that "all the ends he aimed at were his country's, his God's, and truth's," as that he was brave. The love of his countrymen is the spontaneous testimony of the common conscience, to the beauty of holiness. It is the confession of our nature that the virtue of the Sacred Scriptures, which is a virtue purer and loftier than that of philosophy, is the true greatness, grander than knowledge, talent, courage, or success. Here, then, as I believe, is God's chief lesson in his life and death (and the belief encourages auspicious hopes concerning God's designs towards us). He would teach us the beauty and power of pure Christianity, as an element of our social life, of our national career. Therefore he took an exemplar of Christian sincerity, as near perfection as the infirmities of our nature would permit, formed and trained in an honorable retirement; he set it in the furnace of trial, at an hour when great events and dangers had awakened the popular heart to most intense action; he illustrated it with that species of distinction which above all others, attracts the popular gaze, military glory; and held it up to the admiring inspection of a country grateful for the deliverances it had wrought for us. Thus he has taught us, how good a thing his fear is. He has made all men see and acknowledge that, in this man, his Christianity was the fountain head of the virtues and talents, which they so rapturously applauded; that it was the fear of God which made him so fearless of all else; that it was the love of God which animated his energies; that it was the singleness of his aims which caused his whole body to be so full of light, that the unerring decisions of his judgment, suggested to the unthinking, the belief in his actual inspiration; and that the lofty chivalry of his nature was but the reflex of the Spirit of Christ. Do not even the profane admit this explanation of his character? Here then, is God's lesson, in this life, to these Confederate States: "It is righteousness that exalteth." Hear it ye young men, ye soldiers, ye magistrates, ye law-givers; that "he that exalteth himself shall be abased; but he that humbleth himself shall be exalted."

But what would he teach us by his death, to our view so untimely? To this question, human reason can only answer, that God's judgments are far above us, and past our finding out.

One lovely Sabbath, riding alone with me to a religious service in a camp, General Jackson was talking of the general prospects of the war, hopefully, as he ever did. But at the close, he assumed an air of intense seriousness, and said: "I do not mean to convey the impression that I have not as much to live for as any man, and that life is not as sweet. But I do not desire to survive the independence of my country." Can this death be the answer to that wish? Can the solution be, that having tried us, and found us unworthy of such a deliverer, God had hid his favorite in the grave, in the brightness of his hopes, and before his blooming honors received any blight from disaster, from the calamities which our sins are about to bring upon us? Nay; we will not believe that the legacy of Jackson's prayers was all expended by us, when he died; they will yet avail for us all the more, that they are now sealed by his blood. The deliverance of the Jews did not end with the untimely end of Judas Maccabee. The death of William of Orange was not the death of the Dutch Republic. The lamented fall of John Hampden was not the fall of the liberties of England. And, if we may reverently associate another instance with these, the crucifixion of Jesus of Nazareth, was, contrary to the fears of his disciples, but the beginning of the sect of the Nazarenes. So, let us hope, the tree of our liberties will flourish but the more for the precious blood by which it is watered.

May it not be, that God, after enabling him to render all the service which was essential to our deliverance, and showing us in him, the brightest example of the glory of Christianity, has bid him enter into the joy of his Lord, at this juncture, in order to warn us against our incipient idolatry, and make us say: "It is better to trust in the Lord, than to put confidence in princes?" No man would more strongly deprecate this idolatry of human instruments, than Jackson, and never so strongly, as when addressed to himself. None can declare more emphatically than would he, if he spoke to us from the skies, that while man is mortal, the cause is immortal. Away then, with unmanly discouragements, God lives, though our hero is dead.

That he should have toiled so hard for the independence of his country, and so ardently desired it; and then at last, be forbidden to hail the day of our final deliverance, or to receive the grateful honors which his fellow-citizens were preparing for him; this has saddened every heart with a pang both tender and pungent. The medicine to this pain, my brethren, is to remember, that he has entered into a triumph and peace, so much more glorious than that which he bled to achieve for his country. It would have been sweet to us, to hail him returning from his last victory to a delivered and enfranchised country; sweet to see and sympathize with the joy with which he hung up his sword, and paid the sacrifices of thanksgiving in the courts of the Lord's house; sweet to witness, with reverent respect, the domestic bliss of the home for which he so much sighed, solacing him for his long fatigues. That happiness *we* have lost; but *he* has lost nothing. He has laid down his sword at the footstool of his Father God; he now sings his thanksgiving song in a nobler sanctuary than the earthly one he loved so much; he "bathes his weary soul in seas of heavenly rest."

We who loved him, while we bewail our own loss, should not forget the circumstances which alleviate the grief of his death. Surely, it was no ill-chosen time for God to call him to his rest, when his powers were in their undimmed prime, and his military glory at its zenith; when his greatest victory had just been won; and the last sounds of earth which reached him were the thanksgivings and blessings of a nation in raptures for his achievements; in tears for his sufferings. I love to remember, too, that his martyr-life had just been gladdened by the gratification of those affections which were in him so sweet and strong, and which yet, he sacrificed, so patiently, for his country.

Still more do we thank God that it was practicable, as it might not have been at an earlier, or a later period, for him to enjoy those ministrations of love, in his last days, which were the dearest solace of his sufferings. Into the sacredness of those last communings, and of the grief which survives them in his widowed home, we may not allow even our thoughts to intrude. And yet, may not a mourning nation venture to utter their blessing on the mourning heart which blessed him with its love; and to pray, that the breast which so magnanimously calmed its tumult, to make a quiet pillow for the dying head of their hero, may be visited by God, with the most healing balm of heavenly consolation? Will not all the people say: amen?

Nor will they forget the tender flower, sole off-shoot of the parent stock, born to bloom amidst the wintry storms of war, which he would fain have forbidden the summer breeze to visit too roughly. The giant tree which would have shielded it with pride so loving, lies prone before the blast. But His God will be its God; and as long as the most rugged breast of his hardy comrades is warm, it will not lack for a parent's tenderness.

And now, with one more lesson, I leave you to the teachings of the mighty dead. If there was one trait which was eminent in him above the rest, it was determination. This was the power, before whose steady and ardent heat obstacles melted away. This was the force, which caused his battalions to breast the onset of the enemy like ramparts of stone, or else launched them irresistibly upon their shivered lines. It was his unconquerable will, and purpose never to submit or yield.[237] Every one who was near him imbibed something of this spirit, for they saw that in him the acceptance of defeat was an impossibility. To that conclusion no earthly power could bend his iron will. Let this example commend to us the same steadfast temper. In his fall and that of the noble army of martyrs, every generous soul should read a new argument for defending the cause for which he died, with invincible tenacity. Surely their very blood might cry out against us from the ground, if we permitted the soil, which drank the precious libation to be polluted with the despot's foot! Shall it ever be, that our discouragement or cowardice shall make the sacrifice vain? If we consent to this, then was it not treacherous in us to invite it? We should rather have warned them to restrain their generosity, to save the lives they were so ready to lay upon their country's altar, as too precious to be wasted for a land occupied by predestined slaves and cowards, and to carry their patriotism and their gifts to some more propitious clime, and some worthier companionship.

Such are the thoughts which should inspire the heart of every one who stands beside the grave of Jackson.[238] Around that green and swelling hill stands the circle of solemn mountain peaks keeping everlasting watch over the home which he loved and the tomb where his ashes sleep, majestic when the summer sunset bathes them in azure and gold, but only more grandly steadfast, when they are black with storms and winter. So, let us resolve, we will guard the honor and the rights for which he died, in the hour of triumph, and more immovably in the hour of disaster.[239]

Faith[240]

An Expository Sermon

on

Romans 10:6-10

"But the righteousness which is of faith speaketh on this wise: Say not
in thy heart, Who shall ascend into heaven? (that is, to bring Christ
down from above:) Or, Who shall descend into the deep? (that is, to
bring up Christ again from the dead.) But what saith it? The word
is nigh thee, even in thy mouth, and in thy heart: that is, the word of
faith which we preach: That if thou shalt confess with thy mouth the
Lord Jesus, and shalt believe in thy heart that God hath raised him
from the dead, thou shalt be saved. For with the heart,
man believeth unto righteousness; and with
the mouth confession is made unto salvation."

Preached September 6, 1863, at Orange Courthouse, Va. to an assemblage of
officers and men, belonging to the 2nd Corps, Army of N. Va.[241]

The great end, my brethren, of all the exhortations of the ministry to men is, to flee from the wrath to come, and make their peace with God. Just so far as their exhortations are successful, they must be met by the answering inquiry: "What must we do, that we may work the works of God?" And therefore they should be always ready to expound the nature of that *faith*, which answers this great question: that faith which the Redeemer declared, was preeminently the work of God, and which the Scriptures everywhere hold out as the thing whereby the sinner passes from death unto life. I invite you to study this topic today, as it is presented in the text, one of the most striking and profitable descriptions of saving faith within the lids of the Bible. I do it, because I would fain hope that there are at least some here, enough interested concerning their own salvation, to find this an interesting subject. I would appeal to that consciousness of your lost estate which, I well know, lurks in the hearts of the most careless of you. Why may not this be the day for you to awake, and look at the hope which is set before you in the gospel?

The Apostle Paul's language in this place is almost a verbal quotation of the words of Moses in Deuteronomy 30:11 and following verses. He quotes first, the declaration of Moses in Leviticus 18:5 as expressing the condition of the covenant of works. "He that doeth the commandments shall live in them." But the gospel proposes no such plan of salvation. The righteousness of faith which we preach is just the opposite. It depends, not on a perfect obedience, which we know we cannot render; but on a simple faith or trust in the offered righteousness of another. To describe this faith, St. Paul borrows the words of Moses in Deuteronomy, where the great prophet urges upon his charge, the people of Israel, that he had set before them life and death. He says: "For this commandment which I command thee this day, it is not hidden from thee, neither is it far off. It is not in heaven, that thou shouldest say: Who shall go up for us to heaven, and bring it unto us, that we may hear it, and do it? Neither is it beyond the sea, that thou shouldest say, Who shall go over the sea for us, and bring it unto us, that we may hear it and do it? But the word is very nigh unto thee, in thy mouth and in thy heart, that thou mayest do it." A remark may be needed, to explain the Apostle's apparent wresting of Moses' words, in applying to the "righteousness which is by faith," what at the first glance, seems to have been said by him touching obedience to his institutions and precepts. Moses tells his people that the condition of their salvation was now brought near, and made plain to them. It was no longer concealed, remote, or abstruse. No profound speculations, no distant journeys to consult the sages of other lands, no imagination soaring into the secrets of heaven, were now needed by a Hebrew, to know what he must do in order to be accepted of God. The revelation of this was explicitly made by him; and he had taught them what they had to do, publicly, and plainly, so that all might understand.

Saint Paul is to be understood, in the first place, as asserting a parallelism between the teachings of Moses and Christ, in this particular: that the latter, like the former, had published the terms of salvation clearly, so that no sinner could justly complain of not knowing what he had to do. As Moses had set before his people "life and good, and death and evil," by his fulfillment of his mission: so Jesus Christ had wrought out a finished redemption, and had announced its terms with a clearness which left no room for addition: as for instance, when he commissioned his Apostles, and said: "He that believeth and is baptized shall be saved: he that believeth no shall be damned." Obviously, the two dispensations, of Moses and Christ could be alike in this particular, even though they proposed different plans of salvation. So that in this respect, St. Paul might speak just as Moses spake. As the latter reminded the Hebrews, that they no longer had a pretext for asking: "Who shall go up for us to heaven"? because he had met God on the holy mount, and brought back full instructions: so, says the Apostle, none now have a pretext to say that they are waiting for fuller communications with the skies, because Christ himself has come thence, finished his work, and declared his will as to man's salvation. Moses urges, in substance, that his people could not say they were awaiting instructions from beyond the ocean, or from some remote and inaccessible region; for he had published their duty in their very midst, and in the most simple mode. So, Paul reminds us, no one can now pretend that it is necessary the abyss of the grave shall be sounded, or its secrets disclosed: because Jesus Christ, by his resurrection has already taught the sinner all he needs to know of its secrets: namely, that the Captain of his salvation has conquered death, and led captivity captive, and assured the resurrection of all his people. And as Moses declared that the word was very nigh unto the people, that the question of duty was brought home to them, to their very lips and hearts, so, says the Apostle, is the word of faith which we preach. A provided gospel and finished redemption now so plainly offered to you, brings your own salvation to the issue of your own choice. All you have to do is to decide in your heart, and declare Christ with your mouth. Your fate is ready for this immediate decision. But, in the second place: The dispensations of Moses and Christ agree exactly, not only in the above particular, but in the substance of the way which they propose to man for salvation. "Moses spake of me," says the Savior himself. Notice, that the prophet, in v. 10th requires not only a formal obedience to his ordinances, but a "turning to God," with all the soul. What can this be but repentance? And those ordinances which made up the formal part of his system, all pointed to a vicarious sacrifice to come: so that to observe them with the heart, was to exercise faith in the foreshadowed Savior. In a word St. Paul's application of the language is justified by the acknowledged fact, that the feelings with which the pious Hebrew offered the Mosaic sacrifices, and obeyed his precepts, were substantially the same with that faith on the Lord Jesus Christ, and repentance towards God, by which we are saved under the gospel.

Proceeding now to apply the instructions of the passage, we are taught:

I. That there is no work or discovery on the sinner's part, except the simple discovery of his need, which is required to prepare the way for believing. The gospel tells us, vv. 6-7, that there is no righteousness to be brought in by us, no atonement to be invented, no addition to be made to that everlasting righteousness which Christ wrought, when he descended from heaven, went into the grave, and was brought up again from the dead. None of our good works, our forms, rites, sacraments, or superstitions, nor our reformations or repentings, whether unscriptural or scriptural, are needed to supplement his righteousness for our justification. We are to embrace the finished work of Christ just as we are, in our unfitness and unworthiness, except so far as a thorough sense of our guilt and necessity prepares us.

Or, perhaps it is equally important to learn from these words, that saving faith does not consist at all in any profound or far-reaching exercise of the understanding. The sinner is not required to explore the secrets of heaven, or the mysteries of the world of spirits, by the efforts of his philosophy, in order to learn the way of salvation. There is no profound speculation needed. There is no discovery to be made by the force of genius. The believer does not depend on speculation, but on the word of God. He pretends to invent nothing, and to know nothing, except what God has told him: and this he believes, because he has God's word for it. And here, the wisest and most learned are on a level with the babe in Christ. The faith of the learned divine is no more founded on his own wisdom, than that of the humble saint, who knows no more than that his Bible is God's word, and that it offers him Christ. All is revealed, which is to be believed for salvation, and so revealed that its saving reception requires nothing, but a childlike simplicity coupled with humility.

But though faith is not founded on human speculation, it is not opposed to reason. That we should here bow our reason to God's mere word, is the highest dictate of reason. She tells us, by her clearest *dicta*, that this gospel is God's inspired word, and that therefore, all it teaches is unmingled truth, however above, or beyond her comprehension. She pronounces the obvious principle, that the terms on which a sovereign God shall see fit to pardon his rebel creatures cannot be inferred by speculations or deductions, but can only be declared by himself: and when she has heard his voice and recognized it as his, she bows in instant submission. She feels that to admit the dominion of faith here is supremely reasonable.

Say not in thy heart then, O sinner: who shall ascend into heaven, or fathom the abyss, to bring the knowledge of Christ to the soul. All is revealed which you need to know: all is clear and explicit. No laborious invention or ingenuity is required of you. All that is needed is a simple and an humble heart, to embrace God's word.

II. This leads us to the second point of instruction in the text; that saving faith is an exercise natural and easy to him who is truly willing to believe. "The word is nigh thee, even in thy mouth, and in thy heart: that is: the word of faith which we preach." How opposite is this to the thoughts of the unregenerate man? He imagines that faith must be something abstruse and profound, and that some mighty, and almost inconceivable exertion of the soul must be put forth. He looks afar off for it. He supposes that this something which is the hinge of the soul's eternal state, and which transfers from life to death, must be a thing wonderful and difficult. Not so: "The word is nigh thee." To the heart which feels its need of a Savior aright, and is willing to be saved, faith is an exercise so easy, so natural, that it is in fact, spontaneous and unavoidable. It is the reaching forth of the hand of the beggar, when he feels within him the consuming hunger, and sees the bread offered. It is the cry of the frightened disciple, as he found himself sinking in the angry waves, while he grasped the Master's extended hand, "Save Lord, or I perish." "The word is even in thy mouth and in thy heart." It is the spontaneous expression of the soul made willing by the Holy Spirit, coming forth from the heart and lips as naturally, as easily, and as certainly, as the water flows from the living spring.

Hence, the impossibility of conveying to the unbeliever a correct idea of what faith is, needs not be much regretted. All description must, perhaps, fail of conveying a full conception of it; because an affection of the soul cannot be described to one who has never felt it, any more than the idea of light and colors can be conveyed accurately to the mind of one born blind. But there is no danger, that any one truly wishing to come to Christ will be kept away by not knowing how to come. When once the sinner is truly willing, believing on Christ is as easy and spontaneous as the cry of the frightened child for aid, who sees the danger, and his parent near at hand. It is only he who is not willing to come, that does not know how to come.

III. Next, we are taught that the direct object of saving faith is Christ's work of redemption. "Thou shalt believe in thy heart that God hath raised him from the dead." The believer embraces the great fact of Christ's resurrection, as that which he himself had appointed, before his death, for the crowning test of his messiahship. He embraces it as the necessary evidence of the completeness of his atonement. For when the great Surety was released from the prison house of death, it was thereby proved that he had fully paid our debt. The believer sees in Christ's resurrection the proof of His victory over death, and thereby, of his ability to deliver us; and of the fulfillment of the Father's promise to seat him at his right hand, and give all the fullness of redemption into his keeping. To believe in the resurrection, then, is to believe in Christ's completed work of redemption. And this is the direct object of saving faith. Though, all the rest of revelation, except the central doctrines of redemption, be unknown: though the believer may not have heard even, of any portion of the Scriptures, except the single evangel or epistle which tells him of Christ, and convinces him of his truth and fitness as a Savior, saving faith may be exercised, and the soul may pass from death unto life. And yet, wherever true faith [i]n Christ exists, the willing reception of all divine truth will be certain, as fast as it becomes known. When we say that the object of saving faith is not the whole circle of revealed truth, but the doctrine of the cross, we mean that the soul may be saved although (unavoidably) ignorant of all but the doctrines of the cross: and not, that a believing soul can knowingly reject any portion of God's truth. For the same trust in the divine fidelity, which causes him to confide in one doctrine, will ensure his confiding equally in all that God says, as fast as it becomes known.

IV. We are next led to the center of the whole subject, when the Apostle tells us, that "with the heart man believeth unto righteousness." Saving faith is not a mere notion of the understanding: it is an act of the affections and will. By the heart, the Scriptures usually mean the dispositions and will, or the active powers of the soul. And when the text tells us, that man believeth with the heart unto righteousness, it is hoped that you will be led to some understanding of what it is that you lack. Doubtless, when you have heard so much stress laid upon faith, your secret thoughts have answered: I do believe the gospel: I never doubted the truth of the history, which tells how Jesus suffered and died for man's sins, and rose again for his justification, nor of the promises, which offer life in him. And yet, I experience nothing of that mighty change, which is promised to accompany faith: nor of that religious hope and joy which it should beget. How is this? I am told that to believe is all that is needed; and I have never been anything else than a believer, and yet I feel and know that I am not renewed! The text, O sinner, gives you the answer: "With the heart man believeth unto righteousness." You have only believed with the head. You must so believe as to act out your belief. You must so believe as practically to entrust yourself to the Savior. The reality of your belief must be exhibited by your actually setting out on the Christian pilgrimage, and entering upon all the obligations and tasks of the Christian life, in dependence on those truths which your mind professes to receive concerning Christ. A part of this gospel truth is, that you are a lost sinner, condemned to a ruin unspeakably more urgent and vast than all earthly ills. When you so hold this truth, as to arise and flee with instant and constant earnestness from the wrath to come; then you believe with the heart. Another part of the gospel truth is, that "Christ bare our sins in his body, on the tree." When you so believe this, as to entrust your pardon to his advocacy, by a hearty and final act of the inward soul, then you believe with the heart. Another promise of the gospel is, that "they that wait upon the Lord shall renew their strength": that Christ makes "his yoke easy, and his burden light." When you so believe this as to have your dread of undertaking his spiritual service effectually overcome, and so, arise and march forward in the path of his service, then your belief becomes saving faith. Another gospel fact is, that Christ, by his personal excellence, his love, and his sacrifice for us, has earned a right to our supreme, affectionate devotion. When you so believe this, as to bestow that devotion freely and heartily, then the heart believes in Christ, and you are saved. Is it thus that you trust in this Savior? If it is, then I embrace you as my brother in Him: you are a saved soul; and heaven is your inheritance! But alas no! Your faith is a cold, inoperative notion: it dwells only in the unpractical region of the head: it has never warmed and governed your heart and choice.

There are many divines who teach that saving faith should be defined as nothing but the simple, intellectual belief of a proposition. They suppose themselves to be constrained to this view by the force of such passages of Scripture as these: "Now faith is the substance of things hoped for, the evidence of things not seen."[242] "For he that cometh unto God must believe that he is, and that he is the rewarder of them that diligently seek him."[243] "Whosoever believeth that Jesus is the Christ, is born of God."[244] They say, that when we see the exercise so currently and plainly described in the word of God, by the familiar verb 'believe,' and noun 'belief,' we are bound to apprehend it as being simply *belief of facts upon evidence, exercised by the mind.* They appeal also to the nature of the soul: and ask whether it is necessary to predicate any thing more of it. They ask: is it not the nature of man to feel and decide, as his mind sees? Do not all active affections of soul arise by virtue of some view held in the soul's own understanding? And is it not the most obvious law of man's nature, that when he chooses any thing, he does it according to the prevalent view and judgment of his own mind as to the most preferable and reasonable? Is it not this law, in fact, which makes him a reasonable creature in his actions? Now then, say they: by the law of his own nature, according as the mind perceives and judges, the heart will feel and act. Hence we have no need to define faith, as anything more than a thorough conviction of truth in the mind, in order to see how it produces all its practical fruits in the life.

These teachers, among whom are many venerated names, say therefore, that wherever there is a real, clear conviction in the mind, of gospel truth scripturally understood, there is a true, saving faith. If we ask them: 'How is it then, with all those unrenewed persons who indignantly reject the charge of infidelity, and suppose that they believe the Scriptures'? they reply, that they are not sincere and hearty in their conviction of their truth: that, in short, they are, perhaps unconsciously, secret skeptics. They make the difference between a living and a dead faith only this: that the former is full and strong conviction of the understanding, and the latter, wavering and weak.

There is a sense, as will be shown,[245] in which this explanation is true.

But it is perfectly clear that the Scriptures, which aim to give practical rather than scientific views of spiritual exercises, do describe saving faith as embracing two elements, conviction of the understanding concerning gospel truth, and the active embracing of it by the will and purposes. Among these descriptions is the emphatic declaration of the text. "With the heart man believeth unto righteousness." Saving faith is described in the Scriptures, by almost every term which expresses action of soul. It is "trusting in the Son."[246] It is "looking unto God for salvation."[247] It is "receiving Christ."[248] It is "coming unto him."[249] It is "embracing the promises."[250] It is "fleeing unto, and laying hold of Christ."[251] Did inspired truth select these representations, many of them expressive of intense action, to mean nothing?

The intimate connection between faith and repentance shows that faith involves the active powers of the soul, as well as the understanding. Faith implies repentance, and repentance faith. These two graces are twin sisters, so intimately united that their severance would destroy both. Must there not be a community of nature? The active nature of faith is also shown beyond dispute, by the language of the gospel concerning its opposite, unbelief. This is always represented, not as a mere notion, harmlessly erroneous, not as a thing negative and passive, but as a sin, a grievous sin: yea, the head and front of our offending. Now, nothing can be sin in which no active power of the soul is concerned. But since unbelief is both of the heart and head, faith, its contrasted exercise, must be of the heart and head, likewise.

Yet, nothing appears more clear, than that man's feelings and purposes arise according to the light of his own understanding: so that the conclusion seems unavoidable, that if your head were thoroughly convinced of gospel truth, as it is scripturally set forth, your heart would feel and choose accordingly. There is an old-fashioned book, of which I have a high opinion, which defines faith in these words: "A saving grace, whereby we receive and rest upon Jesus Christ alone for salvation, as he is offered to us in the gospel."[252] Now, because I do not see you practically 'resting upon Christ for salvation,' I am compelled to conclude that you do not receive him "as he is offered to you in the gospel," not even with the notion of the understanding. You may honestly suppose that you do: but you are misled by your hearts. You say that you feel you are sinners! Yes: but not in the sense in which the gospel represents you as sinners. You believe that the redemption which you suppose Christ offers will be a desirable thing: but you do not desire such a redemption as God really offers you. When you say that you are not an infidel: that you sincerely believe the gospel history and doctrines; and that you have a high respect for religion, and even a strong desire to possess it; your real meaning is about this: That you are, indeed a sinner, for you have done many wrong things: That sin endangers your soul, because it is just [for] God to punish, if he pleases: That you need a change of purpose and feeling, you scarcely know what, before your heart will be right within: that when you get ready to reform and repent, you must be assisted by Jesus Christ, who procures your pardon: That when you come to die, and so, can no longer possess this world, it will be extremely desirable to possess the Christian's security: That, in short, when you have gotten your own consent, you must secure that blessing, some day before it is too late: which you fully purpose to do: And that, whenever you thus begin to move in the matter, Christ will help and pardon you, as he has engaged. This is your gospel, and it is as different from the true gospel of the Scriptures, as earth is from heaven!

You verily think you are a sinner! But do you believe that "all your righteousnesses are filthy rages," and that those very virtues on which you plume yourself are justly condemned before God? You feel that you need an inward change, and intend to procure it! But do you believe that your soul is "dead in trespasses and sins," that you "are in the bond of iniquity," and that, so far from choosing your own "convenient season" to repent, you will never form the first sincere desire for God, if left to yourself, and will live on in your guilty procrastination until you drop into hell, as surely as rivers flow towards the sea? You think that when death forbids you to enjoy the preferred delights of sin and worldliness, the Christian's impunity will be an excellent thing! But do you believe that it is a desirable thing for you, today, to be "redeemed from all iniquity, and purified unto God a peculiar person zealous of good works"? Ah no: that peculiar sanctity is the very thing which you today dread: and that entire surrender of will and forsaking of sin for Christ is the very thing against which you today reluctate. You hope Christ will help you when you seek him! But do you believe that Christ will faithfully communicate to every sinner who simply trust him, and to you, spiritual strength to carry out a profession of religion consistently and happily, in such a sense that you, even such a poor conscious worldling as you, may leave that seat today, a declared, steadfast child of God, and consistent Christian, by trusting yourself to his hands? No: you do not believe it; not even with the cold speculative notion of the head. Much of this you regard as absurdity and extravagance. But these propositions which I have thus set in contrast with your creed: these are Christ's true gospel! This then, is the just sense in which, as was before indicated, all dead faith is an actual skepticism.

And now, how can this obstinate unbelief of the head be removed? I reply, only by a sovereign renewal of the heart. It may be granted, that if the understanding be thoroughly convinced concerning the preferable good, the will must surely and naturally follow its judgment. But there is a prior question. How shall the head ever be brought to think that holiness, the preferable good, which the heart obstinately eschews, as the object of its native repugnance? And how shall the head sincerely adopt the belief that sin, in all its forms, is a present evil in itself, when the heart loudly declared that, apart from the hell which is connected with it, sin is its preferred delight? It must be remembered that the objects which the gospel presents, to man's soul are all moral objects. It brings not only truths to be understood, but in every truth it also brings a duty, or an obligation, to be felt. The profound [Blaise] Pascal observes, in his *Pensees*: "In natural things, the views of the understanding determine the feelings: but in spiritual things, the feelings determine the views of the understanding."[253] This is true. In the choice between sin and righteousness, the world and Christ, the judgment of the head is but the echo of the native affection of the heart. Here then, is the root of the sinner's unbelief, who professes a historical faith. Christ proposes himself as a Savior from sin itself. Embracing him as such implies then, of course, the intellectual conviction that sin itself, apart from its penalty is a great and present evil, and that the sinner is in bondage to that evil. But how is it possible, that man's understanding can entertain these statements as truths, whose heart cherishes sin, in itself, with a controlling native affection, and only is pained by the fear of its punishment?

This explanation shows us what the text means, when it says, that "with the heart man believeth unto righteousness." And we can now understand also, how faith is the result of that sovereign change of heart, by which the sinner is born again. This native appetite for sin must be revolutionized, before sin can be seen to be indeed a present evil, and a salvation from it the immediate preferable good. But let the almighty Spirit cure this perverse affection of the heart, and turn it to God and right; and then the head comprehends, and the will chooses, Christ, as the desired deliverer. "Thus, by grace we are saved, through faith: and that not of ourselves: it is the gift of God."[254]

V. The text teaches us, that saving faith is not a thing latent and inoperative. "Thou shalt confess with thy mouth the Lord Jesus." Some men cheat themselves with the dream of a covert Christianity: of a compact with Christ to be formed and kept in secret, so as to avoid the reproach of the cross. This cannot be. Such a faith as this of the heart will declare itself with the mouth. It cannot be restrained from publishing its affectionate devotion, but rejoices in glorifying its Redeemer.

And now, O hearer, wilt thou not close with Christ, by believing on him with the heart, and confessing him with the mouth? If only thou art willing to be saved by him, with such a salvation as he offers, a salvation from sin and self-will, as well as from hell, "the word is nigh thee, even in thy heart and in thy mouth." A complete redemption is brought to thy very lips, and only one word, spoken from the heart, is needed to make it yours! Will you close your eyes now upon the outer world, even where you sit, and speak that word to your God in the secret chambers of your soul?

There is momentous solemnity in this thought, that the gift, freighted with all the immense issues of eternity, should be now brought so near us, that only a word of the heart, one aspiration to Christ, should interpose between us and it. For, as nigh as it now is to us, even so remote will it soon become, if we reject it. Between us and this gospel, which is now even in our mouths and in our hearts, there will soon be a gulf fixed, which no man can pass over.

Does any unbeliever object, that now I am inconsistent: because I am urging him to faith: and yet, I have just taught that it is God's gift, which no man exercises until his heart is renewed by sovereign grace? This is true: but wherefore is it true, O sinner? Whose fault are those perverse and sinful dispositions of soul, which blind you to the present evil of sin and the value of a present redemption from it? In adopting sin and the world as your present preferred portion, you are but following your own inclinations. And therefore your incapacity is your guilt. Helpless sinner: guilty for thy very helplessness, cast thyself upon the Savior. Away with proud cavils! If thou art impotent, then fall impotent and submissive upon Jesus' arms, and he will save.

> A guilty, weak, and helpless worm,
> On thy kind arms I fall:
> Be thou my strength and righteousness,
> My Jesus and my all.[255]

The Bondage of Sin

A Sermon

on

Acts 8:23

"Thou art . . . in the bond of iniquity."

Preached in the Tabb Street Church, Petersburg, Va. February 1865. to an assemblage of soldiers and citizens.[256]

This is a part of the rebuke addressed by the Apostle Peter to Simon Magus. It was provoked by an outrageous sin, Simon's attempt to induce the Apostles by a bribe, to bestow on him a share in their spiritual influences. The word "iniquity" is sometimes popularly used among us, to express a high degree of relative wickedness. But the text, of itself, contains no reference to the peculiar enormity of Simon's sin. The word rendered "iniquity" is that common word, everywhere used in the New Testament, to express unrighteousness – disobedience to God's laws. When we address the text to impenitent men, we do not at all intend special reproach against them, as though, like Simon Magus, they had committed sins of great enormity compared with those of their fellows. We use it simply to express by it what St. Peter expressed by it: *that you are in bondage to sin.*

That you are sinners, is a charge which you, my impenitent friends, will admit. But my object is not merely to point your attention to this lamentable fact. I would urge the peculiar form in which this fact is charged home upon unbelieving man: "Thou art in the bond of unrighteousness." Thou art a captive, a bond slave to sin. Your sinful condition is a true slavery: your liberty is gone: sin holds you fast bound in its fetters, so that you cannot deliver yourself from it.

Now, if a bondage were imposed upon you by external force, which you could not resist, there would be no guilt necessarily implied in your condition. Where man is kept back by a physical impossibility, from the performance of any duty, God will not hold him responsi-

"

ble for failing, provided his disposition to obey was good. But it is ever to be pressed upon the sinner; that his bondage is, as this text so clearly expresses it, the bondage of iniquity, and not of external force. It is a bondage: and yet it is not involuntary: because he is only bound by his own sinful inclinations of heart, and by evil habits and other untoward circumstances of his own producing. The ungodly influences of fellow sinners cooperate with this bondage: but they do it only suasively. Satanic temptations assist: but Satan can only allure; he cannot compel. No man, no angel, no demon, nothing but the sinner's own free will, causes him imperatively, to disobey God; and if man or devil did compel him to disobedience by a controlling outward force, his own free will fully purposing to obey, in that act God would not hold him guilty. While other influences concur, your bondage to evil consists essentially in this: that your own spontaneous inclinations prompt you to evil, (in some of its forms) with a force absolutely certain and invariable. If I should say that you are utterly unable to assist your own inclinations to evil, I should use the word, unable, in a peculiar meaning. For it is properly applied to a person who wishes and endeavors to do something: but has not the requisite natural power. But you never wish, or endeavor to resist your inclinations to evil, because it is from these inclinations your wishes proceed, and by them, are directed to the opposite choice. No rational being ever wishes what is contrary to his own inclinations. I will say then, with more strict accuracy of language, it is absolutely certain that you never will, in your own strength, overcome the bondage of your own inclination to sin. For, that inclination is natural, and controlling, and uniform in you: so that of yourself, you will never have a true desire to overcome it. When therefore, I shall say hereafter, that you are wholly unable to deliver yourself, in your own strength, from the bond of iniquity, or that it is impossible: or any such like words are used: you will bear in mind that I do not mean that there is some outward power, which will compel you against your own free choice; but that I mean this: *It is perfectly certain that your own sinful inclinations and habits will always cause you, of your own free choice, to live in sin,* notwithstanding your partial, selfish efforts towards outward reform.

While the bond of iniquity which holds you is thus voluntary, several strands enter into its composition. One of these is habit. Man's soul has always a tendency to do what it has done before. The mere fact that the soul has sinned, creates some propensity to sin again. The oftener it is repeated, the stronger the habit. Consider now, the slighter and more recent bodily habits, which you have formed since your recollection, in things to which no natural inclination impelled you: see their strength: reflect how hard it would be to break them: and how probably such an effort would fail; and ask yourself then, how much strength a habit of sinning may not possess: a habit which has been growing every day and every hour, since you understood the difference between right and wrong.

Another strand in this bond of unrighteousness is the evil power of human example, fashion, persuasions, and ridicule. Man is a social, and an imitative being. Example and fashion decide a vast portion of his actions, and exert a powerful influence over his feelings. It has been found far easier to break through all the social instincts, and separate from our fellow creatures, than, remaining amidst them, to be wholly unlike them. There have been many more of hermits than of unfashionable. But the fashion of the human race is to sin. Even in so unimportant a matter as dress, would it not require a more powerful exertion of resolution than you could put forth, to disregard the universal example of the community, and wear the Hebrew tunic and flowing mantle, instead of the modern European garments? How strong, then, is the bond of the sinful example of a whole world?

Another element of bondage to sin is doubtless to be found in the persuasions and enticements of Satan. He operates by guiding and inciting the suggestions of our own wayward fancies; and therefore, we cannot put our finger upon one enticing idea, and say, this was injected by Satan: and upon another, deciding that this sprung out of our own uninfluenced memory. But we have the word of God for it, that "sinners are taken captive by him at his will." (I Timothy 2:26) It is enough to know that the Scriptures represent his influences as fearfully strong.

But the fourth, and the chief element of your bondage is your own inclination to sin. It is this which gives strength to all the other elements. This inclination was born in you. It has strengthened by indulgence, ever since you began to act as free agents. And this, especially, is the bond of iniquity, which makes you the servant of sin. The text, thus explained, teaches us, that unconverted men are determined to sin by influences of their own free will, which, it is absolutely certain, they will never break.

I. For evidence of this truth, let us look at the frequency and strength of the Scriptural assertions concerning it. In Isaiah 66:1 the Messiah thus announces the nature of his mission: "He" (Jehovah) "hath sent me to bind up the broken-hearted, to proclaim liberty to the captives, and the opening of the prison to them that are bound." And what this captivity, and this prison are, from which Christ delivers men, we will explain by the Apostle Paul. (Romans 6:16) "Know ye not that to whom ye yield yourselves servants to obey, his servants ye are, to whom ye obey? Whether of sin unto death, or of obedience unto righteousness. But God be thanked that ye, who were the servants" (slaves) "of sin, have obeyed from the heart that form of doctrine which was delivered unto you. Being then made free from sin, ye became the servants of righteousness." Or, let Christ himself explain the nature of the captivity and of the deliverance predicted, where he declares his mission to the Jews. John 8:31&c: "If ye continue in my word, then are ye my disciples indeed, and ye shall know the truth, and the truth shall make you free. They answered him, we be Abraham's seed, and were never in bondage to any man: how sayest thou, we shall be made free? Jesus answered them, verily, verily, I say unto you, Whosoever committeth sin, is the servant" (slave) "of sin." To this agree various other expressions, such as that of Romans 7:23: "I see another law in my members, warring against the law of my mind, and bringing me into captivity to the law of sin which is in my members." Galatians 4:3: "Even so we, when we were children, were in bondage under the elements of the world." II Peter 2:19: "For of whom a man is overcome, of the same he is brought in bondage." Does not all this represent your condition as one of helpless bondage in iniquity, from which none but Christ can make you free? You have already "yielded yourselves to obey sin": then, you are the servants of sin, unto death. You have indisputably "committed sin": According to the words of Christ, you are "the servants of sin."

II. Let us look then, at the evidence of it which is given by the analogy of secular vices, and bodily habits. It is the most common observation of your worldly experience, to say that the drunkard, the gambler, the debaucher, is the slave of his vice. Indeed, are there not practices of comparatively trivial importance, and indulgences in certain feeble stimulants, concerning which we are accustomed to say, that they who have long indulged them, are 'slaves to the habit?' The power of secular vices over their victims is, indeed such, as fully to justify the use of this language. Look at the drunkard, for instance, in his reflecting and rational moments. How keen his sense of the vileness of his faults! How strong, distinct, and terrifying the picture which rises to the view of his mind, of the shame and want, the sorrow, disease, and ruin, brought by his vice upon himself and those he loves. See his tears of repentance, so burning and sincere: and hear his vows of amendment, spoken apparently from the bottom of his heart, and with awful protestations to God: vows in which he, at least, imagines himself most sincere. And yet, see how the next temptation drags him astray like a bullock to the slaughter! his own better nature forewarning him, and love, honor, duty, drawing him back. How frequently does he not make these[257] abortive efforts to escape from the deadly grasp of his passion: efforts most intense, earnest, and bitter, and yet most futile, because of the more intense force of his tyrant vice. See how, resolving and re-resolving to stay his course, he plunges down, and yet deeper down, and explores the depths of that degradation which his own soul hates. Say: is not this a bondage? Is not this man a slave? Consider how few vicious men are ever thoroughly reformed, without the grace of God, by all their desires after reformation, and their harrowing foresight of their own ruin. How many efforts are made, which in the end, yield again to the power of vice?

Now, the control of these particular indulgences over their victims consists of similar elements to those, which make up the bond of ungodliness upon the unbeliever. It is formed of the united influences of habit, example, persuasions and ridicule of evil companions, Satanic temptations, and the evil propensity. Hence, it is most natural to infer that, as the power of the secular vice is a bondage, so, the power of the great, spiritual, universal vice of the sinful heart is a bondage still more. Each one of these particular social vices is a part of that general sinfulness: and what we find true of each of the parts, we suppose is more true of the whole. Yea, our inference is greatly strengthened, as we pass from the particular social vice to the spiritual malady. How long has the drunkard's or the gambler's habit of indulgence been growing? It may be, two or five, or ten years. And yet he cannot break it! But your habit of disobeying God has been strengthening with your strength from infancy. How frequently does the gambler or the drunkard repeat those indulgences, by which his habit and passion have been conformed? It may be, sometimes daily, and sometimes with intervals of weeks, and even months. Yet he cannot break them! But you have repeated your neglect of God's authority every hour, and with every act. For "God sees that every imagination of the thought of men's hearts is only evil continually." How much more confirmed then, your habit and passion of sinning? Again: the evil example which countenances and influences the drunkard or the gambler, is far from constant or general. The great majority of men, and all those whom he respects as men of commendable example, frown upon his vice. Yet the evil example of the few wicked companions controls him! But the example and fashion of almost the whole world, and of all whose society you most love, and whose conduct is most congenial to you, encourages you in disobeying God. The drunkard's passion for the wine-cup, the gambler's for his dice and cards, was, for many years, dormant in his breast: when first awakened, it was feeble: and yet, his indulgence has pampered it into a resistless tyrant. Your propensity to ungodliness sprang like a full-grown dragon from your infant heart, and since the days of your childhood, has swayed every moral act, with ever growing mastery. Draw the fair conclusion then: you who know the fearful bondage of one of these secular vices, when it is fully established. Is it natural to expect, that you will ever be able to break out from your bondage of unrighteousness, so much more deeply founded? You who have not been able to break so unimportant a habit as the use of a trifling stimulant, although perhaps you have made strenuous exertions, to do it, will you be so absurd as to expect, in your own strength, to reform the lifelong habit and passion of sinning?

III. That sinners will never deliver themselves from the bondage of sin, is proved by all the abortive attempts which men have ever made to do so, in their own strength. When we see a multitude of people in a house, and great numbers of them making strenuous efforts to escape, but always without success, we conclude naturally that this house is a prison, and that they are captives. So every ineffectual attempt which has been made to serve God in the strength of self-righteousness, by monks, or ascetics, or legalists, or partially convinced sinners, bears testimony to the reality of man's bondage. Men have made mighty struggles to become Christians without divine help: but always in vain. They have imagined to tear themselves[258] from the bondage of sin, by rending themselves away from all human ties, and immuring themselves in caves and cells. They have imposed upon themselves numberless prayers and fastings. They have attempted to subdue sinful propensities by scourgings and penances. But the ever restless conscience has declared that it was all in vain: they were still, in heart, the servants of sin. I can appeal to many of you, my brethren, for similar proof. When you were groaning under your guilt and danger, and were not yet humbled to trust yourself wholly to Christ, did you not make most strenuous exertions to become Christians? Did you not resolve that you would reform your sins, that you would read and pray: that you would live the inward life of a pious man? Did you not watch, and strive, and tremble, and weep, while you struggled against the power of ungodliness? And was it not all in vain? Yes: conscience condemned all your services, and groaned in anguish under her increasing load. Your resolutions were broken: your religious services were soon neglected: your piety soon came to naught: till at last, convinced of the helplessness of your soul, you invoked Christ to set the captive free. We all failed in our self-righteous attempts, because all of us were in the bonds of iniquity.

Indeed, I can appeal to many of you, my unconverted hearers, for proof. Have there not been times with many of you, when you felt the omnipotent force of religious truth, and were convinced that you must attend to your soul's salvation? You made firm resolutions to be Christians, and you began many pious practices, as you supposed them. Where are those resolutions? Where those religious observances? Broken, neglected, forgotten: and you are today more the servant of sin than ever.

But you say, perhaps: "I was not thoroughly in earnest then: I did not make a sufficient effort. Had I put forth all my determination I should have succeeded." Sinner: I defend you from your own charge! You were not hypocritical in those resolutions: you made them before a God who, you knew, could not be mocked. You verily purposed to keep them, yea, you fully expected to do so. But you see the result! Now will you not believe that you are "in the bond of iniquity"; since you yourself have tried the strength of the fetters, and could not break them? All your bitter struggles, your tumultuous beatings against the bars of your prison, have but left you with limbs bruised and bleeding, and strength exhausted.

Yet more painful proof of the text is seen in all the attempts of religious reform, to which men have been driven by the urgent terrors of danger and death, when those efforts were made merely in dependence on natural feelings and principles. This is an evidence of the most practical and experimental kind. It is presented by incidents of real life, known to all observing men. We have seen souls driven out of their carefulness, and impelled to religion by the most mighty and dreadful of natural motives: the instant danger of death, and approach of judgment. We have seen men of clearest minds and most determined wills, whose gigantic purpose triumphed over all other resistances, set about turning to God at such times, with agonizing earnestness: we have heard them pray, and vow, and confess, with all the terrible solemnity of men who thought themselves dying; and yet we have witnessed the speedy and ignominious failure of their religiousness, as soon as the danger was over past. Ah, sinful hearers, physicians and pastors witness things, in sick rooms, where wicked men erroneously conclude themselves dying, which form a biting commentary upon man's ability for God's spiritual service. Almost uniformly, returning health and security explodes these supposed death bed repentances; and sometimes the most tremendous vows of unending gratitude and deathless devotion to the God of mercies are falsified with the first breath of their convalescence; which, one would think, should have been spent in heartfelt ascriptions of praise to the divine Deliverer.

Now, why was this? Did not these men know perfectly, that their restoration was only a reprieve? Surely. Do you say, that they were not in earnest? They were terribly in earnest. Why should they not be, when they knew that they had death and hell at their backs, to lash them to a true repentance? And yet they could not break the fetters of ungodliness. Do you scornfully say: "But they were men of weak and despicable character. I am not a poor, vacillating witling like them: when *I* undertake any thing of importance, I do not so feebly relinquish it." I reply: No. These men were no more weaklings than you are. They were simply what you are, poor, lost sinners in "the bond of iniquity." One of the most immediate, and shameful, even pitiful failures in carrying out a sick bed repentance, which has fallen under my observation, was made by a man notable for an iron will, and invincible determination, before which every opposing will, during his whole life, had been accustomed to bend. But these attempts were made in the mere strength of natural principles, with[out] any true appeal for the help of the great deliverer: and hence their shameful failure.

Again: it has often been found that when the Holy Ghost stood aloof, even an actual death bed has not been sufficient to drive the sinner out of his ungodliness. Men die as Voltaire and [Thomas] Paine died: despairing, yet incapable of that repentance by which despair might have been turned to hope. And lest you should think that their desperate case arose only from their preeminent impiety, God shows us instances in which the outwardly moral, and even tender and amiable females, who had finally banished his Holy Spirit, have died thus. Their consciences were fully awakened to feel the horror of their cases: they fully apprehended their doom: their whole souls were aroused by terror: no difficulty of resigning the pleasures of sin, or braving the ridicule or fashion of the world, had any longer an atom of influence upon their hearts, for they well knew that they were done forever with the world, and its follies and its joys. They cried for salvation with anguish which harrowed the souls of the bystanders: but yet, when the herald of mercy faithfully set before them a free redemption, upon the terms of a true faith and hearty surrender of sinful self to Christ, those conditions were found more obnoxious to their obdurate wills than hell with all its pangs: and they coldly turned their despairing faces away, to resume the lamentations of despair. Thus it is evinced, that not even approaching death, nor imminent perdition are sufficient to loose the chains of iniquity, if the Holy Ghost be absent. Human power, stimulated to its most intense effort by the monitory stings of the never-dying worm, cannot break this bond!

But remember, sinner, in all this bondage, you are yet a free agent. It is not the lack of faculties of soul:[259] you have all the faculties by which, if they were righteously directed, you might serve God fully. It is not any external constraint. It is the bondage of iniquity, of your own iniquity. So far as it "consists in habits of sin, it is a bondage of your own making: and so far as it consists in an ungodly disposition, it is of your own free exercising. Those seeming efforts for godliness which you have made, were never prompted by a true desire to please God, or choice of his service for its own righteousness' sake: if they had been, they would have constituted you a Christian. But they were made merely at the impulse of alarmed selfishness, fear, self-righteousness, or other carnal motives, which, if not sinful, had no positive godliness. Such a piety is simply your old self-will, directed to a new object.

Remember also, sinner, that this bond does not lighten your responsibility. It aggravates your guilt. This is clear, because it is the very strength of your guilty principles and impulses, which constitutes it. Do you spurn the incipient drunkard, who as yet can, and often does, resist his passion; but when he has become the confirmed slave of his vice, do you judge him as now innocent again, and responsible,[260] and reinstate him in your confidence? No: you judge, that the more he is enslaved by his sin, the more is he blameworthy. So judges God, of you.

You talk, ungodly man, with contemptuous arrogance, of "the restraints of religion." You "do not intend to surrender your liberty: Not you"! What is the transgressor's liberty? It is only a license to grovel: to become more vile, to ruin himself. As soon as he aspires to the true freedom, and safety, and elevation of Christ's service, to true honor, or glory, or immortality, he finds the foul constraint of this bond of iniquity upon his limbs. True liberty is only found in the conformity of the will to God. His will is holy, true, wise, and good: harmony with it alone brings man's soul under the sway of the principles which promote its true glory, and concur with his nobler nature. "If the truth shall make you free, ye shall be free indeed." "Where the spirit of the Lord is, there is liberty."

And now, let me speak plainly with you. There are two things perfectly evident to your own minds. One is, that you are not now prepared for death. The other is, that it is a thing not to be thought of, to die as you are. Who can endure infinite, everlasting, hopeless misery? You no more purpose it for yourself, than I do for myself. Your fixed intention is, as you suppose, to do, at some future day, before it is too late, this necessary work of preparation. And this is the expectation which aids in keeping you quiet in your present most dangerous position. If you clearly foresaw that you were destined to live ungodly, as you now are, until you die, and drop into hell: if you knew that this was an absolutely settled fact, you might perhaps be awakened to some sense of your misery. I tell you, so far as you are concerned, it is settled. You may purpose to turn to God at a future day: but when that day comes, you will not turn. You may make earnest resolutions.

You will break them. You may bestir yourself to practice much religiousness, under the spur of fear and selfishness. It will all come to naught. You may hope that the sober and pensive shades of age, or seasons of bereavement, or the wholesome monitions of sickness and approaching death, will be efficacious to turn you in earnest to a better world. All these will fail. Not even the terrors of an unprepared death, although they may wring your heart with despair, will be sufficient to bow it to Christ. I repeat, sin and Satan have you safe in their chains: and so far as your efforts go, they mock your vain dreams of release. "Thou art in the bonds of iniquity."

And now, do you cry in your anguish, "Men and brethren, what must we do?" Evidently, you are in [a] desperate case. What *can* that man do, who is fast bound? I see but one thing: and that is, to raise the cry of the helpless: "Save Lord, or I perish."

Appendix 1: National Fast Day Sermon and Observations

A Discourse,[261]

Preached in the Camp of the 18th Regiment, Virginia Volunteers, at Manassas Junction, on the National Fast Day, June 13th, 1861, by the chaplain, Rev. R. L. Dabney. D. D.[262]

PROV. xiv:34. "Righteousness exalteth a nation; but sin is a reproach to any people."

I preach this day, a volunteer chaplain, to volunteer soldiers. Hence, I feel authorized to assume that we have all satisfied ourselves of the justice of the cause in which we are engaged. For otherwise, you would not have thus embarked yourselves in it. So that I shall not consume time in arguing the righteousness of our country's position in this war.

But the fact that our quarrel is just as against our enemies, is no evidence that we are not great sinners against God; and that it would not be reasonable and righteous with him to punish us through those very enemies. Let us learn hereupon from the instance of Judea and Babylon, detailed in Isaiah 10. The little kingdom of the Jews had sinned most deeply against their God; but against the Chaldean Empire they had done nothing; for indeed they were strangers who had no relations whatever with each other. Yet God permitted the haughty Kings of Babylon to wage a destructive, aggressive war against the Jews who had done them no harm; thus using the ambition of the wicked to chasten them for their sins against Him. And yet, when Babylon arrogantly boasted itself against the Almighty hand which had used it as the rod of his anger, He in turn punished it for its injustice to Judea, with a destruction far more utter than they had visited on their helpless victims.

Let us then observe the clear distinction; and while we courageously justify ourselves against the assailants who would wrong us, humbly bow and confess our personal and [social sins unto our Lord and][263] King, who righteously permits the assault in punishment of our guilt.

The bravest men regard War as a great calamity. The text tells us that the distresses of nations are produced by their sins; while righteousness is the path to prosperity in the favor of our God. The connection between national sins and national calamities, is a topic appropriate to our attitude this day, as contrite suppliants for divine favor.

That connection, I assert, is in the end universally sure. The recorded experience of the human race shows us on every page, that nations have arisen by the virtues of temperance, industry, domestic fidelity, good faith, and piety; and have fallen by their vices. Witness the long drama of Assyrian, Hebrew, Persian, Greek, [and] Roman stor[ies]. All have run one cycle, as regular as if it were fated; first the hardy virtues, then greatness and prosperity as their reward; then arrogance, luxury and the other vices; and then decline and ultimate ruin.

Now shall the thinking man profess to see no cause for this uniformity, deeper than the natural influence of virtue to consolidate and strengthen, and of vice to dissipate and weaken? That influence is indeed perfectly regular. But its very uniformity suggests the farther inquiry: Who ordained the connection? Who gave to human affairs this law? Who constituted human nature so as to cause it to operate? We must recognize in it the same hand which regulates that perpetual providence by which all causes act, and all laws subsist; the hand of the King of kings.

But we are not left to surmise merely, for the influence of righteousness in exalting a nation, and of sin in destroying it. Sacred writ asserts i[t], not only in particular passages too numerous to be recited, but especially with reference to the Hebrew commonwealth. In all their vicissitudes of fortune, their prosperity is ascribed by the prophets to their obedience of God's laws; and their frequent calamities, in every case, to their idolatries and corruptions. Just so surely as national apostasy was committed, it plunged them into national calamity; and so surely as they turned to God by repentance and reformation, they found speedy deliverance.

Let it not be said that these wondrous dealings were peculiar to the Hebrew people because of the special theocratic covenant which bound them in a peculiar relation to God as their political head. For we find the prophets, as often as they turn their warning voices from their own people to the surrounding Gentile nations, assert the same connection between national sins and judgments. In every case the dooms predicted by Isaiah, Jeremiah, and the minor prophets, against Edom, Assyria, Babylon, Tyrus, Egypt, and even distant Greece and Rome, are connected with their crimes as the cause. They were overthrown because they sinned. These pagan empires, surely bore no more intimate relation to Jehovah, than our Christian commonwealth bears. If even over them His providence always asserted this awful law, assuredly we must conclude that God still rules among the Kingdoms of men, and determines their happiness or miseries, according to their public virtues or crimes. To deny it would betray a practical atheism as odious as that by which the Epicurean Greek and decadent Roman plucked down on themselves the inevitable wrath of the heavens. Yet we may well fear that there are many in this soft and prosperous age of ours, who harbor a covert insensibility to that most near and intimate truth, that "verily there is a God that ruleth in the earth." There are men, I fear, among us, who because they have experienced only good from the hand of God, are skeptical of his practical concern in the fortunes of men. Theirs is the sneering atheism which was implied in the remark of Gen. Charles Lee, upon the call of our great [Gen. George] Washington to fasting, humiliation, and prayer, that our fathers might seek the blessing of Divine Providence on their cause. Thus sneered the cynical old unbeliever: "I have always observed that Divine Providence is on the side of the strongest battalion;" plainly implying that *there was no Providence* behind those second causes through which He ordinarily works. Now I might safely propose to all such shallow and senseless thinking, to let the destinies of these two men, the carping, malignant skeptic, and the Christian statesman and devout believer, decide whether there is a Providence who notes the sneers uttered against his majesty, and is armed with the means of refuting and avenging them. I say, let the career of the two men decide which was the happier creed? The unbeliever speedily brought the dense cloud of disgrace, crime, and mortification over his fame, on the field of Monmouth, sank into obscurity and contempt, and spent the miserable remainder of his age, deserted of God and man, in a misanthropic solitude. But the man who knew how to honor and acknowledge God in sincerity, was steadily raised by His Providence to the most enviable pinnacle of glory to which uninspired mortal ever rose: "first in war, first in peace, and first in the hearts of his countrymen."

Away then with this unbelief which thrusts God out of this world, as stupid as it is wicked. Let us humble ourselves before that almighty and most present power, which ties our punishment to our sins as a people. Let the pinching calamities which we now experience waken our sluggish minds to it; the separations which have torn us from our beloved homes, the anxieties, the watchings, the toils, the sultry heat of noon, and the posts of our night watchings. Let us learn to respect in them the anger of an offended Providence, lest some worse thing come unto us, and he teach us in the louder tones of lost battlefields, and wailing widows, the outcry of cities sacked, and the death dirge over the slain.

The fall of the great American Union assuredly forms no exception; we feel the anger of our God upon us; let us then turn and seek its cause in our public and private sins, in order that we may remove that cause. I am not of the number of those who identify this disruption of our fathers' union with the overthrow of the constitutional liberty they bequeathed us. On the contrary, since the means have ceased to conduce to the end, the disruption of our Union has become the only method to pluck the principles of the constitution out of the hands which were perverting them. Yet this disruption is a great and a mournful calamity, though a far smaller one than the dishonor and oppression which were inexorably forced upon us, as the alternative of rending it. The war which follows close upon its destruction is a great evil; though we hold it, with all its expenditure of treasure and blood, its desolated homes, and bloody fields, a far less evil than the submission which else we would have had to choose. Great chastisements should point our eyes to the great sins by which we have provoked them. Let us then review penitently our national profanity, avarice, worldliness, and pride; our official corruptions, and legislative peculations, and bickerings; our arrogant aggressions upon our neighbors. Above all these stands the crowning crime of this confederated cluster of peoples, the covenant breaking, by which the constitutional guarantees of the rights of the several parts have been trampled in the dust. In this series of acts, the only principle, so far as human wit can perceive, upon which the regulated, equal liberty of a great people can be secured is destroyed; and the nations are again consigned to the alternative between consolidated despotisms, or else the rude anarchy of petty commonwealths, each one nominally free at home, but each perpetually tyrannized over by combinations of its neighbors. Here is the *great sin* of America against the human race, against the sacred faith of compacts, and against the God whose jealousy watches over his violated oaths. True, in this great crime, our Southern common-wealths have been on the whole, the injured, and not the injurers. Yet wherever one of us has aided by word, or over-reaching act, or unscru-pulous theory, to weaken the holy bond of covenanted rights, we are in part guilty, and must humble ourselves before God.

Now, can a Christian people, who perceive such a cause lying at the root of their troubles, find any remedy so appropriate as repentance and reformation? This is God's appointed means to secure again his alienated favor. And to do this, is better defense than the armies and bulwarks by which we here see ourselves surrounded. To alienate His good will by unrepented sin, or by deceitful confession, disarms us more effectually than any defeat in the field.

Every soldier especially, should bethink himself of these truths, and seek that strength which is found in turning from our sins. As the appointed, official defenders of the land, they have a peculiar reason to fear the judgments of God upon the sins of the land, and the sins of our soldiers will be visited by God as the *representative sins* of our people. To no class is repentance, piety, humility, purity of life, and trust in God, more appropriate, than to soldiers. I trust there are none here so weak as to imagine that these Christian graces are at all inconsistent with true manhood and courage. When Robert Bruce had marshaled his little army on the field of Bannockburn, to strive for the independence of Scotland, against the three-fold army of Edward of England, the latter saw the Scottish ranks successive-ly kneeling upon the ground, and exclaimed arrogantly: – "They are dispirited: they kneel; they supplicate my royal mercy." "No sire," answered a wise and experienced noble at his side: "they kneel not to you, but to the majesty of Heaven. See, the holy man of God passes along their ranks, and they kneel in order to receive by his hands the benediction of God." And soon the sceptered fool was taught, by the terrible issue of the day, that the humility of the pious Scots was not incompatible with a heroism which swept his proud chivalry as chaff before the whirlwind.

Yes; the sense of God's favor and trust in his omnipotent Providence, are the true basis of courage: (And these are to be sought by sinners, as we all are, only in the paths of repentance.) The man who has an approving conscience, who has God for his friend, and heaven for his home, may be insensible to fear: for death to him is no evil; and death is the utmost that human malice and power can inflict.

The man who cultivates the strongest sense of the world to come is, in all ages, the best soldier. So true is this, that even the military religions of Paganism were found the most potent engines to raise men to an exaltation of martial spirit. What made the old Scandinavian the terror of the feudal ages? He had been taught by his religion, that if he died in his bed, his future state would be obscure and ignoble; but if in battle, with his face to the foe, his immortality would be passed in the Walhalla of the Heroes, in perpetual banquet with princes and conquerors. Mohammed taught the Arabs, that he who died for the Koran was a martyr, who went straight to the bliss of paradise. It was this which made the Saracens the terror of Christendom. The Crusaders were authorized by the Romish church to believe that every one who fell fighting for the holy Sepulchre, should escape the pains of purgatory, and go at once to the highest heavens. If now, these superstitious dreams could inspire men with such indifference to death, what should not be the heroism of the enlightened Christian, who has attained the national evidence that God is his friend; that heaven is his final home; that his life is shielded by an infinite Providence, which makes his injury or death impossible, until death is his truest blessing, and that "all things work together for good to him?" Let facts answer this question. While man is, unfortunately, every where a combative being, the truest instances of martial heroism have ever been found among enlightened Christians. [Thomas] Macaulay stated of [Oliver] Cromwell's famous *Ironside* Regiment, that not only was it never conquered in battle, but it never met the enemy, whether impetuous Cavalier, or steady Scot, or the boasted chivalry of Spain, that it did not both defeat and crush the body opposed to it. Cromwell's letters give us the origin of this corps. He informed the Commonwealth generals, that he found the Parliament's army too much composed of scurvy materials, such as "decayed serving men and tapsters." "But I will go," saith he, "and recruit among the respectable landowners, and godly people." Such was the *material* of his Ironsides; respectable sons of the soil; sons of Christian households, reared in the fear of God; men who, to strict discipline, joined the fear of God; and who [sang psalms while march]ing[264] to the field of battle, with their Bibles girt under their armor. And such is emphatically, the constitution of this Regiment, drawn from the flower of our section, the sturdy children of the soil. May your sobriety, discipline, and elevated fear of God make the 18th to be known hereafter as the invincible Ironsides of this war!

But he who, by his impenitence makes God his enemy, and contributes to make Him the enemy of his country, has no right to be brave. For who can presume to contend successfully against Omnipotence? Who can face a contest with Him who hath power not only to kill the body, but to destroy soul and body in Hell-fire? In view of the truths I have established, the sins of the wicked and impenitent soldier are seen to be a worse assault upon his country, than any which can be made by the weapons of our enemies. The man who professes to take up arms to save his country, and yet helps to array against her the irresistible anger of the Almighty, by his sins, is but a hypocrite and a parricide. Every oath uttered in this camp is a stroke struck against the safety and the triumphs of the regiment, and the liberties of our commonwealth. – Every act of lewdness, or injustice, or intemperance, is a wound deeper than enemies could inflict. And there is perhaps, no blow more mischievous, because no sin more provoking to a jealous God, than the formal and insincere observance of this day. If we do indeed bow ourselves before the throne of divine mercy, with true contrition for our sins, purposes of amendment, and sincere prayer for the divine favor; then this day's work will be the most important one done in this campaign. In this sacred hour, and in this place of prayer, the battle will be virtually won, for God will be won to our side; and if "He be for us, who can be against us?"

Let us then come, with profound and genuine reverence, with holy fear, with godly sorrow, and plead the cleansing blood of the Savior of mankind. Let us make true confession of our sin, and honor God by righteousness, that He may exalt us. It is no slender nor trivial company that we approach the heavenly throne this day. At this hour the President of the Confederate States, with our other rulers, are passing to the sanctuary in solemn pomp. In a thousand places our venerable clergy are assembling their people all over our land – And among these, are the well-remembered shrines, at which we were wont to worship God, and to go up to His courts in company. At those peaceful, those beloved spots, your wife, and yours, my comrade; and mine, are doubtless leading up, at this very hour, the tottering steps of our young children to the footstool of God, and teaching them to lisp the name of husband and father, in intercession for us. Shall these dear prayers be neutralized, be shut out from the ear of mercy, by our sins and obduracy? Let us join the great company of our rulers, our fellow citizens, our families, and supplicating the advocacy of the great High Priest and Intercessor, Jesus Christ, spread our confessions and prayers before God, saying: "Spare thy people, Oh God; and give not thy heritage to reproach."

MANASSAS' JUNCTION,
JUNE 13TH, IN CAMP.

The Jewish historians relate, that in the great war by which the Maccabees delivered Judea from the yoke of Syrian despotism, they at first interpreted the Sabbath law so strictly, that when attacked by their enemies on that day, they would not resist. – Soon, their foes began to select the holy day for all their aggressive movements: and the Jews perceived that if non-resistance on the Sabbath was to be their rule, they would be inevitably ruined. Whereupon they consulted the doctors of the law more carefully, and were told that acts of self-defense came within those works of necessity which were permitted by the law, on God's day.

There is no reason to fear that our leaders will push their reverence for the Sabbath to too punctilious a degree. Indeed it were to be wished that the business of the encampments was arranged so as to reduce Sabbath labors more carefully to their least practicable amount. But there are many duties, especially at a juncture so momentous as this, the omission of which would be equivalent to the disorganization of our camps, and the surrender of our cause to our ruthless enemies. That these should be performed by the Christian soldier, is as right as it is necessary; and he should seek to perform them, however uncongenial to the sanctity of the day, with the same devout spirit, with which the pious Jewish Priest, on the Sabbath day performed the labors of cleaning and serving the sanctuary, and was blameless; or with which the disciples rubbed out the ears of wheat and ate, and were guiltless. Yet, there are many sights and sounds about a camp on the Sabbath, grating and painful to the Christian heart.

Yesterday was the day of fasting, humiliation, and prayer, and appointed by the President of the Confederate States, for our success in defending our liberties. Its observance was marked by the authorities in command, by the omission of the customary morning drill, and the invitation to all the regiments to attend divine service in their respective quarters. Can the happy frequenter of our peaceful sanctuaries frame to themselves the picture of such a scene of worship? Over head there is no roof besides the azure of the heavens. – The place of worship is nothing but an oblong area between two rows of tents; and the pulpit a rude box to elevate the minister a step from the earth, with a rough board before him, draped with nothing richer than a soldier's blanket. On either hand are clusters of glittering arms stacked, soldiers reclining on their pallets, and the open doors of tents, filled with their occupants. The signal of divine worship is the rattle of the drum, the soldier's substitute for the bell; and they come from every side to the meeting-place, some singly, some by twos and threes, some marching in companies with measured tread; rough-bearded men, bronzed and weather-beaten, and almost unrecognizable as the trim gentlemen, who a month or two ago would have been seen at similar occasions, going in holiday attire to their churches. Some bring camp-stools in their hands, some stand, some are seated on logs of wood, some on mother earth.

But see; the man of God has risen and stretched forth his hands in prayer. Instantly every head is reverently uncovered; and bowed in prayer; while Jehovah of Hosts is implored to bless our bleeding country, to crown our arms with success, and to protect the beloved ones at home. Then follows an old, familiar psalm. – There are no strains of woman's sweeter melody to mingle with the stern melody of the men; but the wind sighing through the pine trees around us is the accompaniment, not unfitting, to the hundreds of manly voices which roll the hymn to the heavens. Then follows the sermon, short and informal, but swallowed with solemn eager faces. It is evident that many hearts are busy with thoughts of home, of the peaceful sanctuaries where, in happier times, they were wont to worship, and of the wives and sisters, who at the very hour, sadly passing to the house of God, lead perhaps the tottering feet of their little-ones, to join in prayers for fathers, husbands, and brothers far away. Not a few tears are wiped from those bronzed and bearded faces. But they are not unmanly tears; our enemies will find, to their cost, that the love for homes and households by which the fountains of tenderness have been opened, will make every one of these men as a lion in the day of battle.

It has been customary to speak of camps, as schools of temptation and evil. And there is too much in them, to pain the Christian's heart, and to try the graces. – But our camps are places of much prayer, and afford many shining examples of Christian consistency. Let the people of God abound in prayer for the bodies and souls of our citizen-soldiers. "The effectual fervent prayer of a righteous man availeth much." Now is the time for the people of God to besiege the throne of grace, and prove the efficacy of this agency. For assuredly we are in a great strait. But God can easily deliver us; and to this end the prayer of the humblest, the most infirm, or the most aged saint may avail just as much as the arm of the robust warrior, yea more. Let Christians arise, and conquer in this war by the power of prayer.

It is to be regretted that the supply of ministerial service for our camps is so inadequate. Not one regiment in ten is yet supplied with its stated chaplain, so far as we are informed; although the voluntary labors of many ministers of the gospel partly supply the lack of service. Yet we are credibly informed that numerous applications have been made for the appointment, and that quite a number of meritorious ministers have received it. The failure to supply the present wants of the army arise, doubtless, in part from the neglect of successful applicants, to attend in person to their appointments, and ask for immediate orders to their posts. We have little doubt that a number of appointments are now lying over in this way; and that all that is needed is for the applicants to ask orders for service. Amidst the urgent and multitudinous cares connected with the creation of a great army, our rulers are but too likely to overlook such points; and those who seek the spiritual care of our soldiers should, without waiting, report themselves as ready for service, and ask for orders.

Appendix 2:
Chronological Chart of Civil War Sermons

Date	Scripture	Title	Location	Unit/Congregation	Current Format
05/1861	Philippians 4:4-7	The Christian Philosopher	Richmond	Camp of Instruction	Sketch & Full Manuscript
05/26/1861	Luke 12:4-5	True Courage	Hampden-Sydney	Hampden-Sydney Volunteer Company	Sketch
06/13/1861	Proverbs 14:34	(National Fast Day Sermon)	Manassas Junction	18th Virginia	Full Manuscript
06/1861	Luke 18:7-8	Encouragements to Prayer	Manassas Junction	18th Virginia	Sketch & Full Manuscript
06/1861	I Kings 18:21	The Immediate Decision	Manassas Junction?	18th Virginina	Sketch & Full Manuscript
06/1861	Matthew 5:15		Manassas Junction	18th Virginia?	Sketch
06/1861	II Corinthians 7:10	Spurious and Genuine Repentance Contrasted	Manassas Junction	18th Virginia	Sketch & Full Manuscript
07/1861	I Kings 18:21	The Immediate Decision	Centreville		Sketch & Full Manuscript
07/1861	Matthew 10:29-30		Germantown	18th Virginia?	Sketch
07/1861	Psalm 108:4	God's Eminent Mercy	Fairfax Courthouse	18th Virginia?	Full Manuscript
07/25/1861	Acts 5:1-11		Cub Run	18th Virginia?	Sketch
08/1861	I Peter 2:21		Charlottesville	University of Virginia	Sketch
08/1861	Philippians 4:4-7	The Christian Philosopher	Charlottesville		Sketch & Full Manuscript
08/1861	Philippians 4:4-7	The Christian Philosopher	Culpepper Courthouse		Sketch & Full Manuscript
08/1861	Matthew 11:28-30	The Happy Service	Centreville	18th Virginia	Sketch & Full Manuscript
08/25/1861	Acts 7:59	Our Comfort in Dying	Centreville	27th Virginia, Stonewall Brigade	Sketch & Full Manuscript
08/1861	Acts 7:59	Our Comfort in Dying	Centreville	18th Virginia?	Sketch & Full Manuscript
09/1861	Matthew 22:2-3		Fairfax Courthouse	18th Virginia?	Sketch
04/27/1862	Proverbs 27:1	Procrastination	Swift Run Gap	2nd Virginia Brigade	Sketch & Full Manuscript
04/27/1862	Philippians 4:4-7	The Christian Philosopher	Swift Run Gap	5th Virginia	Sketch & Full Manuscript
05/12/1862	Isaiah 9:12-13	Public Calamities Caused by Public Sins	Franklin	Rockbridge Artillery	Sketch & Full Manuscript
05/18/1862	Matthew 11:28-30	The Happy Service	Mt. Solon	12th Georgia	Sketch & Full Manuscript
05/18/1862	James 4:3	Our Ineffectual Prayers	Mt. Solon	44th Virginia	Sketch & Full Manuscript

05/27/1862	I Kings 18:21	The Immediate Decision	Winchester	2nd Virginia Brigade	Sketch & Full Manuscript
06/15/1862	Psalm 108:4	God's Eminent Mercy	Mt. Meridian	Stonewall Brigade	Full Manuscript
06/22/1862	Ephesians 1:19-20	The Believer Born of Almighty Grace	Frederick's Hall	Hood's Texas Brigade	Sketch & Full Manuscript
12/14/1862	II Samuel 10:12	The Christian Soldier	Hampden-Sydney	College Church	Full Manuscript
06/07/1863	Luke 12:4-5	True Courage	Richmond	First Presbyterian Church	Full Manuscript
07/1863	John 11:21-32	(Funeral Sermon for Lt. Augustus Bass)	Hampden-Sydney	Hampden-Sydney College	Sketch
09/06/1863	Romans 10:6-10	Faith	Orange Courthouse	2nd Corps	Full Manuscript
12/1864	Isaiah 9:12-13	Public Calamities Caused by Public Sins	New Market	Gordon's Division	Sketch & Full Manuscript
12/1864	Isaiah 9:12-13	Public Calamities Caused by Public Sins	New Market	Battle's Alabama Brigade	Sketch & Full Manuscript
12/1864	Isaiah 9:12-13	Public Calamities Caused by Public Sins	New Market	Munford's Cavalry Brigade	Sketch & Full Manuscript
12/1864	Philippians 4:4-7	The Christian Philosopher	New Market	Nelson's Battalion of Artillery	Sketch & Full Manuscript
12/1864	Proverbs 24:10	Fortitude under Reverses, a Christian Duty	New Market	Nelson's Battalion of Artillery	Sketch
12/11/1864	I Kings 18:21	The Immediate Decision	New Market	New Markert Methodist Church	Sketch & Full Manuscript
01/1865	I Samuel 24		Petersburg	First Presbyterian Church	Sketch
01/1865	Proverbs 24:10	Fortitude under Reverses, a Christian Duty	Petersburg	First Presbyterian Church	Sketch
01/1865	Luke 18:7-8	Encouragements to Prayer	Petersburg	First Presbyterian Church	Sketch & Full Manuscript
01/1865	James 4:3	Our Ineffectual Prayers	Petersburg	First Presbyterian Church	Sketch & Full Manuscript
01/1865	II Peter 1:10		Petersburg	First Presbyterian Church	Sketch
02/1865	Acts 8:23	The Bondage of Sin	Petersburg	First Presbyterian Church	Full Manuscript
02/1865	Romans 10:6-10	Faith	Petersburg	First Presbyterian Church	Full Manuscript
02/1865	I John 3:20		Petersburg	First Presbyterian Church	Sketch
02/1865	Acts 8:23	The Bondage of Sin	Petersburg	Tabb Street Presbyterian Church	Full Manuscript
02/1865	Matthew 11:28-30	The Happy Service	Petersburg	Tabb Street Presbyterian Church	Sketch & Full Manuscript
02/1865	John 13:34		Petersburg	Tabb Street Presbyterian Church	Sketch
03/1865	I Kings 18:21	The Immediate Decision	Petersburg	Tabb Street Presbyterian Church	Full Manuscript
03/1865	Psalm 84:11		Petersburg	Tabb Street Presbyterian Church	Sketch
03/1865	Nehemiah 8:10		Petersburg	Tabb Street Presbyterian Church	Sketch
03/1865	I Samuel 24		Petersburg	Walker's Third Corps Artillery Battalions	Sketch

*Dabney's sermon records usually list a month and year only, so the chronology offered here is approximated at times.

Based, in part, on Trotter's "Robert Lewis Dabney Sermons Index," Robertson, *18th Virginia Infantry*, 3-4, 7-8, Withers, 139-142, 149-150, 526, Irby, 10, 13, and Eggleston, "History of College Church."

Appendix 3: The Interests in Education[266]

Wm. H. McGuffey,

R. L. Dabney

The condition of our Southern Confederacy, and especially of our commonwealth of Virginia, has presented an anxious question for our educated young men, and students in literary institutions. We wish, while not discouraging their patriotism, to caution this class against a danger which impends; the making of an unnecessary and irreparable sacrifice by deserting their education for the camp.

We beg our young friends to remember that their situation is unlike that of other citizens. Youth, when gone, never returns; and they will find that the business of education will be practically limited to their youth, in all but exceptional cases. So that in leaving their studies for a year or two, they are not making the sacrifice which others make, of a year or two of comfort or private gain given up for their country. – They are fatally throwing away the efficiency of a whole lifetime, lost in losing the golden season for education, in order to render a temporary service to the State. Surely patriotism itself should forbid such a waste. Let others render the requisite military service, who can do it without so ruinous a cost to themselves and the public. Young men may think that their military career will make only a postponement of their College course. But our experience forewarns us, that they will usually find this expectation, almost before they know it, into a new channel.

If it is wrong for our students to abide by their books at such a time, it would be more wrong for professors and teachers to sit idle at such a time, in schools that had no pupils. Hence this flight of our young men to the camp, if proper, ought to result, consistently, in the thorough disorganization of our Colleges, Seminaries, and Universities. But it is a work of years, often a lifetime, to reconstruct a respectable literary institution. Surely it cannot be right or wise to cut down the tree which it required a lifetime to grow, in order to supply the lack of a stack of timber for a single day!

Without saying anything invidious about that supply of professional men which has been hitherto so largely derived from the North, we may safely assume that it is now absolutely cut off. But we aspire to be an independent, civilized and prosperous people. Surely we shall not submit to living hereafter without teachers, professional men, authors, and ministers! On the contrary, it will be our boast that we shall refute the envious slanders of all our enemies, by displaying a higher and sounder culture, amidst our other elements of social prosperity. – The demand for literary and professional talent must then *recur*, just as soon as the war ends. It will be disastrous indeed, to all these hopes, if the community has to wait for its supply, till a generation of educated young men is raised up anew. Before that is done, a generation of our people will have grown up, with a Boeotian character stamped upon them, which will either entail itself as the permanent trait of our new nation, or will fix upon us a most servile literary dependence on foreign States. Hence it is most vital to the honor and safety of our Confederacy, that during all the time society is busy in this labor of self-defense, it shall be raising up a still larger supply of educated men at home. And fortunate will be that young man who has had the good sense to pursue his studies diligently, so as to be prepared, when peace returns, to step into this teeming field of labor.

All these considerations apply with peculiar force, to the young ministers of the gospel, and candidates for the ministry. In our own denomination for instance, a careful estimate prepared some years ago, revealed the fact that about one-half the ministerial laborers in the Presbyterian church in Virginia, were borrowed from the States North of us. This supply will be henceforth cut off. So that the destitution would soon become alarming enough, were our Seminaries of learning to continue in full prosperity. The churches cannot but suffer much disorganization from the confusions of war at best. Now we appeal to our Christian young men: Will you add to all these cruel losses, the more fatal evil of an absolute dearth of ministerial supply at the end of the war? After all the disasters of the times, must our struggling churches be met, when peace returns, by this answer from their Presbyteries? "We can give you no ministers till we rear a new stock." The education of a Presbyterian minister consumes from five to seven years. Even if no more delay occurred, than would be required for old students to complete their interrupted course of studies, this might be a fatal one, when added to all the evils of a state of war. The only result of such a course on the part of our candidates for the ministry, will be, that our church will retrograde in the South to a point from which a whole generation will scarcely bring it up. As things now go, our church will speedily be in far more ruinous want of ministers, than the commonwealth can be of soldiers.

Surely exigencies of the hour are not so dire, as to justify the raising of soldiers for defense, at such an expense as this. To assume it would be to pay entirely too high a tribute to the prowess of our enemies. It is more worthy of the dignity of Virginia and the South, to show that we are abundantly able to hurl back our insolent assailants, and at the same time to carry on with undisturbed equanimity, all the high functions of civilized society. Virginia does not so need a few hundred soldiers, as to employ her precious educated youth in the work of the camp. We have good evidence that our highest military authorities concur in this view, and lament the ill-considered zeal which has emptied our schools. We believe that our students will best display their patriotism and courage, by laying aside the musket, as autumn returns, and coming back to their studies, in every case where they can honestly do so.

Appendix 4: Dodging Shot and Shell at Malvern Hill

In the first edition of his book, *Christ in the Camp* (1887), J. William Jones provided a humorous anecdote and artistic sketch of Dabney at the Battle of Malvern Hill on July 1, 1862:

> Rev. Dr. R. L. Dabney was a gallant and efficient officer on Jackson's staff, and often preached to the men at head-quarters, and in their camps and bivouacs as opportunity offered. On this march [from the Valley to the Peninsula] he preached a very able sermon on "Special Providence," in the course of which he used this emphatic language: "Men, you need not be trying to dodge shot or shell or minnie [ball]. Every one of these strikes *just where the Lord permits it to strike, and nowhere else*, and you are perfectly safe where the missiles of death fly thickest until Jehovah permits you to be stricken."

> Major [Hugh] Nelson, of General [Richard] Ewell's staff, one of the bravest of the brave and an humble Christian and devout churchman, heard that sermon and did not fully endorse what he called its "extreme Calvinism."

> During the battle of Malvern Hill General Jackson rode, as was his wont, into the very hottest of the fire, and for some time he and his staff sat on their horses at a point at which there was a converging artillery fire; but "old Stonewall" seemed to be entirely oblivious of it until one of his couriers was killed, when he turned to his staff and told them to dismount and shelter themselves. Dr. Dabney chanced to be near a very large, thick, oak gate-post and he very wisely got behind that, sitting bolt upright with his back against it. Soon after he had assumed this position Major Nelson rode up to bring some message from General Ewell to General Jackson, and with a soldier's keen eye at once took in the situation. Delivering his message, he at once rode straight to Dr. Dabney and, with a graceful military salute, said: "Major Dabney, every shot and shell and minnie *strikes just where the Lord permits*. And you must excuse me, sir, for expressing my surprise that you are seeking *to put an oak gatepost between you and 'Special Providence.'"*

But the great theologian was fully equal to the occasion, and at once replied: "Why, major, you do not understand the doctrine of 'Special Providence.' I believe and teach it with all my heart, and *I look upon this thick gate-post as a very 'Special Providence' just at this juncture.*"[267]

After he went blind, Dabney found out about this story in Jones' book. He then wrote to Jones to inform him that "the whole story [was] absolutely false":

> The authentic facts of the case are these: General Jackson was himself present during that terrible artillery fire, having dismounted, as all the officers of his staff were advised to do, and was standing much nearer those noted gate-posts than I was. At last, when the fire became very terrible, he flung himself upon his horse and galloped to the rear, but I was under orders from him to remain near the spot in order to direct movements. This I did until my tasks were finished. The interval between his retirement and mine I spent partly in conference with General [John Bell] Hood, who was standing dismounted in front of his brigade, some forty or fifty yards east of the gate-posts.[268]

Although Dabney did not mention it, his sermon records offer further proof against Jones' story. These records list "The Believer Born of Almighty Grace" (June 22, 1862) as the only sermon he preached during the movement from the Valley to the Peninsula, and it does not reference "special providence" or "dodg[ing] shot or shell or minnie." Dabney's "True Courage" sermon did mention that God "gives each [missile] an aim and a purpose, according to the plan of his wisdom," but this message was only preached on May 26, 1861 and June 7, 1863.[269]

Jones promptly replied to Dabney:

> I had heard this anecdote told a number of times in the camp and since the war, and had seen it in print probably five or six times. I had never heard it denied, or seen its authenticity questioned, and I really believed, until I saw your "open letter," that it was entirely authentic. Your statement, of course, settled the matter, and I shall never repeat the anecdote again; shall ask my publishers to suppress it in future editions of my book, and shall do everything in my power to correct it.[270]

Oddly, the story was republished again in the second edition of *Christ in the Camp* (1904), albeit slightly modified and without the drawing. C. W. Bardeen also retold the story in *A Little Fifer's War Diary* in 1910.[271]

It is possible that this comical story evolved from a similar tale about a fellow Presbyterian during the same battle. As told by Gen. John B. Gordon in 1904:

[T]he particular occasion which I select, and which aptly illustrates his remarkable faith, was the battle of Malvern Hill. At that time [D. H. Hill] was major-general of the division in which I commanded Rodes's brigade. He was my friend. The personal and official relations between us, considering the disparity in our ages, were most cordial and even intimate. He was closely allied to Stonewall Jackson, and in many respects his counterpart. His brilliant career as a soldier is so well known that any historical account of it, in such a book as I am writing, would be wholly unnecessary. I introduce him here as a most conspicuous illustration of a faith in Providence which, in its steadiness and strength and in its sustaining influence under great peril, certainly touched the margin of the sublime. At Malvern Hill, where General McClellan made his superb and last stand against General Lee's forces, General Hill took his seat at the root of a large tree and began to write his orders. At this point McClellan's batteries from the crest of a high ridge, and his gunboats from the James River, were ploughing up the ground in every direction around us. The long shells from the gunboats, which our men called "McClellan's gate-posts," and the solid shot from his heavy guns on land, were knocking the Confederate batteries to pieces almost as fast as they could be placed in position. The Confederate artillerists fell so rapidly that I was compelled to detail untrained infantry to take their places. And yet there sat that intrepid officer, General D. H. Hill, in the midst of it all, coolly writing his orders. He did not place the large tree between himself and the destructive batteries, but sat facing them. I urged him to get on the other side of the tree and avoid such needless and reckless exposure. He replied, "Don't worry about me; look after the men. I am not going to be killed until my time comes." He had scarcely uttered these words when a shell exploded in our immediate presence, severely shocking me for the moment, a portion of it tearing through the breast of his coat and rolling him over in the newly ploughed ground. This seemed to convert him to a more rational faith; for he rose from the ground, and, shaking the dirt from his uniform, quietly took his seat on the other side of the tree.[272]

Glossary

abrogated	repealed, abolished.
abstruse	difficult to understand
accordant	agreeing
actuated	motivated
adepts	experts
adjuncts	helpers
Adolphe Thiers	19th-century author of the 10 volume, *History of the French Revolution*
affronting	insulting
aggrandizement	enlargement, increase
aggregate	collective, mass, sum total
aggregated	combined.
aggregation	accumulation
alacrity	goodwill
amiability	friendliness
amours	love affairs
amplitude	largeness, fullness
anodyne	drug
anomaly	abnormality
approbation	approval, praise, commendation
Arminianism	anti-Reformed system of theology which the Canons of Dort (1619) repudiated with the five points of Calvinism
artifice	trick
ascetics	legalistic self-deniers
aspirant	seeker
assimilate	understand, comprehend
assize	inquest, hearing
auld lang syne	times gone by; also a famous ballad which begins with: "Should Old Acquaintance be forgot"

auspicious	favorable.
avarice	greed
avouch	acknowledge, affirm
azure	blue
baleful	menacing
bandying	arguing
Bannockburn	battle on June 23-24, 1314 in which Bruce defeated a larger English army under King Edward II
beetling	projecting
begrimed	dirty
behests	commands
belie	contradict, deny
benefaction	gift
benign	wholesome
besotted	infatuated, smitten
bestir	ouse
bethink	remind
Blaise Pascal	17th-century Jansenist theologian who opposed the Jesuits
blanched	made pale
Bloody Queen Mary (Mary Tudor)	Roman Catholic Queen of England who persecuted the Protestants in the 16th century
Boeotian	uncultured, unrefined
boggle	stumble
boon	benefit; social, convivial
bosses	raised ornamentations on a shield
bourne	goal
bravo	villain, assassin
broil	uproar
browbeat	intimidate
bulwarks	fortifications
cant	triteness
carping	critical
caterers	providers
Cavalier	royalist supporters of King Charles I during the English Civil War
cavil	complaint, objection
champaign	plain or open country

Charles Lee	general in George Washington's Continental Army who was court-martialed for his actions at the Battle of Monmouth
checkered	marked
clap	loud sounding; possibly a reference to the Ten Commandments
clemency	mercy
communings	discussions, fellowship
compunctions	anxieties, distresses
condign	appropriate
conduce	contribute, lead
conflagration	conflict
congenial	pleasant
consonant to	in agreement with
Constantine	Roman emperor of the 4th century
contingencies	events, conditions
contrition	remorse, sorrow
convalescence	recovery
convulsive	producing convulsions
corporeal	bodily
coterminous	having the same boundaries, bordering each other
covert	secret, concealed
Crusaders	Romanist soldiers who fought against the Muslims for control of the Holy Land in the 12th and 13th centuries
cupidity	greed
death dirge	song of grief at a funeral
delirium tremens	alcohol withdrawal
delusive	deceptive
demurs	objects
deprecate	denounce, disapprove
despot	tyrannical ruler
dicta	statement
diffidence	distrust, reserve
diminution	reduction
dissipate	dissolve, disperse
dissipated	degenerate, perverse; driven off, broken up
dissolute	degenerate, corrupt
dissolution	closure, termination, death

domestic fidelity	faithfulness in marriage
draught	drink
dray	cart
efficacy	effectiveness
effusions	outpourings
egress	exit, escape
elasticity	responsiveness, receptiveness
embower	shelter, enclose
encomium	accolade, commendation, eulogy
endued	endowed
enervating	softening, weakening
enigma	mystery
enjoin	instruct, order, command, bid
enstamps	imprints
entail	necessitate
ephemeral	transient
Epicurean	pleasure-seeking
equanimity	calmness
eschews	avoids, disdains, shuns
essay	try
etymology	the study of words, particularly their roots and development
evanescent	momentary, fleeting
evitable	capable of being canceled
exaction	extortion
exemplification	example, illustration
exigencies	demands, needs, pressures
exonerate	acquit, absolve
expostulations	earnest reasoning
extenuation	excuse
facile	easy
fetters	chains
fidelity	faithfulness, loyalty, reliability, integrity
flinty	hard, unbending
forswear	reject
founder	sink

fratricidal	brother against brother
freighted	loaded
frenzy	passion
frippery	finery, ostentation
gaiety	jollity, happiness
gamester	gambler
garner	storehouse
gay	happy
Geneva, Wittenberg, Leyden	prominent cities of the Protestant Reformation
genial	friendly
George Whitefield	prominent evangelist in Great Britain and the American colonies during the First Great Awakening of the 18th century
Giant Despair	ruler of "Doubting Castle" in John Bunyan's classic allegory, *The Pilgrim's Progress*
gibbet	gallows
Gilbert Tennent	American preacher during the First Great Awakening of the 18th century
Girondists	members of the moderate republican party during the French Revolution
glebe	cultivated land
grated	vexed, irritated
gristle	cartilage; infancy
Grub-street hack	mercenary writer
habitudes	affections; customs
hackneyed	well-worn, commonplace
harpies	ravenous, mythological birds with women's faces; leeches or predators
harrow	torment, vex, distress
have done despite	has insulted
heath	moor
hoary	old
horrent	bristling
husbandman	farmer
hustings	election campaigns
ignominious	despicable, disgraceful, humiliating

immolate	kill
immuring	secluding
impends	looms, threatens
impinge	Infringe, impose
impious	irreverent
import	meaning
importunate	troublesome
importunity	persistent requesting
imposture	deception
impotency	weakness
imprecations	curses
impunity	exemption, freedom, liberty, immunity, license
incipient	emerging
incorporeal	intangible, spiritual
incredulity	disbelief
incredulous	unbelieving
incubus	oppression
inculcated	instilled
inculcation	teaching, admonition
indignant	angry
indisposition	problem
indolence	laziness, inactivity
indomitable	unconquerable
inebriate	drunkard
ineffable	indescribable
inert	sluggish
inexorable	inevitable, unavoidable, unstoppable
inexorably	adamantly; unstoppably
ingenuous	innocent, simple
ingenuous	compunction noble conviction
inlet	entry
insidious	sinister; subtle
insolence	discourtesy, disrespect
intemperance	overindulgence; possibly referring to drunkenness
intercourse	conversation
interlard	intersperse, mix up
intermeddled	interfered

interpose	intervene
inutility	uselessness
inveigled	enticed
invidious	unpleasant
invigorated	energized, animated
inviolable	hallowed
inwrought	made within
Ironside Regiment	cavalry unit organized by Cromwell
irrespected	heedless
irrevocably	permanently
Jockies	people who pragmatically arrange things to their advantage
John Hampden	an Englishman in the 17th century who opposed King Charles I for trying to impose a tax without Parliament's consent
John Knox	great Scottish Reformer of the 16th century
jostling	contending with
Judas Maccabee	Hasmonean general who took back the Jewish temple from the Seleucids during the second century B.C.
juncture	occasion
labyrinth	complex maze
languor	weakness
lassitude	weariness
latent	dead, dormant
laxity	carelessness, neglect, looseness
leaden	heavy
levies	enlistments
levity	lightheartedness, silliness, frivolity
lewdness	unchasteness, vulgarity
libation	offering, sacrifice
limbus	border
lineament	feature
lithe	agile, bendable
Maccabees	Jewish family who led a successful rebellion in Judea against the Seleucids during the Intertestamental Period
magnanimity	generosity
malignant	cruel, evil
maudlin	silly
maw	jaws

mediation	intercession, intervention; going on behalf of someone else
meet	fit
memoriter	by memory
mephitic	foul-smelling, noxious
meum and tuum	mine and yours
miasm	corrupting influence
mien	appearance
minatory	menacing, dire
minced	restrained
misanthropic solitude	cynical loneliness
Mohammed	7th-century founder of Islam, and author of its sacred text, the Koran
monitions	warnings
Monmouth	Revolutionary War battle fought on June 28, 1778 between Continental and British forces, resulting in a tactical draw
morose	gloomy
mortifications	putting to death fleshly desires
multifarious	diverse
multitudinous	countless
obduracy	obstinacy, stubborness
oblong	rectangular
obloquy	censure, condemnation; dishonor, disgrace
obtruding	imposition, intrusion
obviate	remove
odious	detestable
officious	kind, dutiful
Oliver Cromwell	Protestant commander of the Parliamentarian ("Roundhead") armies in the English Civil War (1642-1651), and later Lord Protector of the British Isles
omnipotent	all powerful
oracles of profligacy	expressions of corruption
orthodox formularies	correct sayings
palate	appetite, taste
pallets	bedding
palliation	alleviation, moderation

pallid	pale
palmistry	the Satanic practice of trying to read someone's future from the lines on his or her hand
palpable	perceptible
paltry	despicable
parricide	murderer of one's own relatives
partisans	members
peculating	stealing
peculations	embezzlements
peltings	assault
penal suffering	just penalty or punishment
penetralia	innermost
pensive	mindful, reflective, thoughtful
peradventure	doubt; perhaps, possibly
perdition	destruction, condemnation
perfidious	treacherous
perorations	speeches
perquisites	rights, privileges
perspicuity	clarity
pertinacity	stubbornness
petulance	insolence, rudeness
petulant	rude, irritable
philanthropy	goodwill
phlegmatic	calm, stolid
pinchbeck	counterfeit, imitation
pinions	feathers, wings
pique	resentment
pitchy	black
plaudits	approvals, praises
plausibility	believability
plume	flatter, pride
Popery (Roman Catholicism)	religious system which elevates the pope, his priests, and ecclesiastical tradition above Scripture, thereby rejecting justification by faith alone and a host of other Protestant doctrines
predilections	preferences
prelibation	foretaste
pretense	fake excuse

primeval	primitive, ancient
prodigality	wastefulness
profusion	extravagance
prognosticate	predict
promiscuously	liberally
promontory	projecting cliff
propitiation	an atoning sacrifice
propitious	benevolent
propitious clime	favorable climate
proscriptions	condemnations
prostrate	lying flat
protestations	declarations
Proteus	a Greek sea god who allegedly could take on different forms
proto-martyr	first martyr
proviso	stipulation, condition
provocation	incitement, encouragement
prowess	bravery
punctilious	scrupulous, meticulous
pungent	painful, sharp; powerful
purgatory	Roman Catholics believe this is an intermediate place where departed souls suffer indefinitely for sins which were not previously atoned, thus making them fit for heaven
Puritanism	16th and 17th century Reformed movement which sought to purify the Church of England of Roman Catholic vestiges
purveyors	peddlers
querulous	critical; fretful
raked	scraped, collected
rapacity	greediness
Rationalism	philosophy which elevates human reason above God's revealed truth
recreant	cowardly
rectitude	righteousness, uprightness
regale	divert, amuse, entertain
reluctate	hesitate, loathe
(Protestant) Reformation	16th-century movement which denounced Roman Catholicisim, and advocated a return to the sufficiency of Scripture and salvation by faith alone in Christ alone
remission	forgiveness

remissness	negligence, carelessness
remonstrate	plead; reprove or rebuke
reprobation	rejection
repugnance	disgust, hatred
requiem	elegy, lament
retorting	responding to
retrenched	removed
retrograde	go backward
retrospection	reflection
revivalism	the reliance on the anxious bench, invitationals, altar calls, or other forms of pychological pressure to induce spiritual revivals; popularized by Charles Finney
Robert Bruce	King of Scots who led his people to independence from England in the 14th century
sagacity	discernment
salutary	beneficial, helpful
Samuel Davies	American preacher during the First Great Awakening of the 18th century
sanguinary	bloody
Saracens	Arabic Muslims
sardonic	mocking
satiated	filled
satiety	a disgust at overindulgence
scurvy	despicable
sedge	marsh plants
self-abnega-tion	self-denial
sentient	responsive
Septembris-eseurs	September massacres, September 2-7, 1792
serene	calm
shrines	sacred places, churches
shufflings	rearrangings
sibilant	producing the ssss sound
sinuous	winding
slough	quagmire
smarting	stinging
smited to	taken with

Socianism	liberal system of theology originating with Faustus Socinus (1539-1604)
solace	comfort
solidity	strength
sonorous peal of the clarion	loud sound of the trumpet
sophisms	deceptive arguments
sordid	dirty, vile
sot	drunkard
specious	deceitful, beguiling
speculative	theoretical; questioning
spurious	false
strait	difficulty, problem
suasion	persuasion
sublimity	loftiness, greatness
sublunary	earthly
subserve	serve as a means for
substantiate	validate, prove
subterraneous	underground
succor	help
suffrages	votes
sultry	hot, humid
sundered	broken
supinely	idly
suppleness	adaptability
supplicate	beg, pray to
Surety	security, guarantee; i.e. Jesus Christ
Tamerlane	a Mongolian conqueror (also known as Timur) of the 14th century who tried to restore the empire of Genghis Khan
tapsters	bartenders
teeming	abounding
tenacity	resolve, firmness
tenement	dwelling
terrestrial	earthly
theocracy	God's rule over the nation of Israel in the Old Testament
thespians	actors
Thomas Macaulay	19th-century British author of the five-volume *The History of England*

score	20 years
Thomas Paine	during the American Revolution, he was the pro-patriot author of *Common Sense* and *The American Crisis*; he was also a vocal opponent of Christianity
torrents	fast-moving water
traffic	deal
transcendent	surpassing, beyond comprehension
transmuting	transforming
trenchant	sharp, severe
tropes	figures of speech
trow	think
truculent	hostile, defiant
tumultuous	violent, fierce
ubiquitous	omnipresent; ever-present
uncongenial	disagreeable
ungenial	unpleasant
unmitigated	unrelieved
unscrupulous	corrupt, unethical, unprincipled
unutterably	unspeakably, indescribably
upbraiding	scolding, reproaching
usury	lending money at exorbitantly high rates of interest
utter	thorough
vacillating	fickle, wavering
venality	corrupt bribery
venerable	honorable; respectable person
verdure	greenness, lushness
viaticum	provisions
vicarious	mediated, on behalf of
vicissitudes	changes
vigils	watches
vituperation	railing, vitriol
vivifying	enlivening
volition	will-power
Voltaire	18th-century French philosopher and critic of Christianity
votaress	devoted woman
vouchsafed	granted

Waldenses	Christian sect which predated the Protestant Reformation and eventually aligned with it
Walhalla	banqueting hall of dead warriors, according to Norse mythology
wan	sickly, feeble
William of Orange	he, with his wife Mary, became the monarchs of England in 1688 during the Glorious Revolution
witling	a person of little sense
zenith	peak

Endnotes

1   J. William Jones, *Christ in the Camp, or Religion in the Confederate Army,* 2nd ed. (1904; repr., Harrisonburg, VA: Sprinkle Publications, 1986), 245. All citations from *Christ in the Camp* will be from this edition, unless otherwise noted.

2   The author(s) of Log College Press observed that on the final page of the manuscript for "The Immediate Decision," Dabney wrote out six dates, ending with "June 1882." This seems to indicate that Dabney was working on the *Army Sermon* compilation during this time. "Robert Lewis Dabney (1820-1898)," Log College Press Web site: https://www.logcollegepress.com/robert-lew-is-dabney-18201898 (accessed May 26, 2020).

3   Dabney's Preface. David Frank Coffin, "Reflections on the Life and Thought of Robert Lewis Dabney with Particular Reference to His Views on Divine Sovereignty and Human Free Agency," (PhD diss., Westminster Theological Seminary, 2003), 327-328, 327 n 4, 403-404. Lawrence Calvin Trotter, "Orality in Robert Lewis Dabney's War Sermons," (Regent University, April 5, 2005), 2-3. Robert Lewis Dabney, "A List of My Publications," Union Presbyterian Seminary, Robert Lewis Dabney Papers, Box 6, file 6/1. There is no extant list by Dabney of all twenty sermons he wished to include in *Army Sermons.* In "A List of My Publications," Dabney mentions: "Life of Stonewall Jackson. 8 vo.," then "Army Sermons. 12 vo.," and then "Defense of Virginia. 12 vo." Dabney's biography of Jackson is twice as thick as his Confederate apology, so "12 vo." must not be referring to size.

4   Both Sean Michael Lucas and Russell St. John mention *Army Sermons* in their works on Dabney. I cannot recall for certain, but one of these resources may have been an impetus for me finding the digitized sermons in late March 2020. Sean Michael Lucas, *Robert Lewis Dabney: A Southern Presbyterian Life* (Phillipsburg, NJ: P&R Publishing, 2005), 258 n 31. Russell St. John, "Empty Admiration: Robert Lewis Dabney's Expository Homiletic," (PhD diss., Middlesex University, 2018), 52, 173, 250.

5   The following materials appear in this volume courtesy of the Special Collections, William Smith Morton Library, Union Presbyterian Seminary (the twelve extant Army Sermons have their original roman numerals written beside their titles): "Getting Without Paying", "Profaning God's Name", "A Warning Against Secular Prosperity" (I), "The Christian Philosopher" (III), "Encouragements to Prayer" (V), "Our Ineffectual Prayers" (VI), "Spurious and Genuine Repentance Contrasted" (VII), "The Immediate Decision" (VIII), "The Happy Service" (X), "Procrastination" (XIII), "Public Calamities Caused by Public Sins" (XIV), "God's Eminent Mercy" (XV), "Faith" (XVIII), "The Bondage of Sin" (XIX), and Dabney's Preface to *Army Sermons.*

6   Dabney originally wrote "somewhat" but crossed it out.

7   Dabney engaged in "secular preaching" once while in a Confederate army camp. He may have intended to include this in his twenty *Army Sermons*, but did not get around to writing it out in full (or maybe he did, and the document is lost). The sermon therefore remains in outline and sketch formats. "Fortitude under Reverses, a Christian Duty," Union Presbyterian Seminary, Robert Lewis Dabney Papers, Sk#185, Box 7, File 7/3. For more information on this sermon, see the introduction.

8   Five in this book.

9   The 13th in this book.

10   Hampden-Sydney is located over five and a half miles southwest of Farmville, VA.

11   William S. White to RLD, January 26, 1849 and C. R. Vaughan to RLD, early 1850, in Thomas Cary Johnson, *The Life and Letters of Robert Lewis Dabney* (1903; repr., Carlisle, PA: The Banner of Truth Trust, 1977), 111.

12   An unknown former student, quoted in *LLD*, 173-174.

13   *LLD*, 198-199. RLD to Charles Hodge, Union Seminary, Virginia, April 10, 1860, in *LLD*, 202-205.

14   For a detailed explanation of Dabney's political views, see his *A Defence of Virginia (And Through Her, of the South) in Recent and Pending Contests Against the Sectional Party* (1867; repr., Harrisonburg, VA: Sprinkle Publications, 1991) and "On the State of the Country," in *Discussions, Volume II: Evangelical*, ed. C. R. Vaughan (1891; repr., Harrisonburg, VA: Sprinkle Publications, 1982), 421-429.

15   RLD, "Autobiography," Box 4, Robert Lewis Dabney Papers, University of Virginia Library, Charlottesville. RLD, April 25, 1861, in *LLD*. 232. Half of the student body at Union Seminary would also join the Confederate army by October 1861. RLD to Charles Dabney, October 31, 1861, in *LLD*, 243.

16   James I. Robertson, Jr., *18th Virginia Infantry* (Lynchburg, VA: H. E. Howard, Inc., 1984), 2-3. Enoch Withers, *Autobiography of an Octogenarian* (Roanoke, VA: The Stone Printing & MFG. Co. Press, 1907), 132-134. Edward G. Longacre, *The Early Morning of War: Bull Run, 1861* (Norman, OK: University of Oklahoma, 2014), 3.

17   *LLD*, 236. James Robertson, *18th Virginia Infantry*, 3. Unidentified chaplain, "Camp Life," *The Central Presbyterian*, June 22, 1861. RLD to his mother, June 14, 1861, cited in *LLD*, 237-238. RLD, "Autobiography."

18   "Manassas' Junction, June 13th, in Camp," *The Central Presbyterian*, June 22, 1861. See appendix no. 1. Johnson attributed this letter to Dabney. *LLD*, 236.

19   Dabney's Preface. Lawrence Trotter "conducted [an] experiment of reading out loud in a homiletic style and timing [all] twelve of the full text sermons . . . for Dabney's Army Sermons[, and he] . . . found with little variation that each quarter-sheet took an average of about one minute, ten seconds to read out loud." These *Army Sermons* then averaged over twenty-five minutes in length (nothing over thirty-two minutes), but Trotter recognized that Dabney's "rate of delivery may well have been faster than [Trotter's] experimental average." Trotter, "Blasting Rocks: The Extemporaneous Homiletic of Robert Lewis Dabney," (PhD diss., Regent University, 2007, rev. 2010), 200-201. Trotter, "Orality in Robert Lewis Dabney's War Sermons," 20-22. Maj. Michael Beinham estimated that Civil War sermons, in general, "usually ran between fifteen to thirty minutes." Michael L. Beinham, "Role of the Southern Baptist Chaplains and Missionaries in the Civil War," (master's thesis, U.S. Army Command and General Staff College, 2003), 40.

20   *LLD*, 552-553. Johnson said that Dabney's sermon delivery from reduced briefs "were often the most appreciated by the people. If pushed for time, he took subjects on which he had long pondered, and was red-hot."

21   Dabney's Preface.

22   RLD, "Simplicity of Pulpit Style," in *Discussions, Volume III: Philosophical*, ed. C. R. Vaughan (1892; repr., Harrisonburg, VA: Sprinkle Publications, 1996), 86.

23   John A. Broadus, a Southern Baptist chaplain, wrote on September 12, 1863 that "Lacy, Hoge, and most of the Presbyterians . . . invit[e] men forward to prayer, etc. . . . just like the rest of us." J. William Jones, another Southern Baptist chaplain, also listed a number of ministers (including Dabney) in his book *Christ in the Camp*, and stated that the typical Civil War preacher gave an invitation after a camp service. Considering Dabney's later writings on the subject of revivalism, it does not seem appropriate, however, to include him among those who gave altar calls. John A. Broadus to Charlotte E. Broadus, Beaumont, near Gordonsville, VA, September 12, 1863, in Archibald Thomas Robertson, *Life and Letters of John A. Broadus* (1901; repr., Harrisonburg, VA: Gano Books, 2003), 208. *CC*, 245. RLD, "Spurious Religious Excitements," in *Discussions, Volume III*, 456-475. See also Iain H. Murray, *Revival and Revivalism: The Making and Marring of American Evangelicalism 1750-1858* (Carlisle, PA: The Banner of Truth Trust, 1994), 357-388.

24   *LLD*, 238, 552. Johnson also added that Dabney "had a power of simplification and illustration in a rare degree[, and] . . . he used to capture his audience with . . . bursts of descriptive eloquence."

25   RLD to Dr. Moses D. Hoge, cited in *LLD*, 238.

26   Richard Irby, *Historical Sketch of the Nottoway Grays, Afterwards Company G, Eighteenth Virginia Regiment, Army of Northern Virginia* (Richmond, VA: J. W. Fergusson & Son, 1878), 11. RLD to his sister, Betty, July 22, 1861, in *LLD*, 239.

27   Withers, 66, 150-151. RLD, "Autobiography." *LLD*, 241. James Robertson, *18th Virginia Infantry*, 6-7. Longacre, 415, 421-422. RLD to his mother, July 19, 1861, in *LLD*, 239. RLD to his sister, Betty, Manassas Junction, July 22, 1861, in *LLD*, 241. RLD to Lavinia Dabney, August 29, 1861, in *LLD*, 242. RLD to his sister, Betty, Fairfax Courthouse, July 12, 1861, in *LLD*, 238.

28 RLD, "Autobiography." Lt. Richard Irby (Co. G) indicated that on July 23, the 18th Virginia encamped near Cub Run and stayed there "[f]or many days, . . . picking up muskets" from the battle. According to Dabney's sermon records, he preached a message on Acts 5:1-11 while at Cub Run in July 1861. Presumably, this was the very thanksgiving sermon he referred to in his autobiography. Irby, 13. "Lecture 21. Expository sermon on Acts. V. 1 to 11. inclusive," Union Presbyterian Seminary, Robert Lewis Dabney Papers, Ex#6, Box 9, File 9/4. It does not appear, though, that Withers' profession was genuine. In his autobiography, Withers only mentioned giving up smoking a month after Manassas, saying nothing of a conversion. Withers' references to Christianity were also few in his book, and not very evangelical. Withers, 155-156.

29 Sermon no. 11 on "Our Comfort in Dying."

30 Thomas Jonathan Jackson to Anna Jackson, August 26, 1861, in Anna Jackson, *Life and Letters of General Thomas J. Jackson* (1892; repr., Harrisonburg, VA: Sprinkle Publications, 1995), 193.

31 Wm. H. McGuffey and RLD, "The Interests in Education," *The Central Presbyterian*, August 17, 1861. See appendix no. 4. RLD to Charles Dabney, October 31, 1861, in *LLD*, 243. RLD to Lavinia Dabney, August 29, 1861, in *LLD*, 242. RLD, "Autobiography." Irby, 13. Withers, 152, 156-157. Col. Withers said: "Our army remained in its camps on and around the battle-field [of Manassas] with disastrous consequences, as a perfect epidemic of typhoid fever speedily broke out, from the effects of which we suffered greatly. All the streams and springs were contaminated from the putrifying (sic.) bodies of men and horses, and soon nearly half of our men were in the Hospitals and many died."

32 *LLD*, 244.

33 *LLD*, 245, 247. TJJ to RLD, January 15, 1862, in *LLD*, 261. RLD, "Autobiography." RLD to Board of Directors, Union Theological Seminary, April 21, 1862, UTS, File 2.4, cited in Jeffrey David Ray, "The Education of Robert Lewis Dabney," (PhD diss., The University of Southern Mississippi, 2006), 136.

34 D. H. Hill to RLD, March 26, 1862, in *LLD*, 263.

35 TJJ to RLD, January 15, 1862, in *LLD*, 261. TJJ to RLD, Near Mount Jackson, March 29, 1862, in *LLD*, 261-262. TJJ to RLD, Near Mount Jackson, April 8, 1862, in *LLD*, 262.

36 *LLD*, 263. RLD, "Autobiography." RLD to his mother, Headquarters, Army of the Valley, April 24, 1862, in *LLD*, 263.

37 Sandie Pendleton to William Pendleton, Swift Run Gap, Rockingham County, April 27, 1862, in W. G. Bean, ed., "The Valley Campaign of 1862 as Revealed in Letters of Sandie Pendleton," *The Virginia Magazine of History and Biography* 78, no. 3 (July 1970), 352. Jedidiah Hotchkiss, *Make Me a Map of the Valley: The Civil War Journal of Stonewall Jackson's Topographer* (Dallas, TX: Southern Methodist University Press, 1973), 27-28, 31-32. RLD, "Stonewall Jackson: A Lecture delivered in Baltimore, in November, 1872," in *Southern Historical Society Papers*, ed. J. William Jones (Richmond, VA: Southern Historical Society, 1883), 11:129.

38 *LLD*, 263. "Stonewall Jackson: A Lecture," 129. "Dabney's Last Lecture on Stonewall Jackson," *The Davidson College Magazine* 16, no. 1 (Oct. 1899): 3. See also RLD, "Autobiography."

39 Hotchkiss, Memoranda, Valley Campaign of 1862, Stonewall Jackson Collection: Correspondence & Battle Reports, 1862-1863, New-York Historical Society, New York. RLD, "Autobiography."

40 Bean, *Stonewall's Man: Sandie Pendleton* (1959; repr., Wilmington, NC: Broadfoot Publishing Company, 1987), 89 n 53. Sandie Pendleton was temporarily occupying the position of chief-of-staff before Dabney arrived. By Sunday, April 27, Pendleton was already saying that "Dr. Dabney from the Union Theological Seminary is our Ass't Adj't Gen. now and I have not much to do." Sandie Pendleton to his mother, Swift Run Gap, April 27, 1862, in "The Valley Campaign of 1862," 354.

41 Johnson said that Dabney "was indefatigable in looking after the sick, particularly the Scotch-Irish boys of the Valley." *LLD*, 264-265 n 6. Eight years before the Civil War started, Dabney ministered at a church (Tinkling Spring) in the Valley whose members were predominantly Scotch-Irish.

42 Richard McIlwaine, *Memories of Three Score Years and Ten* (New York, NY: The Neale Publishing Company, 1908), 196.

43 TJJ, Swift Run Gap, unknown date, in *LLJ*, 254.

44 *LLD*, 264. John A. Harman to A. W. Harman, April 25, 1862, Jedidiah Hotchkiss Papers, *Subject File, Circa 1835 to 1899; Harman, John A., Circa 1862*. 1862, Manuscript/Mixed Material, Library of Congress, Washington, D.C., https://www.loc.gov/item/mss265260277/ (accessed May 26, 2020).

45 *MMMV*, 31. Sandie Pendleton to William Pendleton, Swift Run Gap, Rockingham County, April 27, 1862, in "The Valley Campaign of 1862," 351-352. Sandie's comments come from a larger paragraph:

> I firmly believe we shall be victoriously (sic.) wherever we fight them here, for I believe that God will ever, as he has hitherto, bless a cause with so Godly and upright a man as our Genl. [Jackson] at its head. However great the necessary vices of an army, I am honest in the conviction that there is more order and less wickedness connected with our division than any other of the army. The moral effect, to speak psychologically, and not strategically, of having Christianity and sturdy piety, and a religious sense of duty recognized as the only rules of action, and continually represented in the life of the Commander and his Chief of Staff [R. L. Dabney] is very great, and is felt in the whole army.

46 Henry Kyd Douglas, *I Rode with Stonewall* (1940; repr., Marietta, GA: Mockingbird Books, 1993), 104. RLD, "Autobiography." See also *LLD*, 264 and Lucas, 116.

47 Sandie Pendleton to William Pendleton, Swift Run Gap, Rockingham County, April 27, 1862, in "The Valley Campaign of 1862," 351-352. John Esten Cooke, *Stonewall Jackson: A Military Biography* (New York, NY: D. Appleton and Company, 1866), 128-129. Sermon no. 12 on "Procrastination." Frank Buck Jones Diary, March 11- June 27, 1862, annotated transcript and typescript by Charles Cochran, Louisa Crawford Collection, number 424 WFCHS/box 1, Stewart Bell Jr. Archives, Handley Regional Library, Winchester, VA. Harvey Black to his wife, Swift Run Gap, Rockingham County, April 28, 1862, quoted in George McMullen, ed., *A Surgeon With Stonewall Jackson: The Civil War Letters of Dr. Harvey Black* (Baltimore, MD: Butternut and Blue, 1995), 30. Sermon no. 6 on "The Christian Philosopher." *LLD*, 265 n 6. For the morning service, Cooke incorrectly stated that "Jackson stood . . . with his old cap drawn down to shield his eyes from the dazzling sunlight." Cooke additionally claimed that the sermon lasted more than an hour, but this too seems dubious as Trotter later clocked the sermon at 20:28. Trotter, "Orality in Robert Lewis Dabney's War Sermons," 23.

48 Hotchkiss, Memoranda, Stonewall Jackson Collection. *MMMV*, 35. *LLD*, 270. RLD, *Life and Campaigns of Lieut. Gen. T.J. (Stonewall) Jackson* (1866; repr., Harrisonburg, VA: Sprinkle Publications, 1983), 338-339. James Robertson, Jr., Jackson's definitive biographer, believed that these humorous stories involving Dabney and Jackson occurred on two separate days. This interpretation, however, does not seem to fit well with the eyewitness accounts. For one, Hotchkiss specifically recorded that on the mud march of April 30, Jackson's staff "had a ludicrous race across a quicksand field[,] . . . Maj. Dabney cutting a sorry figure in his clerical outfit of leggings, umbrella, sober old horse, etc." Dr. Hunter McGuire (Jackson's medical director) stated in his account that "during the first days of Dabney's service as Chief-of-Staff . . . when Jackson was on the march, his men began to guy his Chief-of-Staff" about his umbrella. McGuire noted that after riding through the woods, "Dabney's umbrella had been reduced to tatters." Robertson placed McGuire's story on April 25, but it does not seem likely that Dabney brought two umbrellas with him to the Valley Campaign, nor is it likely that he purchased another one for Hotchkiss' mud march on April 30. Therefore, it seems best to say that both McGuire and Hotchkiss' umbrella stories occurred on the same day: April 30. James Robertson, *Stonewall Jackson: The Man, the Soldier, the Legend* (New York, NY: MacMillan Publishing, 1997), 360, 368.

49 RLD to his mother, May 6, 1862, in *LLD*, 264.

50 RLD, "Autobiography." RLD to Lavinia Dabney, Near Mt. Meridian, August, June 12, 1862, in *LLD*, 265.

51 Memoranda for Col. Henderson by Maj. R. L. Dabney, Victoria, TX, May 7, 1896, Jedidiah Hotchkiss Papers, *General Correspondence, -1899; 1896, May* 1896, Manuscript/Mixed Material, Library of Congress, Washington, D.C., https://www.loc.gov/item/mss265260155/ (accessed May 20, 2020). RLD to D. H. Pannill, Austin, TX, January 14, 1891, in *LLD*, 572-575. "Stonewall Jackson: A Lecture," 146, 148. *LCJ*, 411-412. Dabney's note from Sermon no. 15 on "God's Eminent Mercy." Robert G. Tanner, *Stonewall in the Valley: Thomas J. "Stonewall" Jackson's Shenandoah Valley Campaign, Spring 1862*, 2nd ed. (1996; repr., Mechanicsburg, PA: Stackpole Books, 2002), 371-372, 379. James Robertson, *Stonewall Jackson*, 431-433. Robert K. Krick, *Conquering the Valley: Stonewall Jackson at Port Republic* (Baton Rouge, LA: Louisiana State University Press, 1996), 52, 72-73, 79, 82-83, 94-97, 99. See the latter three books for a discussion on how the

credit for the Confederate defense could be shared among the participants involved.

52   RLD, "Autobiography." See also *LLD*, 264. It is unknown when Grigsby exactly made this comment. Dabney said it was "some weeks" after he first met him at headquarters. According to Dabney's preaching records, the Stonewall Brigade (of which Grigsby was a part) heard Dabney preach on August 25, 1861 and twice during the 1862 Valley Campaign: April 27 and June 15. Considering this and Dabney's exploits at Port Republic, it may seem best to conclude that Grigsby's profane comment came sometime after the battle (possibly after the last sermon).

53   Sermon no. 15 on "God's Eminent Mercy." F. K. Hitner, "Brief Compend[ium] of the Religious History of the Rockbridge Artillery," quoted in *CC*, 482. *MMMV*, 56-57. Hugh White to sister, Mrs. M'crum, in William S. White, *Sketches of the Life of Captain Hugh A. White of the Stonewall Brigade* (Columbia, SC: South Carolinian Steam Press, 1864), 95-96.

54   Sermon no. 16 on "The Believer Born of Almighty Grace." Robert Dabney's Memorandum for Col. Henderson of Jackson's march from Mount Meridian to Cold Harbor, March 31, 1896, Jedidiah Hotchkiss Papers, *General Correspondence, -1899; 1896, Apr.* 1896, Manuscript/Mixed Material, Library of Congress, Washington, D.C., https://www.loc.gov/item/mss265260154/ (accessed May 26, 2020). J. B. Polley, *Hood's Texas Brigade: Its Marches, Its Battles, Its Achievements* (New York, NY: The Neale Publishing Company, 1910), 36. Frederick's Hall was located a few miles east of Tolersville (Mineral), VA.

55   *LLD*, 271-272. RLD, "Autobiography." Robert Dabney's Memorandum, March 31, 1896, Jedidiah Hotchkiss Papers. Douglas, 106. Rev. Richard McIlwaine, chaplain of the 44th Virginia, had a similar experience to Dabney's. The Valley and Peninsula Campaigns also wore McIlwaine out, and he obtained a furlough for some rest. He eventually met with Dr. Walton and another surgeon, who "told [him] that if [he] returned to the army it would lead to [his] early death. At their [insistence he] was released from further service." McIlwaine, 196-197.

56   Samuel B. Morrison to Dr. Dabney, March 20, 1866, in *LLD*, 272. In contrast to Gen. Jackson's assessment, Lt. Douglas disparaged Dabney's efficiency by focusing on his lackluster performance the day he first fell ill on the Peninsula Campaign. Douglas, 106. After Dabney's departure from the staff, Jackson split Dabney's responsibilities into two separate positions. Sandie Pendleton filled the role of adjutant-general, and Rev. Beverly Tucker Lacy eventually became the chaplain of the Second Corps.

57   TJJ to RLD, December 5, 1862, in *LLD*, 275. Emphasis in original. Jackson was so thrilled to hear of Dabney's prayer meetings, that he wrote his wife a letter on Christmas Day to tell her (among other things) that "[t]his prayer-meeting may be the means of accomplishing more than an army. I wish that such existed everywhere. How it does cheer my heart to hear of God's people praying for our cause and for me! I greatly prize the prayers of the pious." TJJ to Anna Jackson, December 25, 1862, in *LLJ*, 387-388. See also TJJ to RLD, Caroline County, VA, January 1, 1863, in *LLD*, 276.

58   *CC*, 283-390. Steven E. Woodworth, *While God Is Marching On: The Religious World of Civil War Soldiers* (Lawrence, KS: University of Kansas Press, 2001), 199-255. Frank L. Hieronymous, "For Now and Forever: The Chaplains of the Confederate States Army," (PhD diss., University of California, 1964), 238-271. *LCJ*, 656-657. For the first wave of the revival (fall of 1862 to the spring of 1863), Jones conservatively estimated that "at least 1,500 professions of conversion [were made] in Lee's army" (p. 307).

59   John B. Gordon, *Reminiscences of the Civil War* (New York, NY: Charles Scribner's Sons, 1904), 233.

60   "In the army of Northern Virginia, . . . Dr. B. T. Lacy, Dr. R. E. Dabney, and others . . . gave a great impetus to the revival by their unwearied and successful labors." William W. Bennett, *The Great Revival in the Southern Armies* (1877; repr., Harrisonburg, VA: Sprinkle Publications, 1989), 283.

61   Union Seminary had up to four students by December 31, 1862. RLD, December 31, 1862, in *LLD*, 273.

62   *LLD*, 272-274. A. C. Hopkins to J. William Jones, Charlestown, WV, March 22, 1867, in *CC*, 469. Dabney, *Swear Not!* (Petersburg, VA: Evangelical Tract Society, c. 1863). Dabney, *Christ Our Substitute*, No. 1. (Richmond, VA: Presbyterian Committee of Publication, c. 1863). *Swear Not!* was based, in part, on a sermon he preached at Tinkling Spring Church in February 1851 and at Union Seminary in October 1859. See Sermon no. 3 on "Profaning God's Name." He published another tract in 1864, entitled "Memorial of Lieutenant Colonel John T. Thornton, of the Third Virginia

Cavalry, C.S.A.," *Discussions, Volume IV: Secular*, ed. C. R. Vaughan (1897; reprint, Harrisonburg, VA: Sprinkle Publications, 1994), 453-469. RLD, "A List of My Publications."

63   Sermon no. 18 on "True Courage."

64   *LLD*, 282-283. *MMMV*, 174-175. Sermon no. 19 on "Faith." Dabney arrived in the Confederate camps just as a new wave of the revival was beginning along the Rapidan River. Jones estimated that from August 1863 to May 1864, seven thousand professions of faith were made in the army. *CC*, 390.

65   Emphasis in original. *LLD*, 290. RLD to H. G. Guthrie, Newmarket, December 12, 1864, in *LLD*, 290. Henry Alexander White, *Southern Presbyterian Leaders* (New York, NY: The Neal Publishing Company, 1911), 388-389. Trotter, "Robert Lewis Dabney Sermons Index" (unpublished document in the editor's possession). *MMMV*, 246-248. "Fortitude under Reverses." While Dabney preached "Fortitude under Reverses" in a Confederate camp only once, he delivered it six other times in churches, beginning at College Church in January 1864 and ending with the First Presbyterian Church of Petersburg in January 1865.

66   Meanwhile that spring, his wife and children cared for wounded soldiers back at their home in Hampden-Sydney. *LLD*, 291. *SI*. Sermon no. 20 on "The Bondage of Sin." "A Narrative Sermon on I Samuel. 24," Union Presbyterian Seminary, Robert Lewis Dabney Papers, Ex#39, Box 6, File 6/5. As with "Fortitude under Reverses," Dabney may have intended to include his forbearance message as a part of *Army Sermons*, but did not get around to writing it out in full (or maybe he did, and the document is lost).

67   RLD, "Autobiography." Charles William Dabney, "Memoirs," bound typescript, Joseph D. Eggleston II Papers, Hampden-Sydney College Archives and Special Collections, Hampden-Sydney. Johnson claimed that Dabney hid in Buckingham after the surrender at Appomattox Court House. While this is possible, it does not seem likely considering 1) Dabney did not explicitly state such in his autobiography and 2) Gen. Ulysses S. Grant gave generous terms to Lee's army at Appomattox, thus negating the need thereafter to hide. *LLD*, 292. For an evaluation of Dabney's ethnic prejudice and embittered sectionalism, see Lucas, 99-163 and Charles Reagan Wilson, "Robert Lewis Dabney: Religion and the Southern Holocaust," *The Virginia Magazine of History and Biography* 89, no. 1 (January 1970), 79-89.

68   *Presbyterian Banner*, January 12, 1898, in *LLD*, 534.

69   James Power Smith began his seminary training at Union in 1858, but left to join the Rockbridge Artillery during his summer vacation in 1861. Smith eventually joined Stonewall Jackson's staff in September 1862, just two months after Dabney's departure. Smith returned to Union Seminary after the war and graduated in 1866. James Power Smith, "With Stonewall Jackson," in *SHSP*, (Richmond, VA: B. F. Johnson Publishing, Co., 1920), 43:3-6, 13-20. John W. Schildt, *Jackson and the Preachers* (1982; repr., Parsons, WV: McClain Printing Company, 1992), 164, 192.

70   Frank Bell Lewis, "Times of Crisis," in *The Days of Our Years: The Historical Convocations Held April 24-27, 1962, as a Feature of the Celebration of the Sesquicentennial of Union Theological Seminary in Virginia*, Richmond, VA: Union Theological Seminary, 1962), 36. See also *CC*, 396, 462-463, *LLD*, 238, and Bennett, 427.

71   In the latter half of the 20th century, the Banner of Truth Trust likewise sought to follow I Thessalonians 5:21 by republishing Dabney's *Discussions* without his ethnically prejudiced material. Phil Johnson, "How to View the Flaws of the Reformers," I'll Be Honest Web site (December 17, 2017): https://illbehonest.com/flaws-of-reformers (accessed November 18, 2020).

72   B. B. Warfield, review of *In Memoriam: Robert Lewis Dabney, The Presbyterian and Reformed Review* XII (1901), 320-321 and Warfield, review of *The Life and Letters of Robert Lewis Dabney*, by Thomas Carey Johnson, *The Princeton Theological Review* III (1905), 157. Although he did not elaborate on the "extremities of opinion" in either review (possibly out of deference to the recently departed), Warfield most likely was referring to Dabney's ethnic prejudice. See "A Calm View of the Freemen's Case," in *Selected Shorter Writings of Benjamin B. Warfield*, ed. John E. Meeter (Nutley, NJ: P&R Publishing, 1973): 2:735-742, "Drawing the Color Line," in *Selected Shorter Writings*, 2:743-750, and Bradley Gundlach, "'Wicked Caste': Warfield, Biblical Authority, and Jim Crow," in *B. B. Warfield: Essays on His Life and Thought*, ed. Gary L. W. Johnson (Phillipsburg, NJ: P&R Publishing, 2007), 136-168.

73   "Sermon on Exodus XX.15," Union Presbyterian Seminary, Robert Lewis Dabney Papers, No#136, Box 6, File 6/4. The editor created a new title for this sermon.

74   Bracketed material inserted by the editor.

75   Dabney had a note here to offer further explanation to his audience.

76   Dabney originally wrote "turns off his job in a hasty and unfinished manner."

77   Dabney thereafter wrote but deleted the following: "Certain it is, that if the purchaser did not buy, consider it as implied to be a sound article, and free from secret defects, he would not purchase."

78   Dabney seems to have accidentally inserted the word "not."

79   Dabney then writes: "'What is everybody's business.' Etc."

80   Dabney originally wrote but crossed out, "helpless and."

81   Dabney originally wrote "molded."

82   Dabney originally wrote "taking."

83   Dabney then wrote but crossed out the following incomplete phrase, used later in the paragraph: "How full, then, is the word, of covert breaches of the 8th Com[mandment]? How many who hold themselves proudly: and scorn the."

84   Dabney originally wrote "thief" instead of "open offender," but crossed it out.

85   Dabney originally wrote "they" but crossed it out.

86   Rather than writing out these verses, Dabney concludes his sermon with these words: "Quote Romans 3:19:24. Rev. 3:17&18."

87   Dabney, at times, made different versions of his sermons, and this one is a case in point. See RLD, "Our Secular Prosperity," in *Discussions, Volume I: Theological and Evangelical*, ed. C. R. Vaughan (1890; repr., Harrisonburg, VA: Sprinkle Publications, 1982), 699-705. The variants between these two versions are too numerous to list in this publication of *Army Sermons*, so only a few will be mentioned.

88   Dabney's friend and college classmate, Rev. Moses Drury Hoge, was the pastor of this church.

89   The first two sentences of this paragraph plus the two paragraphs above are not found in the 1890 edition of this sermon.

90   "*Diva auri fames ipsa pecunia crescit.*" Horace. (Dabney's note)

91   The two paragraphs above, plus the last sentence of the paragraph before them, were not in the 1890 edition.

92   The last four sentences are not found in the 1890 edition. There, Dabney had: "Hence, it is one of the prime duties of the ministry to inculcate new principles of Christian beneficence. And hence it is the time for the church to go forward with gigantic strides, and give tenfold expansion to all those mans for glorifying God which his temporal bounties can sustain." *Discussions, Volume I*, 705.

93   "Sermon on Exodus. XX.7," Union Presbyterian Seminary, Robert Lewis Dabney Papers, No#127, Box 6, File 6/4. The editor created a new title for this sermon.

94   Also preached at Tinkling Spring Church in February 1851.

95   *Westminster Shorter Catechism*, Questions 54-55.

96   Dabney then references Matthew 12:34 and Proverbs 4:23.

97   Dabney had "often" written above "usually," but he did not cross out either one.

98   After this paragraph, Dabney had the word "Enlarge." He probably elaborated some more upon this point.

99   Following this word, Dabney wrote "deserves" but crossed it out.

100   Dabney originally wrote "where" after this word, but crossed it out.

101   Isaiah 29:13, Matthew 5:8, Ecclesiastes 5:1-2, Psalm 50:16-17, Isaiah 1:15. Dabney listed these with the main text.

102   After this paragraph, Dabney wrote "Hypocritical partaking, for self-interest."

103   Dabney inserted a word or abbreviation here that is illegible.

104   After this paragraph, Dabney wrote, "Flippant talk (professedly pious) about holy things. Matt. 7:6."

105   After this paragraph, Dabney wrote, "The sin of blasphemy literally understood."

106   After this paragraph, Dabney wrote, "Practice of ancient Jews."

107   Dabney wrote above the text "to hurl dam[nation] at a fellow, for our foolish displeasure."

108   James 1:21. It could be translated "superabundance of wickedness."

109   In the sermon manuscript, Dabney wrote: "Excuses. Habit. Ans:"

110   The editor has inserted the bracketed material to fill out Dabney's sketch at this portion of

the sermon. Much of this material comes directly from Dabney's 1863 tract on the same subject, edited by J. H. Varner. RLD, "Swear Not!" in *Discussions, Volume V: Miscellaneous Writings*, ed. J. H. Varner (Harrisonburg, VA: Sprinkle Publications, 1999), 227-233.

111   Also published in *Discussions, Volume I*, 626-642.

112   William Shakespeare, *Othello*, 3.3.184, 188-190.

113   John Milton, *Paradise Lost*, 9.782-784.

114   Also published in *Discussions, Volume II*, 401-412.

115   This sermon was delivered to the author's pastoral charge, under the circumstances indicated, and was printed and extensively circulated, precisely as it is now given, through many channels, in both sections of the United States. The preacher endeavored to bear in mind the truths that if we would indeed propitiate God, the appropriate business for us, on a day of humiliation and prayer, is confessing our own sins, and not those of other people. He was afterwards mortified to perceive a total failure to appreciate this on the part of many, who circulated and used the sermon, not with a generous emulation in a similar exercise of candor and honesty; but only with the design of encouraging aggression, by the hope that Southern Christians would constrain their section to be acquiescent under any aggression whatever. It was printed at the unanimous request of the male part of the author's congregation, and may be, therefore, assumed to have been fairly representative of their opinions. A few months after, nearly every one of these persons (who was not beyond military age) was in arms. These, indeed, were, in the beginning of the recent contest, the sentiments of nearly all whom the wrongs of their opponents compelled to become the soldiers of the Confederacy. Hence it may be seen how exceedingly easy it would have been for moderation and justice in that quarter to have prevented the whole catastrophe. (Dabney's note)

116   See Exodus 18:21.

117   The Brooks-Sumner Affair, May 1856. Senator Charles Sumner attacked Andrew Butler in a coarse speech against slavery. Two days later, Representative Preston Brooks (Butler's cousin) brutally beat Sumner with a cane in retaliation.

118   For another such sermon delivered by a Southern Presbyterian that same month, see James Henley Thornwell, "Sermon on National Sins," in *The Collected Writings of James Henley Thornwell, Volume IV: Ecclesiastical* (1875; repr., Carlisle, PA: The Banner of Truth Trust, 1974), 510-548.

119   Camp Lee (named after Robert E. Lee's father, Gen. "Light Horse Harry" Lee) was also known as the New Fairgrounds or Camp (of) Instruction, and it was located two miles northwest of downtown Richmond. Soon after Virginia's secession, Governor John Letcher requested that the VMI cadets come to Richmond to help drill new recruits. Major Thomas Jackson brought the corps of cadets to Camp Lee in late April, but he was soon detached to Harpers Ferry and missed hearing Dabney's sermon. By the time Dabney arrived to preach in May, Rev. Moses Drury Hoge (pastor of the Second Presbyterian Church of Richmond) was "acting as chaplain" of Camp Lee. As he and Dabney were college classmates and friends, one could assume that Hoge invited Dabney to preach at Camp Lee. However, on May 26 at the Hampden-Sydney College, Dabney preached a farewell sermon on "True Courage" to the newly formed Hampden-Sydney Volunteer Company (Co. G of the 20th Virginia) under the leadership of their President, Capt. John M. P. Atkinson. Dabney, whether on his own initiative or at Hoge's request, may have followed the company to Richmond to preach to them one last time. Or, Dabney may have come to Camp Lee earlier in the month to preach to the regiment he would soon join: the 18th Virginia, which was also training there until May 26. Since he does not date this sermon exactly or detail the name of the troops, one may never know when it was preached or to whom. "Information about Camp Lee in Richmond, VA during the Civil War," Civil War Richmond Web site: http://www.mdgorman. com/Hospitals/camp_lee.htm (accessed May 26, 2020). *Sl.* Irby, 9. Nighttime preaching may have been a regular occurrence at Camp Lee, for Rev. Hoge mentioned in a letter to his sister that he too preached at that time of day. Moses Hoge to his sister, Mrs. Marquess, June 3, 1861, in Peyton Harrison Hoge, *Moses Drury Hoge: Life and Letters* (Richmond, VA: Presbyterian Committee of Publication, 1899), 145-146. Dabney arranged most of the twelve known *Army Sermons* in chronological order, except for "VI" ("Our Ineffectual Prayers"). The missing "IV" may have been "True Courage," which Dabney preached again later (with modifications) after Jackson's death. Dabney listed "The Christian Philosopher" as "III," but this too may have been out of chronological order. Coffin, "Army Sermons List," (unpublished document in the editor's possession).

120   During the Civil War, Dabney also preached this sermon in Charlottesville and Culpepper Courthouse in August 1861, in Cascade Pittsylvania and Prince Edward Courthouse in April 1862, then to the 5th Virginia near Swift Run Gap on the evening April 27, 1862, to Lt. Col. William Nelson's Battalion of Artillery at New Market in early December 1864, and finally to the First Presbyterian Church of Petersburg that same month. *SI.* Frank Buck Jones Diary, April 27, 1862, Handley Regional Library.

121   Original word is illegible.

122   Hor. Ode. III. 3. (Dabney's note) The translated text of this poem may be Dabney's as well.

123   In the original manuscript, Dabney seems to start his sentence here with the word "Will" followed by a colon.

124   Major Frank B. Jones of the 2nd Virginia (Stonewall Brigade) said of this sermon:

In the evening [of April 27, 1862], Dr. Dabney preached at the Camp of the 5th [Virginia] Infantry, 1st Brigade on the text "Be careful for nothing etc., etc.,". Delightful text. Delightful sermon. He said nothing was too trivial or too small to go to God with, but in everything by prayer and supplication with thanksgiving let our requests be made know unto God. Blessed Lord, what a glorious priviledge (sic.), and may I learn more and more to prayer with faith and trust. I enjoyed the sermon. It was a great comfort to me.

Frank Buck Jones Diary, April 27, 1862, Handley Regional Library.

125   According to Union Theological Seminary, "this sermon was [initially] published in the newspaper Watchman and Observer, from which Dabney [took] clippings and added new material to form the document" he developed for the *Army Sermons*. Dabney Army Sermons 006, Union Theological Seminary Library, Richmond: https://cdm17236.contentdm.oclc.org/digital/collection/p17236coll4/id/160/rec/6 (accessed November 29, 2020). This sermon is also available on New Hope Presbyterian Church's Web site: http://www.newhopefairfax.org/files/DabneyLuke%20 18EncouragmenttoPrayer.pdf (accessed May 26, 2020).

126   Dabney also preached this sermon at the First Presbyterian Church of Petersburg in January 1865 during the Siege of Petersburg. *SI.*

127   Dabney hand wrote the introductory material, but then used a newspaper clipping for the first paragraph of the sermon up until this point.

128   Dabney shifted to using newspaper clippings after this paragraph.

129   Dabney hand wrote the first few words of this paragraph, and then continued to use newspaper clippings.

130   Dabney crossed out a word (now illegible) from the newspaper clipping, and added in "implements."

131   Dabney hand wrote the next couple of lines.

132   Dabney then shifted back to using the newspaper clippings.

133   The newspaper originally had "trivial."

134   The newspaper also had "and easy," but Dabney crossed it out.

135   Dabney hand wrote the end of the sermon.

136   Psalm 84:11.

137   Isaiah 40:31.

138   Isaiah 45:19.

139   Psalm 81:10.

140   John 16:24.

141   II Peter 1:5.

142   This sermon actually may have been preached in June 1861, as the 18th Virginia moved out to Centreville in late June, and only briefly marched through Manassas Junction after the battle the following month. Withers, 139, 150.

143   Greek αποινα. Lat. poena. Engl. *pain.* (Because suffering is the appointed price of guilt.) *penalty*: Lat. Poenitere, poenitentia. Italiano, pentimento. Spanish: penitenceieo. Fr. *Penitence.* Engl. Repentance. (Dabney's note)

144   *Westminster Confession of Faith*, Chapter XV: "Of Repentance unto Life." Section 1.

145   Psalm 51:3-4.

146   Psalm 51:10.

147   Ezekiel 36:31.
148   Ezekiel 18:30.
149   Zechariah 12:10.
150   Romans 7:22-24
151   II Corinthians 7:11. (following the text.)
152   Also published as "The Hazards of Indecision Towards Things Eternal," in *Discussions, Volume V*, 201-214. Varner, the editor of this volume of *Discussions*, noted that the sermon he published in 1999 first "[a]ppeared in *The Homiletic Review* under the title 'The Immediate Decision,' September 1887; vol. 14:3, pp. 225-31."
153   Dabney preached this message multiple times during the Civil War. According to Trotter's index, Dabney preached this message first to the 18th Virginia in June 1861, and then again at "Camp Centreville" in July 1861, followed by "Camp Winchester" in May 1862, again at the New Market Methodist Church on December 11, 1864, and finally at Tabb Street Presbyterian Church in Petersburg in March 1865. *SI*. When compiling his *Army Sermons* in the 1880s, Dabney may have accidentally stated that the 18th Virginia heard this message at Centreville in July 1861, and forgot about the previous month. Likely, the July sermon was delivered to another outfit.
154   Shakespeare, *Julius Caesar*, 4.3.225.
155   The 1887 edition of the sermon uses the word "vast" instead. *Discussions, Volume V*, 209.
156   In the original, Dabney has: "it would teach the future destiny of men who have . . ." He, or someone else, scratched out "future destiny of." The 1887 edition of the sermon also deletes these words. *Discussions, Volume V*, 210.
157   Dabney originally wrote "voice" instead of "plea," but crossed it out.
158   Dabney originally added "to day" to the end of this phrase, but also crossed it out.
159   The 1887 edition of the sermon uses the word "taste" instead. *Discussions, Volume V*, 211.
160   Dabney originally wrote "idiot" instead of "imbecile," but crossed it out.
161   The 1887 edition of the sermon uses the word "goods" instead. *Discussions, Volume V*, 211.
162   The 1887 edition of the sermon uses the word "miserable" instead. *Discussions, Volume V*, 212.
163   The 1887 edition of the sermon uses the word "stop" instead. *Discussions, Volume V*, 212.
164   Dabney originally wrote "sin" instead of "judgment," but crossed it out.
165   Dabney originally wrote "to sanction" instead of "with," but crossed it out.
166   Jedidiah Hotchkiss heard this message twice during the Civil War, although he did not seem to realize it. The first time was on Tuesday, May 27, 1862 after the First Battle of Winchester. The second time was on Sunday, December 11, 1864 at New Market Methodist Church. Regarding the first, Hotchkiss recorded the following in a Memoranda after the war: "Tuesday May 27. Spent A. M. in Winchester. in p.m. went with Gen. & Dabney to the 2nd. Br., [William] Taliaferro's, near Stephenson's [three miles north of Winchester] & Dabney preached – rendering thanks very devoutly for our victory. A fine warm day." In his journal for Sunday, December 11, 1864, he wrote: "Went to [New Market Methodist Church] and heard Dr. Dabney on the text, 'How long halt ye between two opinions'? An excellent argument." Hotchkiss, Memoranda, Stonewall Jackson Collection. *MMMV*, 247. RLD to H. G. Guthrie, Newmarket, December 12, 1864, in *LLD*, 290. *SI*. *LCJ*, 383.
167   Also published in Ministers of the Southern Presbyterian Church, *Southern Presbyterian Pulpit: A Collection of Sermons* (Richmond, VA: The Presbyterian Committee of Publication: 1896), 99-117.
168   This sermon was also preached on the morning of May 18, 1862 near the village of Mount Solon. Hotchkiss wrote in his journal: "Gen. Jackson[,] Maj. R. L. Dabney[, Gen. Richard Ewell,] and myself rode via Mossy Creek down to opposite Bridgewater where Maj. (Rev. Dr.) Dabney preached a good sermon to Col. Z. T. Connor's Brigade, encamped in George Gibbon's meadow on the left of the road and along North River." In a letter to his wife, Jackson concurred with Hotchkiss' opinion of the sermon, saying: "Yesterday [May 18] Dr. Dabney preached an excellent sermon from the text: 'Come unto me, all ye that labor and are heavy laden, and I will give you rest.' It is a great privilege to have him with me." In his note to the sermon on "Our Ineffectual Prayers," Dabney said that the morning's message of May 18, 1862 ("The Happy Service") was actually "preach[ed] in the camp of the famous 12th Georgia Regiment," which was a part of Connor's Brigade. *MMMV*, 46. TJJ to Anna Jackson, Near Harrisonburg, May 19, 1862, in *LLJ*, 258. See Sermon no. 14 on "Our Ineffectual Prayers." See also James Robertson, *Stonewall Jackson*, 386 and *LCJ*, 359-360.

Some may wonder if this sermon was one of the gospel seeds planted in Gen. Ewell's mind which brought about his spiritual transformation after 2nd Manassas. See Donald S. Pfanz, *Richard S. Ewell: A Soldier's Life* (Chapel Hill, NC: University of North Carolina Press, 1998), 267-268. For a dramatization of Ewell's religious journey, see *Red Runs the River*, VHS, directed by Katherine Stenholm (Greenville, SC: Unusual Films, 1963).

169   The 1896 edition of the sermon adds in the first word of the sentence. *Southern Presbyterian Pulpit*, 101.

170   John 10:30. Colossians 1:19. Ephesians 1:21-23.

171   John 8:34. Acts 8:23. II Timothy 2:26.

172   Romans 5:6.

173   II Corinthians 5:17.

174   Galatians 2:20.

175   II Corinthians 12:9.

176   Ezekiel 36:26-27.

177   The 1896 edition uses the word "breath" instead. *Southern Presbyterian Pulpit*, 110.

178   Dabney initially wrote what appears to be "reluctating," but the 1896 edition changed it to "reluctant." *Southern Presbyterian Pulpit*, 113.

179   The 1896 edition accidentally had the word "the" before God. *Southern Presbyterian Pulpit*, 116.

180   The sermon was initially "published as 'The Stoning of Stephen' [*Homiletic Review*] 10:1 (July 1885) 39-45; and reprinted with some additions as 'Our Comfort in Dying,'" *Discussions, Volume I*, 602-613. The text used here is taken from the *Discussions*. Coffin, "Army Sermons List." This sermon was also preached at another camp near Centreville (possibly the 18th Virginia) that same month. *SI.*

181   John H. Grabill, "Diary of a Soldier of the Stonewall Brigade," *Shenandoah Herald*, January 8, 1909, transcribed by Jackie Milburn: http://www.vagenweb.org/shenandoah/wars/civil/grabill-diary.html (accessed January 7, 2021).

182   The private correspondence of General T. J. Jackson with Mrs. Jackson was found to contain an account, and quite a full and correct analysis, of the following sermon, in a letter written August 26, 1861. The author has been induced, by what, it is hoped, will be considered a pardonable infirmity, if it is an infirmity, from the knowledge of this fact, to select it for insertion, from among the many preached in the camps. It was prepared and preached many years before to a little social assemblage in the author's pastoral charge, with especial reference to a venerable "mother in Israel" there present. On the 25th of August, 1861, the Sabbath day, the 18th regiment was encamped within a mile of the Stone-wall Brigade. The latter lay on the wooded ridge east of Centerville, Fairfax Co., Va., where the main road to Alexandria crosses it. On the right of the way was the encampment of the infantry and on the left that of the artillery and the quarters of the General. Being requested by him to preach for his command, and having secured a supply for his own regiment, the author delivered this sermon in the woods, in the presence of the General and his staff, and a promiscuous assemblage of men and officers. It seemed to him to present a subject not inappropriate to Christian soldiers, whose business it was to die for their country. It was hoped that the sublime truths revealed to us in this passage of God's word would be impressive to those who were out of Christ, and consoling to those who were united by faith to him; and especially, that the Divine Comforter would bless them to such as, in his secret purpose, might be appointed unto death. Subsequent events have shown that among this number was the great leader himself; and it is felt as no small favor of the Head of the church that this discourse was carried as a message of consolation and strength to that devout and consecrated heart, as was shown by the elevated joy with which he received its doctrine, and his reference to it in his letters. So may it strengthen the souls of all God's chosen ones to whom it comes, and "deliver them who, through fear of death, have been all their lifetime subject to bondage." (Dabney's note)

183   Isaac Watts, "The Death and Burial of a Saint," *Hymns and Spiritual Songs*, Book II, Hymn 3. Sometimes the second line is rephrased: "And scattered all the gloom."

184   *Westminster Shorter Catechism*, Question 37.

185   The *Westminster Confession of Faith* rejected purgatory (Chapter XXXII: "Of the State of Men After Death, and of the Resurrection of the Dead," Section 1):

> The bodies of men, after death, return to dust and see corruption: but their souls (which neither die nor sleep) having an immoral subsistence, immediately return to God who gave them: the souls of the righteous, being then made perfect in holiness, are received into the highest *heavens*, where they behold the face of God, in light and glory, waiting for the full redemption of their bodies. And the souls of the wicked are cast into *hell*, where they remain in torments and utter darkness, reserved to the judgment of the great day. *Beside these two places, for souls separated from their bodies, the Scripture acknowledgeth none* (emphasis added).

186   Romans 8:1, 33.

187   Hebrews 10:14-18. See also Psalm 103:12; Micah 7:19; Romans 5:1.

188   Luke 16:22; 23:43; Acts 7:59; II Corinthians 5:1, 6-8; I Corinthians 15:50; Hebrews 7:23; Revelation 21:27.

189   Revelation 14:13.

190   Shakespeare, *Hamlet*, 1.5.167-168.

191   Alexander Pope, "The Dying Christian to His Soul," 7-8.

192   John 27:24.

193   I Thessalonians 4:17.

194   I John 3:2.

195   Psalm 16:11.

196   As was mentioned earlier, Stonewall Jackson wrote his wife about this sermon. He said particularly:

> I did not have room enough in my last letter, nor have I time this morning, to write as much as I desired about Dr. Dabney's sermon yesterday [August 25]. His text was from Acts, seventh chapter and fifth verse. He stated that the word God being in italics indicated that it was not in the original, and he thought it would have been better not to have been in the translation. It would then have read: 'Calling upon and saying, Lord Jesus, receive my spirit.' He spoke of Stephen, the first martyr under the new dispensation, like Abel, the first under the old, dying by the hand of violence, and then drew a graphic picture of his probably broken limbs, mangled flesh and features, conspiring to heighten his agonizing sufferings. But in the midst of this intense pain, God, in His infinite wisdom and mercy, permitted him to see the heavens opened, so that he might behold the glory of God, and Jesus, of whom he was speaking, standing on the right hand of God. Was not such a heavenly vision enough to make him forgetful of his sufferings? He beautifully and forcibly described the death of the righteous, and as forcibly that of the wicked.

Lt. John H. Grabill (33rd Virginia) also recorded in his diary for August 25: "For the first time since we left camp E. K. Smith[,] I had the pleasure of enjoying a Sabbath. We heard a sermon by Rev. Dr. Dabney in the 27th Regt." TJJ to Anna Jackson, August 26, 1861, in *LLJ*, 193. Grabill, "Diary of a Soldier of the Stonewall Brigade."

197   When drawing up his *Army Sermons* in the 1880s, Dabney incorrectly labeled this one as being delivered on Saturday, April 26, 1862. Sandie Pendleton wrote his father however on Sunday, April 27, 1862:

> This lovely spring morning, as I sit alone in the office, I cannot refrain writing to you. I am alone because . . . Rev. Robert L. Dabney . . . has gone out this fair Sabbath day to hold service among the troops, and all have gone with him. And while they all [are] thus engaged I am left, a sort of higher sentry to receive dispatches from the neighborhood of the enemy and have the bridges across the Shenandoah, one mile in front, burned, if they press on.

Dabney's letter to his mother on May 6, 1862 confirmed Pendleton's statement that this sermon was delivered on April 27. Dabney said: "I have now been in camp two Sundays. The first [April 27] I preached twice to noble congregations. The second [May 4], the whole army was marching, and neither I nor any chaplain could preach at all." Sandie Pendleton to William Pendleton, Swift Run Gap, Rockingham County, April 27, 1862, in "The Valley Campaign of 1862," 351-352. RLD to his mother, May 6, 1862, in *LLD*, 264. Dabney also preached this sermon at College Church in January 1861. *SI.*

198 Two soldiers left eyewitness accounts of the service that morning. Major Frank B. Jones of the 2nd Virginia (Stonewall Brigade) said: "Lovely day. Rev. Dr. Dabney preached at the camp of the 2nd Brigade, his subject, the uncertainty of life and to great stake against the chances. May the Lord bless the discourse to those who heard it. Noticed General [William] Taliaferro and many friends present. General Jackson stood with head uncovered through the whole exercises, whilst the soldiers formed a [semi-]circle and sat upon the ground." Dr. Harvey Black of the 4th Virginia (Stonewall Brigade) also was present, and recounted that "Dr. Dabney preached in an adjoining brigade, and I went to hear him – and a most excellent sermon it was too. From the text that 'no man knowest what a day may bring forth.' He has been recently appointed Gen. Jackson's Adjutant General and was one of the professors at Hampden Sydney." Frank Buck Jones Diary, April 27, 1862, Handley Regional Library. Harvey Black to his wife, Swift Run Gap, Rockingham County, April 28, 1862, in *A Surgeon With Stonewall Jackson*, 30. John Esten Cooke was not present for the sermon, but received the following account from another:

[Gen. Jackson] was riding, on one Sunday morning, along his lines drawn up for inspection, when Dr. Dabney, his chaplain, determined to address the men. He and Jackson accordingly dismounted and tied their horses; the Bible was laid open upon the head of a bass drum; the small drums beat to attention, and Dr. Dabney preached to the troops. During the sermon of more than an hour, Jackson stood perfectly motionless, with his old cap drawn down to shield his eyes from the dazzling sunlight; and throughout the whole sermon an officer directly in front of him declares he did not move, or even "wink his eyes."

Cooke, 128-129. See the introduction for a reconciliation of Cooke's account with the others.

199 On the Monday after the battle of McDowell, the Sabbath having been employed in the pursuit of [Union troops under Gen. Robert] Milroy and [Gen. Robert] Schenk, Gen. Jackson granted his soldiers the half of Monday as a season of rest, and issued the following order:

Soldiers of the Army of the Valley and North West.

I congratulate you on your recent victory at McDowell. I request you to unite with me, this morning, in thanksgivings to Almighty God, for thus having crowned your arms with success; and in praying that He will continue to lead you on from victory to victory, until your independence shall be established; and make us that people whose God is the Lord.

The chaplains will hold divine services at 10 o'clock A. M. this day in their respective regiments.

The author having been invited by [Capt. William] Poague's battery, composed of gentlemen from Rockbridge County, who had no chaplain, to preach for them, availed himself of this opportunity. The men were assembled in the verdant meadow of the South Branch, beside a cluster of haystacks, and there were present in addition, Gen. Jackson and his Staff, Gen. F. H. Smith of the [Virginia] Military Institute, and his distinguished group of offices; when the following sermon was delivered. (Dabney's note)

In his biography of Jackson, Dabney also quoted the aforementioned order and said:

The different groups were soon assembled, beneath a genial sun, along the verdant meadows of the South Branch; and the neighboring mountains, which, on the Sabbath, had reverberated with the bellowings of cannon, now echoed the Sabbath hymns. The commanding General attended reverently the worship of a company of artillery near his tent. After the midday, the camps were broken up, and the march was resumed for McDowell."

LCJ, 353.

200 Although he got his days confused, Capt. Poague agreed with Dabney's description of the preaching venue:

Jackson's next fight was at McDowell (May 8, 1862). Not a single cannon shot from our side. Artillery could not be gotten to the top of the mountain where the infantry had a hot time.

Next day the enemy under Milroy was pursued to the neighborhood of Franklin in Pendleton County. The next day we rested, it being the Sabbath. Major Dabney (the Reverend R. L. Dabney) preached to a large congregation in a beautiful meadow.

Gunner with Stonewall: Reminiscences of William Thomas Poague, ed. Monroe F. Cockrell (Jackson, TN: McCowat-Mercer Press, Inc.), 22.

201   Dabney's original word appears to be "recur."

202   or, wild goats.

203   *Delirant reges, plectunter Achivi.* (Dabney's note)

204   As Dabney's first biographer notes, "it may be admitted as practically certain that [Dabney's] family was a Huguenot one, and that the name went through various changes after the family left France." *LLD*, 3.

205   Pvt. Randolph Fairfax (Rockbridge Artillery) wrote of this sermon:

I was much pleased with a sermon preached for us last Monday by Dr. Dabney—the day set apart by Gen. Jackson as a day of rest and thanksgiving. The services were held within hearing of the enemy's guns and were impressive. Dr. Dabney's view of the war was that it was a visitation of God upon us for our sins, and that it would not cease until the purpose of God was accomplished—that is, until our people repent and turn to God; or else it may cease for awhile, and when our cup of iniquity is full, more terrible punishments may come upon us. He also said, that God sometimes uses a more wicked instrument to punish a more innocent one, but that the punishment of the more wicked instrument would surely fall sooner or later, with terrible vengeance. He spoke of the Babylon of the North, and predicted its downfall and destruction. His view is, that nations, as they cannot be punished in the next world, are punished in this [world] for national sins—a view I think entirely coinciding with the Bible. I think the fate of the country is now in the hands of the praying people, and though I cannot see how or when, I believe God will certainly answer the prayers of His faithful people in the land.

Randolph Fairfax, Foot of Shenandoah Mountain, May 16, 1862, in Philip Slaughter, *A Sketch of the Life of Randolph Fairfax*, 3rd ed. (Baltimore, MD: Innes and Company, 1878), 25-26. After Gen. Jubal Early's failed Valley Campaign two years later, Dabney also preached this sermon three additional times to Gen. John B. Gordon's Division, Gen. Cullen Battle's Alabama Brigade, and Col. Thomas Munford's Cavalry Brigade respectively in early December 1864 in the New Market area. *SI*. RLD to H. G. Guthrie, Newmarket, December 12, 1864, in *LLD*, 290.

206   Also available on New Hope Presbyterian Church's Web site: http://www.newhopefairfax. org/files/Dabney,%20Jam.%204.3%20Our%20Ineffectual%20Prayers.pdf (accessed May 26, 2020).

207   After the battle of McDowell, and the pursuit of Milroy and Schenk, Gen. Jackson returned by forced marches to effect his junction with Gen. Ewell, and to pay his respects to Banks. The point to which his march first tended was Harrisonburg. The Sabbath found him near the village of Mt. Solon, on the Mossy Creek, and there, although most eager to husband every moment, he paused, amidst the luxuriant fields and majestic groves of that beautiful region, to give the troops their day of sacred rest. The Sabbath proved to be one of unrivalled mildness and beauty. The author, then chief of Gen. Jackson's staff, accompanied by him, went in the forenoon to preach in the camp of the famous 12th Georgia Regiment, then without a Chaplain. In the afternoon, he passed to the opposite extremity of the encampments, and delivered the following discourse to the 44th Va. (Dabney's note)

208   Dabney also preached this sermon to the First Presbyterian Church of Petersburg in January 1865 during the siege of that town. *SI*.

209   Matthew 7:8.

210   Matthew 21:22.

211   John 16:23.

212   Hebrews 11:33-34.
213   James 5:16-18.
214   Attributed to Martin Luther.
215   *Westminster Larger Catechism*, Question 178.
216   The previous Sabbath, June 8th the headquarters of the Army of the Valley were at Port Republic. On Saturday, Gen. Jackson had sent away the mortal remains of the heroic [Gen. Turner] Ashby for burial, and had committed to the earth the corpses of those slain in the combat near Harrisonburg, in which he fell. The morning of the holy day dawned with peculiar brightness; and the author asked the General, as was customary, whether it was his wish that he should attempt to hold public worship in any part of the army, while the enemy was so near. His reply was: "Oh yes: certainly, unless he disturbs us. I wish you to prepare for peaching, that, if things remain quiet, we may have public worship." But a very short time elapsed, before the sudden attack of Shields upon the village plunged everything into hurry and excitement. The author was compelled to doff his sacred functions, more hastily than he had donned them, to resume those of the officer, and to spend the sacred hours, not in proclaiming the gospel of peace, but in galloping from point to point to reinstate the order of the surprised troops, in the rapid issuing of commands, and in combat with the enemy's advance. Thus began the two days' battle of Port Republic. This was followed by the withdrawal of the troops into Brown's Gap, and a dreary rain.

But in the middle of the week, Gen. Jackson moved his army from their uneasy *bivouac*, out into the open valley at Mount Meridian; and in that charming region of green woods, and waning fields, and sparkling waters, he allowed it a week's repose. According to his wont after a battle, Saturday, June 14th, was set apart as a day of religious rest and thanksgiving; and public worship was celebrated in those regiments which had chaplains. The following day was again the Sabbath, and a day of peaceful splendor. In the forenoon, the General worshipped with his old Brigade; where the following discourse was preached, in the presence of a large assemblage of men and officers, including Generals [Richard] Ewell, C[harles] L. Winder, and others. In the afternoon, there was a great convocation of believers, with their ministers, in the woods, where the Lord's Supper was administered. At this solemn ordinance, Gen. Jackson attended, with a multitude of devout soldiers: many of whom were destined to taste the sacramental cup no more, 'until they drank it new in the kingdom of their father.' This Sabbath day can never cease to be the source of a flood of sacred and pensive reminisces, to those who assisted at these services: and it is with a mournful pleasure, that they recall especially, the shining countenances of the many young Christians, like Hugh White, Randolph Fairfax, and others, who then promised to be so precious to the Church of God, but whose gallant and devoted spirits were to be breathed out, ere long, upon the field of glory. (Dabney's note)

Dabney also made reference to these events in his biography of Jackson:

> The Saturday following the battle, was proclaimed by General Jackson as a day of thanksgiving and prayer, and all the troops were called to join with their General and their chaplains, in praises to God for his deliverances. The next day, a general communion was observed in the 3rd Virginia brigade, at which the Lord's supper was dispensed, in the wood, to a great company of Christian soldiers from all the army. At this solemnity the General was present, as a worshipper, and modestly participated with his men in the sacred feast. The quiet diffidence with which he took the least obtrusive place, and received the sacred emblems from the hands of a regimental chaplain, was in beautiful contrast with the majesty and authority of his bearing in the crisis of battle.

LCJ, 430.
217   Dabney also preached this message at a camp at Fairfax Courthouse in July 1861. *SI*.
218   Four soldiers commented on Dabney's preaching and the communion service held on the weekend of June 14-15, 1862. Private F. K. Hinter of the Rockbridge Artillery noted:

> Saturday, June 14, 1862, a day of thanksgiving to God for many mercies and protection, which was much enjoyed throughout this portion of the army; preaching and prayer-meetings in the day. June 15, much to our surprise as to our joy, no orders to move, and we spent

the day quietly—preaching in the morning by Dr. Dabney; in the evening enjoyed a communion season, in which many participated and drew near to Jesus.

Pvt. Fairfax (also from the Rockbridge Artillery) mentioned: "Yesterday, June 14th, by special order, services were held in the regiment, giving thanks for our victories and prayers for further blessings. I heard a delightful sermon from Dr. Dabney yesterday evening, and another this morning. This evening the sacrament of the Lord's Supper is to be administered, and I hope I may be able to attend."

In a letter to his wife, Jedediah Hotchkiss (Stonewall Jackson's topographer) said: "We had sacrament today [June 15] in camp, it was a solemn scene, and Dr. Dabney prefaced it by some excellent remarks." In his journal, Hotchkiss also wrote:

Sunday, June 15th. Attended preaching at the First Brigade, Gen. C. S. Winder's camp. Maj. (Rev. Dr.) R. L. Dabney preached a good sermon. . . . In the afternoon we had sacrament at the Qrs. of the Third Brigade[.] . . . Dr. Dabney made some excellent remarks. It was a very impressive celebration of the Lord's Supper, in the woods, amid the din of camps hushed for a brief period to celebrate the Supper of the Prince of Peace. The General attended the meeting, humbly devout.

In a letter to his sister, Capt. Hugh White (4th Virginia, Stonewall Brigade) also declared: "[Dabney] is very busy, but preaches whenever he has an opportunity. I heard him last Saturday [June 14], then twice on the Sabbath, when about two hundred soldiers received the sacrament of the Lord's Supper at his hands. This was a spiritual feast indeed."

F. K. Hitner, "Brief Compend[ium] of the Religious History of the Rockbridge Artillery," quoted in *CC*, 482. Randolph Fairfax to his mother, Camp near Port Republic, June 14, 1862, in Slaughter, 33-34, Augusta County: Jedidiah Hotchkiss to Sara A. Hotchkiss, June 15, 1862, Valley Personal Papers, *The Valley of the Shadow*, University of Virginia Library: https://valley.lib.virginia.edu/papers/A2542 (accessed May 26, 2020). *MMMV*, 56-57. Hugh White to sister, Mrs. M'crum, in *Sketches of the Life of Captain Hugh A.White*, 95-96. Capt. Hugh White was the son of Rev. William White, Dabney's mentor in Lexington, VA. Hugh was also a student of Dabney's at Union Seminary when the war broke out. He was later killed during the Battle of 2nd Manassas in August 1862. His father then compiled Hugh's letters and wrote a brief sketch of his life for publication. Dabney contributed an introduction to this book.

219   Also published in *Discussions, Volume I*, 482-495.

220   General Thomas J. Jackson, during his forced march from the Valley of Virginia to the Chickahominy, halted his command, for the Sabbath, along the line of the Virginia Central Railroad, from Gordonsville to Frederick's Hall, in the county of Louisa. He himself spent the sacred day at the latter place, in the hospitable home of N. Harris, Esq. I ascertained that the brigade of Hood, near us, had at that time no chaplain present, and offered to conduct public worship for them. This offer was courteously accepted by their General, and the afternoon of the bright Sabbath was chosen as the time, and a dilapidated country church, near the encampment, as the place. These troops, having been attached to the command of General Jackson a few days before, were strangers to his person, and naturally anxious to see the far-famed soldier. This desire, with better motives on the part of some, brought the whole brigade to the appointed place. The little wooden church was packed, the open grounds beside it crowded, and the fences and the very trees loaded with human bodies. To provide for the multitude without, General Hood proposed that the speaker should be placed, not in the pulpit, but in a side door, where a table was arranged for him. A long bench next this door was intended for General Jackson. As party after party entered the house, and finding no vacant seats elsewhere, were about to occupy this bench. General Hood arose again and again, and remarked: "That seat is reserved for General Jackson and his staff." This repeated caution seemed at length to beget in all minds the vision of a brilliant cavalcade, dashing up with the far-famed Stonewall Jackson at its head, and displaying any amount of military pomp and finery. After a few moments a "buggy" was seen creeping along, containing the General in a sunburned uniform, and a person in black. The two dismounted, and proceed-

ed with their own hands to detach the horse, and tie him to a "swinging limb." After, this, the General slipped quietly into the house and took his seat. Noticing, as he approached, one or two companies of Texans marching up in regular ranks, though unarmed, he said: "See there, that is what I like." After the close of the service, he saluted the officers near him, returned to the vehicle, reattached the horse with no other assistance than that of his clerical companion, and returned to his quarters. The great multitudes around him behaved throughout with the strictest decorum; and not a man betrayed the slightest manifestation of unseemly curiosity.

As we were returning, General Jackson said to me: "Your subject this evening was of great importance, and some of your views new to me. I wish all my men could read your sermon. I should be glad if you would reduce it to writing, when other duties permit—I know you cannot have time for this now, but hereafter, when operations in the field are less urgent—and let me have it. I will print it myself and supply my command." To this request I could only promise compliance.

The pressure of duties in the field, then protracted sickness, then the death of my revered commander, with a train of subsequent disasters, have long delayed my fulfillment of the pledge. It is, in my eyes, only the more sacred, that he is no longer upon earth to remind me of it. Having at length found another medium

(through the Publishing Committee of our church, which prints it simply for the sake of the great truths of redemption it contains), I now present the sermon to the survivors of those for whom General Jackson designed it. I beg them to receive it as his message; his adopted testimony to the necessity and nature of the new birth. It comes to them as a voice from beyond the grave, as well as an affecting mark of the zeal and love of the departed Christian soldier towards their souls.

Union Theological Seminary, December 20, 1868.   R. L. Dabney.

See also Daniel H. Hill, "Lee's Attacks North of the Chickahominy," in *Battles and Leaders of the Civil War*, ed. Robert Underwood Johnson and Clarence Clough Buel (1887; repr., Edison, NJ: Castle), 2:348-350. *LCJ*, 435.

221 Shakespeare, *The Life and Death of King John*, 3.4.110-111. Dabney substituted "irksome" for Shakespeare's original word: "tedious."

222 Also published in *Discussions, Volume I*, 614-625. Dabney preached another commemorative sermon at Hampden-Sydney College in July 1863 for Lt. Augustus Bass. The Scripture passage for this message was John 11:21-32. Based on Dabney's numbering system for the *Army Sermons*, it does not appear that he intended Bass' funeral service to be included in his Civil War compilation. Therefore, it remains in sketch form. *SI.*

223 The session of College Church adopted a resolution on December 15, 1862:

The Session of this Church having heard with great satisfaction the funeral sermon preached by their request yesterday, in reference to the death of our brother, Lieut. Abram C. Carrington, and believing that its circulation will be productive of good, do resolve, that Rev. R. L. Dabney be requested to furnish a copy thereof for publication.

J. D. Eggleston II, "History of College Church Hampden-Sydney, Virginia 1776-1941," bound typescript, Joseph D. Eggleston II Papers, Hampden-Sydney College Archives and Special Collections, Hampden-Sydney. Prior to his death, Carrington was the treasurer of College Church. William E. Thompson, *Her Walls Before Thee Stand: The 235-Year History of the Presbyterian Congregation at Hampden-Sydney, Virginia* (Farmville, VA: Zebrabooks Publications, 2010), 205, 215.

224 Shakespeare, *Othello*, 1.3.156-159.

225 E. Cobham Brewer says in his dictionary that this phrase comes from Samuel Johnson's poem, "The Vanity of Human Wishes." No such matching phrase, though, can be found in the poem. Brewer also mentions a similar line though in Alexander Pope's "Essay on Man." Brewer, *Dictionary of Phrase and Fable* (Philadelphia, PA: Henry Altemus Company, 1898), 177, 790. Brewer seems to say that the "Macedonian madman" is a reference to Alexander the Great; and the Swede, Charles XII of Sweden.

226 Joseph Addison, "The Campaign, a Poem, to His Grace the Duke of Marlborough," 107-108.

227 Matthew Henry uses this phrase multiple times in his *Expositions of the Old and New Testaments* (1708-1710). See his notes on Exodus 2:1-4, Judges 13:8-14, I Kings 14:1-6, John

21:20-25, and Acts 27:21-44.

228   The editor is unsure of the original source for this quotation. Both the quotation and the sentence before it are found in J. William Jones, *Life and Letters of Robert Edward Lee: Soldier and Man* (New York, NY: The Neale Publishing Company, 1906), 439. Jones said he found these words on a sheet of paper written by Gen. Lee.

229   In an earlier edition of this sermon, Dabney placed the last phrase in brackets. RLD, *The Christian Soldier: A Sermon Commemorative of the Death of Abram C. Carrington* (Richmond, VA: Presbyterian Committee of Publication, 1863), 10.

230   Shortly after the battle, Carrington reported for sick call. Dabney wrote a letter to his wife on August 29, 1861, saying the he was "about to start to Manassas with the ambulance, to see Mr. Abram Carrington off to Richmond to be sick. He is taking this fever, I think, which is prevailing here, and is going to have a spell. I found it prevailing when I came to the regiment [18th Virginia], and now about every second man is down with it." RLD to Lavinia Dabney, August 29, 1861, in *LLD*, 242.

231   In an earlier version of this sermon, Dabney included the following text before the next sentence:

> And especially would I now commend, by his example, the sacred and religious duty of defending the cause for which he died. In the death of him and others who went from our midst, of such noble spirits as Abram and Edgar Carrington, of Peyton and Dabney Harrison, of Hugh White, of John Thornton, and all their noble fellowship of martyrs, I see a new argument for consecrating ourselves to our country's cause, and defending it with invincible tenacity. Surely their very blood should cry out against us from the ground, if we permitted the soil which drank the precious libation, to be polluted with the despot's foot! Shall it ever be that our feebleness or discouragements shall make the costly sacrifice vain? If this is to be, then was it not treacherous in us to invite it? We should rather have warned them to restrain their generosity, to save the lives they were so ready to sacrifice on their country's altar, as too precious to be wasted for a land occupied by predestined slaves and cowards, and to carry their patriotism and their gifts to some more propitious clime, and some worthier companionship. But we have invited the sacrifice; we have received it; and before God, I take you to witness this day, that its blood seals upon you the obligation to fill their places in your country's host, and "play the men for your people and the cities of your God," to the complete vindication of their rights.

The Christian Soldier, 13.

232   Also published in *Discussions, Volume IV*: 435-452. Also contained in this volume is Dabney's "Memorial of Lieutenant Colonel John T. Thornton of the Third Virginia Cavalry, C.S.A.," which originally was published as a tract by the Presbyterian Publishing Committee in 1864. *Discussions, Volume IV*, 453-469. *LLD*, 298.

233   General Jackson died May 10th, 1863. In June following, the author was urgently requested to deliver a memorial sermon for him in Richmond. Having acceded to this request, he prepared the following discourse, and delivered it in the First Presbyterian Church, the evening of the first Sabbath of June [7], before a vast assemblage of officers, soldiers, and citizens. If the reader has happened to have seen also the Life of General Jackson, he will notice a certain similarity of thoughts, and even of language, in the sermon and in some parts of the narrative. The author has not been careful to suppress the whole of these in republishing the sermon, because he was not afraid of the charge of repeating his own matter, where it formed so appropriate, and indeed, so necessary a part of both compositions. (Dabney's note)

234   In an earlier edition of this sermon, Dabney included this succeeding paragraph:

> And so, we may assert, it is with all the best of our land. Just in proportion to the integrity of men's principles, to their magnanimity, to their incorruptible love of right and truth, to their fear of God, have been their decision and zeal to the cause of the Confederate States. Our mothers, wives and sisters, with their disinterested and generous instincts; our most honored and venerable citizens and jurists; the most saintly and reverend pastors in the Church of Christ; have been foremost to justify our defence. If there have been any dissent,

they have been found usually among the ignorant, the mercenary, and the base. This is our answer to the slanderers, who denounced our revolution as a scheme of wicked politicians, an artifice of the ambitious and factious few.

RLD, *True Courage: A Discourse Commemorative of Lieut. General Thomas J. Jackson*, 2nd ed. (Richmond, VA: Presbyterian Committee of Publication of the Confederate States, 1863), 10.
235 See appendix no. 4.
236 Watts, "Protection from Death, Guard of Angels, Victory, and Deliverance," Psalm 91, Part II, *The Psalms of David Imitated in the Language of the New Testament.*
237 An earlier edition of this sermon had a different ending:

Every one who was near him felt that defeat was a result wholly excluded from his contemplation. Let us imbibe this spirit. As we, visit the soil which drank his blood! or the grave where his body rests in the bosom of his beloved valley, we will adopt them as new seals to our pledge to be free or die. Let us resolve that as the solemn mountain peaks keep their everlasting watch around the home and the tomb of Jackson, even so immovably will we guard the honor and the rights for which he died.

True Courage, 2nd ed., 26. After this concluding paragraph, this edition included an appendix entitled, "Sketch of the Life of Lieut. Gen. T. J. Jackson."
238 Jackson's grave is in Lexington, VA, near where he taught at Virginia Military Institute.
239 A different version of this sermon (minus the comments on Jackson) was preached at the Hampden-Sydney College on May 26, 1861 to the Hampden Sydney Volunteer Company (Co. G of the 20th Virginia) under the leadership of their President, Capt. John M. P. Atkinson. Coffin, "Army Sermons List." See Sermon no. 6 on "The Christian Philosopher."
240 This sermon was also preached at the First Presbyterian Church of Petersburg in January 1865. *SI.*
241 Johnson said that Dabney was "at Orange Courthouse, in August 1863[.] . . . While he was there a grand review of A. P. Hill's [3rd] Corps was held a few miles east of the courthouse. It brought to witness it many prominent men[, including] . . . General Lee." James Robertson noted in his biography of Gen. A. P. Hill: "Late in August, Hill reviewed [several of his] divisions. . . . At noon on September 12, Lee arrived with his daughters for another review of the Third Corps." To complicate matters, Hotchkiss (now under Gen. Richard Ewell) said that Dabney "came up today [Friday, September 4] to [our camp to] obtain materials for his life of Jackson and we had a long talk on various topics about him." Two days later, Hotchkiss recorded that "Dr. Dabney gave us a short morning discourse, then I went to the Presbyterian Church and heard a good sermon on 'Faith.'" Then on September 9, Hotchkiss wrote, "Dabney copied my map of Chancellorsville. There was a fine review of [Ewell's] Second Corps by Gen. Lee; said to have been a grand affair." In light of all of these records, it seems best to conclude that Dabney arrived at Orange Court House possibly in late August, eventually made it over to the Second Corps' camp on September 4, stayed for a few days to talk matters over with his old comrades, preached on September 6, and observed a grand review of the Third Corps on September 12 before departing. *LLD*, 282. James I. Robertson, Jr., *General A. P Hill: The Story of a Confederate Warrior* (New York, NY: Random House, 1987), 231. *MMMV*, 174-175. Hotchkiss noted that at least for the evening of September 6, Dabney resided with Lt. James Power Smith, another former member of Jackson's staff (who joined in September 1862, two months after Dabney's departure). Smith also began his ministerial training under Dabney at Union Seminary before the war, and would finish his degree there after the war. Schildt, 164, 169-170, 192.
242 Hebrews 11:1.
243 Hebrews 11:6
244 I John 5:1.
245 Dabney originally wrote "explained" instead of "shown."
246 Psalm 2:12.
247 Isaiah 45:22.
248 John 1:12.
249 John 6:44.

250   Hebrews 11:13.

251   Hebrews 6:18.

252   *Westminster Shorter Catechism*, Question 86.

253   The exact location of this quote from Pascal's *Pensees* ("Thoughts") is unknown.

254   Ephesians 2:8.

255   Watts, "Faith in Christ for Pardon and Sanctification," *Hymns and Spiritual Songs*, Book II, Hymn 90.

256   Trotter's index does not list this sermon as being preached at the Tabb Street Church but at the First Presbyterian Church of Petersburg. It is possible that Dabney preached the sermon at both churches that month. *SI.*

257   Dabney originally added "bitter, but" before the word "abortive," but crossed it out.

258   Dabney added the word "away," but then crossed it out.

259   Dabney originally added "by which, if they were rightly directed," but eventually deleted this phrase.

260   Dabney wrote "irresponsible," but given the context, "responsible" seems the better choice of words.

261   Taken from *The Central Presbyterian*, July 20, 1861.

262   Much of the material in this sermon can also be found in Sermon no. 13 on "Public Calamities Caused by Public Sins" and Sermon no. 18 on "True Courage." This may be the reason why Dabney did not include his Fast Day discourse in his *Army Sermons*.

263   This section in the newspaper is unclear, so the editor added in these words based on Sermon no. 13 on "Public Calamities Caused by Public Sins."

264   The editor added these words as most of this section of the newspaper was illegible. The first word in Dabney's text, however, looks like "passed." In his book on the revival in Southern armies, William W. Bennett mentioned that the Ironsides "marched into battle singing psalms and shouting such watchwords as, 'The Lord of Hosts!'" Bennett, 12.

265   Taken from *The Central Presbyterian*, June 22, 1861. *The Central Presbyterian* incorrectly printed the date of this letter as June 13, but it should be June 14. Thomas Carey Johnson attributes this letter to Dabney. *LLD*, 236.

266   Taken from *The Central Presbyterian*, August 17, 1861. It appears that Dabney obtained a leave of absence from the army in early August 1861, for his sermon records indicate that he preached once at Culpepper Courthouse and twice in Charlottesville that month. One of the latter messages was particularly delivered at the University of Virginia, where William H. McGuffey taught as a Professor of Moral Philosophy. Dabney and McGuffey must have written their article then, and submitted it to *The Central Presbyterian* for publication. *SI.*

267   Jones, *Christ in the Camp or Religion in Lee's Army*, 1st ed. (Richmond, VA: B. F. Johnson & Co., 1887), 252.

268   An Open Letter from Dr. R. L. Dabney to Dr. J. William Jones, Austin, TX, December 15, 1891, in *SHSP*, ed. R. A. Brock (Richmond, VA: Southern Historical Society, 1891), 19:376-377.

269   *SI.* Sermon no. 16 on "The Believer Born of Almighty Grace." Sermon no. 18 on "True Courage."

270   Dr. J. William Jones' Reply to the "Open Letter" of Rev. Dr. R. L. Dabney, Atlanta, GA, January 5, 1892, in *SHSP*, 19:377-379.

271   *Christ in the Camp*, 2nd ed., 252. C. W. Bardeen, *A Little Fifer's War Diary* (Syracuse, NY: C. W. Bardeen, 1910), 137.

272   Gordon, 67-68.

Bibliography

Abbreviations

CC	J. William Jones, *Christ in the Camp, or Religion in the Confederate Army,* 2nd ed. (1904; repr., Harrisonburg, VA: Sprinkle Publications, 1986).
TJJ	Thomas Jonathan Jackson
LCJ	Robert Lewis Dabney, *Life and Campaigns of Lieut. Gen. T.J. (Stonewall) Jackson* (1866; repr., Harrisonburg, VA: Sprinkle Publications, 1983).
LLD	Thomas Cary Johnson, *The Life and Letters of Robert Lewis Dabney* (1903; repr., Carlisle, PA: The Banner of Truth Trust, 1977).
LLJ	Anna Jackson, *Life and Letters of General Thomas J. Jackson* (1892; repr., Harrisonburg, VA: Sprinkle Publications, 1995).
MMMV	Jedidiah Hotchkiss, *Make Me a Map of the Valley: The Civil War Journal of Stonewall Jackson's Topographer* (Dallas, TX: Southern Methodist University Press, 1973).
RLD	Robert Lewis Dabney
SI	Lawrence Calvin Trotter. "Robert Lewis Dabney Sermons Index."
SHSP	*Southern Historical Society Papers*

Manuscripts

Handley Regional Library
    Frank Buck Jones Diary

Library of Congress
    Jedidiah Hotchkiss Papers

Hampden-Sydney College Archives and Special Collections
    Joseph D. Eggleston II Papers

New-York Historical Society
    Stonewall Jackson Collection

Union Presbyterian Seminary
    Robert Lewis Dabney Papers

University of Virginia
    Robert Lewis Dabney Papers
    Valley Personal Papers

Periodicals

The Central Presbyterian, 1861
The Davidson College Magazine, 1899
The Presbyterian and Reformed Review, 1901
The Princeton Theological Review, 1905
Shenandoah Herald, 1909
Southern Historical Society Papers, 1872, 1892-1893, 1920
The Virginia Magazine of History and Biography, 1970

Other Sources

Annals of the War. 1879; repr., Edison, NJ: The Blue & Grey Press, 1996.
Bardeen, C. W. *A Little Fifer's War Diary.* Syracuse, NY: C. W. Bardeen, 1910.
Blackburn, George A., ed. *The Life Work of John L. Girardeau, D. D., LL.D.* Columbia, SC: The State Company, 1916.
Bean, W. G. *The Liberty Hall Volunteers: Stonewall's College Boys.* Charlottesville, VA: The University Press of Virginia, 1964.
__________. *Stonewall's Man: Sandie Pendleton.* 1959; repr., Wilmington, NC: Broadfoot Publishing Company, 1987.
Beinham, Michael L. "Role of the Southern Baptist Chaplains and Missionaries in the Civil War." master's thesis, U.S. Army Command and General Staff College, 2003.
Bennett, William W. *The Great Revival in the Southern Armies.* 1877; repr., Harrisonburg, VA: Sprinkle Publications, 1989.
Brewer, E. Cobham. *Dictionary of Phrase and Fable.* Philadelphia,

PA: Henry Altemus Company, 1898.

Brinkley, John Luster. *On This Hill: A Narrative History of Hampden-Sydney College, 1774-1994.* Hampden-Sydney, VA: Hampden-Sydney College, 1994.

Brinsfield, Jr., John Wesley. *The Spirit Divided: Memoirs of Civil War Chaplains: The Confederacy.* Macon, GA: Mercer University Press, 2006.

Cairns, Alan. *Dictionary of Theological Terms.* 2nd ed. Greenville, SC: Ambassador-Emerald International, 1998.

Cockrell, Monroe F., ed. *Gunner with Stonewall: Reminiscences of William Thomas Poague.* Jackson, TN: McCowat-Mercer Press, Inc.

Coffin, Jr., David Frank. "Army Sermons List."

__________. "Reflections on the Life and Thought of Robert Lewis Dabney with Particular Reference to His Views on Divine Sovereignty and Human Free Agency." PhD diss., Westminster Theological Seminary, 2003.

Cooke, John Esten. *Stonewall Jackson: A Military Biography.* New York, NY: D. Appleton and Company, 1866.

Dabney, Lewis Meriwether. *Lewis Meriwether Dabney: A Memoir and Letters.* New York, NY: J. J. Little and Ives Company, 1924.

Dabney, Robert L. *Christ Our Penal Substitute.* 1898; repr., Harrisonburg, VA: Sprinkle Publications, 1998.

__________. *Christ Our Substitute*, No. 1. Richmond, VA: Presbyterian Committee of Publication, c. 1863.

__________. *The Christian Soldier: A Sermon Commemorative of the Death of Abram C. Carrington.* Richmond, VA: Presbyterian Committee of Publication, 1863.

__________. *A Defence of Virginia (And Through Her, of the South) in Recent and Pending Contests Against the Sectional Party.* 1867; repr., Harrisonburg, VA: Sprinkle Publications, 1991.

__________. *Discussions, Volume I: Theological and Evangelical*, ed. C. R. Vaughan. 1890; repr., Harrisonburg, VA: Sprinkle Publications, 1982.

__________. *Discussions, Volume II: Evangelical*, ed. C. R. Vaughan. 1891; repr., Harrisonburg, VA: Sprinkle Publications, 1982.

__________. *Discussions, Volume III: Philosophical*, ed. C. R. Vaughan. 1892; repr., Harrisonburg, VA: Sprinkle Publications, 1996.

__________. *Discussions, Volume IV: Secular*, ed. C. R. Vaughan. 1897; reprint, Harrisonburg, VA: Sprinkle Publications, 1994.

__________. *Discussions, Volume V: Miscellaneous Writings*, ed. J. H. Varner. Harrisonburg, VA: Sprinkle Publications, 1999.

__________. *Evangelical Eloquence: A Course of Lectures on Preaching*. 1870; repr., Carlisle, PA: The Banner of Truth Trust, 1999.

__________. *Life and Campaigns of Lieut. Gen. T.J. (Stonewall) Jackson*. 1866; repr., Harrisonburg, VA: Sprinkle Publications, 1983.

__________. *The Practical Philosophy*. 1897; repr., Harrisonburg, VA: Sprinkle Publications, 1984.

__________. *True Courage: A Discourse Commemorative of Lieut. General Thomas J. Jackson*. 2nd ed. Richmond, VA: Presbyterian Committee of Publication of the Confederate States, 1863.

__________. *The Sensualistic Philosophy*. 2nd ed. 1887; repr., Dallas, TX: Naphtali Press, 2003.

__________. *Swear Not!* Petersburg, VA: Evangelical Tract Society, c. 1863.

__________. *Systematic Theology*. 1887; repr., Carlisle, PA: The Banner of Truth Trust, 2002.

Denney, Robert E. *The Civil War: A Day-by-Day Chronicle*. New York, NY: Gramercy Books, 1992.

Douglas, Henry Kyd. *I Rode with Stonewall*. 1940; repr., Marietta, GA: Mockingbird Books, 1993.

Faust, Drew Gilpin. *This Republic of Suffering: Death and the American Civil War*. New York, NY: Alfred A. Knopf, 2008.

Freeman, Douglas Southall. *Lee's Lieutenants: A Study in Command: Volume One: Manassas to Malvern Hill*. New York, NY: Charles Scribner's Sons, 1942.

Gordon, John B. *Reminiscences of the Civil War*. New York, NY: Charles Scribner's Sons, 1904.

Greene, A. Wilson. *Breaking the Backbone of the Rebellion: The Final Battles of the Petersburg Campaign*. Mason City, IA: Savas Publishing Company, 2000.

Henderson, G. F. R. *Stonewall Jackson and the American Civil War in Two Volumes*. 1898, repr., Secaucus, NJ: The Blue and Grey Press.

Hieronymous, Frank L. "For Now and Forever: The Chaplains of the Confederate States Army." PhD diss., University of California, 1964.

Hoge, Peyton Harrison. *Moses Drury Hoge: Life and Letters*. Richmond, VA: Presbyterian Committee of Publication, 1899.

Hotchkiss, Jedidiah. *Make Me a Map of the Valley: The Civil War Journal of Stonewall Jackson's Topographer*. Dallas, TX: Southern Methodist University Press, 1973.

In Memoriam: Robert Lewis Dabney. Knoxville, TN: The University of Tennessee Press, 1899.

"Information about Camp Lee in Richmond, VA during the Civil War." Civil War Richmond Web site. http://www.mdgorman. com/Hospitals/camp_lee.htm (accessed May 26, 2020).

Irby, Richard. *Historical Sketch of the Nottoway Grays, Afterwards Company G, Eighteenth Virginia Regiment, Army of Northern Virginia*. Richmond, VA: J. W. Fergusson & Son, 1878.

Jackson, Anna. *Life and Letters of General Thomas J. Jackson*. 1892; repr., Harrisonburg, VA: Sprinkle Publications, 1995.

Johnson, Gary L. W., ed. *B. B. Warfield: Essays on His Life and Thought*. Phillipsburg, NJ: P&R Publishing, 2007.

Johnson, Phil. "How to View the Flaws of the Reformers." I'll Be Honest Web site. entry posted December 17, 2017. https://illbe-honest.com/flaws-of-reformers (accessed November 18, 2020).

Johnson, Robert Underwood and Clarence Clough Buel, eds. *Battles and Leaders of the Civil War, Volume II*. 1887; repr., Edison, NJ: Castle.

Johnson, Thomas Cary. *The Life and Letters of Robert Lewis Dabney*. 1903; repr., Carlisle, PA: The Banner of Truth Trust, 1977.

Jones, J. William. *Christ in the Camp or Religion in Lee's Army*. 1st ed. Richmond, VA: B. F. Johnson & Co., 1887.

__________.*Christ in the Camp, or Religion in the Confederate Army*. 2nd ed. 1904; repr., Harrisonburg, VA: Sprinkle Publications, 1986.

__________. *Life and Letters of Robert Edward Lee: Soldier and Man*. New York, NY: The Neale Publishing Company, 1906.

Krick, Robert K. *Conquering the Valley: Stonewall Jackson at Port Republic*. Baton Rouge, LA: Louisiana State University Press, 1996.

Lewis, Frank Bell. "Robert Lewis Dabney: Southern Presbyterian Apologist." PhD diss., Duke University, 1946.

__________. "Times of Crisis." In *The Days of Our Years: The Histor-*

ical Convocations Held April 24-27, 1962, as a Feature of the Celebration of the Sesquicentennial of Union Theological Seminary in
Virginia*, 21-40. Richmond, VA: Union Theological Seminary, 1962.

Longacre, Edward G. *The Early Morning of War: Bull Run, 1861*.
Norman, OK: University of Oklahoma, 2014.

Lucas, Sean Michael. *Robert Lewis Dabney: A Southern Presbyterian
Life*. Phillipsburg, NJ: P&R Publishing, 2005.

McIlwaine, Richard. *Memories of Three Score Years and Ten*. New
York, NY: The Neale Publishing Company, 1908.

McMullen, George, ed. *A Surgeon With Stonewall Jackson: The Civil
War Letters of Dr. Harvey Black*. Baltimore, MD: Butternut and
Blue, 1995.

Miller, Francis Trevelyan, ed. *The Photographic History of the Civil
War* (10 Volumes). 1911, repr., New York, NY: The Blue & Grey
Press, 2011.

Ministers of the Southern Presbyterian Church. *Southern Presbyterian Pulpit: A Collection of Sermons*. Richmond, VA: The Presbyterian Committee of Publication: 1896.

Murray, Iain H. *Revival and Revivalism: The Making and Marring of
American Evangelicalism 1750-1858*. Carlisle, PA: The Banner of
Truth Trust, 1994.

__________. "Life of Robert L. Dabney." SermonAudio
Web site. https://www.sermonaudio.com/sermoninfo.as-
p?SID=1080263842 (accessed March 24, 2020).

Pfanz, Donald S. *Richard S. Ewell: A Soldier's Life*. Chapel Hill, NC:
University of North Carolina Press, 1998.

Polley, J. B. *Hood's Texas Brigade: Its Marches, Its Battles, Its Achievements*. New York, NY: The Neale Publishing Company, 1910.

Rable, George C. *God's Almost Chosen Peoples: A Religious History
of the American Civil War*. Chapel Hill, NC: University of North
Carolina Press, 2010.

Ray, Jeffrey David. "The Education of Robert Lewis Dabney." PhD
diss., The University of Southern Mississippi, 2006.

Red Runs the River. VHS. Directed by Katherine Stenholm. Greenville, SC: Unusual Films, 1963.

"Robert Lewis Dabney (1820-1898)." Log College Press Web site.
https://www.logcollegepress.com/robert-lewis-dabney-18201898
(accessed May 26, 2020).

Robertson, Archibald Thomas. *Life and Letters of John A. Broadus.* 1901; repr., Harrisonburg, VA: Gano Books, 2003.

Robertson, Jr., James I. *18th Virginia Infantry.* Lynchburg, VA: H. E. Howard, Inc., 1984.

__________. *General A. P Hill: The Story of a Confederate Warrior.* New York, NY: Random House, 1987.

__________. *Stonewall Jackson: The Man, the Soldier, the Legend.* New York, NY: MacMillan Publishing, 1997.

Schildt, John W. *Jackson and the Preachers.* 1982; repr., Parsons, WV: McClain Printing Company, 1992.

Sears, Stephen W. *To the Gates of Richmond: The Peninsula Campaign.* New York, NY: Ticknor & Fields, 1992.

Slaughter, Philip. *A Sketch of the Life of Randolph Fairfax.* 3rd ed. Baltimore, MD: Innes and Company, 1878.

St. John, Russell. "Empty Admiration: Robert Lewis Dabney's Expository Homiletic." PhD diss., Middlesex University, 2018.

Sweetser, Jr., William B. *A Copious Fountain: A History of Union Presbyterian Seminary, 1812-2012.* Louisville, KY: Westminster John Knox Press, 2016.

Tanner, Robert G. *Stonewall in the Valley: Thomas J. "Stonewall" Jackson's Shenandoah Valley Campaign, Spring 1862.* 2nd ed. 1996; repr., Mechanicsburg, PA: Stackpole Books, 2002.

Thompson, William E. *Her Walls Before Thee Stand: The 235-Year History of the Presbyterian Congregation at Hampden-Sydney, Virginia.* Farmville, VA: Zebrabooks Publications, 2010.

Thornwell, James Henley. *The Collected Writings of James Henley Thornwell, Volume IV: Ecclesiastical.* 1875; repr., Carlisle, PA: The Banner of Truth Trust, 1974.

Trotter, Lawrence Calvin. "Blasting Rocks: The Extemporaneous Homiletic of Robert Lewis Dabney." PhD diss., Regent University, 2007, rev. 2010.

__________. "Orality in Robert Lewis Dabney's War Sermons." Regent University, April 5, 2005.

__________. "Robert Lewis Dabney Sermons Index."

Warfield, Benjamin B. *Selected Shorter Writings of Benjamin B. Warfield, Volume II.* ed. John E. Meeter. Nutley, NJ: P&R Publishing, 1973.

Wert, Jeffry D. *From Winchester to Cedar Creek: The Shenandoah Campaign of 1864.* Mechanicsburg, PA: Stackpole Books, 1997.

White, Alexander. *Southern Presbyterian Leaders*. New York, NY: The Neal Publishing Company, 1911.

White, William S. *Sketches of the Life of Captain Hugh A. White of the Stonewall Brigade*. Columbia, SC: South Carolinian Steam Press, 1864.

Wiley, Bell I. *The Life of Johnny Reb*. 1943; repr., New York, NY: Book-of-the-Month Club, 1994.

Wilson, Howard McKnight. *The Tinkling Spring Headwater of Freedom: A Study of the Church and Her People 1732-1952*. Richmond, VA: Garrett and Massie, Inc., 1954.

Withers, Robert Enoch. *Autobiography of an Octogenarian*. Roanoke, VA: The Stone Printing & MFG. Co. Press, 1907.

Woodworth, Steven E. *While God Is Marching On: The Religious World of Civil War Soldiers*. Lawrence, KS: University of Kansas Press, 2001.